A Picture History of
NEW BEDFORD

© 2016 Spinner Publications, Inc.
All Rights Reserved.

Library of Congress Cataloging-in-Publication Data

A picture history of New Bedford / edited by Joseph D. Thomas, Alfred H. Saulniers, Natalie White, Marsha L. McCabe, Jay Avila.
    pages cm
Includes bibliographical references and index.
ISBN 978-0-932027-24-5 (v. 2 : hardcover) -- ISBN 978-0-932027-23-8 (v. 2 : pbk.)
1. New Bedford (Mass.)--History--Pictorial works. I. Thomas, Joseph D., editor.
F74.N5P53 2013
974.4'85--dc23
                    2013020781

A Picture History of
NEW BEDFORD

Volume Two ~ 1925–1980

edited by

Joseph D. Thomas • Alfred H. Saulniers

Natalie A. White • Marsha L. McCabe • Jay Avila

Spinner Publications, Inc.

New Bedford, Massachusetts

Grant Support ~ (Gifts of $3,500 – $10,000)

Bristol County Savings Bank

CHT Foundation

Furthermore: A Program of the J. M. Kaplan Fund

Mary Morley Crapo Hyde Eccles Fund

Massachusetts Cultural Council

New Bedford Cultural Council

Whaling City Donor ~ (Gifts above $1,000)

Gotta Have It! Inc. ~ **Lisa V. Bindas** (NBHS 1978) **& Jacilyn E. Barnett**

In Honor of Apolonia Holziewich & the Bindas Family ~
John, Valentyna, Jan, Randy, Lisa, Bradford, Mary Kate, Deidre & Anya.

Palmer's Island Donors ~ (Gifts of $1,000)

Cheryl J. C. Blanchard and Stuart C. Dickinson

Carney Family Foundation

Neto Insurance/Neto Family

Ann Sheehan

Rumrunner Donors ~ *(Gifts of $500)*

Deborah A. & Benjamin B. Baker

In Memory of Alvin and Helena Bodzioch

Bourassa True Value Hardware

Laurie & John K. Bullard

Everett & Ruth Caswell

Clean Uniforms and More!

Natalie White & Jeremy Crockford

William do Carmo

Albino & Joan E. Dias
Grandchildren Ellie, Jack, William, Alex, Paxton & Beckett

Epec Engineered Technologies

Kathleen Mullen Guarino

Diane M. Gilbert & Lee W. Marland

Mary Louise Nunes & Randall B. Mello

Donna Huse & Jim Sears

Sue & Calvin Siegal

Ray & Claudette Veary

Dr. and Mrs. John S. Wolkowicz

Dias, Lapalme & Martin, LLP
Albino Dias, David Lapalme, Anthony J. Martin

Pier 3 Donors ~ *(Gifts of $300)*

Elizabeth J. Atkins

Vernon & Ann Barclay

Zelinda & John Douhan

Sheldon Friedland, Esq.

Sheriff Tom Hodgson

Gail & Arne Isaksen

David S. Martin

Cindy & Corbin Pettway

Attorney Paul J. Mathieu & Janet R. Mathieu

Sylvia Group ~ Maureen Sylvia Armstrong & Beth Sylvia Caldwell

Isaksen Fishing Company

Southcoast Health

Mr. & Mrs. David Teixeira

Worleybeds Factory Outlet

Margaret D. Xifaras

Acushnet Avenue Donors ~ *(Gifts of $175)*

Adamowski & Adamowski PC, CPA

Annette Almeida

Mary Jean Blasdale

Lucy Bly

Ken & Tamia Burt

Mark Coholan

Crystal Ice Co. Inc.

Janet S. DaSilva

Bruce DeMoranville

DHM Oil

Enos Home Medical

Kreg R. Espinola

Fabulous Foundations by Nancy

Fernandes Masonry, Inc.

Rev. G. Kenneth & Mary L. Garrett

Halloran, Lukoff & Smith, PC

Max & Karen Isaksen

Elizabeth Isherwood & John Moore

Nicholas Iwanisziw

Bob and Debi Jorge

Roger P. Levesque

Frank & Jane Linhares

Joyce D. Lopes Realty Corp.

Joanne Mello

Rick and Rose Miller

Elise Mock

Betty Jeanne & Wendell Nooth

E. J. Pontiff Real Estate

Bill & Martha Reed

Anthony Sapienza

Ron Saulnier

Subtext Bookshop

Ramon Tarini

Paul & Paulette Thomas

Bill Walsh from his Little Brother

William P. Walsh

Waterfront Grille ~ Kevin Santos

Sally & Jerry Wheeler

Nicholas Whitman

Amaral's Linguica & Chourico
Est. 1928) ~ Antonio Rodrigues, President

Donna A. Bobrowiecki
NBHS Class of 1978

From Your Friends at Dunkin Donuts
New Bedford/Fairhaven ~ Daly-Kenney Group

Gembala Family ~ Arrived 12/24/1948
John, Ewa, Theresa, Josephine, Jane, Stanley, Mary, Etta & Raymond

Glaser Glass Corp.
In Memory of Alvin Glaser

Frederick M. Kalisz, Jr.
Mayor of New Bedford ~ 1998-2006

Kitchen & Baths
Est. 1975 ~ George & Denise Reiniche

The Lariviere Family
Paul and Jackie, Paul Jr., Peter, Julie & Ted

In Honor of Elaine Lima
"The Queen of Downtown" ~ Your friend, Julie

Master Urban Educators, LLC.
Jo-Anne Mello Hodgson, Executive Director

John & Diana Meldon
J.J. Best Banc & Co.

New Bedford YMCA
In Honor of CEO & President, Gary Schuyler

Polish Women's Business & Professional
Club *Established 1937.*

Ponichtera & DeNardis, P.C.
Ann Ponichtera DeNardis, A. Daniel P. DeNardis

Regal House
Santos Family & Holden Family

In Memory of
Jerrold, Carol & Scott Rogers

Sandwich Lantern
Steve Sherman, NB Voke Class of 1976

Sea Lab Marine Science Education Center
In honor of Paul Levasseur, Arthur A. Dutra & Simone P. Bourgeois

Souza & Branco Electric, Inc.
Dan Souza, NB Voke 1980, Louis Branco, NBHS 1976

In Honor of Ms. Sandra "Sandy" Sylvia
The Best Teacher Ever!

In Memory of The Sylvia Family
Dad, Mom, Norman & Gary - Love, Sandra Sylvia

In Honor of Our Parents
Honorable John A. & Rosemary S. Tierney

In Memory of our friend Ronald W. Teser
Norris H Tripp Company Inc.

New Bedford-Fairhaven Bridge Donors ~ (Gifts of $100)

Dr. & Mrs. George H. Abbot
Fred & Marcia Anselmo
Kathleen Anthony
Mr & Mrs. Frank Allen
Janet Thomas Barnard
Peter & Joan Barney
Judith Barry
Dawn Baxter & Spence Smith
Teri Bernert & Paul Krause
Chuck & Jan Bichsel
Sandra Bilodeau
Lee Blake
In Honor of Emile G. & Barbara E. Blier
Norma L. Bosse
Brewer Banner Designs
Diane Brodeur & Bill Moniz
Gertrude T. Burr
Capt. Greg Freitas
Claire T. Carney
Gardner Chace
Chas. Ashley Insurance Agency
Susan & Andrew J. Chlebus
Gloria Clark
The Cleveland Family
Tom Coish
Cornell Dubilier Electronics, Inc.
Jeff Costa Fitness
Attorney Jan E. Dabrowski
Carlos DaCunha
Brooke & Reid Davis
Joanne Demers
Bruce & Melanie Demoranville
Dorothy Cox's Chocolates ~ Est. 1928
John & Mary Beth Dowd
Dr. & Mrs. Charles Eades
Fairfield Inn & Suites & Waypoint Event Center

Anne Folino
Gallery X
Garlington Florist, Inc.
Mark & Jeannie Gates
Bill & Joyce Hillier
Robert E. Horne
Robert & Deborah Huckabee
Diane Buckley Jacob
Kenneth & Linda Jensen
Jewish Federation of Greater New Bedford
The John & The Bruno Families
Susan (Ashley) Kaput
Mark & Nancy Keighley
David N. Kelley II
Karin Buckley Kingsland
Cynthia L. Burt Knowles
Stuart A. Lawrence
Paul & Elizabeth Lestage
Councilor Joseph P. Lopes
Carl & Christine Loria
Judy & Ned Lund
Kathleen & James Mandly
Ron & Nancy Manzone
Laura E. McLeod
James J. Mello
Neil Mello
Attorney Joseph L. Michaud
Laura J. Morales
Darryl & Georgette Murphy
Susan Nelson
New Bedford Antiques at Wamsutta Place
New Bedford Historical Society
New Bedford Symphony Orchestra
W. Patt & Tania Nicolet
Nancy Nissen
Theresa C. Nowell

Oceans Fleet Fisheries
Jason K. Paiva
Andrew & Cathy Paven
Elizabeth Pimentel
Georgianna Pimentel Contiguglia
Robert C. Pina
Richard A. Pline
Roger Poirier
Marlene Pollock & Dan Gilbarg
Roger F. Poulin
Leonard M. Poyant
Project Independence Adult Day Health
Marjorie & Tom Puryear
John Querim
Mary Jane Richard & Jack Nelson
Dr & Mrs. Thomas Ridzon
Joanne Robinson
Alice Sylvia Rose
Thomas C. Sargent Sr.
Jody Gonsalves Seivert
Andrew & Diane Setera
Everett B. & Pamela A. Sherman
Ray and Charlotte Smith
Tom & Jo-Ann Souza
Paul A. & Toy T. St. Pierre
Nancy and David Sylvain
Maureen & Ed Sylvia, CPA
Richard & Patricia Taylor
Louise Tervo
Charles T. Toomey
Donald Veronneau
Sid Wainer & Son, Gourmet Outlet
Waterfront Historic Area LeaguE
Richard A. Weeks & Bernadette Appleyard
Susan White

Amaral Family
Ronald, June, Michael, Mark & William

Baszak Family
Bruno, Theresa, Ted, John & Mary Ann

Bay State Window & Door, Inc. ~ Est. 1951.
In memory of my Dad "Butch Silva." Love, Michelle

The Berche Family & The Roy Family
with love from Paula Berche Roy and Marc P. Roy

In Honor of Gilbert & Lois Botelho
Best Nana and Grampa Ever!

Down to Earth Natural Foods
In Honor of Dolores Caton, NBHS Class of 1951

Executive Mitsubishi
Bob Burgess & Jim Burgess

Luzo Auto Center
John & Victor Pinheiro

Gene Manzone
Neighborhood Auto Services, Inc.,

In Memory of Manuel & Alice Oliveira
From your Loving Family

Attorney Paul J. Santos
New Bedford High School Class of '78

Linda M. Taber
Bishop Stang High School Class of '68

In Memory of
Antone & Almorinda Ventura

Wings Auto Inc.
Jesse & Fatima Gaudencio

Mike Young
New Bedford High School Class of '64

Acknowledgments

*F*irst, we would like to recognize the authors, editors and contributors for the thousands of collective hours poured into this book at very little recompense. Al Saulniers, economist emeritus by trade, wrote most of the material on education, music, industry, immigration and anything to do with statistics, percentages, census findings and unemployment. Marsha McCabe, in her spirited and passionate style, contributed most of the person-to-person and oral history accounts, as well as chapter overviews and articles on social organizations, community groups and neighborhoods. Natalie White, in addition to contributing beautifully crafted essays, had the pleasure of editing everyone's work and was the guiding force and glue that kept everyone working together with focus. Joseph Thomas and Jay Avila sculpted the content, assigned writing topics, selected photographs, created the design, constructed the layout and contributed research, writing and editing.

Spinner is indebted to several major contributors who have been a part of the organization for many years, and we are thankful to have them by our side. We leaned heavily on Claire Nemes for the bulk of copyediting and for her keen insights. Contributing writer and longtime Spinner author and associate Dan Georgianna wrote the Strike of '28 and essays on the fishing industry. Zachary White provided library research, photography and general assistance. We are also grateful to Jennifer White Smith for allowing us to freely use material from her thesis on South Terminal urban renewal; and to Kathryn Grover and Carmen Maiocco for allowing us to mine their writings on the history of Acushnet Avenue.

Much appreciation goes to Spinner staff Susan Grace and Karen Gravel for their dedication, for helping in all areas of production and for keeping the organization afloat while we labored over five years putting the two volumes together. The authors wish to thank their spouses for their longstanding and unyielding support: Jane Thomas, Suzanne Saulniers, Jeremy Crockford, Bob McCabe and Stacey Avila. And we're beholden to project volunteers—Claire Nemes, Sonia Pacheco, Marsha Onufrak, Gloria de Sá and Paula Saunders— who helped raise money, locate resources and provide guidance.

Spinner would like to offer special thanks to Lisa Bindas, owner of Gotta Have It! Inc. in Fairhaven, who generously gave to this project in so many ways. Grateful to Spinner's mission to preserve local history, Bindas single-handedly set out to raise a remarkable $10,000 for this book—and she did. Caught up in her infectious enthusiasm, friends and customers coming through her gift shop joined in her fundraising goal. Having grown up in New Bedford, she was touched by the outpouring of support and struck by the affection and connections many donors have for the city, its history and the families who have lived here.

A sincere thank you goes out to the institutions and individuals who graciously made their photographic collections, historical materials and personal knowledge available. In particular, we thank the editors, writers and staff of the *Standard-Times* newspaper who gave their time, expertise and encouragement. We are also grateful to the staff at the New Bedford Free Public Library for their assistance.

Finally, a most heartfelt thank you to all of our sponsors, small and large, who provide much-needed support to the Spinner organization. We are flattered and honored that so many members of the community see our mission as worthwhile and share our vision of preserving local history. It would be impossible to publish books of this nature if it were done solely on a for-profit basis. New Bedford is, after all, a small fish in a very expensive ocean. Demand for picture history books in small markets is just not strong enough to pay for such projects.

And so, *A Picture History of New Bedford: Volume 2 ~ 1925-1980* belongs to the contributors, the sponsors and the readers, as well as to future generations who will call New Bedford home.

Contributors

Writers / Editors
- Jay Avila
- Marsha L. McCabe
- Alfred H. Saulniers
- Joseph D. Thomas
- Natalie A. White

Proofreading
- Robert Barboza
- Tamia Burt
- Susan Grace
- Karen Gravel
- Alexandra Harrison
- Liz LaValley
- Richard Pacheco

Writing / Editing / Research
- Daniel Georgianna
- Claire Nemes
- Jennifer White Smith
- Zachary M. White

Volunteers
- Christina Connelly
- Claire Nemes
- Sonia Pacheco
- Marsha Onufrak
- Gloria de Sá
- Paula Saunders

Resources
- Fort Rodman/Fort Taber Military Museum
- Library of Congress / National Archives
- Mass Memories
- Museum Madeiran Heritage
- Millicent Library
- New Bedford Fire Museum
- New Bedford Free Public Library
- New Bedford Musicians Hall of Fame
- New Bedford Whaling Museum
- Our Lady Of Assumption Church
- The *Standard-Times*
- UMass Dartmouth Archives

Donors of Photographs & Other Contributors

- Baldwin Family
- Jan Baptist
- John Baptista Jr.
- Joan Barney
- Mark L. Baron
- Lucille M. Barbero
- Joan Beaubian
- Arthur Bennett
- Lee Blake
- Kirsten Bendiksen
- Norman Bergeron
- Mary Jean Blasdale
- George Blier
- Tony Branchaud
- David Brenneke
- Jane Oliver Britto
- Hazel Britto
- Raymond Buckley Family
- John K. Bullard
- Linda Whyte Burrell
- Edward Camara
- Claire T. Carney
- Leo J. Carney Family
- Patrick Carney
- Ruth Caswell
- Sylvia Ann Chariton
- Roger Chartier
- Normand Chartier
- Gloria Clark
- Jimmy Connors
- Gilbert and James Costa
- Paul Cyr
- Jeffrey Dawson Family
- Debrosse Family
- George Diggle
- William do Carmo
- Louis Doucette Jr. Family
- John P. & Mary Beth Dowd
- Ferreira Family
- David Fauteux
- Rosemary Ferro
- Judith Farrar
- Fontaine Family
- Diane Gilbert
- Peter Grace
- Kathryn Grover
- Donna A. Halper
- William R. Hegarty
- Natalie Hemingway
- Lou Henderson Family
- Janice Hodson
- Cecelia Hurley
- Jack Iddon
- Max Isaksen
- Olga Jacques
- Eric Johnson
- Richard A. Kellaway
- Landry Family
- Scott W. Lang
- Cynthia Le Roux
- John Linehan
- Isabelle Livramento
- Ann Marie Lopes
- Anne Louro
- Ned Lund, MD
- Carmen Maiocco
- John A. Markey
- Florence Marshall & Family
- Richard Marshall
- John Mckenna
- Joanne Evans Mee
- Joanne Mendes
- Gerald Messier
- Jon Mitchell, Mayor
- Richard Moniz
- John Mullins
- N.B. Symphony Orchestra
- Teresa Nielsen
- Paul Nunes
- Sonia Pacheco
- Tony Pacheco Family
- Phil Paleologos
- Maggi Peirce
- Frank Perry
- Jim Phillips
- Coleen Pina-Garon
- Richard A. Pline
- Eleanor Pontes
- Susan Poyant
- Jack Radcliffe
- David Reis
- Rice Family
- Raymond Rivard
- John K. Robson
- Charles Russell Family
- Jackie Santos
- Anna Senna
- Calvin Siegal
- J. Michael Smith
- Michael & Joe Silvia
- Lionel Soares Family
- George Sylvia Family
- Tadeusz & Jeanne Swiszcz
- Buddy Thomas
- Andy Tomolonis
- Al Tremblay
- José & Ana Vinagre
- Bobby Watkins Family
- Neal Weiss
- WHALE
- Glenys L. Walcott
- John & Martha Worley

Foreword

*A*t last, the second volume of the history of New Bedford is in hand. Covering just a bit more than half a century, it would seem a simple task. After all, how many interesting events could have transpired in a small city such as ours in five decades? It turns out quite a lot. These events and so many individuals—industrialists, shopkeepers, musicians, sea captains, nurses, teachers and others—have left their marks. Though many are long gone and some forgotten, they nonetheless have shaped the arc of New Bedford's story. Some we celebrate, some we are still trying to figure out.

It may be a cliché to say that we are the sum of the individual accomplishments and failures of those who came before us. But in small-city America, that history is what gives us character. I have asked myself, what does my life have to do with whaling, fishing or going to sea? I'm a landlubber. I was not, I thought, shaped by the sea in any way. My ancestors came here to work in factories, to escape the hardships of famine and religious persecution pervasive in the "old country." As far as I know, the only thing my Middle Eastern ancestors knew about the sea is that they had to cross it in order to build a new life. Yet, I find myself boasting of our seafaring heritage as if I experienced it firsthand. Well maybe I have, unwittingly. Anyone who spends time in New Bedford can hear the sea in the city's voices and feel the sea in its heart. We are all influenced in tangible and intangible ways by the culture around us. For example, I speak New Bedford. I carry the strains of the Portuguese neighborhood I grew up in; the French Catholic school I was reared in; the Irish parochial high school I matured in; and the local university that brought me to adulthood. I've shared the New Bedford experience. Each New Bedford generation has its own stories of Friday night hangouts, dances and drive-ins. But we all have walked the same streets, cruised the same strips, and for some, worked in the same brick sweatshops for however long it was necessary.

Like the first, this second volume of illustrated history portrays a local twist to major events of the period. It is highlighted by portraits of high-profile as well as little-known people. The book exemplifies the American experience in many contexts—war, industry, sports, recreation, politics, social rebellion, urban demolition and revitalization, family life and artistic expression. It is in no way complete, but touches on many of the large and small moments in history that helped create New Bedford's identity.

– Joseph D. Thomas, Publisher

Contents

Sponsors and Donors	iv
Acknowledgments	viii
Contributors	ix
Foreword	x
New Bedford Mayors	xii

Chapter 1 ~ 1925–1941 Stacks to Masts 3

Introduction: New Bedford between the Wars; The Textile Strike of 1928; Prohibition and Rumrunning; The Great Depression & the WPA; The Hurricane of 1938; The Last Whaling Voyage; The New Bedford Fishery, 1925–1942; Manufacturing Industries; The Needle Trades, 1825–1960; New Bedford Municipal Airport; Trains, Trolleys, Buses & Cars; Port of New Bedford; Acushnet Avenue & the North End; South Water Street & the South End; South Central Neighborhood; Ice Cream, Lunch & Gas Stations; Recreation, Sports & Entertainment; Music; Immigration & Social Activities; Education.

Chapter 2 ~ 1942–1960 War & Peace 149

Fort Rodman during WWII; The Home Front; Mostly Women; Honor & Sacrifice; The Hurricanes of 1944, 1954 and 1960; Industry at Mid Century; From Textiles to Apparel; Acushnet Process Company; Old, New and Renewed Industries; Home Brew; Transport Services; St. Luke's Hospital, 1942–1960; The Fishing Industry during World War II; The Longshoremen; Boats & Bridges; Planes & Trains; Lunch Counters, Diners & Cafés; Bakeries & Pie Makers; The Old West End; WNBH and WBSM; Presidents; Basil Brewer and the *Standard-Times*; Sporting News; World Premieres & Moby Dick; "Sweet Daddy" Grace; New Bedford Schools; St. Mary's Home; A History of Music of New Bedford.

Chapter 3 1960–1980 Winds of Change 254

Hurricane Protection; South Terminal Urban Renewal; Highway Development; The Waterfront Historical Area LeaguE; Hot Town, Summer 1970; West End Development; Vietnam; Protests, Rallies & Marches; Model Cities; Claremont Companies; Immigration; Industrial Park and the Acushnet Cedar Swamp; New Industries; Hospitals; The Needle Trades; Outlet Stores; Fishing Industry 1960–1980; New Bedford Schools, 1960–1980; Film, Television & Radio; Sounds of New Bedford: Rock and Rythym & Blues; Feast of the Blessed Sacrament; The Photography of E. Milton Silvia & The *Standard-Times*; Photos Around Town.

Index	360
Bibliography	370
Index to Photographs and Photographers	372

New Bedford Mayors ~ 1847–1905

1847–1851
Abraham H. Howland

1852
William J. Rotch

1853–1854
Rodney French

1855–1856
George Howland Jr.

1857–1858
George H. Dunbar

1859
William Nye

1860–1862
Isaac C. Taber

1863–1865
George Howland Jr.

1866–1867
John H. Perry

1868–1869
Andrew G. Pierce

1870–1872
George B. Richmond

1873
George H. Dunbar

1874
George B. Richmond

1875–1876
Abraham H. Howland Jr.

1877
Alanson Borden

1878
George B. Richmond

1879–1880
William T. Soule

1881–1884
George Wilson

1885–1888
Morgan Rotch

1889–1890
Walter Clifford

1891–1892
Charles S. Ashley

1893
Jethro C. Brock

1894
Stephen Allen Brownell

1895–1896
David Parker

1897–1905
Charles S. Ashley

New Bedford Mayors ~ 1906–2017

1906
Thomas Thompson

1907
Charles S. Ashley

1908–1909
William J. Bullock

1910–1914
Charles S. Ashley

1915–1916
Edward R. Hathaway

1917–1921
Charles S. Ashley

1922–1924
Walter H. B. Remington

1925–1926
Edward R. Hathaway

1927–1936
Charles S. Ashley

1937–1940
Leo E. J. Carney

1941–1942
Mathew A. Glynn

1943–1951
Arthur N. Harriman

1952–1953
Edward C. Peirce

1953
Francis J. Lawler, Interim Mayor

1954–1955
Arthur N. Harriman

1956–1961
Francis J. Lawler

1962–1969
Edward F. Harrington

1970–1971
George Rogers

1972–1982
John A. Markey

1983–1985
Brian J. Lawler

1986–1991
John K. Bullard

1992–1998
Rosemary S. Tierney

1998–2006
Frederick M. Kalisz Jr.

2006–2011
Scott W. Lang

2012–
Jon Mitchell

Chapter I ~ 1925–1941
Stacks to Masts

Fishing vessels at City Pier 4, 1942. Fish dealer L. S. Eldridge & Son, located on City Pier 4, led the transformation of New Bedford into one of America's richest fishing ports. At the time of this photograph, New Bedford handled 62% of the nation's supply of yellowtail and 70% of its scallops.

Introduction: New Bedford between the Wars

In the years between the world wars, New Bedford witnessed the heady heyday and desperate downfall of the textile industry. It saw the end of a once dominant whaling industry and the burgeoning of the port's prominent fishing industry. During these years, immigration and population peaked and then plummeted. The automobile shifted the transportation landscape, radio revolutionized news and entertainment and "talkies" took over the theaters. Markets crashed. Mills collapsed. Storefronts closed. At times, the city struggled to provide its citizens with education, jobs, food and housing, but New Bedford's spirit still prevailed with song and sport, invention and innovation—and always a strong sense of community. Despite desperate circumstances and historically high unemployment, city folk found ways to celebrate, gathering for sport competitions, growing community gardens and pitching in on federal and local work programs to build piers, parks and roadways. Although challenged, New Bedford nurtured some of the best musicians in the region, entertaining folks with marching bands, concerts and vaudeville.

In 1920, at the cotton industry's height, 70 cotton mills operated 3.4 million spindles and employed 33,708 men,

women and children. The city thrummed with round-the-clock textile work, rolling out fabrics to be sent around the world. Workers often toiled for 10 hours or more a day, and even young children filled factory shifts. By 1938 though, only 30 mills remained. Production had plunged an incredible 93 percent. The number of spindles dropped by 81 percent to 644,000 and mill employment fell 77 percent to 7,799.

New Bedford went from a magnet for immigrants seeking jobs to a down-and-out city abandoned by many families and individuals fleeing to find better lives elsewhere. In 1937, its unemployment rate reached 32.5 percent, the country's second highest for mid-sized cities with populations of 100,000 or more. It ranked only one-tenth of a percent behind the nation's leader, Scranton, Pennsylvania.

Weave room of the Nashawena Mills Corporation, 1920. *Organized by William Whitman in 1909, Nashawena Mills began production in 1910 with the manufacture of rayon and silk fabrics, jacquard novelties and fine cotton cloth. Nashawena began as one of the largest fine cotton mills in the country with 125,000 spindles and 1,200 looms. In 1925, the mill expanded, buying the Manomet Mill #3, renaming it Plant B and converting it to a weaving plant. Thus, with 272,000 spindles and 6,100 looms, Nashawena became the largest single manufacturer of combed goods in the country. In the 1930s, the mill began to divest assets, selling Plant B to Aerovox. In 1941, it leased Plant A to States Nitewear Manufacturing Company. Among today's occupants are Joseph Abboud Manufacturing and the Hatch Street Studios.*

A complicated set of political, economic, business and labor forces from within and without the city drove the dramatic decline.

Competition from Southern mills had left New Bedford lagging irrevocably behind. Because many of the city's mill owners had been slow to invest in modern, more efficient machinery such as automatic looms and ring spindles, its mills stood in marked contrast to newer Southern mills with more modern equipment that embodied the latest efficiency gains. New Bedford mills proved unable to keep pace. Supported and managed in large part by a small, insular group from prominent local families, they suffered as their owners clung to inefficient, incompetent and unprogressive ways. Managers siphoned off high salaries, reinvested as little as possible, and employed questionable accounting practices that proved disastrous. After mill owners announced a 10 percent wage cut, a seasoned and organized industrial workforce rebelled. Textile workers went on strike for six months in 1928.

Southern mill owners, meanwhile, enjoyed comparatively untroubled labor relations. Strike actions were practically unknown in Southern mills, where workers coming from farms and small villages proved to be more complacent and less expensive. In the 1920s, average yearly wages were 48 percent higher in New Bedford than in cotton-growing states.

The situation worsened during the Great Depression. New Bedford had weathered previous downturns, partly because it

A slice of the North End district—from Wamsutta Street to Earle Street—shows city cotton mills along the west bank of the Acushnet River in 1938. From left to right are Wamsutta Mills, Grinnell Manufacturing Company, Fairhaven Mills / Columbia Spinning Company, Bennett Manufacturing Company, Soule Mills, Pierce Manufacturing Company (center) and Whitman Mills. At far left sits the large vacant lot, a remainder from the just-razed Bristol Mill.

could draw on ready labor from an increasing pool of immigrants and eager workers displaced by the demise of the whaling industry. It had also benefited from lower transportation and fuel costs because of superior rail-to-water shipping links and use of steam power. Even as Southern mills began operating in the early 1900s—taking market share for coarse textile goods away from many Northern mills—New Bedford had flourished because it concentrated on finer cotton textiles. During the Depression, however, demand for the city's fine goods, such as plushes, velvets, damasks and voiles, tumbled.

By the end of the Depression, only 13 textile mills remained, and wages had fallen by two-thirds. New Bedford worked to attract new industries and keep the ones it had. In 1927, the Board of Commerce formed an Industrial Development Division to help local firms expand and to convince new businesses to settle here. From 1927 to 1939, Frank J. Leary, the New Yorker who ran the division, reported that it had brought in new companies that provided 8,002 jobs for the community. In 1939, it brought two firms to the city: cranberry packager Stokely Brothers & Co. and Seaview Fish Company. Stokely Brothers did not last long, closing in 1942. Seaview Fish was still operating at the end of the 1940s.

In February 1938, Mayor Leo E.J. Carney, backed by newspaper publisher Basil Brewer, created the Industrial Development Legion and urged city workers to contribute weekly to fund its activities. Police, firefighters and teachers,

some who were concerned that failure to pay would jeopardize their jobs, contributed. By the end of the drive, city workers had raised more than half the legion's funds. In 1938, the legion spent $42,500 of those funds to cover partial costs of bringing Aerovox Corporation, a maker of radio and refrigerator condensers, from Brooklyn to New Bedford. As no local firm produced anything similar, Aerovox's arrival helped diversify the city's industrial base. In 1941, the Aerovox presence induced Cornell Dubilier, another electronics manufacturer, to also locate in the city.

The legion attracted several apparel firms to the Grinnell Mill on Kilburn Street. The American Huarache Company, later known as American Playshoe Company, made Mexican-style leather sandals. Epstein Brothers made flannelette pajamas and nightgowns. New Bedford Hosiery Company knit men's socks. Star Garment Manufacturing Company made ladies' sportswear, skirts and blouses. Tru-Line Dress Company produced women's dresses. In the Whitman Mill, N.A. Textile Company made chenille bedspreads. All had ceased operations by 1943.

Flooded basement of the Nonquitt Mills, 1938. *Four feet of water in the basement of the riverfront factory destroyed merchandise and equipment.*

Funding secured by the legion from the Reconstruction Finance Corporation also allowed Taber Mill keep operating, providing jobs for 750 employees for an additional six months and helped the Naushon Mills repair damage caused by the 1938 hurricane, enabling it to remain open through World War II. With the legion's aid, the Acushnet Process Company bought Nashawena weave shed B, Strand Leather Company expanded its space, and Monarch Wash Suit doubled its floor space.

Pierce Mill on Belleville Avenue at the foot of Tallman Street, 1941. *Even before America entered World War II, its defense industry was driving full throttle providing European allies with equipment, supplies and ammunition. In making this image, Farm Security Administration photographer John Collier recorded the wheels of industry running around the clock, pulling a work-hungry citizenry out of economic depression.*

On the Waterfront

During this time, whaling receded into the city's economic past. In 1925, the schooner *John R. Manta* made the last successful American whaling voyage, returning to New Bedford with a disappointingly small haul; in 1927, it aborted its voyage and returned empty, a definite end to whaling.

But New Bedford did not give up its ties to the sea. As the whaling era faded, and the textile era withered, some turned to harvest the ocean's bounty of fish. A small commercial fleet began to grow around 1910.

A 1925 *Providence Journal* article highlighted the city's emergent fish business. Although New Bedford then ranked "nowhere" as a commercial fish port—city boats had to unload and sell their catches at Fulton Fish Market in New York— fishing provided a growing bright spot in the city's economy. The article described the waterfront's new seafarers:

> The spirit which took New Bedford's men down to the sea in ships to barter their lives against a living is not yet dead...The humming looms of New Bedford's mills have drowned out the rattle of the anchor chain and the creak of the cordage, and the boll weevil and its activities are of more concern to this city than good weather at sea...But as long as there are fish in the sea there will be men to go and get them.

At the time New Bedford's fleet comprised more than 14 fishing boats worth at least $25,000 each and many smaller boats. Even so, few thought the fishing industry would amount to much. That soon changed. With fishing providing some of the city's few employment opportunities during the Depression, many looked to the port for jobs—and found them.

Soon Linus S. Eldridge and others began buying fish from New Bedford's fishing boats and trucking seafood to New York and other markets. This bolstered the city as a major fishing port and created allied industries such as filleting, freezing, ice-making, outfitting, packaging and transport.

The waterfront also developed certain dark and dangerous aspects. Some fishermen and other seafarers turned to rumrunning during Prohibition (1920 to 1933). Cash-strapped men from Maine to Florida loaded their boats not with fish but with whiskey, gin, rum or champagne. They tried to outwit authorities to deliver their liquid catch, usually under cover of darkness. In the early days of rumrunning, an almost congenial relationship existed between the US Coast Guard and the smugglers. But as time wore on, smuggling became more dangerous and the stakes more serious as a more violent criminal element entered the picture and enforcement efforts grew more deadly.

New Bedford's small dragger fleet iced in at Pier 3, 1935.

The Textile Strike of 1928

On Easter Monday April 9, 1928, the New Bedford Cotton Manufacturers' Association, representing owners of the city's 27 major mills, announced a general 10 percent wage cut effective Monday, April 16. The proposed cut infuriated workers. For them, the 1920s had brought speedups, stretch-outs, automation, layoffs and wage cuts totaling 30 percent. By 1928, a city textile worker earned a yearly average of $1,037, about half of the federal government's estimated minimum budget covering health and decency. In sharp contrast, mill owners had seen a decade of high profits with record output and profits occurring in 1927. The *Evening Standard* reported that profits for the association mills exceeded $2.5 million. They had paid out $47 million in dividends during the previous decade alone.

At the time of the proposed 10 percent cut, about 5,000 of the city's 30,000 textile workers belonged to one or more of seven craft unions. These were loosely organized into the New Bedford Textile Council. The remaining workers, mostly Portuguese, Poles, French Canadians and Cape Verdeans, were not union members either by choice or because their jobs were not unionized.

As the pay cut approached, William Batty, head of the loomfixers union and secretary of the Textile Council, pressed for a strike vote. Having learned of the pending wage cut, outside labor organizers Fred Beal and William Murdock arrived in New Bedford to form the Textile Mills Committee (TMC), meant to be an industrial union of all textile workers. At a tumultuous meeting on April 12, the Textile Council voted 2,572 to 188 to strike if owners cut wages. When the Cotton Manufacturers' Association refused to back down, workers streamed out of the mills on Monday, April 16.

William Batty, Secretary of the New Bedford Textile Council.

Initially, the strike had a holiday atmosphere with spouses and children joining the festivities. Batty played his cornet and led strike songs in Brooklawn Park. Strike funds collected by the Textile Council from throughout New England provided soup, bread and lollipops that were handed out at the South

First day of the strike, Nashawena Mills. *"There was some uncertainty about whether or not to go to work," wrote the* Evening Standard*. "Some hoped they might find a sign, 'No Cut,' posted to cancel the strike. A few workers entered the mill to get personal belongings. Others were overheard to say, 'If you'll go, I'll go in too,' but no one started in. Machines could be heard running near the doors where the crowd gathered. The noise gave the impression that some workers were in the mills, but with four or five cars in the parking lot, it was obvious the bosses were running the machines. Outside the Nashawena, a shout went up and the crowd of workers streamed away after the gates were closed."*

End's Washington Club and other locations all over the city. Meanwhile, the TMC, growing in influence among Portuguese and Polish workers, distributed fish and bread donated by fishermen and bakers.

To strikers, victory seemed assured. TMC-organized mass picketing kept the mills closed. The Textile Council published a 12-part series written by nationally renowned labor economist Dr. Norman Ware, who called the wage cut unnecessary because New Bedford's finely woven cloth did not compete with the coarse cloth produced by low-wage Southern mills and other manufacturers. Ware also argued that wage cuts were unfair at a time when profits were rising. Liberal churchmen, mostly Protestant, called for a return to the higher wage. A headline in the *Evening Standard* reported, "CONSIDER MILL WAGES FIRST, PROFITS LATER, PLEAD PASTORS." In the article, Rev. Linden White declared that private detectives were offering bribes to clergy willing to preach that workers should return to work. Local merchants, whose sales fell because their worker-customers had no paychecks, said "the burden of proof lies with the manufacturers." Even the city's newspapers favored the workers. An editorial in the *New Bedford Times* chided mill owners, "Among the newspapers of their own city they could not find a single editorial comment in their favor."

Mill owners were not united in their reactions. The Dartmouth Mills and the Firestone, Goodyear and Fisk tire plants, the largest mills in the city, refused to cut wages. The Beacon Mill withdrew from the association and rejected the 10 percent cut. Two silk mills settled separately with the Textile Council; three others had not cut wages.

However, the Cotton Manufacturers' Association refused to negotiate and in mid-summer went on the offensive. John Sullivan, agent for Taber Mill as Association president, broke the three-month silence in a series of newspaper articles that accused city police and the courts of being too lenient on pickets and Mayor Charles S. Ashley of negligence for failing to protect mill property.

Police and the courts responded by taking quick action against the TMC. Beal and Murdock, who had been arrested several times for singing, whistling and creating a "nuisance"

STRIKE IN 27 MILLS STARTS, HUNDREDS AT GATES ORDERLY

Binns States Walkout 100 Per Cent Effective—Batty Says Non-Union Workers Co-operate

MACHINES HEARD IN FEW PLANTS

Morning Shift Spinners Go in at Page—Throng Outside Sharp Indulges in Cheers and Snake Dance

Evening Standard headlines on the first day of the strike.

Fred Beidenkapp, president of the Workers International Relief (WIR), addresses a large crowd at the Cove Road landfill near County Street.

on the picket lines, were jailed for 30 and 60 days respectively. Police repeatedly arrested Elizabeth Donnelly, Augusto Pinto and Jack Rubenstein along with hundreds of rank and file strikers. Courts imposed lengthy sentences and assessed bail of hundreds of thousands of dollars. Police stepped up surveillance of TMC headquarters and disrupted deliveries there of bread and milk by issuing traffic violations. City newspapers picked up the cry of the "Red Menace," applying it to the TMC. Sullivan labeled sympathetic clergymen, Quakers and liberal legislators as being among the city's 800 "Reds." The *Evening Standard* responded: "The Mayor will spare no resources to see that the communists cannot rule in New Bedford."

Confrontations intensified. When owners announced the mills' reopening on Monday, July 9, Mayor Ashley refused to issue a permit for a TMC-organized parade. Instead, he called in the National Guard and 150 police from other cities. The attempted parade collapsed when police arrested its leaders and dispersed marchers. Still, the mills failed to reopen; 20,000 striking workers from the Textile Council and the TMC picketed peacefully, each in separate lines.

Clashes escalated between the Textile Council and the TMC, which had been rivals since the latter's establishment. While the Textile Council never welcomed the TMC (Batty punched Beal the first time he saw him on the picket line), by midsummer hostility extended to every aspect of the strike. Each union had its own legal defense system, rallies, demands and picket lines. The mayor, press, clergy, police and mill owners treated each union differently—most favored the Textile Council over the TMC.

But by summer's end, the Textile Council also found itself in disfavor with many of its former supporters and under attack by the police, courts and other city institutions. The YWCA evicted tenants and Textile Council organizers Sadie Reisch and Josephine Kaczor. On the picket lines, police arrested Batty and three associates, Frank Manning, Donald Thompson and Mike Shulman.

By September, with winter looming, workers were increasingly desperate. Their strike benefits had expired. Grocers, meat markets and landlords faced bankruptcy from extending credit. Mill owners also suffered, losing markets and profits as the strike dragged on. Nevertheless, the Cotton Manufacturers'

225 GALLONS OF SOUP CONSUMED

2,200 Loaves of Bread and 2,000 Lollipops Distributed to Children

Washington Club's Line of More Than 2,000 Longest Since Strike Began

The Washington Club is praised for its generosity.

Pickets gather for the July 4th parade. *The TMC planned two parades—one beginning in the South End and the other in the North End—that would meet in the city center. Police Chief Samuel D. McLeod refused to grant marchers a permit saying it was really a demonstration, which the courts deemed illegal. Nonetheless, the parade took place. McLeod called out every police officer, blocked both routes and arrested more than 30 people.*

Association still refused to budge; more was at stake than the wage cut. The textile and financial editor of the *Evening Standard*, A. A. Talmage, said that the strike's greater importance involved the "question of union domination and factory discipline that would result from a labor victory."

Both the Textile Council and the Manufacturers' Association needed a way out. In September, both groups negotiated a five percent cut, which went to a vote of Textile Council members, excluding the TMC. Despite enormous pressure from the city's clergy, merchants and newspapers to accept the offer, Textile Council members voted 963 to 748 to reject it; TMC members picketed polling places urging workers not to give in. Less than two weeks later, the Textile Council called for another vote. This time, as New Bedford police blocked TMC pickets from the polls, the negotiated compromise carried by an estimated vote of 1,200 to 850. The strike of 1928 was over.

The Great Depression quickly followed. One by one, the mills fled. Falling demand for New Bedford's finely woven cloth, combined with the South's lower labor costs, enticed mill owners to abandon this city's antiquated machinery and old buildings and move south.

Nonetheless, the outcome of the 1928 strike had a strong impact on the region's textile industry. Immediately after the

Crossing the line. *Woe be to him, and his car, if he crossed a picket line during the strike. Onlookers seem amused at the graffiti on this car, parked on South Water Street just a block away from the Acushnet Mills.*

New Bedford settlement, Fall River and Providence mill owners rescinded half of the 10 percent wage cut that they had forced on workers six months earlier. Also, New Bedford union leaders used the experience they gained during the strike to organize the city's textile and clothing workers over the next two generations. Others dispersed throughout New England to organize workers into the new Textile Workers Union of America during the 1930s and 1940s

Arrests at the Whitman Mills. *On July 30, 256 picketers were arrested in an attempt to demoralize demonstrators. "People were hungry," recalled Al Saulnier, "and when the police brought those big moving vans, people jumped into them to get arrested, just to get a free meal. That was quite a stunt!"*

Voices of Strikers

At first, they said it would not last any longer than two weeks. At first, people were in a holiday spirit. Women decided to clean their homes for it was spring—a nice spring. The men were working in their yards as it seemed to me that it wasn't going to last very long, but it lasted. The summer came along and soup kitchens opened up. The bluefish ran in the river, and there was so much fishing that you couldn't get a place on the bridge to fish that year. On Friday, we had bluefish in the chowder. Things got pretty bad as the summer went along, because now all the money that people had was spent. People were not paying their rents and the little stores suffered.

– Gladys Howcraft, cloth inspector

On a typical strike day, I would get up and picket one of the mills. Then I would walk around to the bigger mills and pick a soup kitchen and stay to eat with the people. And very often I would have a speech to make before some particular group. People would come to see me about some problems that they had, and very often at night, I would be invited to one of the striker's homes for supper. No difficulty in understanding the language. They had good humor, some that I didn't always catch. They had their own songs and were always singing, "I want a pie with a plum in it," and so forth.

– Frank Manning, union organizer

We went back with what we thought was a 10% cut. Once we got inside it was 20%, and in some crafts it was more than that. A weaver who was paid piece work would look at his pay and realize the size of the cut. When he went to complain the boss would tell him, "Look, be quiet. If you don't want it, move. The next guy will take it." My wages in the spinning room were clipped 15%. There was nothing we could do. Anyway, once we went back we were just individuals. After the strike there was no unity. You could have said to me, "Hey Pete, I got a $5 cut in my pay." I would have said, "Hey, you're lucky. I got a $7 cut." Then they threw out the old-fashioned looms. A weaver who had run eight looms was given 16. They knew we were at their mercy, so they speeded up the machinery. Looms running 126 picks-a-minute before the strike ran at 240 picks; double speed. Finally, the manufacturers started spreading the rumor that they were going south, and they did.

– Pete Fauteaux, card room worker

Well, you didn't have to go very far to tell these people that they were downtrodden, when kids making 13¢ an hour got 3¢ an hour taken out of their pay. Jobs were closer to people than they are today, because the main vein of their existence was getting each week's pay, each hour's pay. Their living was so closely connected with working.

Back then, there was no 'something else.' You work in the mill and that mill was your life. That's the place you went to; that's the place you came back from; and there is very little in-between because there wasn't enough income to take care of in-between. I don't think you could get a group of workers to go through with what they did then, to strike for six months. In a sense, they have something to lose now, no matter what their status is. In those days, they had nothing to lose.

– Jack Rubenstein, union organizer

Workers International Relief (WIR) Food Station. Located at TMC headquarters on Potomska and South Water Streets, the WIR promised financial support but like other unions delivered little. However, it did administer food donated and collected by supportive unions throughout New England. Much of the outside support came from textile working families in Fall River, who were solicited door-to-door by local organizers.

1928 Strike Songs

> On the line, on the line
> On the picket, picket line
>
> Boys and girls together
> In all kinds of weather
> Singing on the picket, picket line.

Music underpinned the textile strike. Union organizers used songs to promote solidarity among workers and encourage them to embrace collective action. The TMC drilled workers of mainly Portuguese, French Canadian and Polish descent with the words of "Solidarity Forever," sung to the tune of "John Brown's Body." Music also energized and excited strikers. At the Pemaquid Mill, women operatives marched up and down the street singing, "Hail, Hail, the Gang's All Here." On July 30, while 256 arrested strikers sang and chanted at the Central Police Station, Chief of Police Samuel D. McLeod summoned bayonet-wielding National Guardsmen to disperse a crowd of their supporters.

Union members taught children to sing. On August 9, police arrested children's organizer Elizabeth Donnelly and picket captain Marion Botelho for teaching songs and strike cheers to children in a public park. The women were sentenced to 30 days in the House of Correction. Strikers cleverly rewrote songs to mock local authority. They taunted Police Sergeant William H. McCarty by singing, "They bought McCarty for 50¢. The son of a bitch he jumped the fence," to the tune of "Mademoiselle from Armentières." Other songs glorified union leaders. Strikers lionized William Murdock after his jail sentence by chanting, "Strawberry jam, cream of tartar. Who's the TMC's greatest martyr?"

Immigrant strikers sometimes sang in their native languages. An Azorean folk song adapted to the picket line went:

> A rambóia, a rambóia,
> Anda sempre a rambóiar
>
> Quem casar com a papo-seco
> Não precisa de trambalhar.
>
> A woman who loves to dance
> Is always dreaming
>
> Whoever marries a dandy
> Does not need to work.

The pun on papo-seco meaning "dandy" as well as the bread familiarly known as "pop" revealed the family's concern for getting enough food on the table during the strike.

Former speeder tender Esther Cabana had a similar concern in a French-language song that she composed to support her striking husband:

> Ça fera bientôt près de six mois
> Qu'on mange rien que d'la
> soupe aux pois.
>
> Il faudra aller voir M. Poirier
> Se faire donner des bons souliers.
>
> Car il faut être bien chaussé
> Pour pouvoir aller piqueter.
>
> It will soon be almost six months
> That we eat nothing but
> pea soup.
>
> One must go see Mr. Poirier
> To be given some good shoes.
>
> For one must be well shod
> To be able to go picket.

At the time, Charles A. Poirier was secretary of the Board of Overseers of the Poor.

A city growing hungry. Children of striking workers received food at bread lines. The Department of Welfare did what it could and several private groups opened up soup kitchens and bread lines. The Washington Club on South First Street distributed 2,000 to 2,500 loaves of bread and 250 gallons of soup every Tuesday, Thursday and Saturday. The Citizen's Relief Committee issued from 500 to 1,000 grocery orders a day to strikers' families. Many stores did not demand payment from their striking customers. Nonetheless, lost income compelled some workers to leave New Bedford during the strike, and by the end of September everyone was suffering. Strike benefits had run out, and store owners found themselves unable to keep extending credit.

Prohibition and Rumrunning

In the days of Prohibition, local fishermen, many of whom had never been on the wrong side of the law before, suddenly found themselves in demand as rumrunners during one of the most lawless and chaotic periods in American history. Reformers believing "demon rum" and other alcohol led to social ills such as poverty and family disintegration had successfully lobbied for passage of the 18th Amendment, banning liquor's manufacture, transport and sale. Instead of enhancing civic virtue, however, the ban ushered in a period of lawlessness lasting from 1920 to 1933. Smuggling, robbery, piracy and murder became commonplace. As money got scarce during the Depression, even the most unlikely suspects turned to smuggling.

Most illicit alcohol arrived by sea from Europe and the Caribbean in mother ships that anchored and opened for business in infamous Rum Rows, near large ports just outside U. S. territorial waters. The rumrunners would zip under cover of darkness to the mother ships, load up with whiskey or other spirits, and return to shore. They were highly skilled navigators and, more often than not, easily outfoxed the Coast Guard, who pursued them in recovered rumrunning boats called "chasers."

The Casey Boat Yard in Fairhaven built many rumrunners. Designed for speed and concealment, the 40- to 60-foot vessels could hold 1,000 cases of liquor in their double bottoms and false bulkheads. Trucks and horse-drawn wagons would wait on shore to take the goods to local barns or large cities.

The Dorothy Earle Incident

On January 31, 1927, the schooner *Dorothy Earle* was smuggling liquor when it foundered about 175 yards off Westport's Horseneck Beach. Town constables Charles Hitt, Harry Sherman, Phillip Sherman and Omar Brightman salvaged 563 cases. They commandeered storage space in the name of the town at the Ocean House hotel, expecting to get a hefty reward. Instead, New Bedford prohibition agent Dennis Driscoll arrived and arrested the constables for smuggling. He took the liquor, some of it leaking, to the Custom House, which sold it to a Worcester drug firm. As the contraband was leaving the Custom House, a spark from a passing trolley ignited the leaking alcohol and the fire destroyed most of the liquor and two transport trucks. Firefighters rescued only a few cases. A jury acquitted the constables of the smuggling charge.

The *Black Duck*

The skipper of the *Black Duck* was a notorious local smuggler named Charlie Travers, who came to be admired as the speediest rumrunner on the East Coast. The *Black Duck*

Rumrunner *Auf Wiedersehen* at the Coast Guard base in Woods Hole, June 2, 1932. *Owned by Morris Handler of New Bedford, the streamlined speedster was carrying $15,000 worth of liquor on its maiden voyage when captured off Cuttyhunk Island. In this photograph, taken shortly after the seizure, cases of contraband still sit on the deck. While under chase by Coast Guard vessel CG-2296, 75 rounds of gunfire were shot at the boat, wounding one of the crew. Like the* Black Duck, *the* Auf Wiedersehen *was powered by two Liberty aircraft engines. The boat's estimated worth was $70,000.*

Boston Globe *headline, December 30, 1929.*

The *Black Duck* (center) detained in New London, Connecticut, January 1930. *Outfitted with two V-12 Liberty aircraft engines capable of producing 500 horsepower, the diminutive* Duck *could travel at 32 knots—faster than anything in use by the Coast Guard.*

(painted black to blend in with the night) had two successful years, but smuggling turned deadly on December 29, 1929 when the boat was shot up by the Coast Guard, killing its three crewmen. Travers was shot through the hand and nearly bled to death, but he lived to tell about it.

Many versions of the story were told in court: As the boat approached Dumpling Light buoy off Newport, the *CG-290* loomed out of heavy fog and shots rang out. Coast Guard skipper Alex Cornell testified that he had first warned the rumrunner with a horn and searchlight but got no response.

Travers maintained that the *Duck* was never warned but simply gunned down. According to newspaper accounts, Travers claimed, "Everybody knew what we were doing. Hell, we used to moor the *Duck* in the slip next to the Coast Guard cutters during the day! We weren't exactly friends, but we all knew each other, and the rules of the game were that the Coast Guard had to catch you with the alcohol on your boat."

Travers' friends claimed he used his rum money to buy groceries and coal for those in need. Travers went to jail, but charges against him were dropped. The *Black Duck* was refitted and taken into service as a Coast Guard boat.

Motorboat *E885*, 1924. *In an April 1924 raid, the Coast Guard tug* Acushnet *seized the 60-foot-long motorboat* E885. *Merely based on the fast vessel's position near rumrunners off Block Island, authorities charged the people onboard, Joseph P. Jason of New Bedford and Herbert Days of Fairhaven, with "intending" to get liquor and smuggle it ashore in violation of Prohibition, which banned alcohol sale, transportation and manufacture.*

Captain Louis A. Doucette Sr., 1940. *During the Depression, Captain Doucette always brought in three or four 500-pound boxes of fish for the hungry down at the waterfront. He also sent barrels of fish to feed the children at Saint Mary's Home. Tempted by a rich haul of rum, scotch and rye, he succumbed to the lure of contraband and paid the price.*

The *Addie Mae*

Stories of Prohibition characters, catches and near misses abound, but the capture of the Addie Mae is one of the biggest from the era.

Louis Doucette Sr., skipper of the *Addie Mae,* was more than a well-liked, remarkably skilled New Bedford fishing captain; he was also a hero who had been awarded the Carnegie Medal for his brilliant acts of rescue at sea.

He once saved 14 people from drowning, making seven dangerous trips in a dory to rescue the captain and crew of the *Mertie B. Crowley* when it wrecked on the backside of Martha's Vineyard. In another heroic effort, Doucette rowed 150 miles to shore when his schooner *Progress* was torpedoed by a German submarine off Georges Bank during World War I. But in the wild days of Prohibition, Captain Doucette fared less well.

On September 25, 1932, the *Addie Mae* left New Bedford for Vineyard Sound for a day of trawling. That night the Coast Guard noticed a mother ship looming nearby and a shadowy exchange taking place. They moved in and found the *Addie Mae* packed with 850 sacks of imported liquor, the government's largest catch in months, worth $40,000.

There were no shots fired, no speedy getaways. Captain Doucette and his crew were apprehended and taken to Falmouth for questioning. The capture was made by a notorious former rumrunner boat named *Je T'Aime*. In Falmouth, Doucette asked not to be separated from his dog, Daisy, a four-year-old Scottish spaniel who always accompanied him on his trips. He also requested that all the provisions on the boat (minus the liquor) be given to the poor of Falmouth. In the end, he and crew received a scolding and a fine.

Players at the Bergeron Farm Shootout, 1927. *From left to right: Dartmouth patrolman William J. Reynolds, New Bedford businessman Max Fox, and farm cook Jack Antone Burgo. Reynolds served 15 years on the force despite several suspensions. Max Fox, millionaire junk dealer, retired as an auto dealer for Metropolitan Motors in the 1950s. In 1927, Jack Burgo lost his suit for injury benefits against the Cape Verdean Beneficent Association—according to the judge, he should have known better than to engage in illegal activities.*

Shootout on Bergeron Farm

At times, the stakes of smuggling ran dangerously high and violent, and the tales grew more twisted, as with the shootout at Bergeron farm in Dartmouth. Max Fox, a junk dealer turned real estate broker turned bootlegger-smuggler, was smack-dab in the middle of this story. He and his brother Louis were district lieutenants under Charles "King" Solomon, a racketeer who controlled narcotics and illegal gambling in the Boston area in the 1920s and 1930s. Louis ran the Revere area for Solomon, while Max ran the New Bedford region.

On January 6, 1927, Max Fox sent word to Dartmouth Police Chief Thomas C. Barnes that chicken coop raiders were hitting the Bergeron farm. Fox didn't raise chickens, but he stored illegal liquor in the farm's barn. Chief Barnes sent four officers to the farm, and a gunfight involving 50 men ensued. Fox's stash was being raided not by chicken thieves, but by hijackers coming to steal his illegally gotten alcohol. In the midst of the shootout, Fox and his men were able to remove the liquor as the police officers were pinned behind stone walls fighting it out with the hijackers. Some of the liquor was loaded into a sedan bearing Rhode Island plates, which the hijackers had to abandon after crashing into a stone wall. Hundreds of broken liquor bottles littered the ground. Bullets pierced the clothes of two Dartmouth police officers and another bullet shattered the rear window of a third officer's car before lodging in the driver's seat. The battle left farm cook Joaquim "Jack" Antone Burgo with a 25-caliber bullet resting between his skull and brain. Heading to the farm with reinforcements, New Bedford and Dartmouth police spotted suspicious men entering a garage on Kempton Street in New Bedford. Rushing the doors, they found a small amount of liquor, some liquor transport vehicles with warm motors, rifles, revolvers and shotguns. They arrested 14 men hiding in the garage.

Meanwhile, Burgo was brought to St. Luke's Hospital and he later turned state's evidence. Fox's fate, for the crime of conspiracy in connection with the illegal keeping, intended sale and transport of liquor, was three years in prison with a $700 fine. Others received lesser fines and jail sentences.

Later investigations revealed that rogue federal Prohibition agents from New York had sent hijackers from New York and Connecticut to target Fox's shipment, part of a consignment valued at $250,000. Some local police reported they were offered bribes to "not remember" details from that night. One officer resigned, saying he was unhappy with the way police handled the situation.

The End of an Era

In the end, despite some high-profile raids and destroyed stills, Prohibition did little to stop the flow of alcohol. Instead, it opened up black-market and smuggling opportunities, enabling organized crime to build powerful empires. Meanwhile, state and federal governments lost billions of dollars in taxes before Prohibition was repealed by the 21st Amendment in 1933.

Custom House Lane, 1927. *New Bedford Fire Chief Edward Dahill and US Customs Agent Dennis Driscoll guard seized liquor after dousing a conflagration in the alley on the south side of the Custom House. Much of the liquor was lost when a spark ignited some leaking alcohol.*

The New Bedford Liquor Squad, 1934

At left, members of the New Bedford Liquor Squad—police officers Owen Cox, Al Davis and Bill Smith—destroy a still furnace in a raid in the city's North End, 1934. At right, US Customs Inspectors William J. Fitzgerald and Leslie F. Hart heft a cask of Scotch whisky from Islay, the southernmost of the Inner Hebrides Islands, into the New Bedford Custom House, 1934. The Islay Scotch was later among the lots auctioned off by the US Customs Service in Boston. Fitzgerald and Hart attended the auction to witness the fruits of their endeavors.

The Great Depression & the Works Progress Administration (WPA)

New Bedford struggled with crippling unemployment during the Great Depression. In 1934, nearly one in four people could not find work, with 22.5 percent of the city's labor force unemployed. By 1939, unemployment had reached 29.1 percent. The Depression hit workers younger than 21 hardest—during the same years, their unemployment rate soared from 40.0 to 47.4 percent. Many jobless fled. From 1920 to 1940, the city lost almost 11,000 inhabitants.

Mayor Charles S. Ashley tapped into federal funds released after President Franklin D. Roosevelt took office in March 1933, establishing programs and projects that would put people to work and forever change the face of New Bedford.

Several idle mills that had reverted to the city in lieu of unpaid taxes were razed using federal funds, giving temporary jobs to almost 1,200 residents. City workers leveled the Bristol, Acushnet and Potomska Mills and also a Whitman Mills weave shed. After demolishing the buildings, they graded the lots and turned them into city parks. Demolition materials were cleaned and recycled, providing bricks to build the

View east across Rural Cemetery from Rockdale Avenue, 1936. *Expanding Rural Cemetery by 15 acres turned into the city's single largest WPA project, lasting two years and creating more than 800 jobs. Workers cleared weeds, brush and trees from overgrown and heavily wooded acres, then dug the entire area down to grave depth by hand, moving almost 100,000 cubic yards of soil. They removed boulders, then leveled, graded and seeded the land. They also laid new avenues and built fieldstone walls with rounded caps topped by a row of cobblestones. When completed, Rural Cemetery extended west to Rockdale Avenue and north to Grape Street. The WPA paid $500,000 in labor costs while the city paid a mere $55,000 for materials, expecting to recoup that by selling hundreds of newly added cemetery plots. The WPA later built an onsite garage and maintenance building for storage of tools, equipment and cemetery vehicles.*

Wharfinger Building on City Pier 3, the Municipal Garage, the Children's Bathhouse, a 14-car garage at the Water Department, a coal and wood storage building at the City Infirmary, the Buttonwood Park recreation center, a high school addition, and New Bedford Vocational School's welding shop and two-story gymnasium. Recycled planking was used to repair the Coggeshall Street Bridge.

Rural Cemetery projects provided 816 jobs clearing brush from 15 overgrown acres, grading the land, installing avenues and building walls. At Oak Grove Cemetery, laborers built walls and landscaped. In all city cemeteries, they surveyed graves of Civil, Spanish-American and World War veterans.

Opposite city hall, workers constructed the iconic Police Traffic Tower. Built as a 25-foot-tall ornamental lighthouse, it allowed officers to oversee the municipal parking lot. Later, laborers reassembled it at the "octopus" intersection of Mill, Kempton and Pleasant Streets.

Several projects transformed Clark's Point with a concrete seawall along Rodney French Boulevard, rip-rap along the shore, a new stone pier and several jetties. Workers cleaned the beaches, seeded parks, laid out walks and planted trees. Rodney French Boulevard was also the site of the city's largest sewer project, connecting several small sewers that had previously emptied directly into the inner harbor to a new pumping station via one central line. Sewer and pumping station work provided 213 jobs.

Hauling wood along North Front Street, January 1941. *During the Depression, many people scavenged for wood and coal to fuel their stoves. The background buildings are part of the Wamsutta Mills blocks, bound by North Front, Logan and Washburn Streets and Hampton Court.*

In the city's Plainville and West End sections, flood-control sewers were installed. The two-mile-long, six-foot-diameter West End sewer was set 18 feet deep, enabling it to capture runoff and prevent floods around St. Luke's Hospital.

Federal funds were used for much-needed maintenance throughout the city. Thirty-nine streets were resurfaced, while ten miles of old concrete and bluestone walks—some with flagstones as old as New Bedford—were replaced with cement sidewalks. Bricks at city hall were repointed and the public library's exterior lanterns restored. Police and fire stations, the

Dismantling the Bristol Mill, 1933. *One of the first WPA projects was the Bristol Mill demolition, providing employment to 296 workers who cleaned and sorted brick and lumber. More than half a million bricks, 247,730 linear feet of three- and four-inch planking and assorted materials were salvaged for other projects. The razing of the mills left open a tract of 17 acres fronting the Acushnet River. Eleven acres were graded and turned into a playground, and the remaining six became community gardens. By the late 1940s, the lot was developed into John J. Cawley Stadium.*

incinerator plant and many school buildings were repaired. At New Bedford High School, interiors were painted, exterior bricks were cleaned and deteriorated terra cotta was replaced with carved limestone.

At Buttonwood and Brooklawn Parks, workers cleared brush and enhanced water features. Old park buildings were upgraded and new ones added; tennis courts were built at Buttonwood, Brooklawn and Hazelwood Parks. At Brooklawn, workers installed a cricket field and a "bear den" for the zoo. They graded the surface and sunk water mains at Marine Park and converted a former city dump into the Cove Road Playground. Ashley Park received a baseball diamond backstop and Mount Pleasant Playground was furnished with three baseball diamonds and a football field.

The city also used federal funds for out-of-town projects. The water department hired workers to build a new garage at Freetown's Quitticas Pumping Station; plant 15,000 red pines; drain and clear Pochsha Swamp; erect a storage building at Black Brook; and clear 1,200 acres at Great and Little Quitticas Ponds distributing the wood from felled trees to the needy.

Some New Bedford workers took daily buses to help with sand abatement projects on the Cape Cod Canal or to work on the nation's largest emergency relief project: the construction of the Bourne National Guard Facilities (Camp Edwards), designed to accommodate 16,000 people.

Federal funds also provided more intellectual, less physically demanding jobs. Writers and researchers indexed and published historical information, compiling key reference works on New Bedford's ship registers, whaling masters, crew lists and passenger lists. At the county jail, they discovered a prisoner pardon signed by President Abraham Lincoln on June 6, 1862.

Special needs created other work. In the aftermath of the 1938 hurricane, hundreds of federally funded workers toiled along the battered waterfronts where 16 were killed. Along Clark's Cove and in the North End, they rescued marooned survivors from wrecked cottages and tenement houses.

In 1939, the Works Progress Administration became the Work Projects Administration. A year later, construction of the municipal airport began. The city would later transfer it to the US War Department.

Modernizing City Piers 3 and 4, 1935. *The WPA financed the new Wharfinger Building on Pier 3, comprised of 50,000 bricks salvaged from the demolished Bristol and Potomska Mills. The building boasted an office, workshop and storage areas. In 1937, the WPA engaged marine salvage and construction firm Merritt-Chapman & Scott to enlarge the old 200-foot-long City Pier by 240 square feet. Workers replaced worm-eaten wooden pilings with steel-reinforced concrete and the wooden deck with concrete slabs coated with asphalt. Many New Bedford ships, including the whaler* Dartmouth, *launched from this historic location, once the site of Rotch's Wharf. The old city Wharfinger Building can be seen bottom left.*

Police Traffic Tower at municipal parking lot, 1937. *The 25-foot-high, octagonal-shaped tower—built with stones recycled from the Rural Cemetery project—provided a clear view of the lot, enabling the police officer on duty to direct motorists to available spaces. A spotlight sits atop the copper dome.*

New Bedford Vocational School gymnasium, 1937. *The largest WPA-built structure in the city was the two-story, 140-foot-long gymnasium. The project, along with construction of the nearby municipal garage, consumed more than half a million bricks and 250,000 feet of planking salvaged from the Bristol Mill.*

In addition to providing jobs, federal money lifted spirits in other ways. The federally funded circus visited the city and put on a free show for 5,000 children and their parents at Buttonwood Park. A New Bedford sponsored band put on local concerts and traveled to statewide competitions.

Despite the number and variety of city work projects, only one unemployed worker in five was hired. Because funded jobs were offered only to heads of households, the projects did nothing for unemployed youth or married women who, given the opportunity, might have entered the workforce.

To help meet their needs, community centers provided practical training in bookbinding, stenography, speedwriting, woodcraft, sewing and stage work or as household aides and—after 1941—defense training.

Rebuilding a seawall and roadway along Clark's Cove, 1938. *Between 1933 and 1938, the WPA spent millions on an all-out beautification project to improve South End roads, parks and beaches. Workers constructed concrete and stone seawalls, extended Hazelwood Park to the waterfront and built bathhouses at Municipal Beach. Around the peninsula, they laid miles of macadam roads, built piers and breakers along beaches, installed walkways and planted trees. Unfortunately, a hurricane in September 1938 destroyed much of it. Following the storm, WPA workers were back at it. Here they are rebuilding the Clark's Cove seawall, resurfacing Cove Road near Orchard Street and installing new sidewalks.*

WPA Woodcraft Project, January 1940. *Instructors Jesse L. Silva and Francis C. Moore of the Woodcraft Project test planers, lathes, drill presses and other power machinery to be used by craftsmen enrolling in night classes at the Mary B. White School. Begun in January 1936, the project was one of the first WPA recreational programs in the city.*

Sewing Class at the City Mission (later Dennison Memorial Building), South First Street, 1938. *The WPA began administering the Sewing Project, directed toward women and young girls, in 1933. By 1938, New Bedford workers had produced more than 210,000 apparel items for adults and children, as well as comforters and mattresses. Employment in the project reached 571.*

WPA workers, 1935. *Taken in the city's North End or nearby Acushnet, this photograph of a WPA work gang includes George Ferreira (middle row, eighth from left) and his brother-in-law Manuel Simmons (next on right). They were among the 162 working on the Water Department's 1,200 acres surrounding Little and Great Quitticas Ponds. To protect the water supply system, they cleared dead wood and brush along the watershed and planted red pines around the reservoir. The project produced more than 1,000 cords of cut wood for distribution to the needy.*

Community Gardens

Community gardens grew much needed food during World War I and the Great Depression. To feed troops and fend off starvation in allied countries during the war, Herbert Hoover, head of the United States Food Administration, encouraged voluntary food conservation and small gardening at home. In New Bedford, school students tilled vegetables and citizens competed for War Savings Stamps for the best war gardens. Morse Twist Drill provided willing workers with seeds, tools, fertilizer and a tilled garden plot of 40 by 60 feet.

City folk continued the garden tradition during the food scarce days of the Depression. In 1932 and continuing for many years, the Standard-Times, the Mercury and the Council of Women's Organizations of Greater New Bedford cooperated to supply plots, seed and fertilizer to the jobless and needy. Residents worked plots near the Poor Farm, on the former Beacon Mill site on Mount Pleasant Street, the Moore Lot at Shawmut Avenue and Hathaway Road and the former Bristol Mill site on Coggeshall Street.

Many families kept the same plot for years, and putting food on the table was often a family endeavor. In top left photograph, **Domingos Moura** uses his homemade water system inside his garden plot at the Bristol Mill Community Gardens. The well lining and cover were salvaged from the mill ruins.

The young boys in top right photograph proudly show off two sacks of just-harvested potatoes.

In the middle photograph, **John, Gil, Manuel and Charlie Rebello** of 77 Rivet Street tend a garden plot alongside Clark's Cove with Page Mill in the background.

At bottom, home-canned and fresh garden vegetables grown and put up by community gardeners **Arthur and Johanna Richard** of 227 Eugenia Street are on display as part of the Standard-Times' call for entries to the Greater New Bedford Victory Garden Harvest Show, October 8 through 11, 1942 at Bristol Arena.

Community gardens. Domingos Moura (left) of 153 Belleville Avenue, accesses his water system, July 1934. At right, brothers Walter and Henry Correia tend their family garden, September 1940.

The Rebello family tend their community garden, June 1940.

Preserves from New Bedford community gardeners, September, 1942.

Taking Care of the Kids

At the **soapbox derby** on the **Municipal Golf Course**, two cars suffered mishaps rounding the curve. Luckily, contestants wore protective helmets. In 1939, a Pathé newsreel of the Boston Traveler Soap Box Derby played locally to enthusiastic audiences in the Empire, Baylies Square and Strand Theaters.

Soapbox derbies exploded in popularity during the Depression-hit 1930s. Within a few years of their "discovery" by Myron Scott, a photographer for the Dayton Daily News in Ohio, who stumbled across three boys racing hand-made, motorless cars down a local hill in 1933, the races became a nationwide phenomenon.

WPA administrators found them a low-cost option to reach boys who might otherwise get in trouble. According to race rules, only boys 8 to 15 years old could compete. Intended to stretch mechanical skills, the races required boys to build their own cars. Only wheels, bearings, tires, axles and steering wheels could be repurposed. Cars had to cost less than $10 and could use no auto parts except steering wheels. Builders had to meet strict rules on length, width, height, weight and materials—including absolutely no glass.

A graduate of the New Bedford school system, **Domenica Bollea** returned to the city to teach **nursery school** under WPA auspices. The program hired teachers and supervisors for a day nursery program for low-income children 2 to 4 years old, freeing parents to seek employment. Later, as Domenica (Bollea) Bellenoit, she taught Special Education at the DeValles School for many years until her retirement.

Although communities cut back on library appropriations, WPA funds led to library initiatives. These included three regional **bookmobiles** operated by the state's Division of Library Services. With holdings of 600 books and a traveling librarian, they concentrated on bringing books to readers in rural areas, but one of them stopped in New Bedford for a demonstration and photo opportunity.

Soap box derby at the site of the Municipal Golf Course, circa 1938.

WPA Nursery School, Clifford School, May 1940.

The WPA Library Project, February 1941.

The Hurricane of 1938

Called "the most destructive storm ever to strike this city," the Great New England Hurricane arrived with little warning on September 21, 1938. Everett Allen was working his first day as a cub reporter for the *Standard-Times* when he saw a woman blown off her feet in front of city hall, as he later recounted in his book, *A Wind to Shake the World*.

Although New Bedford was on its fringes, the hurricane brought the city a record-breaking high tide. Coming with a new moon tide, a southeasterly gale forced water into the bay and caused devastating flooding. The Acushnet River rose 11 feet above mean high tide, inundating the waterfront, swamping stores and buildings and stranding hundreds of cars. Bridges were impassable. A trolley car and more than 100 autos were stranded on the New Bedford-Fairhaven Bridge. The New Bedford Yacht Club on Pope's Island was battered to splinters. The Coggeshall Street Bridge was knocked askew and its east end rose three feet above the connecting roadbed while the central section twisted away from either end span. The Wood Street Bridge to Acushnet washed away. Nine cotton factories closed. Floodwaters ruined stock, damaged machinery and drenched power cables. More than 10,000 workers temporarily lost jobs, although most mills managed to partially reopen within a week.

In the North End, water completely submerged Riverside Avenue and one side of Belleville Avenue. At the New Bedford Rayon Company, water flooded the basement and reached the first floor, damaging electrical equipment and raw materials.

Southeast corner of County and Cove Streets. *A police officer guards a listing house that bore the hurricane's true force. Winds and water twisted it off its granite foundation, stripped roofing shingles and peeled off clapboards. A broken streetlight bears mute testimony to the dark day's destruction.*

At Revere Copper and Brass, lower floors stood under water, ruining machinery and production equipment. The storm swept away a 65-foot dredge and pile driver once anchored at Revere, releasing it a mile up the Acushnet River on Coggeshall Street, where it completely blocked the roadway. St. Mary's Church on Tarkiln Hill Road was so badly damaged that it was razed as a safety measure.

Downtown, the river rose to Water Street. Plate glass windows blew out onto sidewalks. Torrents of rain quickly damaged the exposed offices and showrooms. The storm left the port and docks in shambles. Seven feet of water devastated the office and warehouse contents of Eldridge and Company's buildings. Water above the railway loading platforms destroyed the wire room, sail room and lower floor of the building owned by Daniel Mullins.

Page Mill at Clark's Cove. *Founded in 1906 as a spinning and weaving mill, Page Mill operated until 1933. Later, the Industrial Development Legion found a likely occupant for the space. Aerovox planned to buy it on September 22, 1938, bringing 300 jobs to the city. However, with hurricane floodwaters extending inland up to Jouvette Street, the Page Mill was surrounded by water, causing Aerovox to change its plans.*

Wind and water tore boats from moorings, winter storage areas or boatyards, scattering them along the riverbanks. Small sloops and motorboats littered the shore at Clark's Point and along Cove Road. The storm leveled the boathouse on East Rodney French Boulevard.

The city's fishing fleet was hit hard. Some fishermen rode out the storm at sea. Sadly, some went missing.

Initial reports showed 96 people had died, 40 were missing and many more had been injured in Greater New Bedford alone. Damages were set at $5 million, leaving 2,695 families in need of rehabilitation aid. Many were homeless after their houses flooded and sustained damage.

One who perished was Rev. George A. Jowdy, pastor of Our Lady of Purgatory Church. He and a nephew sought refuge from rising waters on the roof of his Pope Beach summer cottage in Fairhaven when the hurricane forced the building into a pole, knocking them both off. Rev. Jowdy died while his nephew was saved.

Meanwhile, the fiancé of renowned city pharmacist Charles A. Fernandes watched helplessly as the hurricane swept her betrothed away from his cottage, which drifted off Fairhaven's Winsegansett Heights. His body washed up on Silver Shell Beach on Sconticut Neck days later.

Another who died was Mabel Small, wife of Captain Arthur A. Small, keeper of the light on Palmer's Island. As he headed toward the lighthouse to light the lamp, the seas

Ruins at Acushnet Park. *Designed by Daniel E. Bauer, the impressive Acushnet Park roller coaster opened in 1916. In mid-afternoon, shortly after the hurricane struck, its top rail collapsed bringing down the rest of the structure and sculpting it into a sad remnant of twisted iron rails.*

knocked him off his feet and began to sweep him away. He had regained his footing when he spotted Mabel preparing to launch a boat to rescue him. He watched in horror as a heavy wave slammed into the boathouse, which collapsed on her. The next swell swept her away with the building. Injured and suffering from shock, Captain Small hauled himself to the lighthouse, where he kept the light and fog signal operating through the hurricane.

The hurricane spurred many other heroic rescue attempts. Alexander Riviere of Phillips Avenue, for example, rescued several children marooned by rising waters in the North End. Unfortunately, he suffered a massive heart attack in the act and later died.

Westward view of the New Bedford-Fairhaven Bridge. *Gawkers on foot and in cars line the bridge, trying to grasp the extent of nature's ferocity. Searchers found boats, buildings parts, wharf sections, barrels of fuel oil and the sign to Kelley's Boatyard in the mass of debris jammed against the bridge on the Fairhaven side. The newly planted Marine Park extends into the harbor in the middle background.*

The Last Whaling Voyage Out of New Bedford

This was the notice that changed the course of Raymond A. Buckley's life. "I had no intention of going blubber hunting at all, but I happened to see this ad in the Sunday paper," he would later write in his log aboard the schooner *John R. Manta*. "My brother did his best to show me where I was making a mistake," Buckley wrote. "Of course, he was looking at the financial point and I could see where he was right. But when I looked at it from the other side, I could see and feel the glamour, romance and glory of it."

Indeed, he had imagined life at sea since he was a kid jumping in and out of old whaling ships tied up at the New Bedford docks; later, too, he would feel the pull of the sea as he watched the waterfront from an upstairs window at C. F. Wing, where he worked as an interior designer.

So, despite his brother's misgivings, 25-year-old Buckley set out for the Hatteras whaling grounds aboard the two-masted *John R. Manta*, a 100-ton schooner that relied solely on sails and carried a crew of 15 white and 6 men of color. He worked as a forecastle hand, or common sailor—"a bailer, no. 5 on stroke oar"— assigned to port watch and larboard. Although Captain Antone J. Mandly had advertised an old-fashioned voyage employing lances and harpoons, Buckley and his mates would sometimes use modern darting guns and bombs. The voyage began on May 2, 1925. Just over a week later, Buckley wrote, "May God give me the strength to finish this trip." More excerpts from his log give glimpses of the punishing rigors of whaling, his complicated home life and yearnings for the future:

May 10th. *Had all the whaling I want. Next time I'll be satisfied to get it from a book.*

Raymond A. Buckley, seaman aboard the schooner *John R. Manta*, and an excerpt from his journal.

Whaling schooner John R. Manta *under sail, 1925.*

May 19th. *My birthday. 25 years old. Planning big things for the next 5 years if I ever get off this boat....This life is making me religious. I pray that God will bring me back each time we go for whales. Oh, if only I get back. This is terrible. What a hell.*

May 25th. *Terribly cold. Whale sighted at 7am and went after him. Larboard boat got right on top of whale before we could see it. After whale was struck he went right under boat and struck us several times. Then as he left us he gave us his flukes and capsized us. I pulled Jack up on top of boat....We had hard work to stick on top of boat as waves were running heavy. Other boat picked us up.*

May 30th. *Have decided to go in restaurant business if I ever get out of here. And stick to it. I'll be able to eat anyway. I was longing for some bread and butter. Well, they gave us some yesterday. It is terribly rancid--- but it tasted good. Hope we get more....When I get off here, I'll hear the ship-pump in my sleep. Also, I'll hear—"Come here, YOU! You swine."*

June 11th. *Feeling blue again today. Looked at Helen and (baby) Ray's pictures. And asked God to keep them safe for my return. Bodies of 3 whales on deck. Well, the deck is covered with muck, oil and blood again. What a filthy mess. Oh, Helen, do you remember when we were in Washington, D.C. The breakfast we all had together. And the shopping we did. You bought a hat and I bought 2 shirts.*

June 13th. *What a fool I made of myself coming on this trip. Never will I put up with unnecessary hardship again. I will always try to stay where it is warm, comfortable and plenty of food.*

June 15th. *Dear Helen, I've been boasting of your cooking and housekeeping all day. I wish I could send out to the delicatessen and have you fix up a meal for me. I asked God to bring us together again. May he answer this prayer and may we be considerate of each other and live happily together. Amen.*

June 18th. *Been thinking of you all morning, Helen. Oh, I hope we get together again. I can't say I love you but I think a great deal of you and respect you. I am always thinking and planning how we will get ahead when I get back.*

June 24th. *Too rough for masthead. Cleaned ship with lye and water by hand. They told us it wasn't work—it was resting. I lost the deck bucket overboard and the mate tried to make me pull on the ropes. But I would not do it. I can't. The hospital for me as soon as I land.*

June 25th. *Thinking, thinking, thinking. I guess I've reviewed all my past life.*

June 26th. *Pouring rain. Boys sleeping on starboard side thrown out of their bunks....Words can't describe it when it's wet and rough. Oh, Helen, if this trip only does you as much good as I think it has done me. This will be a good test for us.*

July 5th. *Crowie gave me bawling out this morning. Called me all kinds of names and made little of me. Made a motion to strike me but I told him he better not. They can't break me. My side pains me a good deal and I can't put any weight on the ropes. Sighted steamer in distress. Captain jibed over and ran away from it.*

July 6th. *Boy!!! We got our joyride today. Going so fast that it blew my hair back. Had to bomb whale. Lopes threatened to swash us with the gun.*

Aug. 2nd to 8th. *If only we knew where we are? How far away from New Bedford? But we can't find out a thing. When we go back aft to work, we sneak a look at the chart and then try to pick out where we are on my map. But we can't get near enough to the captain's chart to pick out a town or mark to go by. I think we have only 3 or more empty casks on board. We have 40 full ones now and have caught 30 whales.*

Aug. 12th. *I've been looking through the magazines at the hotel ads and they have a strong appeal to me. I think that's going to be my vocation alright. Ever since I was ten, I've wondered what I would do for a living. I've worked at a good many different jobs and positions and the hotel game paid me best and I like it better than anything else.*

Cutting into a sperm whale aboard the *John R. Manta*, 1925.

Aboard the *John R. Manta*, 1925. *Raymond A. Buckley feeds blubber "bible leaves" into the trypot (left), and later gets his hair trimmed.*

Aug. 20th. *Passed Col. Green's at 7am. Land Ho!! New Bedford. I had my first meal ashore with Tripp and I sure did enjoy it. Had fresh vegetables, milk and appetizing food for the first time in four months. I then got some tobacco and went to visit my friends at C. F. Wings. You ought to see the people stare at me. You see I came ashore with a four-month beard and long hair.*

Aug. 21st. *Went down to the 5 & 10 to see Arthur, then get my bags at the Whaling Outfitter. My wife did not seem to think much of my washing.*

After his whaling expedition, Buckley did make his way into the restaurant business and the "hotel game." By 1930, according to that year's federal census, he was working as a hotel waiter, living with his wife Helen, a hotel waitress, and seven-year-old son, Raymond, on County Street.

Hauling the head of a sperm whale aboard the *John R. Manta*, 1925.

The New Bedford Fishery ~ 1925–1942

New Bedford carved its niche in the late teens as a port specializing in small-boats that made short runs in shallow waters. By 1925, the *Standard-Times* noted, the port had become "worthy of notice" with a fleet of more than 14 fishing boats worth at least $25,000 each and many smaller boats.

Flounder became New Bedford's specialty—particularly blackback flounder found nearer to shore in the southeast waters off Georges Banks and in channels off Nomans Island and Martha's Vineyard. Throughout the 1930s and into the 1940s, New Bedford also became known for yellowtail flounder. By 1942, 60 percent of flounder landings were yellowtail, which required slightly larger boats working in deeper waters than those fishing for blackback. The fleet expanded, and its groundfish catch was made up almost exclusively of flounder. Vessels grew in tonnage and ventured farther upon Georges Bank and the South Channel, where they could also harvest scallops, cod and haddock 100 to 200 miles from port.

Early Fish Dealers

Chatham-born Linus S. Eldridge went to sea as a teenager. By the time of his marriage in 1902, however, he had left fishing to become a fish dealer. He and his wife, Harriet Nelson Dexter, settled in her hometown of Mattapoisett, operated a fish trap there, and began dealing in seafood. They bought scallops and quahogs from local fishermen, stocked the goods in their garage and resold them to wholesalers.

Linus S. Eldridge.

Mrs. Eldridge told me many times how many a night she and Linus sat in the garage with little kerosene heaters. They kept the chill off the shellfish so they wouldn't freeze before getting to market. They were very poor when they started, but Linus was a great businessman, and Mrs. Eldridge was right there with him. – Captain Louis Doucette, Jr.

Among the flounder fleet, 1925. *New Bedford fishing vessels, docked alongside J. S. Child's New Bedford Fish Company on City Pier 4, include small draggers converted from schooners such as the Mary and the John M. Hathaway. The Chas. E. Beckman was a newer, slightly larger vessel in the process of being fitted out. Modern draggers with double-drum winches dated only to 1920, when mechanic Chester Hathaway adapted one to use steel cable. In 1924, Dan Mullins built the city's first baby trawler, . It had power proportional to its size matching the larger Boston trawlers.*

Fishing vessel Bernice, Pier 4, 1932. *The L.S. Eldridge Fish Co. owned the three buildings on the pier. It also operated a "packing out" house on the north side of Pier 4 (behind these buildings). The small "eastern rig," Bernice, was built in Thomaston, Maine, in 1922 for Paul Mathieson of Nantucket. Also known as Nantucket sloops, small draggers such as this fished primarily off Nantucket Shoals, also called the "Rips," that lie southeast of Nantucket. They would only occasionally venture to Georges Bank in warmer weather.*

Swordfishers, 1949. *Crew of the scalloper 3+1+1 (left) look out for swordfish as they head home. Captain Louis Doucette Jr. "always tried to get a few fish on the way home to put some cash in the boys' pockets," recalled his son and crewman Al Doucette. At right, Gerry Shawnbeck and George Bower aboard the swordfishing schooner Alpar, skippered by the elder Doucette, showing off their harpooned fish. The Alpar once brought in an 800-pound swordfish measuring 17 feet from the tip of its tail to the point of the sword.*

Years later, to break into the New Bedford market, the Eldridges had to outmaneuver the politically connected J. S. Childs family, who ran the New Bedford Fish Company on Pier 4, eventually buying them out. Boats began landing fish there for Eldridge in 1928. By the mid-1930s, he renamed the company L.S. Eldridge & Son and eventually built new buildings on each side of the pier, handling fish on one side and scallops on the other. With 500 feet of dockage, Eldridge could unload four boats simultaneously. He became the city's first major commercial seafood buyer and processor.

Some places you can walk right in, but not New Bedford. Politicians, bankers, or whoever's running the city says, 'We don't want this fella down here. Keep him out.' This is what happened. So, Eldridge came down around the Union Hall in Fairhaven and started buying quahogs and bay scallops. He'd buy a little bit of fish when he could. Finally—how he did it I don't know—he landed a place down there, and he bought. Linus Eldridge told Mr. Childs, 'I'll have you out of business in six months.' The New Bedford Fish Company didn't even last six months. Mr. Eldridge took over. – Captain Louis Doucette, Jr.

At first Eldridge bought fish from "broken trips," catches from boats returning to New Bedford earlier than expected due to bad weather or other reasons that made it difficult to land and sell at New York's Fulton Fish Market. It turned out New Bedford skippers liked selling locally, avoiding the time-consuming round trip to New York and the uncertainty over prices paid by New York dealers. Eldridge would transport the seafood in refrigerated trucks to New York, Boston and other ports. Skippers began deliberately landing more fish in the city, starting a trend that made New Bedford one of the world's most significant seaports, consistently ranking as a top port for annually landing the highly valued catch.

One day (Eldridge) bought a trip of 100,000 pounds. I think it was the Mary R. Mullins, one of Danny Mullins' boats that caught it. One hundred thousand pounds! That was a big day. Nobody in New Bedford ever thought that one person could buy that much. Well, everybody's saying that Eldridge was going to go bankrupt, but they were wrong. Linus Eldridge is the man who made New Bedford what it is today. I don't care how many fish companies you have down there. Eldridge is the man who made New Bedford the place to sell fish. There's no better place. – Captain Louis Doucette, Jr.

With the increased market for yellowtail and its adaptability for filleting, New Bedford dealers started building fillet houses on and near the waterfront.

The development of this port has come with the development of the plants in the South Terminal, the buying power that's distributed there. We had the guys who started it, like Danny Mullins and myself. People themselves, they began it. The A&P and the First National had a lot to do with buying fish here. They were pioneers of the products that we were catching, yellowtail flounder and other kinds of flatfish. It was a new thing, because flatfish were never filleted and processed like that. Boston and Gloucester would just process cod and haddock. They never used to process flatfish in Boston until we started catching it here. – Captain Louis Doucette, Jr.

Joseph Goulart Fish Company on Homer's Wharf, circa 1938. Goulart had been buying and shipping quantities of seafood throughout the northeast. After the Sea View Fish Company on Homer's Wharf was established, filleting fish and shipping seafood nationwide began to assume ever more important roles for New Bedford's fish processing industry. During January 1939, city dealers handled 38,500 gallons of scallops, 1,714,000 pounds of groundfish and 283,000 pounds of mackerel from large ships in addition to a large quantity of fish from small boats..

View from Fish Island shows the north sides of State Pier and City Piers 3 and 4, 1939. L.S. Eldridge & Son's new building on Pier 4 can be seen through the assembled masts at center. After Linus Eldridge bought out New Bedford Seafood Company, he tore down existing structures on both sides of the pier and erected the long building for processing and shipping seafood. In 1939, city vessels landed 22.5 million pounds of fish worth $733,425, of which 10.7 million pounds were yellowtail flounder. They also landed 525,871 pounds of scallops worth $609,570.

Joseph Goulart began buying fish in 1932 at a facility on Homer's Wharf soon after Eldridge. In 1936, Captains Dan Mullins and Frank Parsons teamed up to establish Acushnet Fish Company on the Pennsylvania & Reading Wharf (P & R), just south of Homer's Wharf. Seaview Fillet Co. followed in 1939 and New Bedford Fillet Co. in 1942. The owners of these five plants constituted what became know as "primary" dealers—buyers located on the waterfront with the facilities to purchase from boats directly and unload catches. Secondary dealers, wholesalers who bought fish from the primary dealers, would clean, resell and ship to market. They did not buy direct from fishermen and were often located away from the docks.

We all started it, the buying of fish in New Bedford, Goulart, Eldridge, Danny Mullins, and me. In fact, before I even went into the business, I sold a few trips to Joe Goulart in the summertime. I came here because I was told by a guy in New York to come, because he wanted my fish, because (it would get to him the next day if unloaded in New Bedford). The fish was already being shipped to New York by truck. In 1937 Danny Mullins got together with a man named Kurtz from New York, and they approached me. "We'd like you to become partners with us and start a business in New Bedford," they said. Well, at that time there was only Goulart and Eldridge here.

There was line-fishing and quahogging and some swordfishing, but most of the boats in New Bedford were running to New York to unload and come back.

We started out at the P & R Wharf, near the Gas and Edison Company. We put a platform there and a catwalk and put a pillar at the other end of it so two boats could be unloaded at the same time. We started buying from the middle-sized boats, the sixty, sixty-five footers. They came into New Bedford every week on a Saturday or Sunday to unload. They'd go to Eldridge's, then come to me, and then to Goulart's until they'd get the final price. Sometimes it would take two or three hours before you'd come to a final price. We thought about establishing a place to buy, but no one looked into it until right around 1945 or 1946. That's when we started buying fish in an auction.

We have a lot of Portuguese fishermen here now [1980]. It's changed from Norwegians and Newfoundlanders to Portuguese. They have produced a lot of fish and they're doing very well. Some of these fellas have gone out with a small boat, then in a couple of years bought a little bigger one, and now they've got highly-placed boats. You can see they're conscientious guys. They're hard-working. They save what they can save and they invest it in something, and that's the fishing. Give them progress, that's the progress for this city. – Captain Frank Parsons

Cleaning shad at L.S. Eldridge plant, circa 1930. *Vessels landed spring shad caught while schooling before proceeding upriver to breed. They were simply gutted and sold in fresh fish markets. Shad was one of the lesser species that came to fish processors along with rosefish, sea bass, scup, sharks, skate, tilefish, weakfish or gray sea trout, whiting and wolffish, whose combined landings amounted to only 130,511 pounds worth a mere $4,292 in 1939. The US Commerce Department's Bureau of Fisheries classified shad as miscellaneous and did not maintain consistent records on its catch.*

Activity on Piers 3 and 4, circa 1940. *By 1935, the city fish processors benefited from rapid freezing techniques that preserved their products' freshness with little change in taste or texture. Refrigerated trucks transported the frozen fish and seafood to areas unable to get fresh fish because of distance or difficulty of passage. Mullins Fishing Gear at the head of Pier 4 was the only one of the city's four ship chandlers located at the city pier in 1940. Ernie Clattenberg recalled that Dan Mullins repeatedly extended credit to fishermen initially fitting out.*

Fishermen splicing twine on Pier 3, circa 1940. *George Sylvia stands foreground left. To attain the pilothouse and become a mate or captain, a fisherman had to learn how to splice rope or wire and mend twine. Splicing on a pier in balmy weather was easier than doing it aboard a tossing fishing vessel in winter. Captain Louis Doucette, Jr. recalled that if he held the twine incorrectly, his Newfoundland shipmates spat tobacco juice on his freezing fingers. His father advised: "There's only one way to get out of that. You learn how to mend twine." Doucette did.*

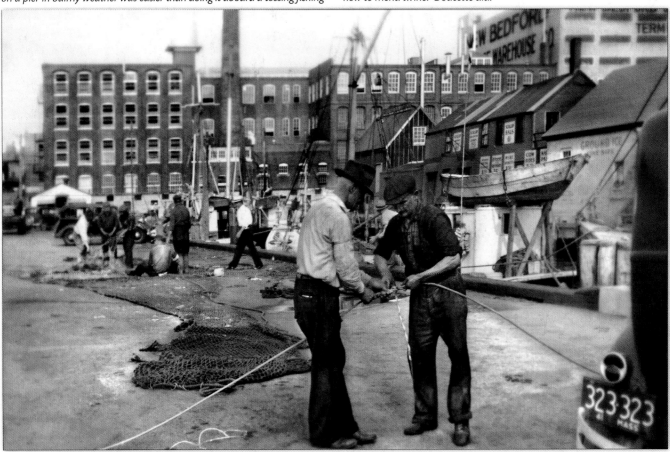

New Bedford's growth can be attributed to the confluence of four factors: its closeness to the fishing grounds, its protected harbor, its ship supply and services sector and its ability to move product overland by refrigerated truck rather than by rail. Taking advantage of better roads and improved transportation, New Bedford boats could land their seafood in the city and get it to market quicker than if they steamed to New York from the fishing grounds. Other ports too began trucking seafood. In 1924, only five percent of the seafood coming into New York City—said to be the largest seafood distribution center in the world at the time—was carried over the highways. By 1938, nearly half came that way.

"The fish—capable of many outlandish means of locomotion in water, such as sitting upright like the sea horse, squirting along like a squid and living on one side like the halibut or flounder—has acquired, because of his food value to man, several new means of transportation, not the least among them being trucks on the highways," proclaimed the *New York Times*. It attributed the shift to "fast roads" maintained by "constant improvement of road networks during the last fifteen years." The newspaper noted that the Fish Forwarding Company Inc., with freight depots from New Bedford to Portland, outfitted its trailers with bunkers that contain dry ice.

Scalloping

Before the 1930s, fishermen kept sea scallop bycatch for local consumption, as scallops had no organized market. Eldridge boosted demand for scallops by buying them and trucking them to New York for resale to the Fulton Fish Market.

When I was scalloping in 1935, there was no auction going on. I'd walk over to Joe Goulart's building and tell him, 'I got a trip of scallops!' He'd ask how many I got. 'Well, eleven hundred pounds! What can you pay me? Make me an offer.' Joe said, 'I have no idea what I can pay. Go see Mr. Eldridge and see what he'll give you.

I was in Dan Mullins' boat at the time. He and Frank Parsons were partners in a fish company with a fella from New York. They had a place at the P&R dock. I'd walk over there and look for Frank. He was in charge. I'd say, 'Hey, Frank, I got a trip of scallops in!' Don't forget. This was the company's boat, Mullins' boat. Frank answered, 'What is Eldridge going to pay.' 'I haven't seen him yet,' I replied. 'Well, go and see him then come back to talk to me.'

So I'd walk down the dock by the Gas Company, all the way to the City Pier, to see Mr. Eldridge. He'd be sitting there with his wife and his son, Bill. 'Young man, you want to see me about

Mary J. Hayes unloading catch, Homer's Wharf, circa 1940. *On this bright, sunny day, everything seems peaceful aboard the 89.3-foot-long wooden dragger. Nonetheless, the Mary J. Hayes later knew serious troubles. On February 7, 1951, the boat was discovered drifting up the harbor, propelled by the wind and tide before it grounded in the mud to the east of Crow Island. It was successfully salvaged. Yet, its bad luck was not over. On August 31, 1954, Hurricane Carol left the Mary J. Hayes high and dry on Crow Island.*

something?' he asked. 'Yea, I got a trip of scallops.' After I told him how much I had, he said, 'That's a nice trip. What are those other fellas offering you?' 'I'm going to be truthful with you, Mr. Eldridge. They're a bunch of jokers. This is what they did. I went to see Joe Goulart. He couldn't give me a price. I went to see Frank Parsons. He didn't give me a price either. They're both waiting for you to give me a price.' He smiled, 'Alright, we'll do just that. You go back and tell them that I offered you 35¢ a gallon.' We didn't make any money on the deal. Nobody knew anything about scallops at that time. All we did was begin to introduce scallops on the market. Then it became what it is today. – Captain Louis Doucette, Jr.

As Eldridge-inspired demand for scallops grew, more local buyers came on the scene, and the city's fishermen developed specialized scallop dredges, landing even more scallops, which would eventually become the most successful product developed by New Bedford's fishing industry. So much so that by 1950, New Bedford had become the nation's leading scallop port. Fishing was one of the few bright spots in the Depression, and many looked to the port for jobs. Not only were there jobs at sea, but as the port solidified, allied industries such as filleting, freezing, ice, supplies, packaging and transporting also grew.

Many early scallopers came from Maine, Newfoundland and Nova Scotia. Aware of the opportunity on New England's

The New Bedford fleet, 1936. *Fishing boats berthed at City Pier 3 alongside the Wharfinger Building, site of the fish auction. The fleet chiefly consisted of small inshore flounder trawlers with a few fair-sized vessels. Department of Commerce records of the fleet's composition date only from 1943. That year, the city's fleet of 267 vessels, exclusive of duplication from seasonal gear changes, included 189 small trawlers, 40 medium-sized trawlers, 22 swordfishing harpooners, 2 handliners, 6 drift gill net boats, 33 purse seiners and 33 scallop dredgers. They made a total of 3,729 trips during the year.*

south coast, and frustrated with the hardships and competition on the Grand Banks, they made their way south.

The scallop business came to New Bedford from Maine. When we found a big run of scallops off of Provincetown, the fellas from Maine commenced to come here. The scallopers started landing at Eldridge's. That was in the '20s and '30s. They went down to Pollock Rip and went to the shoals more. They kept finding new grounds. The boats from Maine, they were the great scallopers. They're the ones that opened the eyes of the guys around here. – Captain Frank Parsons

Unlike in Boston, Gloucester and Portland, no smoking, salting, dressing or drying of fish products took place in New Bedford. And without a substantial mackerel, herring or menhaden industry, no canning or fish by-product businesses emerged. Fresh fish products have always been the city's calling card. Large northeastern cities made up the main markets for New Bedford's growing fresh fish trade. New York topped the list, but large quantities also went to Boston, Philadelphia, Baltimore, Pittsburg, Springfield and elsewhere.

Over time, New Bedford's strong market position led to indictments of several city seafood dealers for violating the Sherman Antitrust Act. They were accused of and fined for excessive control of the scallop market and fixing prices. Still, the seaport became well established and continued to be a dominant force in the seafood industry.

Soon, some Norwegian fishermen who had settled in Brooklyn began coming here to fish for scallops—and more came directly, many came from Karmøy Island. Initially working with 3' or 4' quahog dredges, they eventually improved and designed a wider, heavier scallop dredge to bring in even larger catches.

Acushnet Process Company

In 1910, Philip E. "Skipper" Young, an MIT-trained engineer at Goodyear Rubber in Akron, Ohio, developed a method to extract rubber from the guayule plant grown in Mexico. Goodyear did not want to fund Young's new development, so he turned to Allen Weeks, a college friend from a wealthy Marion family. Weeks agreed to put up the money if the company located near Buzzards Bay, where he loved to sail. Young approached the city of New Bedford, but the "Cotton Textile Town" rebuffed his idea. He bought a vacant building in nearby Acushnet instead.

Disaster struck almost immediately. In 1912, war in Mexico cut off Young's supply of raw material. In 1914, he developed a process to reuse unvulcanized rubber waste and scraps. For years, all Akron rubber companies sent their rubber scraps to Acushnet and bought the processed materials back. After World War I ended, Acushnet became the main source for reclaimed, uncured rubber. When rubber prices fell in the 1920s, Young's engineers began molding it into toys, teddy bears, hot water bottles, and bathing shoes and caps. Young opted for a process of steady, reliable product development, which has long marked the Acushnet Company.

Many of his ideas failed, but a few succeeded. His best idea was a better golf ball. In 1930, Young x-rayed a ball that he blamed for losing a bet on the golf course and noticed that the core was off center. He x-rayed many more and found that cores rarely sat in the center. He began experimenting with machines to wind rubber yarn evenly around the core. He called the result the Titleist.

Young had solved the technical problem of producing a good golf ball, but his greatest breakthrough came in marketing. Golf balls were mainly marketed through testimonials from pro golfers, who were paid to use them.

Young hit upon the better idea of selling his golf balls exclusively through pro shops. Golf pros recommending Titleist balls wouldn't have to worry about their customers buying balls at a sporting goods store at a lower price. Titleist became the ball used by most pros, giving Young an advantage in the higher priced, most profitable sector of the market. During the Depression, when businesses failed all around them, Acushnet Process Company actually grew.

In 1937, with war looming, Young designed and produced a gas-mask mold, winning a government production contract and later becoming the sole-source supplier for US and Allied forces. The Allies

Military inspection, circa 1939. At the press, an inspector from the US Army's Chemical Warfare Service examines a mold used for making flexible exhale valve parts for gas masks while a gloved pressman looks on.

also exclusively used the masks for pilots and an oxygen-control system developed by Acushnet Process and Harvard Medical School. In 1938, seeking additional manufacturing space, the company expanded into New Bedford. With help from the Industrial Development Legion, it bought a barely used Nashawena weave shed. In 1939, the state legislature authorized Acushnet Process Company to build and maintain a bridge over the Acushnet River to link its two plants although the bridge was never built.

Acushnet Process Company, Plant B (bottom building), 1946. Aerovox purchased the long building at center in 1938. Acushnet bought the top building in 1959, called it Plant C and used it for corporate research and development.

Rayon and Rubber

An offshoot of the Delaware Rayon Company, the New Bedford Rayon Company was established in June 1928 and began operations the next year in the Manomet Mill #1 and #2, at the intersection of Belleville and Riverside Avenues, at the site of a former silk mill. Fittingly, the company produced a silk substitute, making rayon out of cellulose derived from chemically treated fine wood pulp put through mechanical processes. The firm wove rayon-based fabrics and supplied rayon yarn to meet growing demand for rayon fiber by New England textile manufacturers. After 1951, it became a division of Mohawk Carpet Mills, of Amsterdam, NY, concentrating on producing rayon for carpet pile.

Three firms made specialized cotton fabric to reinforce rubber tires. Goodyear Rubber Company and Fisk Rubber Company—two of the three firms — both came to New Bedford in 1924, buying the buildings of the Rotch Spinning Company on Orchard Street. In 1927, the Firestone Tire & Rubber Company bought Manomet Mill #4. It had been built in 1920-1922 specifically for making tire fabric, at a cost of $6.5 million, but had already been liquidated. Built for $6.5 million, the mill sold to Firestone for only a fraction of the cost.

Tire styles changed, and consumers preferred balloon tires with larger cross sections and lower pressure to the narrower cord tires. Balloon tires could be woven with fabric made from lower-quality yarn, and eventually Southern mills beat out New Bedford for that market. New Bedford mill owners moved their machinery south.

Inspecting yarn at New Bedford Rayon Company, 1931.

Fisk Rubber Company/Goodyear Rubber Company, Orchard Street, 1939.

Firestone Tire & Rubber Company, Church Street, circa 1940.

More Industry

The 1920s and '30s brought changes to local industry. In 1920, Carl Beckman bought out his father's partner at Briggs & Beckman, sailmakers and ship chandlers. The company had been doing business since Carl's father, Swedish immigrant **Charles Emil Beckman,** teamed up with James C. Briggs in 1905. After the buyout, Carl renamed the company C.E. Beckman. In addition to making sails and cordage, the company sold marine hardware, engines, electrical supplies and, later, automotive parts. With the end of New Bedford whaling, C.E. Beckman stopped making most sails in the 1930s. The Beckman firm, however, continued to supply maritime supplies to New England boatyards and retailers.

The Industrial Development Division of the Board of Commerce attracted **Stokely Brothers and Company** food canning factory to locate in the former Whitman Mills in the late 1930s. Its Cape Cod Cranberries equipment began producing thousands of cans of cranberry sauce for nationwide distribution in 1939 and continued until the company closed in spring 1942.

At left, the man in the extreme upper right corner feeds empty cans onto a runway that carries them to the filling machine. Once filled, the cans head to the capping machine. From there they move along another runway to the cooling channel. In the foreground, the filled cans emerge just before dropping into the cooling channel.

Machines gradually came to local post offices, too, improving efficiency here and across the country. The canceling machine, seen at right, replaced hand canceling of mail. The round table allowed several employees to properly face the outgoing mail before cancelation. After postmarking and cancellation, mail was passed to a stacker, the empty box-like arrangement at far right.

C. E. Beckman Sailmakers George Braga, William Larseu and Ernest Smith, April 1941.

Stokely Brothers & Company food canning factory, 1939.

Postal workers sort and cancel mail using state-of-the-art equipment, circa 1938.

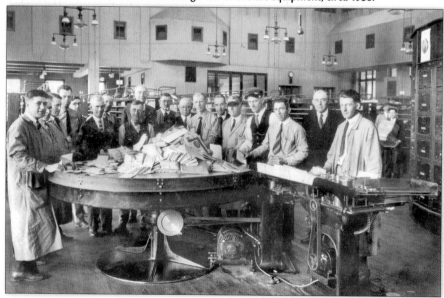

The **Beacon Manufacturing Company** produced quality blankets using a specialized, jacquard-like process to weave with multicolored, pre-dyed fibers. When reorganized in 1904, Beacon had 2,400 spindles, 60 looms and 200 employees. By 1926, it had 18,000 spindles, 740 looms and 1,600 employees plus a new mill, storehouse and weave shed. In 1925, Beacon treasurer Charles D. Owen II opened a plant in Swannanoa, North Carolina to take advantage of the South's low costs and less organized labor. That plant made coarse wool blankets, while New Bedford-made blankets offered a finer weave. By 1932, both mills were operating at partial capacity. That same year, the federal government sued Beacon for advertising Beacon Indian Blankets as Navajo-made. Facing bankruptcy, Beacon consolidated. It dismantled the New Bedford plant brick by brick, reassembling it in North Carolina and outfitting it with machinery from New Bedford. The city took over Beacon's buildings on Purchase Street near Deane Street. Several were demolished by the WPA, and others were purchased by Arlans Department Store or Sid Wainer Fruit.

In 1923, while the textile mills were thriving, Hugo E. Schmidt's firm was one of the city's five specialty reed makers. Made for looms, the reeds consisted of hundreds of flattened wire strips bound between two wooden ribs, forming long comb-like frames with vertical slits. They separated and kept warp threads from tangling, then pushed the weft threads into place. Founded in 1903, when **Schmidt** partnered with fellow German, Herman Tetzner, shortly after coming to the United States, the firm stayed in business through the Depression.

Around the time Hugo Schmidt's business closed, the repeal of Prohibition brought good news to **Smith Brothers Brewery.** Owned by brothers Joseph T. and James F. Smith, New Bedford's second-largest brewery opened at 777 Purchase Street in 1905, moved to 425 Coggeshall Street in 1918 and remained idle from 1920 to 1933, during Prohibition. After reopening, Smith Brothers became known for its ales, bocks, stouts and porters. The brewery closed for good in 1950. Its building burned some years later. Pictured here, workmen Joseph Mitch and Alphonse Bessette clean vats in preparation for the plant's reopening.

Dismantling the Beacon Mill, 1933.

Foundry workers at H. E. Schmidt & Co., 116 Front Street.

Smith Brothers Brewery, back in business after repeal of Prohibition, 1933.

New Bedford Needle Trades, 1825–1960

Fashion historians credit New Bedford merchants with the introduction of ready-made clothing—an innovation that sprang from the whaling industry's needs. Heading out to sea on short notice, as they often did, whalemen needed to fill a slop chest with clothing overnight. And by the time they returned to port after a voyage, their clothes were often in tatters. Whether coming or going, whalers needed cheap clothing immediately and could not wait for a custom tailor to make an outfit. The solution? Sometime around 1825, dry-goods merchants started to provide a full line of nautically appropriate, already-made clothing. Naturally, to avoid tying up substantial capital in the venture, they often used the coarsest materials and workmanship.

From New Bedford, the off-the-shelf clothing idea rapidly spread to Boston, then to New York. Large-scale production started in 1831, when George Opdyke, former mayor of New York City, began making ready-made clothing on Hudson Street. Opdyke had a store in New York and opened branches in New Orleans, Charleston and Memphis. Other firms entered the field to supply markets in the South and East. Around mid-century, miners in the California goldfields generated strong market growth, but real expansion took place with the Civil War. More than a century later, during the 1930s,

Advertisements. At top left, James Cannon sells cheap, used men's clothing through the New Bedford Mercury, September 5, 1817. New ready-made clothing (bottom left)—as well as beans, peas and tobacco—is advertised in the Daily Mercury, June 1, 1827. At right, a Civil War-era broadside promotes Oliver G. Brownell and Reuben R. Howland's clothier on Union Street. It lasted until Howland became Sealer of Weights and Measures.

New Bedford industrial development boosters would look to the apparel industry to fill the city's empty mill buildings, seeking to entice New York business owners—stymied by high rents and persistent labor difficulties—to move operations to the Whaling City. They were successful with more than 2,200 people employed making clothes and other textile products in New Bedford by 1940.

Heart of the Garment District, 1890s. A three-block stretch of Union Street housed one third of New Bedford's clothing stores and merchant tailors. Edward T. Taber, William F. Read and Darius P. Gardner owned Taber, Read & Gardner at Union Street and Acushnet Avenue. Charles H. Gifford and Eugene F. Brown did business as Gifford & Co., and brothers Joseph and William R. Wing also outfitted whalemen at their clothiers at 111 Union.

Pocketbooks & Pajamas

The **Fairhaven Corporation** began making pocketbooks on the fifth floor of the Fairhaven Mills in May 1931. When 500 people showed up to apply for 50 job openings, management called in police to keep order. Three weeks after opening, workers struck to protest the new piecework system that paid them as low as 48¢ per day. Company president Raphael Mutterperl disparaged the strikers. He called new workers "green help" and claimed they were mesmerized by New York labor agitators who wanted to use the strike to drive the company back to New York City.

In August 1931, the Massachusetts State Federation of Labor Convention met in New Bedford and unanimously adopted a resolution disapproving the actions of the New Bedford Police Department in arresting the "peaceful and inoffensive strikers." It also condemned the Third District Court of Bristol County for "persecuting" them and called on newspapers to use their full powers to discourage such practices and expose them as "an un-American and reprehensible abuse of power." In June 1932, the Massachusetts Pocketbook and Leather Goods Wage Board adopted the state's first cost-of-living budget since the start of the Depression. It set the minimum needed for a self-sustaining woman in the industry at $12.50 per week.

Ten years later, the **New England Pajama Company** began operations on Easter Monday morning, 1942, on the top floor of the Booth Mill. Plant manager Samuel Habid, standing at right, told the Standard-Times that the company would hire about 50 workers at once and increase the workforce to between 75 and 100 by year's end. The factory was part of the Colonial Textile Company, which had a similar plant in the Fairhaven Mills on Coggeshall Street.

Striking pocketbook workers of Fairhaven Corporation, Coggeshall Street, May 1931.

The New England Pajama Company in the Booth Mill building, East Rodney French Boulevard, circa 1942.

New Bedford's 20th-Century Boatyards

During the 20th century, New Bedford's boatbuilding traditions dissipated. Many companies moved to outlying towns with more accessible and plentiful waterfronts. Others survived by diversifying and becoming general ship chandlers. Among boatmakers in the first half of the century were Peirce & Kilburn, Palmer Scott, J.C. Beetle, Asa Thomson and William Wood.

Beetle Boatyard

The Beetle family, well known for their high-quality "Beetle Whaleboat," lived on Clark's Point for generations. They developed the technique of wrapping steam-bent cedar planks around a skeleton before putting in the oak frames, enabling builders to complete a whaleboat in one day.

In 1920, James Beetle built a 12-foot sailboat for the family children, creating the first Beetle Cat Boat. It sported a wide, six-foot beam and shallow rudder; with the centerboard lifted up, it drew only eight inches. Ideal for youngsters, it had a single sail and no ballast, and it was unsinkable. John H. Beetle, the designer's son, began manufacturing the Beetle Cat using the company's cost-cutting techniques. When John died in 1928, his daughter Ruth took over, becoming the country's only female boatwright at the time. The 1938 hurricane swept away the company boat shed on East Rodney French Boulevard; World War II interrupted production; and a 1945 fire destroyed key patterns and buildings.

Ruth's brother Carl Beetle, in business for himself, focused on fiberglass and resin boats. In January 1947, he exhibited a fiberglass prototype at the New York Boat Show. It received no interest and no sales. One month later, he sold all of his available boats to the public at the Boston Boat Show. He had replaced the fiberglass foredeck and cockpit coamings with polished mahogany. In 1949, he tried all fiberglass catboats again without success, eventually ruining the family's finances. The family sold the company in 1951.

Beetle Boat Yard, East Rodney French Boulevard, 1933. Tom King (left), veteran whaleman and rigger, and Isaac Sampson, a rigger who owned a Bourne Counting House loft, helped turn out this classic whaleboat commissioned by a private collector. This yard was located near the foot of present-day Rodney Street, across from Peirce & Kilburn's waterfront location.

A New Bedford 35 cruising-racing yacht, 1939. Carl Beetle built the 35-foot sloop-rigged yacht in his boatyard in the City Mill at the bottom of South and Grinnell Streets. Samuel Crocker designed the yacht, outfitted with a teak deck, mahogany planking and a world class Hyde feathering propeller on a Monel shaft to boost racing capabilities.

Peirce & Kilburn

Middleboro-born Charles Edward Peirce settled in New Bedford as a carpenter after serving in the Fourth Regiment of Massachusetts Volunteer Infantry in the Civil War. About 1915, during the height of the city's building boom, Peirce formed a partnership with Clifford H. Kilburn, a New Bedford-born carpenter. They owned a carpentry and building firm at the foot of Leonard Street. Gradually, they shifted to boatbuilding. For a few years, they worked from two locations, also building boats from a yard on East Rodney French Boulevard.

In 1926, they moved both New Bedford operations to the former Atlas Tack works at Rodman's Wharf on Fort Street in Fairhaven. The 1938 hurricane flooded the boatyard facilities with more than seven feet of water, caused several buildings to collapse, floated boats from their cradles, threw a nine-foot draft vessel on the marine railway and sank four boats in their slips. The business quickly recovered, however. During World War II, Peirce & Kilburn repaired and performed alterations to naval vessels.

Sloops on the ways at Peirce & Kilburn yard, circa 1926. The old yard, across from the Beetle property on East Rodney French Blvd., was refurbished by Peirce & Kilburn in the 1920s, only to be swept away by the 1938 Hurricane.

Palmer Scott

An MIT-trained naval architect, Palmer Scott wanted not only to design but also to build boats. In 1935, he bought the William Hand boatyard in Fairhaven and moved to New Bedford's North End in 1936. Scott built custom wooden yachts. One sported a spiral staircase down to the main cabin, with a bannister sculpted as a snake ending with a carved cobra's head.

During World War II, Scott resigned his naval commission to build boats. His yard worked full-time on government contracts. His company built 20 26-foot cable boats, 124 40-foot passenger landing craft, 42 50-foot passenger landing craft, 20 46- and 47-foot tug boats and eight 50-foot salvage boats.

After the war, Palmer Scott & Company followed the trend to fiberglass boats, establishing subsidiary Marscot Plastics to make them. Some Scott-built fiberglass sailboats are still actively raced, including the Wood Pussy, a 13½-foot catboat, and the Dolphin 24, molded by Marscot Plastics. He also built two small fiberglass fishing boats called the Angler 18 and 23.

After Concordia Company bought the rights to the original Beetle Cat in 1946, it received more orders than anticipated and turned to Scott for help. He put Leo Telesmanick in charge of the catboat building.

In 1954, Hurricane Carol submerged the entire plant. Water swept a landing craft through the office, totally wrecking it. Wind and water carried a 24-foot air/sea rescue craft nine miles to a field in Dartmouth. Overwhelmed by recovery efforts, Scott retired in 1960. Catboat production was transferred to Concordia, which set up separate Beetle Cat operations on Smith Neck Road.

Marscot Plastics workers put spray guard on a 22-foot power boat, 1956.

Palmer Scott Boat Company, Logan Street waterfront near Revere Copper & Brass, 1940.

Palmer Scott Boat Company testing boats built for US Navy, August 1942.

Transportation

During the interwar years, New Bedford transportation changed swiftly and irrevocably. Freight volumes shrank after the 1928 textile strike and the subsequent Depression-linked demise of the cotton industry. From 1925 to 1938, the production of thread from cotton fell sharply as the number of active spindles dropped by more than 80 percent and many of the city's spinning mills closed. Remaining mills wove and shipped less finished cloth, and the value of New Bedford's cotton production dipped by 85 percent.

In a rippling effect, the dwindling number of mill boiler rooms needed less coal to power the steam-driven looms and spinning machinery. The remaining mills transitioned to electricity. Due largely to drops in cotton and coal shipments, the volumes of sea- and rail-borne freight coming to and leaving New Bedford plummeted dramatically.

Passenger transport also suffered. Fewer passengers needed the city's train service to and from Boston. In 1938, the New York, New Haven and Hartford Railroad Company shuttered the Weld Square train station. In 1937, the railroad discontinued New Bedford's rail-island steamship link, which mostly served vacationers. The photo shows a desolate rail yard devoid of people at the end of the 1930s. Because the Great Depression slashed available jobs in the mills and elsewhere, fewer people

needed transportation to get to work. Daily urban commuter volume plummeted on the Union Street Railway. Ridership levels dropped from 27.2 million paying passengers in 1925 to 11.2 million in 1940. More than 9,000 people left New Bedford from 1925 to 1940 searching for a better life.

Consumers who had money drove a different transportation revolution, buying automobiles, whose prices kept dropping. New and used car dealerships sprang up to meet demand. More cars on city streets required better and wider roads, new gas stations, more repair services and additional parking. These demands forever changed the urban landscape.

They also generated employment. By 1940, nearly 1,000 people worked selling, repairing, storing and fueling automobiles in New Bedford.

The quest to modernize led to the city's transition from electric trolleys to new buses and from delivery wagons to small trucks. Individual, maneuverable cars, buses and trucks could better share the streets with one another than they could with wagons and trolleys restricted to fixed rails.

Long-distance trucking of fish in refrigerated vehicles provided another shift in the city's transportation horizon. By the 1940 census, trucking services employed 310 people in New Bedford, the first time trucking appeared as a census category.

Railyard, 1938. *View looking south shows the Pearl Street Depot at right with a passenger train alongside its queue. Idle freight cars are at left and center. In the distance sits the three-story New Bedford Manufacturing Company, the city's oldest spinning mill, incorporated in 1884.*

New Bedford Municipal Airport

Charles Lindbergh's solo flight across the Atlantic in May 1927 captivated the nation, inspiring aviation enthusiasts across the country. In New Bedford, Isaac Dawson, of the Prohibition-closed Dawson's Brewery family, ran the area's earliest aviation facility during the late 1920s. The New Bedford-Acushnet Airport, located in Acushnet just over the New Bedford line, near Pontiac Street east of Acushnet Avenue, featured a grass landing strip and a rickety hangar next to Mrs. Jennie Bartlett's apple orchard.

Pilots disliked the field, which often became swampy after spring rains. A student pilot's plane once landed in Mrs. Bartlett's apple trees. In 1929, Acushnet's extension of Westland Street from Middle Road to Acushnet Avenue ended the airfield. Dawson found an alternative in Fairhaven near Mill Road and Bridge Street. Named the New Bedford-Fairhaven-Acushnet Airport, people called it Baylies Flying Field to honor of Frank L. Baylies, a New Bedford pilot killed in France while serving in the Lafayette Escadrille air squadron.

In November 1929, Sound Airways bought land from the Duff family, which they had used to pasture horses that hauled their coal delivery wagons. Sound Airways flew passengers and freight to Martha's Vineyard, Nantucket and Long Island and also ran a flight school. Isaac Dawson sat as president and New Bedford automobile dealer David Sher as general manager. Fairhaven resident and pilot Henry Olden operated the airport. They converted the Duff barn into a hangar. To guide pilots, they painted its roof with "NEW BEDFORD" on one side and "FAIRHAVEN" on the other. The airport opened on December 2, 1929 in front of 10,000 people. On April 19, 1930, New Bedford Mayor Charles S. Ashley presided over its formal dedication, which was followed by a two-day air show.

Sound Airways operated successfully through the first summer and offered summer trips to the islands in 1931, but closed for good at year's end, a victim of the Depression. Pilots used the East Fairhaven Airport sporadically for flying lessons and charter flights. On May 19, 1938, to honor National Airmail Week and National Ice Cream Week, the first—and only—official airmail flight left for Taunton and lasted nine minutes. The mail and ice cream arrived safely. In 1941, pilots and crews of the First Observation Squad of the Massachusetts State Guard used it to practice takeoffs and landings. In 1943, it was sold to become a dairy farm.

In nearby Dartmouth, meanwhile, Col. Edward H. R. Green, son of financier Hetty Green, transformed a natural saltwater marsh into manicured grass runways. He long loved

flying, but his mother had threatened to disown him if he took it up. After her death, he pursued his dream, building a state-of-the-art airfield and hangar at his Round Hill estate. Dedicated in 1928, it was one of the nation's most modern airports, with runways lit for night landings. Huge, red neon tubes on the mansion's roof spelled out "ROUND HILL" for fliers. A hangar housed the MIT-leased Goodyear blimp for aerial experiments.

The nation's top pilots came to Green's airport: Charles Lindbergh, Eddie Rickenbacker, Jimmy Doolittle and William Randolph Hearst Jr. Col. Green provided free fuel and services for all who landed there. The airport closed in 1936 after his death. The 1938 hurricane irreparably damaged it. In 1939, Henry Olden, then president of the local air club, lobbied officials to build a new airfield. A survey identified the Plainville Road–Shawmut Avenue area as the best option. Ground was broken on April 9, 1940, and the New Bedford Regional Airport still operates at the site today.

Portuguese aviators at New Bedford Airport, September 18, 1932. *The local Portuguese community enthusiastically welcomed Lieutenant Plácido António Cunha de Abreu, pilot, and Sergeant António José Gonçalves Lobato, mechanic. Sadly, each would suffer an early aviator's fate. Lieutenant Abreu died instantly when his plane crashed at the World Aerial Acrobatic Championships in Vincennes in June 1934. Sergeant Lobato died when his "Tiger-Moth" had an accident at Viseu airport (subsequently named in his honor) during a leg of the Second National Air Rally in June 1935.*

Baylies Flying Field, New Bedford Airport, January 24, 1930. *Engineers for the Curtiss Flying Service surveyed the 86-acre Duff Farm in Fairhaven, pronouncing it one of the best natural fields on the Atlantic coast. The sod-covered field measured roughly one-half-mile long by one-quarter-mile wide. Because it was level and had excellent natural drainage, airplanes could use the entire area. The barn was converted into a substantial hangar. It had room for aircraft maintenance and an office for general use. A garage extending from the hangar sheltered automobiles. The Fairhaven Star objected to having "New Bedford" painted on the hangar roof, but Isaac Dawson explained that it was done for the convenience of the pilots, most of whom had New Bedford as their destination. Known as Baylies Flying Field, it was nicknamed after World War I flying ace Frank L. Baylies.*

Crowds turn out to view Colonel Edward H. R. Green's body at Pearl Street Depot, June 1936.

The Pearl Street Depot

The Pearl Street Depot clung to existence despite persistent efforts by the New York, New Haven & Hartford Railroad to end service in the Old Colony division. In February 1929, citing continued losses, the company abandoned ferry service from New Bedford to Fairhaven and then razed the Fairhaven train station without prior notification, replacing it with a car opened for boarding just 30 minutes before departure.

In December 1931, the rail company discontinued one round-trip train from Boston to New Bedford and all train service between New Bedford and Providence. In March 1933, with continued drops in passenger traffic, it cut three trains from Boston to New Bedford and two return trains, later restoring one on Saturdays and Sundays. After its bankruptcy, the railroad abruptly closed the Weld Square Depot. By 1940, it argued before regulators that it earned revenue of only 47¢ per train mile to Boston, compared to costs of $1.10 per train mile from New Bedford to Taunton and $1.21 from Taunton to Boston. In April 1940, it cut the passenger train schedule from twelve trains per day to eight, and then to four in May. Critics griped that the line had never properly promoted traffic to the area, pointing to only one picture-cycle excursion for hobbyists to Martha's Vineyard via New Bedford in 1938 and a similar hobby train excursion for cyclists to Martha's Vineyard and Nantucket in 1941.

Sailors of the 7th Division US Naval Reserves return from a two-week training cruise, 1939.

US Army draftees await the train to Fort Devens as family and friends see them off, 1942.

Crossing the Bay

Seaplanes and ferries long used Buzzards Bay's inlets and harbors for access to the city and its intermodal transport. The **New Bedford, Martha's Vineyard and Nantucket Steamboat Company** ran ferries between New Bedford, Woods Hole, Hyannis, Vineyard Haven, Edgartown and Nantucket. It initially transported goods and passengers by side-wheel steamers, then by steamboats. In 1922, it became part of the New England Steamship Company, a subsidiary of the New York, New Haven & Hartford Railroad. The merger led to a loss of individuality and concern for local development. In 1911, its board had had five men from New Bedford, two from Boston, one from Nantucket and one from Vineyard Haven. After absorption, all but two directors came from Connecticut or Boston.

In 1925, New Haven cut the New Bedford-New York summer passenger service from six to three days per week, transferring boats used on the other three days to its New York-Hyannis line.

By the 1930s, a two-hour trip from New Bedford to the Vineyard cost $1 on the New England Steamship Company ferry. A four-hour trip to Nantucket cost $2.20.

While the ferries remained popular, more and more people looked to the sky for alternative transportation. Curtiss Flying Service hoped to establish a seaplane base in New Bedford, claiming, "the conditions are ideal." In 1929, Major Gil Ervin and Bob Foote of Curtiss delivered their survey of the city's options to the Board of Commerce. Meanwhile, Colonel Edward "Ned" H.R. Green built his own $1.5 million seaplane airport at Round Hill in Dartmouth. His wife had so liked her first flight in a seaplane that Col. Green bought her the plane and built the airport for it.

By 1932, Island Airways seaplanes flew five daily round trips between New Bedford, Woods Hole, Vineyard Haven and Nantucket. A one-way ticket from the city to Nantucket cost $6.50. That same year pilot Philip Mostrom, manager of Sound Airways, and Phillip S. Powell, a local undertaker, died when British Commander Augustus W. S. Agar's seaplane fell into the Acushnet River and sank in a sudden rain and hail storm.

Curtiss NC-4 flying boat, October 1919. *In May 1919, the NC-4 became the first aircraft to cross the Atlantic. Designed by Glenn Curtiss, it had three tractor engines and one "pusher" engine. After the trip, the navy sent it on a recruiting mission before donating it to the Smithsonian. Most of the original crew came to New Bedford, including Lieutenant Commander Albert C. Read, sitting on the nose, and Lieutenant Walter K. Hinton, the pilot standing in the cockpit.*

Aviator Henry T. Olden and his seaplane at Fairhaven's West Island, 1937. *Following a special commission on aviation's recommendation to build seaplane ramps at New Bedford, Martha's Vineyard and Nantucket, Henry Olden and Arthur Kelly began a passenger service from New Bedford to the Islands. After the 1938 hurricane destroyed their facilities, Olden relocated to Rochester. His Cape Cod Airlines operated from there until 1942, when the government closed airports within 80 miles of the coast.*

Uncatena, the line's last sidewheel steamer (1908-1928), leaving New Bedford Harbor, 1925.

Trolleys

As more residents adopted automobiles during the 1920s, trolley ridership fell steadily. The number of city-registered automobiles more than doubled from 1920 to 1925, while the number of Union Street Railway passengers fell 14 percent. To make up the deficit, the company doubled the fare to 10 cents in May 1927.

The company also introduced interstate bus service on the New Bedford-Providence line via Fall River in May 1925. Initially, the deluxe motor coaches carried only interstate passengers. Later that year, after being licensed by New Bedford and Fall River, they carried intercity passengers as well. In 1926, buses replaced many trolleys on the New Bedford-Fall River line.

To reduce labor costs, Union Street Railway began one-man operation on the Rivet Street Line in 1926. The motorman would now also collect fares, a job previously performed by conductors. From 1928 to 1929, the company converted cars on most trolley lines to one-man operations. It also reduced the labor force through normal attrition and a hiring freeze.

The 1928 textile strike dealt the Union Street Railway a sharp blow. During 1927, when many workers commuted on trolleys to their jobs in the textile mills, it transported 23.3 million passengers. During 1930, the number of passengers had dropped to 14.4 million. Profits evaporated. Despite repeated cost cutting, the company continued to lose money through the rest of the decade.

Motormen outside car barn. *Union Street Railway motormen took exceptional pride in their work and aimed to provide riders with outstanding service. The job provided excellent training. Before 1950, practically all corporate officers of the Union Street Railway rose from the ranks.*

During the 1930s, it introduced buses on some city routes. Viewed as more modern, buses had another advantage on New Bedford's narrow streets—flexibility. A car or truck parked too close to the track held up a trolley, making riders late and sabotaging company efforts to provide regular, punctual service. Trolleys could not leave the track to swerve around obstructions. Buses, with no such constraints, could more easily maneuver around obstructions and continue on their routes. Buses also had an important financial advantage for a cash-strapped company since they didn't require investment to build and maintain tracks. Instead, cities built and kept up the roads.

Streetcar 416 on Acushnet Avenue near Brooklawn Park, 1930s. *Built by the Osgood Bradley Car Company of Worcester in 1918, it could carry 44 passengers on cane-upholstered seats. It ran until the end of trolley service on May 3, 1947, when it was scrapped.*

The Replacements ~ Buses

In 1931, buses began running from Lunds Corner to Sassaquin, with extra weekend excursion trolleys. That trolley service ended in June 1934 when city workers tore out tracks to widen Acushnet Avenue up to Sassaquin Hospital.

In September 1933, trolley service between New Bedford and Fall River ended. Elsewhere, buses began replacing trolleys. In May 1935, buses ran to Padanaram; by September of the same year, they also ran to East Fairhaven and Mattapoisett. In February 1938, buses replaced trolleys on the Arnold Street and Mount Pleasant lines.

The September 1938 hurricane felled miles of overhead wires serving the city's seven remaining trolley lines, isolating trolleys and buses throughout the city and disrupting service. The Union Street Railway Company eventually replaced downed poles and wires, but hurricane damage created unexpectedly high repair costs and additional revenue loss due to a lengthy shutdown. The Valentine's Day Storm of 1940, called the "worst blizzard in years," blocked trolleys and buses with heavy snows. Closed for nine days, the company experienced further heavy financial losses.

Union Street Railway car barn on Pope's Island, circa 1949. *Originally built to serve trolleys, the car barn housed only the line's new buses after 1947.*

Rear view of the Union Street Railway Bus Terminal, Middle Street side, 1943.

Automobiles

Velie, 8-column, beveled glass hearse body manufactured in New Bedford by William A. Carroll on a Buick D-6 55 chassis, 1920s.

Car makers proliferated during the early automotive years. Massachusetts had about 180, but none were located in New Bedford. The city's artisans and tinkerers, however, made custom parts. Joseph Chausse and Joseph Bolduc's Air-Tight Piston Ring Mfg. Co. produced piston rings. Hyman Brooks and Harry Miller's New England Auto Radiator Co. repaired and made custom lamps, hoods, fenders and mufflers. Philip S. Briggs, Walter L. King and Delphis D. St. John crafted custom soft car tops. Oliva Metthe painted cars, giving customers color options beyond Henry Ford's basic black.

The George L. Brownell Carriage Works had the potential to move into cars. It made hearses, ambulances and coaches. However, in a 1910 preemptive move, James Cunningham, Son & Co. of Rochester, New York bought out Brownell, filled the order book, and then closed the company. Cunningham succeeded in converting Brownell customers into his own.

Two of Brownell's most skilled craftsmen, father and son carriage body builders William E. and William A. Carroll, moved to Merrimac, a key car manufacturing center. In 1911, they built a few motorized hearses and ambulances for S.C. Pease & Sons of Newburyport. In 1912, Pease went into receivership. The Carrolls bought the fixtures and machinery, shipped them to New Bedford and erected a four-story factory on North and Jenney Streets to build bodies for fire and patrol wagons, automobiles, motor hearses and ambulances.

In 1923, H. William Tierney Jr., manager and distributor of the Massasoit Motors Company, assembled the Gray sports car in New Bedford. Painted gray with white stripes and ample nickel trimmings, the fuel-efficient Gray averaged 33.8 mpg.

Another body maker, Cape Verde-born Peter J. Duarte, came to the US as a child. He learned car repair and opened Pete's Auto Body Shop. In the mid-1930s, he advertised the production of custom car bodies. When the venture did not succeed, he returned to the mechanics trade.

Municipal parking lot, circa 1925. *City officials allowed free parking daily until midnight under the eye of police to free up New Bedford's narrow streets. The lot was located where today's bus terminal stands. The view looks north from city hall between Pleasant and North Sixth Streets.*

The spiraling increase in the number of automobiles after 1920 posed parking problems and disposal challenges. Far-sighted entrepreneurs built garages throughout the city to house vehicles. Others provided parking or cleaning services while car owners went about activities downtown. A few supplied taxis and drivers for those needing a ride. Used car dealers also popped up. Unfortunately, **unsalvageable vehicles** were often junked with little thought to environmental concerns.

Colonel Edward "Ned" H.R. Green owned a fleet of electric vehicles, but he really wanted a gasoline-powered car. However, as an amputee, he could not drive a standard-shift, three-pedaled vehicle. As a major stockholder in General Electric, he convinced GE to build a hybrid car by converting a gasoline-powered, manual-transmission vehicle to electric drive and personally pumped more than $1 million into the project. GE sent a 1929 Stearns-Knight M 6-80 cabriolet to carmaker Rauch & Lang of Chicopee Falls to carry out the conversion. Delighted with the car, Colonel Green ordered a second and then a third, each built on a Stearns-Knight chassis but with traditional Rauch & Lang bodies. The Depression ended plans to put the hybrids into production.

The automotive sales industry attracted dynamic first-generation immigrants—who would often move quickly into new business fields—to the city. George A. Emin, the son of a French-born father and French Canadian mother, established **Emin Motor Car Sales** and sold Chevrolets. Next door, Edward J. Lafferty, son of a Scottish-born man and Irish woman, owned the Union Motor Corporation. He sold new Fargo Trucks, Desoto Sixes, Plymouths and some used cars. The Depression eventually took its toll on auto sales. Lafferty dissolved the Union Motor Corporation of New Bedford in early 1932.

Clark's Cove automobile graveyard, 1931. *There is always plenty of space, free parking and no limit. Note the two recyclers scavenging for anything useful from the automobile carcass in the foreground.*

Colonel Green visits downtown in one of his custom-made electric cars, 1927.

Emin's Used Cars dealership, near the junction of Mill and Kempton Streets, 1930.

Port of New Bedford

With whaling's demise, harbor activity waned. Whaling ships moored several deep disappeared from the wharves. Seaweed-covered barrels of whale oil and tall stacks of baleen no longer crowded the waterfront. In the aftermath of the Strike of 1928 and with the onset of the Great Depression, harbor business grew even quieter. From pre-strike levels in 1927, port traffic dropped by more than 350,000 tons annually by 1932. Tonnage arriving in the harbor fell by one-third, while shipments plunged by two-thirds. New Bedford shrank to a minor Massachusetts port, ranked well below the state leader, Boston. New Bedford lagged well behind the state's second port, Fall River, which in the 1930s boasted more than a hundred times the international trade and two-and-a-half times the domestic coasting traffic as New Bedford.

Raw cotton for the city's remaining mills made up part of the incoming cargo. In addition, the Greene and Wood lumberyard opened a pier served by a private channel to attract large steamers carrying lumber, cotton or general cargo. Greene and Wood owned a chain of warehouses that later supplied lumber for the building boom in year-round and summer houses on Cape Cod, the construction of Camp Edwards in Bourne and the post-1938 hurricane reconstruction throughout the region.

In the mid-1930s, the Federal Housing Administration's programs to finance home purchases or repair and its development of plans for small, affordable, housing led to a surge in building. In 1939, the United States Housing Authority

Storage of cotton bales at State Pier, 1925. *At its 1925 peak, the port took in roughly 750,000 cotton bales. Many were stockpiled in the second floor storage space above the State Pier transit shed. In 1926, the value of the city's cotton production tumbled 15 percent. Cotton's decline had begun.*

Freighter *Clevedon* at State Pier, 1941. *The steamship brought 23,506 bales of British wool and wool products from Australia, part of the effort to build up supplies in the run-up to World War II. The New Deal's Reconstruction Finance Corporation financed the purchase, and the harbor easily handled the ship's 27.6-foot depth. Dockworkers unloaded the entire cargo in 40 hours. To speed paperwork, Boston Customs agents lent a hand.*

approved slum clearance to build 398 family dwellings in New Bedford.

New Bedford fell behind in port technology while others adopted new technologies to better accommodate bigger and deeper boats. By 1910, dredging had deepened the 300-foot-wide channel to 25 feet at mean low water. But the channel was allowed to refill. In 1922, the Cunard Line's *Italia* went aground at low tide while tied up at State Pier to load passengers bound for the Azores and the Mediterranean. The pier had been rated for 27 feet and the *Italia* drew only 23.2 feet. After refloating, the *Italia* had to remain in port until it obtained a certificate of seaworthiness from the line's insurers. A 1928 report to the Board of Engineers for Rivers and Highways later confirmed common knowledge, stating the channel had been maintained to a depth of only 21 feet. It proposed further deepening to 30 feet to avoid danger.

As time went on, piers needed to accommodate increasingly longer ships. The 750-foot-long State Pier, completed in 1917, had limited capacity. Public works funds regularly paid to upgrade it during the 1930s. Greene and Wood lumber company built its own pier at the foot of Pine Street in 1925 and began attracting longer, ocean-going ships. Among them was the Munson Steamship Line's 400-foot-long *Munmystic*, which in 1931 delivered 14,200 bales, the largest cotton shipment ever offloaded in New Bedford. It took four days to discharge at the Greene and Wood pier.

Dredging alongside State Pier, 1936. *Trimont Dredging Company of Boston carries out maintenance to keep the recommended depth for ships coming into New Bedford harbor. In January 1936, the state budgeted $54,000 to dredge the extensions to the harbor's western maneuvering area.*

Munson Line freighter SS *Munindies* unloading cotton and lumber at Greene & Wood Pier, 1934. *Most lumber cargo was landed at Greene & Wood Pier, home to the company's 10-acre yard. Greene & Wood had been operating at the former Leonard's Wharf since 1845. In 1926, the terminal was deepened for larger steamers carrying lumber from Pacific and southern ports. The company operated huge cranes to offload freight. A large planing mill on site produced custom woodwork and building materials for housing. The Munindies was later sunk by a naval mine during World War II.*

The City

Between 1925 and 1942, the cityscape shrank as New Bedford's population fell by more than 9,000 people. Tall ships disappeared from the harbor with smaller fishing vessels taking their place. Sprawling textile mills along the waterfront and rail lines closed, giving way to vacant lots or parceled out to several smaller tenants. Inside houses and tenements, less visible changes took place as average family size decreased from 4.5 in 1920 to 3.7 by 1940.

In this photo, circa 1942, dark clouds allow thin streams of sunlight to illuminate the old town. Just east of Palmer's Island, vessels leaving the harbor and entering Buzzards Bay cut a floating trail into the thin ice. Church spires and the remaining mill chimneys pierce the haze hanging low over New Bedford. The dark bulk of Saint Anthony of Padua Church dominates while at bottom left, on Church Street, a wisp of factory exhaust emerges from the Firestone Mill, producers of defense products and ordnance. At bottom center, a frozen Nash Road Pond reflects the weak sunlight. At lower right center, the new, treeless Presidential Heights Federal Housing Project on Mount Pleasant Street welcomes new families seeking comfort and convenience. Across the street and at bottom right, Sacred Heart Cemeteries #1 and #2 stand set to accept future generations.

The Heart of Downtown, 1925–1942

During whaling days, New Bedford's financial and commercial center came together at the Four Corners, where Union and Water Streets intersect near the waterfront. This financial-commercial center brimmed with banks, counting houses, law offices and many ancillary firms that sustained whaling. As whaling waned, the center moved up the hill to eventually settle around the crossing of Union and Purchase Streets, known as Lawton's Corner, which became one of the busiest places in town. Two brothers, Horace and Charles Lawton, opened a drug store there in 1873 on the northwest corner. The store closed 23 years later, but the name stuck.

For decades, locals dubbed downtown Purchase Street "The Strip." This one-block stretch between Lawton's Corner and William Street evolved into the city's new banking and commercial heart. It held three of the region's largest financial institutions: the New Bedford Institution for Savings, New Bedford Five Cents Savings Bank and Merchants National Bank. The strip also boasted four flagship department stores: the Star Store, Steiger-Dudgeon Company (until its closure and sale to Charles H. Cox Company, which closed in turn in 1937), Cherry & Company and C. F. Wing & Company. These downtown merchants occupied more than 150,000 square feet of retail floor space on 16 stories. Regular customers came from as far away as Provincetown, Nantucket, Providence and

Purchase Street, looking north from William Street, 1927. *The North Congregational Church looms at the corner of Elm Street. The Olympia Theatre showed both film and vaudeville. The movie marquee touted Mary Astor and William Collier in* The Sunset Derby. *Vaudeville-goers could take in the Brown Demont Revue with the Leila Shaw Company and Ed White.*

Brockton. The strip's other department stores included Enterprise, W. T. Grant Company, Lincoln Stores, S. S. Kresge, and Sears Roebuck & Company. The rest of the 22-block downtown district was crammed with clothiers, toy stores, furniture dealers, theaters, government buildings, churches, restaurants, drug stores, confectioners, tobacconists and more.

The New Bedford Institution for Savings began in a modest bookstore at Four Corners and moved twice more before settling into its glorious Greek temple at the corner of Union and Purchase Streets. This final move signaled that commerce had indeed moved uptown. New Bedford greeted 1925 with optimism for a promising economic era. Although the *Wanderer*, the last whaling bark to sail from the city, had run aground on the rocks off Cuttyhunk the year before, the city's new economic motor of textile mills registered its best year and the port's new commercial fishing fleet was growing. But the promise was short-lived. History would soon intervene with disastrous labor issues, the collapse of the local textile industry, a sharp drop in population, the stock market crash, the Great Depression and World War II.

C. F. Wing Department Store, Purchase Street, circa 1918.

C. F. Wing Sporting Goods Department, Acushnet Avenue, 1940. *Manager Dennis A. Sylvia (right) demonstrates a saltwater, level-wind casting reel to sales clerks Trudy Litz, Natalie (Hemingway) Sylvia and Frank Jarvis. Wing's store on the Avenue abutted the rear of the main store, which faced Purchase Street.*

Lawton's Corner and the Bristol Building, southeast corner of Union and Purchase Streets, 1925. *The Bristol Building (center) was built in 1914 at 740-768 Purchase Street with room for 10 stores at street level and office space upstairs. Over the years, it has housed many different retailers.*

On a Saturday afternoon in May 1939, a mixed crowd of pedestrians of different ages, ethnic groups and social classes cross this busy William Street intersection at the **Cherry Building** (right).

In 1898, George Cherry opened a small shop on Purchase Street with five employees. He sold high quality ladies' garments and furs. Cherry was both buyer and janitor. As his shop expanded and prospered, he opened a bigger store in a new building in 1917.

After the Depression hit, Cherry showed his faith in the city's future by buying the former Union Street Railway Company waiting room on the corner of Purchase and William Streets in 1931. There, he built a massive Art Deco style store designed by Lowell-born architect Herbert R. Hunt. It was the city's only sizeable business project since 1926. In January 1932, to help it meet its payroll, Cherry loaned the city $100,000 against future taxes.

Shoppers and students cross William and Purchase Streets, in front of Cherry's, 1939.

The Cherry Building, Purchase and William Streets, 1931.

At right, a section of the Purchase Street strip shows the **New Bedford Five Cents Savings Bank** (left) and the Merchants National Bank (far right) with two commercial buildings in between—old China Hall (housing Mason's Furniture) and the Cummings Building.

Below, the **Star Store** (left), designed by Louis E. Destremps, opened in 1915 and reigned as the city's premier department store for nearly a century. Its imposing building towered over the southwest corner of Union and Purchase Streets and its chic window displays drew customers inside. During Christmas season, it hired hundreds of temporary employees to accommodate the festive shoppers. People fondly remember the restaurant, the escalator and friendly sales staff who knew their customers' names.

The eight-story **First National Bank building** (right, rear) at the corner of Union and Pleasant Streets stood as New Bedford's tallest "skyscraper" for decades. The bank's history went back to 1832. It moved into its new quarters built by William Coulson Company of Cambridge in August 1925. The last major building erected in the city before the Depression, it exemplified the enthusiasm of the time for the city's future.

West side of Purchase Street between Sears Court and William Street, 1925.

View west on Union Street from Purchase Street with Star Store and First National Bank, 1932.

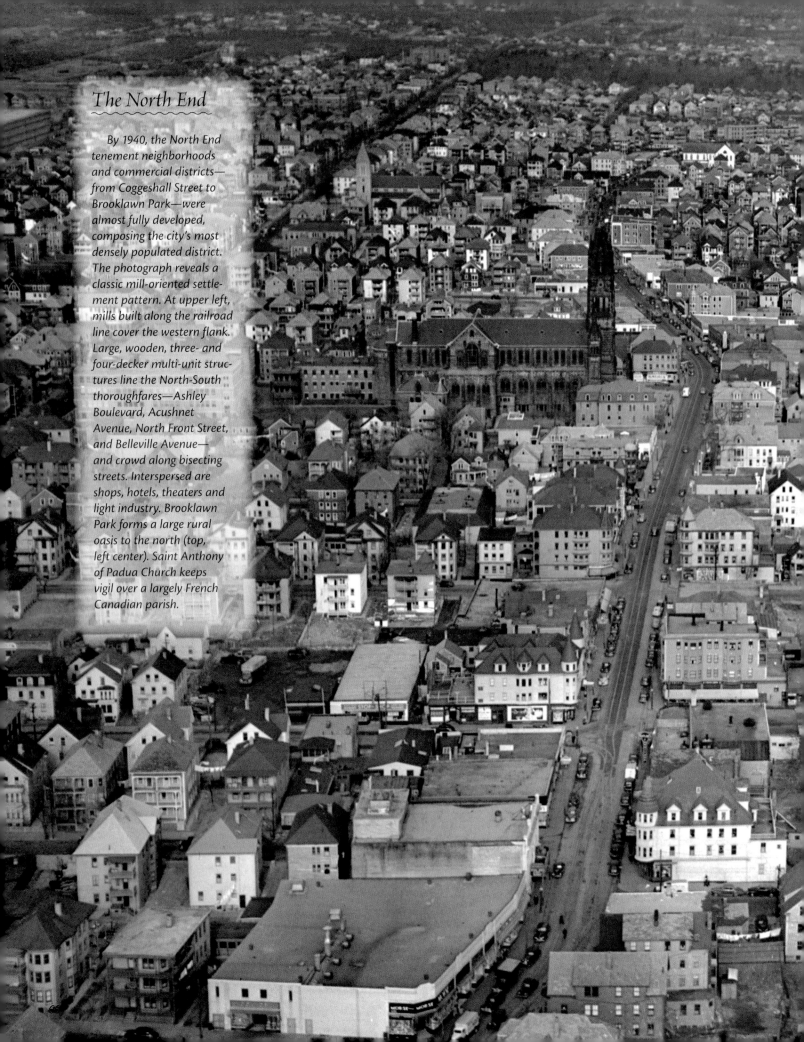

The North End

By 1940, the North End tenement neighborhoods and commercial districts—from Coggeshall Street to Brooklawn Park—were almost fully developed, composing the city's most densely populated district. The photograph reveals a classic mill-oriented settlement pattern. At upper left, mills built along the railroad line cover the western flank. Large, wooden, three- and four-decker multi-unit structures line the North-South thoroughfares—Ashley Boulevard, Acushnet Avenue, North Front Street, and Belleville Avenue—and crowd along bisecting streets. Interspersed are shops, hotels, theaters and light industry. Brooklawn Park forms a large rural oasis to the north (top, left center). Saint Anthony of Padua Church keeps vigil over a largely French Canadian parish.

Acushnet Avenue & the North End

Affectionately called "The Avenue," Acushnet Avenue runs through the city's North End, revealing its immigrant, commercial and cultural roots. Acushnet Avenue, between Weld Square to the south and Tarkiln Hill Road to the north, traces the stories of Native Americans, old Yankees and each new immigrant wave. With time, the Avenue became one of the city's most extensive and busiest commercial districts.

An ancient Native American trail extended south along Acushnet Avenue, County Street and Cove Road, providing access to the river, harbor and inner bay. From Plymouth, east-west paths crossed the Acushnet River farther north and intersected with the avenue. One path roughly aligned with Tarkiln Hill Road, a second with Nash Road and a third with the Coggeshall Street Bridge. A 1795 map of New Bedford shows an avenue with its abrupt jog to the northeast running to the Head of the River near Tarkiln Hill Road. Residents called this northern part "the road to Acushnet" or the "old county road."

In the early days, large farms and rural estates covered the area north of Coggeshall Street. City dwellers largely viewed it as a rural retreat. Only in 1849 did the city directory list a street named Acushnet Avenue. During the 1880s, as mills grew in the formerly rural North and South Ends, 90 percent of the foreign-born migrants to the city settled in these areas. Housing boomed to the east and west of Acushnet Avenue, but much of the avenue itself remained undeveloped until 1895, when extensive building began. At the same time, some older

Christopher A. Church Mansion, later owned by A. Davis Ashley, 1908. *As Acushnet Avenue developed, commercial properties often emerged around stately homes. John A. Ruggles Jr. and Henry W. Ellison located their North End dry goods store in the newly built Arcade Building on the southwest corner of Coggeshall Street and Acushnet Avenue.*

buildings were re-purposed; the old Coggeshall/Pope house at 300 Acushnet Avenue, for example, became the hotel known as Avenue House.

By 1910, more than 64 percent of the city's residents of French Canadian origin lived in the North End's Ward 1. Church authorities added two new Catholic churches on Acushnet Avenue to serve them: Holy Rosary, between Hicks and Logan Streets, which opened in October 1908 for those living south of Coggeshall Street, and St. Joseph's, at the corner of Duncan Street, which opened in August 1910 for those living north of Nash Road. Both churches joined the venerable St. Anthony of Padua, which opened in 1895 at the corner

Coggeshall Street and the North End looking east from the reservoir standpipe on Mt. Pleasant Street, circa 1897.

of Bullard Street. In 1926, as the area's French-speaking population continued to migrate ever further north, St. Theresa's Church was established farther up on Acushnet Avenue adjacent to Pine Grove Cemetery.

With time, "The Avenue" developed as a mixed commercial and residential area. Along its length, hundreds of small, often competing stores offered every conceivable kind of goods and services. Ground floors provided retail space for small businesses, with residential living space above. Chain stores appeared in the early years, especially five and dime stores. Some had a downtown or South End location as well as a spot on the avenue. F. W. Woolworth Co. had an Acushnet Avenue store by 1910. The Great Atlantic & Pacific Tea Co. opened an avenue store in 1912. J. G. McCrory launched a store at South Water and another at the busy commercial hub of Acushnet Avenue and Coggeshall Street in 1913. Thom McAn Shoe Co. and Puritan Grocery Stores joined them later.

By 1924, people of 15 nationalities owned and operated businesses on Acushnet Avenue in the 16-block area between Coggeshall Street and Nash Road. Of 256 listed business owners, 105 were Franco-American—mostly French Canadian—who operated 35 different types of enterprises. Russian and Polish Jews ran 51 businesses; Anglo-Americans

Dr. Norbert Romulus Brault house at 1325 Acushnet Avenue, north of Tallman Street, 1932. *Franco-American builder Joseph Sorrelle Jr., who emigrated from Quebec in 1882, built the house in 1898 to display his skills. Brault, a physician who owned and operated Union Hospital, sold the house around 1930 to Aldège Chaussé, who converted part of it to a funeral parlor.*

(born both in this country and in England) ran 46; Greek Americans ran 15; Irish Americans, 10; and Portuguese Americans, 7. Franco-Americans tended to specialize in millinery, grocery, barber shops and poolrooms, with Jewish merchants focusing on clothing, dry goods and variety stores. Greek Americans tended toward fruit stores, confections, restaurants and delicatessens and Chinese Americans ran laundries and restaurants.

Acushnet Avenue looking north from Deane Street, circa 1922.

View south from Coggeshall Street shows the Arcade Building (at right) after a second-story addition. In the early 1920s, the three short blocks to Kenyon Street formed the core of New Bedford's French Canadian community. Along with homeowners and boarders were institutions including the Franco-American Chamber of Commerce, three French Canadian fraternal organizations, a temperance society, the Comique Theater and more than thirty small businesses owned by French Canadian immigrants or their children. Medical doctor Hormidas Choquette and pharmacist George J. Dion were born in Massachusetts of Canadian-born parents.

The area was not monolithically French; instead, it reflected New Bedford's varied immigrant mix. Fourteen Russian Jewish families owned small businesses there. It also had English-born hotelkeepers, an Armenian-owned shoestore, a Czechoslovak grocery and a furniture store, a Polish druggist and two provisioners, a Portuguese restaurant, a hardware store and a clothing store, a Chinese laundry and a restaurant and Greek, Syrian (as Lebanese were called) and Turkish confectioners. First- or second-generation textile mill workers living on the street represented even more ethnic groups. The Great Atlantic & Pacific Tea Co. at 1032 Acushnet Avenue and F.W. Woolworth at 1081 had already begun to displace small shopkeepers.

Although Portuguese-speaking residents played a minimal role in the North End's early economic years, an enclave of almost 3,000 Portuguese lived in the neighborhood of Our Lady of the Immaculate Conception Church on Earle Street in the North End. In 1915, four Madeiran Island immigrants formed a group to recreate the religious festivals of their home island. To this day, the Club Madeirense S.S. Sacramento continues to annually hold what has become the largest Portuguese feast in the world and the largest ethnic festival in New England.

By 1945 the ethnic composition of retailers along Acushnet Avenue had not changed greatly since 1924. Franco-American retailers still predominated.

Several of their stores prospered and gained strong reputations. The shoe store at 1071 Acushnet Avenue, originally owned by Joseph Champegny and Charles I. Leblanc, was among them. Champegny had come to the US in 1905; Leblanc was born to French Canadian parents in Millbury, Massachusetts. They opened their shoe store on Acushnet

Schick & Son Funeral Home, circa 1920. *An ethnic Pole, Leo Schick left his Austrian-ruled village for the US in 1906. He readily found a job in the city's cotton mills. By 1920, he and almost 650 of his countrymen had clustered near the Polish church, Our Lady of Perpetual Help. Schick rose to become a loomfixer at the nearby Bristol Mill, later advancing to second hand. His wife Katherine, after having seven children, went back to work as a weaver. When the Bristol Mill closed, Schick became an undertaker along with his son Stanley. The family lived in a three-decker on Cedar Grove Street.*

View north up Acushnet Avenue from Holly Street, circa 1928. *Local residents had many options for food. The A & P (Great Atlantic & Pacific Tea Company) appears behind the first telephone pole at left. Elsewhere on the block, Edmond Patnaude and Thomas Daley each had restaurants, Mrs. Minnie Norris had a delicatessen and the Harris Brothers supplied confections. Mary Farrady, I. Margolis & Son, Beaulieu & Mandeville and Max Greenstein had provisions or variety stores. Other merchants sold clothing or household items.*

Avenue around 1910. By 1923, Champegny had bought out his partner and prospered. Going to Champegny's for a new pair of shoes remained a rite of passage for many generations of North End children.

A little farther north, at 1430 Acushnet Avenue, Bouchard's Tavern was established during the 1930s by Canadian-born J. Alfred Bouchard and continued under his son Alfred "Fred" Louis Bouchard. Local historian Carmen Maiocco later noted that the tavern—which became a well-known watering hole—was "famous for its French meat pies sold all over the city and its baked beans…which attracted politicians from far and wide. One fellow told me more deals were finalized by a handshake at the bar at Bouchard's than at any bank in town."

Franco-American George Poyant and his son Leon ran a well-known shoe repair business called Poyant Shoes at 1494 Acushnet Avenue.

Among the early immigrant retailers, Jews were right behind the Franco-Americans in number. Several Jewish merchants had stores in both the South and North Ends. Both Abram Kroudvird's Sanitary Bakery and Kaplan Brothers Furniture had stores on South Water Street and Acushnet Avenue. Other well-known Jewish retailers included Laurence Sadow, who operated Sadow's clothing store from 1938 to 1957; William Saltzman, who ran four United Fruit stores in the city, one at 1497 Acushnet Avenue; and Harry Goldberg and his son Julius, who ran Harry the Hatter's from 1927 to 1979.

Meanwhile, Greek immigrant retailers focused on candy and ice cream stores, restaurants, shoeshine and bootblacking services. Only two Greeks appeared in the 1900 New Bedford

View south on The Avenue from Collette Street, 1920s. *The building at the far right edge was built for French Canadian entrepreneur Ulric E. Collette, for whom Collette Street is named. Its tenants, like most others, were retailers and residents hailing from many different countries.*

census; by 1915, there were 446 Greek-born residents and half of them lived in the North End, where 32 Greek-owned and -operated businesses had sprung up. Peter M. Panaretos ran the Tip Top Restaurant at 1174-1178 Acushnet Avenue until 1936 when John Rampias, also of Greek descent, opened the space as Tip Top Lunch until 1941. Brothers Arthur and George Courosis ran Palace of Sweets and later Capitol Candy Kitchen.

View south along The Avenue from Phillips Avenue, circa 1932.

View north from Beetle Street, 1925. *The French Canadian Vien family built the Touraine Hotel (formerly the Waverly) and the Strand Theater in 1901 and 1909 respectively. They also owned many buildings and lots on both sides of The Avenue. New Bedford architect Samuel C. Hunt designed the hotel with a three-story round turret suspended above a corner store entrance. The vaudeville theater was initially known as the Vien Theater. Later, the Marcus Lowe chain bought it and renamed it the Strand. Both the hotel and theater were precursors of the large-scale buildings that soon set the Acushnet Avenue streetscape apart from those on the city's other North- and South-End thoroughfares.*

Soup line at Harisee's Grocery Store, North Front and Holly Streets, during the strike of 1928.

Nahum and Annie Joseph's grocery and soda fountain, The Avenue and Tinkham Street, 1930.

View north up Acushnet Ave from Weld Square Hotel, 1930.

George Darwish Harisee of Ganem & Company grocery store, with the help of some friends, proved to mill workers that he not only appreciated them in good times but also cared when times were bleak. Harisee, of Syrian origin, served more than 100 gallons of hot spaghetti soup made with 50 pounds of beef to a crowd that newspapers estimated exceeded 400 people. The photo was taken on the second occasion Harisee gave out food. At the front of the line are those who helped make and distribute the fare: Mr. Harisee, Charley Deeb, Marie Tabet, Sophie Hamid, George Ganem, Armand Brothers, Ted Ryder, Henry Tabet and Claude Jalbert.

Syrian-born **Nahum Joseph** came to the US at 18, in 1903, and joined many relatives in New Bedford. After marrying, he and his first wife opened a confectioner's shop at 1668½ Acushnet Avenue, near Nash Road. Following the deaths of his wife and young son at the end of the influenza epidemic, he remarried in 1925. He continued running the candy store until his death in 1932. His widow Annie maintained the business for many years.

Weld Square attracted a mix of commercial businesses. John B. DeMello Jr.'s Gulf gasoline station appears at right, across from the Franco-American Federation building. This view is just north of Weld Square. The only building shown that still survives is the Touraine Hotel, in the far distance where the street bears left and runs out of view. Braudy's Department Store abuts the Weld Square Barbershop, next to the Weld Square Pharmacy. Elsewhere, a plumber, grocer, tailor, bakery, fish market and a kosher meat and poultry provider cluster near each other.

In addition to bicycles, Camara's bicycle shop offered new Victrola talking machines and a variety of records under the Emerson Records label, including the "Bardanella Fox Trot."

The owner, Madeira-born Manuel Camara, came to the US after serving six months in the Portuguese infantry. He started out repairing bicycles and later sold them in his shop along with related equipment including Goodrich tires and not-so-related items such as Victrolas and records. As bicycles took a backseat to automobiles, Camara moved to Fairhaven to work as a gas station attendant.

At 16, young **Alice Audette** *(right in middle photo) briefly attended millinery school in Boston to learn her craft. Working with her sister Adeline (left), Audette opened a millinery shop at 1725 Acushnet Avenue and later moved to 1531 Acushnet Avenue. She married Andre Sirois, and in her later years (1950s), ran a neighborhood groceries and dry goods store on Durfee Street.*

New Bedford-born **J. Alfred Fredette** *(at right in bottom photo) lived most of his life in the North End. He grew up on Sawyer Street and as a youth worked in a nearby cotton mill. After marrying Aldea Sutherland in 1907, he worked for a while in Manuel Sylvia's hardware store at 1147 Acushnet Avenue. Later, he opened his own hardware store down the street at 1533 Acushnet Avenue. His older brother, Louis N. Fredette, owned a large furniture store across the street at 1560-1562 Acushnet Avenue.*

Manuel J. Camara's bicycle shop, Coggeshall Street and Belleville Avenue, circa 1925.

Adeline and Alice Audette's millinery, 1531 Acushnet Avenue, near Phillips Avenue, 1925.

Hardware store of J. Alfred Fredette, 1533 Acushnet Avenue, near Phillips Avenue, 1925.

New homes on the site of the former **New Bedford Athletic Field**, Central Avenue west of Acushnet Avenue, 1921.

Looking north on Acushnet Avenue near Phillips Road, 1934.

Lunds Corner, 1929.

Northern Expansion

By the 1920s, multifamily homes dotted the neighborhood north of Baylies Square. At left, in place of the **old New Bedford Athletic Field** along Central Avenue rose one- and two-story homes, many of which still stand. Later, John C. Motta built the Motta Building, a long, one-story commercial structure on the Acushnet Avenue side of the ballpark.

Lunds Corner, where Tarkiln Hill Road intersects with Acushnet Avenue, was a busy commercial hub for the northern part of the city. Businesses included auto supplies, druggists, restaurants, barbers, a physician, a jeweler and a grocer. The First Congregational Church (the oldest church in New Bedford), the Jireh Swift School and a pool hall were also here. Lunds Corner supplied farmers with feed and machinery as well as harness and blacksmith services.

The area north of this busy corner retained its rural character in the early 20th century. Farmhouses and single-family homes on generous lots lined both sides of Acushnet Avenue from Mill Road at Ball's Corner to **Kosciuszko Square**, where Acushnet Avenue and Ashley Boulevard merge. A few small streets off Acushnet Avenue comprised narrower lots; these, however, were surrounded by farmland and large homesteads belonging to the Washburn, Russell, Tobey, Barlett, Paige, Hamlin, Darling, Ashley and other families.

Sassaquin

Named for a local Indian chief, the Sassaquin section of New Bedford's far North End surrounds Sassaquin Pond, a 37-acre kettle pond encircled by cottages and woods. A small cemetery on the pond's eastern shore holds the graves of about 20 members of the Tobey family, who came to Sassaquin before the Civil War. Farmers and woodcutters were the first to settle here, but in the late 1800s city folk began building summer cottages around Sassaquin to enjoy the country air and the pond's pure waters. They had a simple life with dirt roads and backyard outhouses. Sunday drivers referred to the area as "the country in the North End."

St. Joseph Church organized a mission chapel at Sassaquin in 1925. Later, St. Theresa's Church assumed responsibility for the chapel, which it renamed Ste. Thérèse du Lac. For 35 years it served French Canadians with some observances conducted in French. In 1966, it became Our Lady of Fatima Parish. It graces the far northern part of Acushnet Avenue with its tall steeple and simple interior.

Just south of Sassaquin Avenue near Braley Road was Sylvan Grove, a delightful but at times troublesome neighbor. In 1872, Otis A. Sisson bought 30 acres of land on the west side of Acushnet Avenue in the far North End and called it Sylvan Grove. His clambakes attracted enormous crowds, and the enterprise stoked his ambitions. "The King of New Bedford Hospitality," as Sisson became known, constructed a large pavilion with a dance hall, bowling alleys, baseball diamonds and croquet fields. He planted vineyards and made his own wine. After Sisson died in 1900, parcels of land were sold to developers, but the clambakes, picnics and entertainments continued on the remaining land, sometimes drawing unruly crowds. In 1954, a dance at the pavilion attracted 1,000 people and fights broke out. North Enders, fed up with the shenanigans on the privately owned land, persuaded the city to take it over. Sylvan Grove became a public park in 1963. Polish groups soon influenced the Park Board to change the name of Sylvan Grove to Casimir Pulaski Park in honor of the famous Polish hero of the American Revolutionary War. Since then, Pulaski Park has become a quieter place.

Alfred Dion's Cider & Fruit Stand, Acushnet Avenue and Peckham Road, Sassaquin, 1944.

Sassaquin Pond, 1925.

Looking north over frozen Sassaquin Pond, 1946.

South Water Street & the South End

South Water Street became the city's third thriving commercial artery, serving the densely populated working-class neighborhoods that grew around South End mills and factories. It developed later than the city center or the near North End because mills came to the South End later. Once they did, however, the transition from undeveloped farmland, pastures, groves, beaches and salt works to bustling city settlement came quickly to the area, formerly known as South Bedford. Along streets perpendicular to Brock Avenue (once called Middle Point Road because it was the only road through Clark's Point) farms gave way to one-, two- and three-story buildings.

Long before the British settled in the area, Native Americans regularly gathered here for clambakes, often at the Smoking Rocks, where Potomska Mills later stood. When

the early settlers plowed the meadows into farmland, they routinely turned up quantities of arrowheads and clamshells.

By the end of the 19th century, apartments teemed with people living above the storefronts in the heart of South Water Street's commercial district. By the early 20th century, French Canadians proved the largest group, accounting for almost a third of the adults living between Rivet and Cove Streets. Many came directly from Quebec, but others from across New England, born of French Canadian parents, made their way here. Immigrants from England, Poland, Russia, Portugal and the Azores each accounted for more than four percent of the residents along South Water Street. Lesser numbers came from thirteen other countries and six other states.

The South End did not have ethnic enclaves. Instead, its residents readily lived together in religious and social tolerance. For example, in 1920, the 49 adults lodging in the

Polish National Building/Woodrow Wilson Hall, Rodney French Boulevard, 1932. *Built in 1916 by the Fédération Franco-Américaine Conseil No. 2, the building initially housed the Colonial Theater. After the theater closed in 1930, it passed to the Woodrow Wilson Club, Lodge 1667 of the Polish National Alliance, which used the venue for spectacles and boxing matches.*

Meaney Hall, South Water and Division Streets, 1934. *Irish-born Thomas J. Meaney came to New Bedford in 1868. He served on the police force, then worked in real estate. One of the building's tenants, Industrial Workers of the World, often suffered police raids and vandalism.*

rooming house at 1076 South Water Street hailed from Quebec, England, Massachusetts, Albania, Ireland, the Azores, Turkey, Portugal, France and Austria. Similarly, the 34 residents of another lodging house, at 988 South Water Street, were born in Massachusetts, Quebec, Greece, England, Italy, New Hampshire, Maine, Madeira, Connecticut and the Azores. Different floors in tenement houses often held people from different countries. The high rate of ethnic intermingling inevitably led to intermarriages. By 1920, one in every seven couples was made up of spouses from different ethnic groups, bringing together different cultures, interests, languages and menus.

South Water Street offered a wide variety of goods and services. In 1923, its 169 businesses included fruit, fish, meat and grocery markets, a bank, hotels, confectioners, cobblers, shoe stores, tailors, dry goods, dress and corset shops, pharmacies, hardware stores, barber shops, beauty salons, soda fountains, restaurants, photographers, physicians and opticians, billiard parlors, a penny arcade and a clairvoyant. Most were small businesses, but the national chains had already begun to make inroads, including The Great Atlantic & Pacific Tea Company, F. W. Woolworth and J. G. McCrory, with stores in both the North and South Ends. Some local stores also did the same, including jeweler Stanislas T. Benoit, milliner Henry L. Bonneau, Eugenie Robillard's remnants, Moses Weiner's shoe store, Hudner's Market and the Giusti Baking Company.

Patrons often favored their own ethnic groups. Thus, residents could choose among English, Italian, French Canadian and Portuguese bakeries. Men could choose French Canadian, Irish, English or Portuguese barbers. Similarly, women had their choice of French Canadian, English, Scottish, Russian, Azorean or Portuguese milliners. To get a competitive edge in different ethnic markets, larger stores often hired French-, Portuguese- and Polish-speaking staff.

South End churches answered the spiritual needs of many different faiths and ethnic groups. There were two French Canadian parishes—St. Hyacinthe's Church on Rivet Street, which dated to 1888 and St. Anne's Church on Ruth Street, built in 1908. St. Hedwig's Church at the corner of Delano and South Second Streets served the Polish community. Our Lady of Mount Carmel on Rivet Street dated to 1913. With Rev. Antonio Pacheco Vieira as pastor, it ministered to the Portuguese-speaking community from the Azores, Madeira and mainland Portugal. St. Martin's Episcopal Church, also on Rivet Street, looked after the English and Scottish communities.

Ahavath Achim Jewish Synagogue on Howland Street was built in 1898. Its second rabbi, Hyman Papkin, served from 1900 until his death in 1960. A small Jewish community lived within walking distance of the synagogue. Most of its members

André Fontaine's Pharmacy, corner of South Water and Cove Streets, 1941. *Daughters Evelyn and Dorothy joined their father in the business until Dorothy left for the Navy in 1942.*

Gaston A. Jarry's Pharmacy, northeast corner Brock Avenue and Rodney French Blvd, 1945. *A brother Roger owned a pharmacy on South Water Street as had their father before them.*

had emigrated from Russia, Poland, Hungary and elsewhere in Eastern Europe, escaping harsh economic and social conditions. They began arriving in 1877. Many established businesses on South Water Street to serve the thousands of newly arriving mill workers. By 1920, however, many Jewish business owners had moved out of the area into Ward 5.

The Family Welfare Society of New Bedford maintained a strong presence both at 1006 South Water Street and at 1566 Acushnet Avenue. South Water Street's clubs included the Peace & Harmony Social Club, the South End Social Club and the French Sharpshooters Club. Nearby South End clubs included the Washington Social and Musical Club and the New Bedford Power Boat Club (both on West Rodney French Boulevard), the Portuguese National Club on Rivet Street and the Cercle Champlain Social on Cove Street.

The French Sharpshooters Club built the impressively large Orpheum Theater on South Water Street. The area also included the Royal Theater, Police Station #2 and the local headquarters of the Industrial Workers of the World in Meaney Hall.

South Water from Cove Street, circa 1941. *Across from Fontaine's Pharmacy, an assortment of merchants grace a one-half block of South Water Street. They include South End Hardware Store, Royal Fruit Store, Avila Poisson's jewelry, Boisclair's Fish Market, Harry's Shoe Store, Kroudvird's Sanitary Bakery, A & P Tea Company, Harvey Shoe Store, United Fruit Stores, Stevenson's Dry Goods Store and the New York Shoe Store.*

Big 4 Clothing Company, Lithuanian-born brothers Herman and Israel Shapiro, 907 South Water Street, circa 1912. *The brothers quickly parted ways. Israel left New Bedford to run a dry goods store in Lewiston, Maine and Herman became a nationwide traveling salesman. Another brother, Hyman, managed the New Bedford store for a few years.*

The Orpheum Barber Shop. *Newly married Portuguese-born Umberto Anibal Baldo immigrated to the United States in 1919. On settling in New Bedford, he Anglicized his name to Humbert. The next year, he brought over his mother and sister. Baldo ran both his own barbershop and a nearby poolroom on South Water Street.*

The Orpheum was the center of community activities, housing meeting areas, an armored shooting range and a fine ballroom in addition to the 1,500-seat theater. It opened on April 15, 1912, but news of its opening was driven from the headlines by the sinking of the *Titanic*. Many of New Bedford's French Canadian soldiers during the First and the Second World Wars acquired their firearms proficiency at the Orpheum's shooting range. It originally hosted vaudeville shows, but later converted to movies, snagging many important first-run movies. During the week of August 23, 1915, it hosted the city premiere of D. W. Griffith's *The Birth of a Nation*, boasting that the theater's new $12,000 lighting system boosted the picture's clarity.

On Saturdays, when they showed kiddie movies, the Orpheum and Royal were packed with 13- and 14-year-olds. The Orpheum was nice but the Royal looked like a garage. Both had been built as vaudeville theaters but now showed movies. Kids got a double feature, usually cowboys and pirates, with a serial, which continued from week to week. If the movie projector broke down, we stamped our feet until it went back on.

Many older residents fondly remembered Fontaine's Pharmacy, run by André and Laurina Fontaine. Harold Pilkington, who worked there as a teenager, married one of the Fontaine daughters, Evelyn.

Fontaine's was on the corner of Cove and Water Streets.... Evelyn worked in the pharmacy and learned from her father—she apprenticed with him—she was the only daughter in the business. She ended up getting a couple of licenses and passed a state test. She and her brother Rene (Andy) took over the pharmacy in 1945.... She stayed in the job for several decades until she retired.

I loved the soda fountain at Fontaine's. Evelyn and her mother were so proud of it. There were six tall stools and you could sit there and look out the big window and see everything going on out there on South Water Street. The street itself was very narrow and the trolley barged through, picking shoppers up and dropping them off. The street was full of people—all nationalities. It was a very colorful scene.

Four Generations of Silversteins

When Barnet Silverstein emigrated from Russian-controlled Lithuania, around 1892, he settled in New Bedford and began business as a door-to-door peddler. With a pack of household goods on his back, he knocked on doors in the South End and if he didn't have what his customers wanted, he got it. Soon he traded his backpack for a warehouse in a busy South Water Street location, where he specialized in dry goods and fancy goods. His wife Fannie played an ever-larger role and managed the business after Silverstein died. Later their son Harry and his wife Anna took over.

The business soon occupied half a building at 937 South Water Street. Harry Silverstein did not want his three sons to take over because of the hard work and worry of storekeeping, but Joseph, Bernard and Louis successfully continued the family tradition, with a new focus on boys' wear. The store left South Water Street in the 1970s due to vandalism and street rioting. Its move to New Bedford's center presented a grand opportunity. Its South End customers came with it, and the store began drawing from Providence and Cape Cod. It survived until 1997, when its fourth-generation president, Stephen Silverstein, and merchandise manager, David Silverstein, told unhappy customers that they were closing after a 97-year run.

Kitchen of A-1 Restaurant, 29 Rodney French Boulevard, 1941. *At center is Edward Dumont, proprietor and Fairhaven resident. The restaurant burned down shortly after the photograph was taken. Dumont managed the Bridge Diner before opening the A-1. After the fire, he worked at Romeo's Diner on Acushnet Avenue at the foot of Maxfield Street.*

Armand Piche's grocery store, 712 Brock Avenue, 1921. *Piche is at left, clerk Donat Bessette stands in the center. Butcher J. Leonidas Fournier proudly stands to the far right behind a variety of sausages and prepared meats. A pile of fresh corn, baskets of local blueberries and other produce tempt customers.*

F.W. Woolworth Company, 1069 South Water Street, 1939. *The company opened its third New Bedford commercial location about 1913. The large window display of seeds met Depression-era needs to grow vegetables in small kitchen gardens, with a few flowers for color.*

Around the South End

English-born Samuel Thomas Rex came to the United States as a young man. He learned the stonecutter's trade in Westerly, Rhode Island, and then relocated to Quincy, where he worked at his trade in the late 1880s before going into business for himself. He later moved to New Bedford. In 1894, he bought the Swithin Brothers marble works from its non-resident owners. It was conveniently located on Dartmouth Street across from Rural Cemetery, near the cemetery's main entrance, where Rex displayed his artistic monuments and blocks of raw stone to potential customers. He renamed the company S. T. Rex and Company, and in another name change it became **Rex Monumental Works**. In addition to Italian and American marble, Rex specialized in granites from the United States, Scotland and Sweden.

Fourteen-year-old **Guilherme M. Luiz** of Angra do Heroísmo, Azores, immigrated to the United States in 1891. He first worked in the city's textile mills. In 1909, he founded a travel agency that launched his successful career. Later, his conglomerate combined community banking with the travel agency, which sold steamship passages on the Fabre Line. Luiz was authorized to remit funds to Portugal and its possessions and to serve as a foreign exchange bureau. In 1917, Luiz purchased a newspaper, A Alvorada, and renamed it Diário de Notícias in 1919. At that time, it was the only Portuguese-language daily newspaper in the United States. He also owned the Livraria Colonial bookstore on Rivet Street.

Designed by architects Brown & Poole and built for Lebanese immigrant **Joseph S. Thomas** in 1922, the landmark commercial building had six storefronts and four four-bedroom apartments. In the 1920s, when working capital was easy to secure, Thomas aimed to establish Rivet Street as a commercial adjunct, if not an alternative, to the bustling shopping district on South Water Street, 15 blocks to the east. He moved his dry goods business from lower Rivet Street and within two years began lobbying the city council to establish the corner as Goulart Square, in memory of Walter Goulart, the first Portuguese resident of New Bedford to die in combat during World War I. Next, Thomas and neighboring business owners formed the Goulart Square Business Association to lobby for a streetcar to run between the square and downtown. Although Rivet Street never developed like South Water, it became an important South End business district and was the only throughway connecting the waterfront to Dartmouth Street.

Rex Monumental Works, 1922. *A stonecutter is at work beneath the awning in background.*

Guilherme M. Luiz & Company, Rivet Street and Acushnet Avenue, circa 1936.

The J. S. Thomas Building, Goulart Square, Rivet and Bolton Streets, 1923.

Famous for its all-you-can-eat clambakes at $2.50 per person, **Dan's Pavilion** served nearly 3,000 people weekly at summertime events. Dan's traditional hot-rock clambakes used seaweed cut and gathered from beach rocks at low tide. The seaweed was stored between the pavilion pilings, where the ebb and flow of the tide kept it fresh all week. Dan's Pavilion boasted a refined yet boisterous atmosphere conducive to dancing, fine dining, entertainment and socializing—hosting formal gatherings, conferences and weddings. So popular was Dan's that it took three hurricanes to finally bring it down. Owner Dan Bauer rebuilt with a loan from the city after the 1938 hurricane demolished the pavilion. In the 1944 hurricane, Dan's lost part of the side of its structure. With each loss, Bauer was determined to resurrect the business. However, in 1954, Hurricane Carol washed the pavilion away, leaving Bauer with little emotional and physical energy to rebuild. Finally, in 1959, soon before Dan's death, the Bauers sold the beachfront property to the city.

Southeast winds and rain crash waves over **Cove Road at morning high tide**. City maintenance crews waged a continual battle against the sea, which repeatedly eroded the embankment, undercut the rock and stone foundation and collapsed portions of the road surface. In 1952, a seawall was constructed and the area was filled in to create Jacintho F. Dinis Memorial Playground. The new park consumed the adjacent land formerly known as Joseph F. Francis Playground.

During the early 1940s, the junction of **County and Cove Streets** ranked among the city's most dangerous intersections. At least a dozen accidents occurred here annually, sometimes leading to deaths and more often resulting in numerous injuries. Nonetheless, it took more than 70 years to install traffic lights.

An outing at Dan's Pavilion, East Rodney French Boulevard, 1927. *View taken from the roof of Danceland, dance and function hall.*

Cove Road near Bonney Street, 1920s.

Looking east on Cove Street from County Street, 1941.

South Central Neighborhood

New Bedford's South Central neighborhood and the adjacent Old Bedford district contain some of the city's most ancient streets and oldest dwellings. The neighborhoods are sandwiched between the waterfront and County Street: Old Bedford includes downtown between School and Kempton Streets; South Central lies between School Street on the north and Potomska Street to the south. The grid represents a classic example of the stratification of a New England city: a social and economic hierarchy of streets define the settlement, beginning at the waterfront and culminating at the crest of the hill—County and Orchard Streets—upon which the wealthiest whaling and textile magnates built opulent homes overlooking the sea.

A gateway for immigrants, South Central first welcomed the founding settlers. As the rich whaling families moved further up the hill, new waves of immigrants came and made their homes here. The neighborhood streets were a mixture of transient seamen, tradesmen and laborers who worked on the waterfront. But merchants, lawyers, bankers and sea captains also lived in the neighborhood in homes along Pleasant, Sixth and Seventh Streets before later building finer houses on the hill crest that is County and Orchard Streets.

Also among the early inhabitants were fugitives escaping slavery, having arrived here through the Underground Railroad. Some of these fugitives quickly departed for sea and safety on whaling ships while others continued onward to Canada. Many settled here in New Bedford, finding a welcoming community and safety amongst Quakers.

Howland Street Club, circa 1938. *Henry Pina, shown at far right, lived nearby and helped found the club. An unidentified man stands at left. Behind the bar are Tony Ramos (left) and George Barboza. Members wanted a friendly place to meet, play cards, shoot dice and have a beer. It became a popular gathering place for the Cape Verdean community. By 1939, it was renamed the United Social Club. Finding the place too small, members bought a larger building at 31-33 Howland Street.*

Through the years, immigrants from Canada, Cape Verde, Portugal, Eastern Europe and Central America have been among those who have found homes here.

Walnut Street looking west from South Second Street, August 1938. *Arched by graceful sunlit elms, cobblestoned Walnut Street gave no hint here of impending disaster. A month later, hurricane-uprooted elm trees clogged the road above Second Street; below it, telephone and electric poles, floated up from the Front Street storage yard, littered the road. People in boats made heroic rescues of those stranded in the neighborhood and along the waterfront.*

OLOA & the Synagogue

The heart and soul of the Cape Verdean community, Our Lady of Assumption Church was the first Cape Verdean Catholic Church in the nation. It began in 1905 as a Mission Church on Water and Leonard Streets when a handful of people purchased a chapel that had once been a synagogue, a kindergarten and a storehouse. Father Stanislaus Bernard rode his bicycle in from Fairhaven to celebrate mass, and he also acted as church organist. The coal man, Mark Duff, came around regularly to provide free coal for heating. Many Cape Verdeans were still attending St. John's (at that time a wooden structure located at South Sixth and Wing Streets) or other churches. A key group from the Mission Church met in 1925 to figure out how to increase their numbers, and they came up with a winning formula.

Besides urging neighborhood residents to return to the church, they created a new OLOA Club. They sponsored dances, suppers and social affairs. Their biggest success was opening a youth center in the vacant store next to the church and filling it with Boy Scouts, Girl Scouts and Sunday night movies. Eugenia Martin, affectionately known as Aunt Jenny, taught the parish children catechism in English in her home and Ana Araujo taught them in Portuguese.

In 1935, attorney Alfred "Lawyer" Gomes initiated the popular OLOA basketball team in the CYO League (Catholic Youth Organization). Players and coaches were required to attend church regularly if they wished to play or coach basketball.

In 1957, the growing congregation moved into a new building on Sixth Street. The day of the move, Emilia Ramos cried out, "We must save our bell!" The old bell on their beloved chapel was dismantled and installed in the new church. Its tones had summoned people from their homes and children from the park for half a century.

Our Lady of Assumption Church, South Water and Leonard Streets, circa 1940. *Parishioners celebrate St. Anthony's feast day. Among those present are Bonnie Fermino DeGrasse, Anthony "Butch" Fermino, Barbara Fermino DePina, Henry Fermino, Maria "Bach" Santos, Agnes Lopes Thomas, Maria Guimar Gomes, Mary Gomes, Sebastian Rozario, Mrs. Ramos, Roger Souza, Theoff Almeida, Manual Almeida, Manual Burgo, Manuel Santos, Milton Ramos, Mary Santos Semedo, Gregory Centeio, Tom Lopes, Rev. John Godelaer and Rev. Edmund G Francis.*

Dedication of the Tifereth Israel Synagogue, South Sixth and Madison Streets, 1924. *For many years, the South Central neighborhood was home to many Jewish businesses and families. Around mid century, many families and eventually the synagogue moved westerly toward Buttonwood Park. Shown, left to right, front row: Isaac Barron, Louis Manelis, Samuel Goldfarb, David Kaufman, David Weitzman, Abram Herman, Rabbi Hyman Papkin, Mayor Walter Remington, Rabbi Arnoff, Cantor Boris Alper, Bernard Luiansky, Ike Abramson, Ellis Willis, Abraham Epstein, William Shapiro and Fisher Abramson. Second Row: Harry Queen, Abram Cohen, Louis Israel, Solomon Shuster, Barnet Russotto, Albert Goldsmith, Samuel Fleisch, Nathan Liss, Abram Kaplan, Henry Queen, Harry Lumiansky and Dr. Julius Abramson. Back row: Dr. Jacob Genensky, Dr. Herman Groh, Samuel Genensky, Jacob Horvitz and Abraham Levy.*

Growing up in South Central with Bill Carmo

Born in 1929, Bill Carmo (William do Carmo) grew up in the multicultural South Central neighborhood of New Bedford, the eldest of 11 children. His family lived on South First Street and struggled to make a living during the Great Depression.

"My father worked at the Quisset Mill and my mother stayed home to raise us kids," said Carmo. "The neighborhood kids were Cape Verdean, Jewish and Portuguese and we were all good friends. We did not know what prejudice was. Everybody knew us—we played in the streets and down by Pairpoint Glass and around the Portuguese Navy Yard. In the middle of all this was the massive Morse Twist Drill. We also played on old mill lots and used sticks for baseball bats and made footballs out of cloth. Or we'd swim out to Palmer's Island—naked because we had no bathing suits."

A whaler from the Cape Verdean Island of Brava, Carmo's grandfather settled on Nantucket. As whaling declined, Cape Verdeans bought old whalers and turned them into packet steamers. They began a brisk trade with the economically distraught islands, taking products there and returning with islanders. From 1901 to 1920, about 17,000 Cape Verdeans arrived in New Bedford, many settling in the South Central neighborhood. Carmo remembers a neighborhood of many cultural landscapes. "Most stores were Jewish owned, though a few French people owned hardware stores," he recalled. "I was a hustler and did all sorts of jobs from the earliest age. I worked for Jewish businesses—plucking chickens, helping in delis and bakeries; I hawked the *Morning Mercury*; I took my red wagon behind the factories where they disposed of coal, filled my wagon and sold coal to the Chinese laundry. I worked alongside Cape Verdeans as a box boy during cranberry season and I was a runner for the old ladies who liked to play numbers—I'd take their numbers to the barbershop and the United Social Club."

The neighborhood continues to be a gateway for the latest groups of new arrivals—Hispanics, Mayans and Puerto Ricans.

Cape Verdean Women's Social Club's New Year's Ball, circa 1939. *In 1937, following the example of groups of Portuguese-speaking women elsewhere, Maria L. Livramento of São Nicolau organized a Cape Verdean women's club. At first, members met at each other's homes. For a few years, they met at the Cape Verdean Beneficent Association. As their numbers increased, they later met at the Ultramarine Band Club. At the club's first social gathering, Manuel Gomes, husband of member Maria Gomes, unimpressed with the formality of the occasion, dubbed the group "The Cuckoo Club." The name stuck as a humorous epithet for more than 75 years. Among the those enjoying the Ball are Anna Silva, Julianna Cruz, Caroline Rocha, Maria Soares, Maria Cruz, Lucy Fortes, Sabina Silva, Mary Fernandes, Guimar Gomes, John Duarte, Mary Duarte*

The industrial waterfront of South Central neighborhood, 1940s. *The photograph is taken from the roof of a City Mills storage shed near the foot of South Street. It shows the so-called "Portuguese Navy Yard" at center. Most of the shacks are make-shift fishing cottages to serve the needs of itinerant harbor fishermen and their fleet of dinghies and small craft. Behind the fishing shacks are vacant lots once occupied by Potomska and City Mills. At far right is the Dartmouth Manufacturing Company and in the distance are the Butler Mills on East Rodney French Boulevard.*

Bay Village Housing Project

The South Central neighborhood hosted one of the nation's first public housing developments built from 1939 to 1941. The Bay Village Housing Project offered 22 handsome brick buildings with slate roofs accommodating as many as 200 low-income families. The project fell under a nationwide slum clearance and urban renewal program sponsored by federal Housing and Urban Development.

The chosen area met stringent requirements as it was filled with dilapidated and substandard housing. Bordered by Acushnet Avenue and Second Street, the site encompassed Walnut, Madison, Cannon, Griffin, Howland, Grinnell and Coffin Streets. The New Bedford Housing Authority directed the project. Demolition crews razed 115 structures, mostly wooden houses, and the three-story brick Monte Pio Hall on Acushnet Avenue, which housed the oldest Portuguese Society in New England. As new buildings went up, workers planted grass and trees and installed benches. Crews also built the Cannon Street Playground, later renamed Monte Playground, for older children and smaller play areas in courtyards for younger children.

The project stalled twice, once when the original contractor, D'Amore Construction

Sandlot baseball game, Cannon Street, 1937. During the Depression, city-organized and business-sponsored summer league competitions took place in 11 playgrounds across city neighborhoods. Although the summer league season ended Labor Day weekend, local kids mustered a couple of bats and balls for a pick-up (or scrub) game on this mid-September afternoon. On November 11, 1938, dignitaries including Mayor Leo E. J. Carney and Portuguese Consul Dr. Goulart da Costa honored Joseph J. Monte by renaming the playground after him. During World War I, Fogo-born Monte fought in the 307th Infantry until captured by German soldiers. He was a prisoner of war and the first Cape Verdean awarded a Purple Heart.

Company of Cambridge, experienced financial difficulties and could not complete the job, and again when 23 carpenters left, attracted by higher wages on Cape Cod. But Bay Village finally was finished and hosted its first public open house in 1941, drawing close to 1,800 visitors. New apartments went first to those whose homes were destroyed to make way for the project. Only city families of two to nine people living under substandard conditions were eligible for project housing. Heads of household had to be citizens. For a three-room unit, the monthly rent ranged from $14.40 to $22.00 and four-room units rented for $15.60 to $25.00 a month.

Bay Village Housing Project under construction, February 1941. View looks south with Acushnet Avenue at far right.

Ice Cream

In the early 19th century, wealthy New Bedford residents took to carbonated beverages. Pharmacists, accustomed to working with fruit and vegetable extracts, served up drinks with fizz, using flavored powders that combined sodium bicarbonate, fruit juices and artificial flavors. The 1820s witnessed a running press battle between druggist Wing Russell on Water Street and apothecaries Alexander Read and Elisha Thornton on Union Street, with each touting the virtues of his proprietary soda powder flavors.

Soda powders soon become old hat. By 1829, city coppersmiths Timothy I. Dyre and Anthony D. Richmond were building ornate soda fountains that dissolved carbon dioxide gas in beverages. Druggists competed for fountain customers. In 1910, Henry Corson installed a nine-foot fountain at 639 County Street and Stanislas Lamoureux put another at 1598 Acushnet Avenue. William Higham bested them with a 10-foot fountain at 212 Cross Street. In May 1913, Union Street's Browne's Pharmacy claimed "the largest seating capacity of any drugstore in the world." It seated 250 people around a central soda department.

Under Prohibition, soda fountains filled part of the social void left by bars closing. Even after Prohibition, a neighborhood's social center often revolved around its soda fountain. By 1939, of the city's 74 drug stores, 70 touted fountains. All ages came for conversation as well as refreshing coffees, chocolate frappes, coffee milks, phosphates and ice creams.

Wartime labor shortages left soda fountains with fewer customers and fewer staff. After the war, soda fountains competed with television for leisure-time activity. By 1948, New Bedford had only 51 drug stores.

Many clung to their role during the 1950s still featuring soft drinks, ice cream and meals. In the 1960s, pharmacy chains opened self-service stores with expanded product lines and didn't need space-hogging soda fountains, counters and seats.

The soda fountain as the neighborhood social center became less important as many people moved out of the city, frequented fast-food and drive-thru restaurants and drank more mass-marketed, canned sodas. In 1962, downtown institution Higham's Drug Store at the northwest corner of Union and Pleasant Streets closed after 85 years. By 1963, 48 drug stores remained in the city and many had scrapped their lunch counters and soda fountains.

Browne's Pharmacy interior, Union Street, circa 1910. Located in the Masonic Building at 189-203 Union Street, Browne's served ice cream, shakes and other confections. The pharmacy sold items such as photographic supplies, patent medicines, pharmaceuticals and cigars.

Ice Cream in Iconic Containers

The **Gulf Hill Dairy Bucket**, circa 1930, built alongside the Acushnet Park roller coaster, moved to the Gulf Hill Farm in South Dartmouth sometime after the 1938 hurricane. **Willow Tree** sported one of its iconic milk cans at the southwest corner of Tarkiln Hill Road and Ashley Boulevard, 1934. The **Frates Dairy Bottle**, 1976, built adjacent to the original Frates Farm on Acushnet Avenue and Victoria Street, still stands and continues to serve food and ice cream.

Lunch

Nova Scotia-born Annie Edith Barrows managed and later owned a quaint **tea room at Sears Court**. During the 1930s, she decorated the tavern/restaurant with a speakeasy flavor and a Mexican theme. Painted in silhouette on the wall, a guitarist wearing a sombrero faced a full-skirted dancer. A nautical mural completed the right wall. Candles set in old wine bottles provided a romantic, low-light atmosphere. She also owned and operated Anchorage by the Sea, a restaurant and gift shop on Water Street in Mattapoisett, where she and her husband Arthur lived, and where he owned a provisions store at the corner of Church and Main Streets.

Clifford Hurley ran **Hurley's Lunch**, a popular spot located on the south side at the bottom of Union Street. Pictured from left to right are Clifford, his brother Chester, Chester's wife Barbara and two unidentified waitresses. Their brother Clinton and their father Andrew Sr. worked as cooks in the lunchroom kitchen where two other brothers, Andrew Jr. and Lloyd, were assistant cooks. Their father, a Barbados-born seaman of Irish extraction, chose New Bedford for the family to settle. Many decades later, in the same location as the earlier Hurley's Lunch, Catwalk and then Sláinte Irish Pub also would provide warm Irish welcomes to their customers.

Born in Quebec, André D. Fontaine came to the United States as a child. He served a long apprenticeship in the Pease and Dandurand Pharmacy on South Water Street until he passed his exams in 1908, and was certified a pharmacist. He then opened **Fontaine's Pharmacy** at one of the South End's prime locations. His highly visible drug store had prominent signage, towering billboards and a distinctive corner entrance. It clearly stood out at the busy intersection of two important streets. With the A & P across the street and the hall of the Fédération Franco Américaine next door, Fontaine could count on substantial foot, trolley and vehicular traffic to ensure the pharmacy's commercial success. The pharmacy made an effective transition to a second generation when some of André and Laurina Fontaine's children continued the business.

Sears Court tea room, circa 1935.

Hurley's Lunch, 34 Union Street, 1942.

Fontaine's Pharmacy, circa 1920. André Fontaine is behind the soda fountain at right; assistant Ed Sylvia is at the tobacco counter. Signs offer cod liver oil extract and Murad Turkish cigarettes.

Gas Stations

At the turn of the century, only the wealthiest could afford cars. In 1908, New Bedford had 153 registered cars and nine dealers that sold or serviced them. Only William F. Nye advertised gasoline for sale. That year, Henry Ford introduced the Model-T. His mass production aimed at universal ownership. He changed the city's car ownership and its service options.

By 1922, New Bedford had 7,618 registered passenger vehicles, 354 motorcycles and 1,941 trucks. Car dealers stocked about 660 additional cars. To meet their needs, according to the 1929 census of retail trade, the city had 32 automobile dealerships, 88 filling stations and 44 garages or repair shops that also offered gasoline filling, lubrication and tire-mending services.

During the 1930s, filling stations multiplied. To open one required little capital or expertise, which appealed to some of the city's newly unemployed. By the 1939 retail census, the city had 131 filling stations and 40 dealerships that sold new or used cars, tires, batteries or accessories. Together, they provided almost 600 jobs. The census did not include garages or repair shops. Also during the 1930s, major oil companies began to lease filling stations to independent dealers. As a result, the city's filling stations were small, typically with only a proprietor and the equivalent of one full-time employee.

Debrosse Oil Co., affiliate of Tide Water Oil, makers of Veedol, North Front Street, 1936.

Richfield gasoline and service, 2142 Acushnet Avenue, 1920s.

Weld Square, 1941. *Gasoline is 18.9¢ per gallon at Mobilgas, Acushnet Avenue and Washburn Street.*

At right, Blanche Meunier pours water from a galvanized gooseneck can, cooling down her customer's radiator. The **SOCONY (Standard Oil Company of New York) station** belonged to John A. and Mary DeSautels. The family would later change to Richmond Oil products.

The iconic beacon overlooking the junction of Kempton and Mill Streets just west of Rockdale Avenue was a replica of the **Butler Flats lighthouse.** Constructed for Sumner E. Gifford in 1930, it housed his Lighthouse Oil Company gasoline station. As an eight-year-old in 1898, Gifford watched the original Butler Flats lighthouse being built and dreamed of recreating it. His round, five-story brick building stood 56 feet high, was adorned with two lifeboats hanging from davits on the second story and was topped with a red flashing beacon. The lighthouse filling station was a magnet for tourists, who were allowed to climb to the top. On clear days, a panoramic view of the Elizabeth Islands in the distance rewarded climbers. The station was later sold to Pacific Oil Company and leased to Torres Oil Company. When Pacific razed the building in 1960, company district manager Howard B. Tripp stated, "The lighthouse has outlived its usefulness. Its newness and unusualness has worn out."

In **Kosciuszko Square**, hand-written pleas on freshly painted clapboard of the newly built Colonial Gasoline station implored: "Let us change your oil," and "Have your oil changed here." The do-it-yourself advertising wasn't enough. Owner Henry M. Carroll sold the rural way station around 1929 to Wilfred Bourque. In all, it lasted less than a decade. Today, Pa Raffa's Italian Restaurant occupies the site.

SOCONY filling station, Wood Street near Ashley Boulevard, April 1930.

Lighthouse Oil Company, Kempton Street, circa 1930.

Kosciuszko Square, where Acushnet Avenue and Ashley Boulevard meet, March 1927. *Dedicated in 1927, Kosciuszko Square takes its name from Thaddeus Kosciuszko, the Polish-born engineer and Continental Army colonel who designed key fortifications along the Delaware and Hudson Rivers during the American Revolution, later achieving the rank of brigadier general.*

Chief Dahill and driver, circa 1912.

Dahill Air-Hoist Aerial Ladder, 1908.

The Dahill Hoist at the Methodist-Episcopal Church fire, Pleasant & Sycamore Street, 1934.

Chief Edward F. Dahill

In 1902, Fire Chief Edward F. Dahill (1862-1950) invented a new method of raising ladders. Using a storage tank for compressed air, two cylinders could lift a 70-foot extension ladder to full height in seven seconds. The Pneumatic Aerial Fire Appliance Co. of New Bedford made early versions of Dahill's invention. Later, others such as Ahrens-Fox and The Cornelius Callahan Co. adopted it but Dahill's air hoist retained its technological edge until the late 1930s.

Dahill became a nationally recognized firefighting authority and one of the fire department's longest serving members. He began in 1888 with the Hook and Ladder Company No. 2. Named first assistant chief in 1900 and chief in 1904, Dahill held the latter position until retiring in 1946. He steered the department from all horse-drawn apparatus to gasoline-propelled pumpers and ladders. He also shifted from small on-call, untrained crews to highly trained, permanent firemen. In 1921, Dahill served as president of the Massachusetts State Firemen's Association. From 1904 to 1922, he received five patents for ladder improvements involving the mechanics of raising and lowering them and speed controls on the lift. In his later years, Chief Dahill went only to big fires. A chauffeur would drive him in the chief's official car.

Firefighters used the Dahill Air-Hoist Aerial Ladder to quell the **Pleasant Street Methodist Episcopal Church fire**, at the corner of Sycamore Street, December 11, 1934. Caused by an overheated stovepipe, the blaze swept the recently renovated church and quickly destroyed the wooden building. Five firemen were injured when a huge 900-pound bell crashed through the bell tower and collapsed the belfry. Shortly after, the metal ceiling gave way, wrecking the interior. Then the roof and tower went up in flames. Sparks ignited the nearby Lincoln Hotel and Mary B. White School but firemen contained the secondary blazes.

Rescue at Methodist-Episcopal Church, 1938.

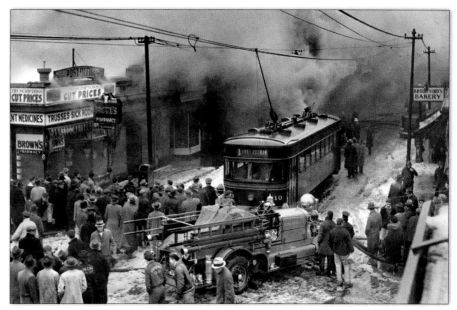

Allen's Theater, 1514 Acushnet Avenue, November 26, 1940.

A dramatic rescue took place at the **Pleasant Street Methodist Episcopal Church** fire. Endangering their own lives, Deputy Chief Frederick F. Ricketson and Fireman Thomas W. Bell rescued trapped Fireman Mariano M. Pacheco of Engine 2. Removing the debris that pinned Pacheco, they carried him through smoke and flames to drop him from a third-floor window to firefighters below, who caught him in a fire net. Brain and spine specialist Dr. Donald Munro came from Boston to operate on Pacheco's fractured spine.

Fire destroyed Allen's Theater and damaged nine nearby stores. It devastated the entire block of one-story wooden structures between Coffin and Phillips Avenues. Other damaged businesses included J. C. Brown's Pharmacy, Gudgeon's Bakery, McDermott's Fish Market, Gauthier's Furniture Store, Lipson's Shoe Store, Ann's Beauty Shoppe and Joseph Z. Boucher's Real Estate. Total losses were estimated at $175,000.

Just as the **Soule Cotton Mill** was set to reopen after a week's closure to repair damage caused by a 10-foot flood during the 1938 hurricane, the four-story spinning plant caught fire. The blaze destroyed two adjoining two-story storage buildings used for cotton bales and cotton waste. Called "the worst mill fire in the city's history," the fire caused damage estimated at $2,000,000 and injured three firemen and one spectator. After fighting for five hours, firefighters finally brought the flames under control, saving several adjoining weave sheds and a cotton shed. Soule later bought the recently closed Neild Mill on Nash Road and transferred its operations there.

Soule Mills fire, foot of Sawyer Street, September 28, 1938.

Recreation, Sports & Entertainment

Despite—or perhaps because of—the city's hard times, recreation took on an increasingly important role during the 1930s. Helping to reduce stress during difficult economic times, recreation often brought together like-minded people to enjoy activities and companionship.

People opted for less costly recreational activities. As a result, movies suffered. From 1925 to 1941, five movie theaters closed, including Allen's Theater, Theatre Comique and Federation Hall on Acushnet Avenue, the Savoy Theater on Union Street and Colonial Theater on West Rodney French Boulevard. Some recreational activities actually could put food on the table. The bluefish run drew hundreds of anglers, many hoping for a quick dinner.

Recreation—including winter skating and summer swimming or lounging at Municipal Beach—could come with a low price tag for equipment. Neither skates nor bathing togs had to be new; hand-me-downs often sufficed. Spectator sports, including soccer and boxing, boomed. When attendance lagged at Acushnet Park, managers jumped on the nationwide craze of sponsoring dance marathons. Down-on-their-luck couples stayed on the dance floor for days hoping to win cash.

Not all activities were organized. Neighbors gathered to play games or cards or simply talk and share the local gossip. Church socials and school programs drew on local audiences. Radio

Racing at Buttonwood Pond, February 1936. *Wearing white socks, Armand Bernard races down the stretch. More than 1,500 turned out to cheer the 200 contestants aged 16 and under at the 1936 Standard-Times skating contest. Bernard won the second 100-yard dash heat. In the final races for the older boys, William Bradshaw won the 100-yard dash and Ernie Spence won the 440-yard dash. Eileen McKenna won both the 100- and the 440-yard dash for the older girls.*

connected the city to the world. People enjoyed listening to news, sports, daytime soap operas, comedy shows and music.

The New Deal legislation recognized the importance of leisure and recreation. The Works Progress Administration took the lead in repairing and building recreational facilities including the warming house at Buttonwood Park. The Federal Music Project and the Federal Writers' Project gave work to the unemployed and made their materials available to the general public.

Whaleboat Race, 1929.

Angling for bluefish from the **Coggeshall Street Bridge**, New Bedford, late September 1938. The bluefish run from late August until October. Anglers fished with long branches, bamboo poles and fishing rods baited with sand eels, small silversides, killifish or mumpers. The bridge was a popular fishing spot after being closed to traffic on September 21—the day the Great Hurricane of 1938 struck the region.

Whaleboat races in New Bedford Harbor date from July 4, 1857, once crowning the city's Fourth of July celebrations. However, as whaling waned, so did the races. In 1929, the contests returned as part of the Board of Commerce's Bigger and Better New Bedford Campaign, topping off a day of water sports at the Municipal Bathing House. In the intense rivalry of a two-boat race, city policemen bested city firemen over the one-mile course. Trojan Athletic Club won the four-boat race shown in the photo. Its boat was pulled by coxswain Jesse F. Roderick, stroke rower John Cabral, and rowers Louis Santos, Gilbert Roderick, Anthony Perry and John Botelho.

Morse Twist Drill took second, with a boat pulled by coxswain Martin Bowman, stroke rower William Carney and Albert Frates, Edward Tripp, Everett Cooper and Raymond H. Eldred. Colonel Edward Green's Round Hill Crew came in third. Curator of the museum whaleship **Charles W. Morgan** and legendary Arctic whaleman Captain George Fred Tilton served as coxswain, Anthony Perry as stroke; rowers were Louis Travers, George Sisson, Adrien Bourbeau and Ernest Jennings. Lalime's Pirates sponsored by City Councilman Napoleon Lalime came in last. The Pirates included Joseph Jason, coxswain, Frank Ponte, stroke, and rowers Antone Jason, Gilbert Perry, Manuel Silva and M. Paul Alexander.

Fishing off the Coggeshall Street Bridge, September 1938.

Municipal Beach

Clockwise from left: **Mayor Charles S. Ashley**, upper left, and local notables visit the beach, as bathers stand under the open showers, August 1936. The bathers seem far more interested in posing for photographs than greeting politicians. **Seeking relief from the stifling heat**, *a group of friends lounge* on the sand near the entrance to John Halliwell Memorial Park, June 1939. The park was originally named for a Ward 6 mule spinner elected to the House of Representatives and then to the state senate. It was later renamed Hazelwood Park. The beach was set to officially open in two weeks after finishing touches to remedy the massive destruction caused by the 13.5-foot tidal surge during the 1938 hurricane. Nonetheless, the swimmers, one of whom was trained in lifesaving, readily enjoy themselves. A group of "old-timers" sitting on a bench enjoy the beach scenery. **Free-style racing, September 1939.** Closely monitored by a lifeguard following behind in a rowboat, a heat of junior girl swimmers compete in a 25-yard dash at the Annual Water Carnival. In 1940, the winners of the 100-yard race were Shirley Langford (who also won the 50-yard race), first place; Anita Laferriere, second place; and Adelia Avila, third place. The city only appointed its first female lifeguard in 1967.

Gar Wood Skating Rink and Warming House, Rockdale Avenue & Durfee Street, December 1936. *Three Gar Wood players in crisp blue-and-white uniforms pose in the new rink before the first game of the newly formed New Bedford Hockey League. Play stopped during the second game when the seventh and last available puck disappeared under broken ice behind one of the goals. Earlier, opposing player Jack Boucher had fallen through the ice into knee-deep water, but play continued. Only the loss of a puck ended the game.*

Cooling down at Buttonwood Pond, 1935. *In 1917, a city-commissioned architect drew up plans for "a warming house and convenience station" at Buttonwood Park. By the 1930s, however, the old wooden structure had outlived its usefulness and was on the verge of collapse. In 1934-1935, the Works Progress Administration built a new warming house with bricks recycled from the demolished Potomska Mills. To accommodate ice skaters, workers enlarged the pond by dredging an adjoining swamp. In summer months, the pond's many bathers used the brick warming house as a changing house. The WPA also renovated the zoo's black bear exhibit to replace an older one that often flooded during rains.*

Acushnet Park

New Bedford's beaches with their calm and clean waters, fine sands and plentiful parking remain among the city's hidden treasures. Locals sometimes refer to East Beach as Acushnet Beach because it sits next to the long gone but once popular amusement park known as Acushnet Park.

Acushnet Park's draws included a Ferris wheel, roller coaster, merry-go-round and the ever-favorite Custer Cars, iron cars that traveled along a track. A tunnel-of-love and a "pretzel" ride attracted lovers and thrill seekers. The Eastern Consolidated Amusement Company situated the park on just 15 acres of land. Its builder Dan Bauer specialized in roller coaster work.

Some 30,000 people attended the park's opening on May 30, 1916. Financially, the park experienced a slow start and Bauer went unpaid. Instead, Eastern signed the park over to him as compensation. The 1938 Hurricane mangled the out-and-back roller coaster (five cents a ride) and heavily damaged the park. Bauer rebuilt parts of the park and stayed in business until a fire sealed its demise in the 1950s, destroying the tunnel-of-love, dodgem cars and other attractions.

Visitors entered the park from Brock Avenue through a densely wooded area on a walkway flanked by whaling try pots. The roller coaster ran along part of East Rodney French

Gateway to Acushnet Park, East Rodney French Boulevard, 1923.

and swooped back along the road near the fort. Danceland, a lively dance hall, later a skating rink, kept the far end of the park jumping, near Portland and East Rodney French. Dance marathons held here in the 1930s caused controversy, as people criticized endurance dancing for money.

On the water and just south of the bathhouses sat Dan's Pavilion, a seafood restaurant and function hall, also owned by Dan Bauer. Here, the Bauer family presided over popular Sunday clambakes. Dan's withstood many ocean storms, but the 1938 Hurricane leveled the pavilion. It was rebuilt, only to have storms in 1944 and 1954 destroy the building again and again.

Rides, dancing, food, swimming and entertainment abound at Acushnet Park, 1916–1956.

Ferris wheel, built in 1920.

Midway showing roller coaster, tip top ride and carousel shed (right), circa 1916

Bumper Kiddie Coaster, 1939.

Summer day at Acushnet (or East) Beach, circa 1920. Fort Rodman is at far left.

Sporting News

New Bedford High School embraced football early on. An early star, **James P. Murphy**, class of 1912, went on to become a beloved coach. A quarterback for Brown University between 1913 and 1917, he returned to NBHS in the 1920s to coach football and became head coach in 1927. Considered the best of its era, his 1931 team won the regular season and missed winning the state championship against Brockton by one touchdown. In 1932, Murphy suffered a heart attack during halftime at a game in Quincy and died before the end of the game. His former players organized the James P. Murphy Memorial Club, which fielded its first team in 1933 and entertained local semi-pro football fans through the 1950s.

In 1936, bicyclist **Albert Crossley Jr.**, became the first city resident to win a world sports championship, despite losing two fingers on his right hand in a Cycledrome accident 14 years earlier. In the 1930s, he was New England five-mile and pro-sprint champion, motor sprint titlist and national champion. Sports writers called him America's greatest sprinter.

During his 15-year professional career, he rode more than 300,000 miles in 126 six-day races. Between 1932 and 1940, he cycled in at least 68 races in the US and Canada, finishing first 10 times. Crossley retired from professional racing in 1940, then returned home to coordinate and compete in a race at the former Baylies Stadium on Coggeshall Street.

In 1930, 17-year-old **Elsie Greenwood** entered the New England Swimming Championships in Boston with no competitive experience. Remarkably, she finished second in the junior girls' division of the 100-yard dash, one foot behind the defending champion, with a time of 1:14. Later, after winning the 1934 New England 400-meter championship, she defeated an all-male field in the 200-yard open at the Inter-City Water Carnival at Municipal Beach. Greenwood helped form New Bedford's first competitive swim club, the Sharks, and Fall River's Amazon Athletic Club. She also saved two young men from drowning: one at a swim meet off Acushnet Park in 1934 and the other in a Dartmouth stream in 1938.

Meanwhile, Amelia Earhart inspired many young women to take to the skies in the 1930s, including New Bedford teenager **Mildred Santos**. She took flying lessons from pilot and instructor Henry T. Olden at Rochester Air Field and New Bedford Airport. On Memorial Day in 1940, she became the city's first licensed female aviator.

Holy Family High School basketball star **Ernest Hassey** brought skill to the local circuit. His high-arc, one-handed jump shot stood out in an era of two-handed set shots. "Whenever we played Bristol Aggie, a little old lady would throw holy water

Hibbits wins high jump at Sargent Field, June 1938. *New Bedford High School star Jack Hibbits cleared 5 feet 8.5 inches to win the dual meet. He also excelled in the broad jump and pole vault. In later life, Hibbits fought in World War II and wrote a book titled* Take 'Er Up Alone Mister!, *about intensive pilot training. It was a local best seller.*

on me as I ran by," Hassey said. "She said anyone who can shoot like you has to be possessed by the devil." Between 1940–42, Hassey led Holy Family to three straight undefeated seasons and three Class B Principals Tournament championships. After serving in World War II, he returned home to help run the family's garment manufacturing business.

New Bedford produced standout competitors in track and field. **Leo E. Larrivee** was the city's first athlete to compete in the Olympic Games. During his junior year at Holy Cross, his friend, runner William Peters, asked for help in winter training. He expected Larrivee to keep pace but Peters ended up chasing him. Peters convinced Larrivee to compete. In his first race, he entered a city track meet and won the mile event. He returned from the 1924 Paris Olympics with New Bedford's first Olympic Medal—a bronze for the third-place 3,000 meter team race. Tragically in 1928, while a medical student at Loyola University of Chicago, Larrivee died, at 25, in a car accident.

Walter "Zyggie" Janiak captained the 1930-1931 New Bedford Vocational School track team. He stood out in the 100-yard dash, 220-yard dash, running high jump and shot put. At Holy Cross, he excelled and Boston sports writers dubbed him the "New Bedford Comet." In 1934, as part of the Polish American track team at the Polish Olympics in Warsaw, Janiak helped his team win the sprint relay with his record-setting 10.9 second, 100-yard dash time. He returned to Voke as teacher, coach and administrator before becoming school director. Named in 1971 the first head of New Bedford Regional Vocational Technical High School, he held the post until 1984. The school's field house proudly bears his name.

In 1934, 16-year-old **Miriam Nelson**, who competed for the Boston Athletic Association, narrowly missed securing a berth on the upcoming Olympic team in the 50-meter dash. She raced locally in the 50-yard and 100-yard dash.

Legends in Their Time

*Clockwise from top left: Portrait of New Bedford High School football star **James P. "Jimmy" Murphy,** December 1917, who returned after college to become a beloved football high school coach; **Leo E. Larrivee**, Olympic Bronze Medal winner in Paris,1924 was nicknamed the "Whaling City Wonder" and attracted national attention; **Al Crossley Jr.** (right) and racing partner Jimmy Walthour Jr. (center) jockey for position before finishing eighth at the New York Six-Day Bicycle Race, November 20-25, 1939; Holy Family High School hoops star **Ernest "Tally" Hassey**, 1941, nicknamed for his accurate shooting and high-scoring prowess and who won three Narragansett League championships and three Class B Principals Tournaments and played in two state Catholic Tournaments; Aviatrix **Mildred Santos** is honored by Mayor Leo E. J.. Carney (right) and other dignitaries as she christens the city's new seaplane dock at Marine Park on Pope's Island, August 19, 1940; and 17-year-old speed swimmer **Elsie Greenwood** shows off her trophies following her third-place finish in the 100-meter dash of the Boston A.A.U. championship swim on August 2, 1931. Other local track and field notables in the 1930s included Omer Monty, Carl Zeitz, Melville Vincent and Jack Hibbits.*

New Bedford Whalers at the Polo Grounds, New York City, 1929. *The Whalers played the New York Nationals in a three-game series to compete for the Lewis Cup and become American Soccer League champs. The Nationals swept the series. The Whalers also reached the championship game in 1928 but lost to the Boston Wonder Workers.*

Arnie Oliver and America's World Cup team, Uruguay, 1930. *Team USA parades across the Centanario Stadium field during opening ceremonies. The Americans shut out Belgium and Paraguay to advance to the semifinals, but their World Cup title dreams ended shortly after the kick-off, as Argentina crushed a short-handed US team 6-1 in front of 112,000 people.*

Soccer-crazed City

During the 1920s and 1930s, local fans saw some of the nation's best soccer played in New Bedford. City teams repeatedly won state, division and national championships.

The New Bedford Whalers were one of the most successful teams of the original American Soccer League (ASL), the first Division 1 professional soccer league in the US. Reorganized in 1924 by former members of the Fall River Rovers, the Whalers joined the ASL in the 1920s. In 1926, they defeated the New York Giants 5-4 to win the ASL's Lewis Cup.

Despite finishing as ASL runners-up in the fall 1929, spring and fall 1930 seasons, the Whalers failed to finish the spring 1931 season, as the Great Depression sapped the team's finances. In the fall of 1931, a newly reorganized Whalers team evolved from the former New York Giants and merged with Fall River Football Club. This team took the American Soccer League championship for the fall 1931 and spring 1932 seasons and won the 1932 National Challenge Cup. The team folded during the fall 1932 season.

During these days, New Bedford buzzed with soccer. In 1926, New Bedford Defenders defeated Pittsburgh Heidelberg Club, winning the national amateur soccer championship 1-0 with a last minute goal. Also that year, the New Bedford Pirates defeated St. Mary's of Lynn for the junior championship of New England.

In 1927, the La Flamme Cobblers won the eastern division but lost the National Amateur Cup to Pittsburgh Heidelberg. In 1931, the New Bedford Black Cats took the eastern division national amateur soccer cup but lost the national championship to Akron Goodyear during a rain-soaked game before a crowd of 5,000. Only boys born in New Bedford and who learned soccer here could join the Black Cats.

In 1932, New Bedford's Santo Christo Club won the eastern division of the national amateur soccer league, but lost the championship to the Cleveland Shamrocks.

New Bedford Vocational School's soccer team won the United States Football Association title in 1932 as state and New England champions. In an unbroken streak, the school's team won the Massachusetts State top soccer trophy each year from 1927 to 1935. In 1933, the New Bedford High School team also had an undefeated regular season.

Professional teams regularly played before local crowds of 7,000 to 10,000, with national championship matches often drawing more than 20,000 fans. The 1928 textile strike did put a damper on local crowds as hard-pressed strikers could little afford bus fares, entry fees and snacks.

Several local key players left after team winning streaks. Sam Chedgzoy, who in 1926 forced a change in the soccer rules governing corner kick scoring, left the Whalers in 1930 for the Montreal Carsteel. New Bedford Soccer Club's crack goalie Joe Kennaway joined Glasgow Celtic in 1931, returning from 1946 to 1959 to coach the Brown University soccer team. High scoring center halfback James Baird "Jimmy" Montgomerie retired from the Whalers in 1931.

Then came the drought for four decades, no New Bedford team made the finals for the National Amateur Cup, until 1972, when the New Bedford Portuguese lost to St. Louis Busch.

Arnie Oliver, Hall of Famer

Arnold Oliver is the only New Bedford athlete ever inducted into a national professional sports hall of fame. The son of Lancashire immigrants, Oliver left school at 14 to work as a winder in the Quisset Mill. He played for its soccer team in an industrial league. In 1925, he joined the Defenders, the South End's leading amateur soccer team. He and the team won the National Amateur Soccer Cup championship in 1926.

After the Defenders narrowly defeated Philadelphia's Heidelberg Club before a capacity crowd in Cleveland, Ohio, the local heroes arrived at the Pearl Street train depot, where they were greeted by a raucous crowd that included Mayor Charles S. Ashley, city dignitaries and a marching band. At 20 years of age, Oliver turned professional. He played inside forward for the New Bedford Whalers and teams from Hartford, Fall River and Pawtucket. He finished his amateur career with the Santo Christos of the New England League in 1938.

He was named to the US team in 1930 for the first World Soccer Championship, held in Montevideo, Uruguay. The team lost to Argentina in the semi-finals. Taking third place, the team advanced further than any other male American World Cup team since. Oliver appears in the official team photograph of the 1930 United States FIFA World Cup soccer team. Two teammates in the photo also had local connections: Pawtucket-born team captain Tommy Florie played for the New Bedford Whalers; and Fall River's Billy Gonsalves—Oliver's lifelong friend—also played with New Bedford teams. All three men are in the National Soccer Hall of Fame as athletes. One of the five founders of the New Bedford Whalers, John Fernley, was also inducted into the National Soccer Hall of Fame, not as a player, but as a builder of the sport of soccer. He served for years as president of the US Football Association.

Oliver (left) defends during an Industrial League game on the Quisset Mill grounds in the 1930s.

After Oliver retired from playing, he coached. In 1966, he became the first head coach of the UMass Dartmouth men's soccer team.

The Defenders Football Club of New Bedford, National Amateur Champs 1925-26. *Arnie Oliver is in front row, fourth from left.*

Boxing-crazed City

On a cool September evening in 1923, more than 3,000 people packed every available space within range of the loudspeaker mounted outside the *Evening Standard* building at Market and Pleasant Streets to hear the title bout. The next day's newspaper told the story: Jack Dempsey had knocked out Luis Angel Firpo in the second round, retaining the heavyweight championship. So quick was Firpo's fall that the microphone announcer did not have time to finish the play-by-play description of round one before being called upon to announce the flash, "Dempsey wins by knockout."

Before the widespread adoption of radio, most people turned to newspapers for news. For major battles, election results or late-breaking sporting events—such as the Dempsey-Firpo bout—newspapers fed up-to-the-minute headlines to information-hungry crowds. Reporters worked news tickers or telephone lines in the newsroom; some wrote stories, others wrote bulletin board copy or spoke into microphones. However, some people heard the bout at home because radio station WJZ broadcast it and stations throughout the country retransmitted it.

Downtown was not the only place fight fans gathered that Friday evening. Loudspeakers bellowed to eager audiences at city parks, the Elks Club, the Knights of Columbus and the Trojan Athletic Club.

Thousands of automobiles thronged the Round Hill estate of Colonel Edward H. R. Green to hear returns over his radio. One of his employees, assigned to count cars, reported that he lost count shortly after 6,000. Nearly all the caretakers were pressed to direct traffic—including estate manager Ernest R. Duff. After the broadcast, it took two hours to lead a procession of autos out the gate. "Not a single accident or disorder of any kind marred the gathering," wrote the *Standard*.

Following the fight, stores throughout the country promoted the slogan, "Every home should have a radio."

Fans gather outside the *Evening Standard*, September 14, 1923. *The crowd jammed the intersection of Market and Pleasant Streets, covering the library lawn and steps and extending along William Street. Fans stood for hours in the chilling, late summer night to hear the announcement that the boxers were ready to square off at center ring. It was hardly worth the wait. No sooner had they settled in to hear the story of the fight than it was over by knockout. "Cheers for Victory of Dempsey Greeted Knockout Announcement," read the Evening Standard's headline.*

Early Boxing Legends

Boxing ruled New Bedford's sports scene during the 1920s. Fans could see some of the city's best boxers in the ring. New Bedford boasted three boxers who each fought more than 1,350 rounds professionally.

Frankie "Young" Britt, born Frank Pacheco in São Miguel, Azores, met the leading champions and challengers. He won New England feather, light and welterweight championships.

Al "Bearcat" Shubert, born Albert Schellenberg in Rhode Island, won New England bantamweight championship. Fans called him "Buzzsaw" for going at his opponents until they fell exhausted. Edward "Chic" Suggs, promoted as the World's Colored Bantam Champion, was the first African American fighter in a main bout at Madison Square Garden. Each of the three had career wins of more than 80 fights; Suggs won 104—30 of them by knockouts.

Among other early New Bedford ring notables, bantamweight Bobby Dyson retired in 1925. In 1921, during a 10-round Boston bout with Earl Puryear, Dyson fractured his wrist in three places toward the end of the fourth round. For the rest of the bout, Dyson ably fought with only one hand while his injured arm hung useless. He could not lift it to defend himself. His exhibition of grit was one of the most remarkable ever seen in the ring and Dyson won the fight.

Charles Manty was born Louis Gonsalves in the Azores. Respected as a master along the ropes, locals often called him "New Bedford's Johnny Dundee" after the Sicilian-born champion rope fighter.

Quebec-born featherweight Leopold "Young Paulie" Demers won 51 of his first 74 fights. He retired from boxing in 1927 and moved to Vermont, where he won that state's lightweight title. In 1928, he returned to New Bedford and spent the rest of his life working in various mills.

In 1923, Tony Thomas, of a family that included his boxing brothers Al, Thomas and Joe, fought and lost to the greatest flyweight champion, Pancho Villa of the Philippines. New Bedford's own Pancho Villa, a welterweight who fought 1,014 rounds during his professional career, alleged in 1936 that he was forced to take a dive in Brooklyn when an assistant promoter held a gun to his ribs between rounds.

Dave Lumiansky, son of Russian immigrants, managed many leading boxers from his Palmer Street office. He was the era's most-suspended boxing manager, having been suspended by the National Boxing Association, the British Boxing Control Board, the French Boxing Federation and the International Boxing Union.

Frankie Britt, 1916.

Left to right, Paul "Kid" Demers, 1919; bantamweight "Panama" Al Brown—boxing's first Hispanic world champion—with his manager, New Bedford's Dave Lumiansky, 1928; city transplant Darcey Whyte, circa 1930; and bantamweight Bobby Dyson, circa 1920.

On Stage in New Bedford, 1900–1950

New Bedford set the stage for a colorful vaudeville era. Many performers were born here; others lived here during their formative years. Although some found fame while living in the city, most did so after moving away, but continued to proudly proclaim their New Bedford ties.

Lionel F. "Leo" Dias and his friends formed an early vaudeville group, singing, dancing and playing skits in New Bedford. They got their first out-of-town gig in 1911. Known as the Capital City Comedy Four, Albert Livesey played a college boy, Antone Marshall played a messenger, William Viera was a "Sport" and Leo played the stereotype of a Jew. When Albert left, the group reorganized as the Capital City Trio. To sound more "American," Dias became "Dwyer" and Viera became "Vera." The group broke up with the start of World War I. On Livesey's draft registration in New Bedford, he listed his profession as vaudeville actor in New York's Palace Theater. In Hull, England, Dias gave his profession as "music hall artist."

Pawtucket-born Lucy Harney moved here as a young girl when her loomfixer father came to the mills. She studied at the Fifth Street Grammar School at the corner of Pleasant and Russell Streets. After graduation, she sang and danced professionally. In 1901, at 16, she married loomfixer Fred C. Greene, but the marriage was short-lived and Lucy became comedienne Lou Lawrence. In 1912, after touring Alaska, Kansas City

Wichita Beacon advertisement to see Miss Lou Lawrence, February 1911.

and Providence, she returned to perform at the New Bedford Theater. She teamed up with Jack Lee in an act known as Lee and Lawrence. In 1923, she teamed with a New York customs inspector, Lowell-born Sidney W. Cornock, who had changed his name to Billy Curtis. They married and became the team of Curtis and Lawrence. He wrote the material that she performed with such an infectious laugh that newspaper headlines referred to her as "Laughing Lou." While on tour, she would regularly send letters to the *Standard-Times* describing interesting features of the cities she played. She noted: "I've been up and down America, in every state in the Union, and in Mexico and Canada, but my feet always point toward New Bedford at the end of each tour.… I like to come home." She and Curtis stayed here for two months every summer.

Vaudeville revival at the New Bedford Theatre, September 1949. *On January 22, 1928, the New Bedford Theatre showed the first sound movies in the city. These consisted of a short speech by entertainment executive Will Hayes followed by* Don Juan *with John Barrymore and Mary Astor. In 1953, the theater presented the city's first 3-D films; the audience used polarized spectacles to view the short films that changed every week.*

Ohio-born Thomas H. "Tommy" Griffith and Springfield-born Walter J. "Rabbit" Maranville each came to New Bedford to play baseball with the New Bedford Whalers as 19-year-old rookies, Griffith in 1909 and Maranville in 1911. Both soon moved on, Maranville joining the Boston Braves in 1912 and Griffith following in 1913. After that year's baseball season ended, they tried vaudeville. Together on the same bill, Maranville sang popular songs and used pantomime and clowning to act out humorous anecdotes from his baseball career, while Griffith played piano and sang his own compositions, such as "Ireland, Dear Old Ireland" or "Take Me Back to Old Ohio." Performing in Lewiston, Maine after the Braves won the 1914 World Series, Maranville demonstrated how he stole second base in the series. Unfortunately, he slid off the stage into the orchestra pit, breaking a leg. Griffith kept his New Bedford home until his wife died in November 1913. Maranville moved to Springfield to live with his family.

When he retired in 1935, Maranville had played 23 seasons in the National League, a record not broken until 1986. Griffith moved to the Cincinnati Reds and Brooklyn Robins. Baseball remained their first love, but vaudeville, based on their New Bedford experience, provided them winter income before enthusiastic audiences.

Baseball Hall of Famer Walter J. "Rabbit" Maranville performs magic at the ballpark, 1934.

New Bedford-born Mary F. Goggin toured New England on the vaudeville circuit in the early 20th century. Her billing as The Blind Melba referenced her physical disability while comparing her singing ability to that of the famed classical musician Dame Nellie Melba. Critics called Goggin "an extraordinary attraction." She retired from the stage after marrying Charles F. Joerres in 1911. After his death, she lived in New Bedford with their children.

Meanwhle, Azorean-born city resident Edmund Amaral changed his name to Eddie Ford and formed a song-and-dance team with a New Bedford-born bellboy named Leonard C. Manning. Beginning in 1909, the "Golden Boys" hoofed from Fall River to New York, Los Angeles and points in between. In 1911, Amaral started a dog act with his new partner, a mutt named Truly. Critics called Truly a "veritable marvel" whose two-legged walk imitated Charlie Chaplin. After Truly died, Ford trained a succession of fox terriers named Whitey, touring South America, South Africa and Europe. Ford felt that dogs made great partners— he bought them for next to nothing, paid them only a daily meal and, in return, they grossed Ford a high weekly rate.

New Bedford native Arthur D. Rousseau toured vaudeville in a song-and-dance act that the *Boston Globe* hailed as "one of the most original, off-the-beaten-track acts in Boston."

Baylies Square Theater Orchestra, 1949. *Pat Healy was the rare vaudeville musician from New Bedford who stayed in the city. He led the orchestra that accompanied visiting performers at the Baylies Square Theater on Acushnet Avenue. During a 40-week season, the theater featured the best vaudeville in the city. Many of its comedians, dancers, musicians and other live acts needed a musical background. Healy and his orchestra supplied it. Later, he felt strongly that television brought about the death of vaudeville because people "stayed home and watched the shows for free."*

He and his wife performed in theaters and clubs along the East Coast and in the Midwest as Artie Brooks and Margie—a play on the mispronunciation of his name as Ruisseau, the French word for brook. In a musical comedy act, she tap-danced on roller skates while he tap-danced in hockey skates on the stage, floor, tables and chairs. They retired to Lakeville to run Harmony Haven Cottages, but fire destroyed their home along with their collection of vaudeville memorabilia. At Lincoln Park, a benefit to help them establish a fund to build a new house drew them out of retirement for a final performance.

Artie Brooks, 1964.

Armand J. Landry was born in Fall River. He began performing at 15 as a single act, and moved to New Bedford to work a day job as a cotton mill speeder tender. He met and married another speeder tender, New Bedford-born Yvette Desjardins, in 1929. She became his assistant, "Yvette, Queen of Escapes." On the US and Canadian vaudeville circuits Landry was variously billed as the "French Court Magician," "The Parisian Escape Artist" or "The World's Youngest Escape Artist." He often traveled with Hardeen, brother of Harry Houdini, who shared family secrets with Landry, including the steel milk can escape. Landry often staged publicity stunts. In September 1930, he escaped from a locked cell at the Central Police Station in one minute and 32 seconds. Later, he moved into comedic magic, and on leaving the road in 1950, ran Landry's Magic and Joke Shop in the North End. At the Olympia Theatre opening of the 1953 movie of Houdini's life starring Tony Curtis, Landry performed on stage, escaping from one of Houdini's straitjackets. Still later, he sold souvenirs and novelties from a booth at Lincoln Park.

James Albert "Al" Trahan got his start in New Bedford. A typesetter with the *Standard-Times*, he also sang baritone with *Le Cercle Gounod*. He turned his piano playing and singing into a top vaudeville musical comedy act, traveling through North America and Europe. After a royal command performance in 1931 before King George V and Queen Mary of England, the king commented: "That man, Al Trahan, the American comedian, made me laugh very much." Trahan became known on both sides of the Atlantic as the man who made the king laugh. In 1937, with the St. Louis Opera Company, he reprised "Louie the 14th," a Florenz Ziegfeld comedy, to rave reviews. Soon after, Trahan gave a command performance for President Franklin Delano Roosevelt, who laughed as well. Trahan

Magician Armand J. Landry performs Houdini-like magic near his home at 164 Rivet Street.

Guffawing with firefighters, circa 1940. *Comedian Al Trahan laughs it up with firefighters at Fire Station #2 on Pleasant Street.*

Carol Haney in *The Pajama Game*, 1957. *After dancing together in* Kiss Me, Kate *in 1953, Bob Fosse recommended that Haney be cast for a dancing part in* The Pajama Game. *Her performance won her a Tony Award.*

regularly visited his mother and grandmother in New Bedford. In 1940, he performed in a Community Fund benefit at New Bedford High School.

Another New Bedford native, Abel Correia, spent long hours at the YMCA as a boy, practicing gymnastics, acrobatics and strength training. Returning in 1947 after US Naval service in World War II, he joined a well-known vaudeville group, The Three Glenns. They toured the country performing acrobatic, gymnastic and strength moves. They opened for Vegas stars such as Tommy Dorsey and other big bands, including Harry James, at the time when a young Frank Sinatra sang with him. In 1949, when the act performed in Sydney, Correia met his future wife and left the group. After 10 years in Australia, he moved his family to Worcester, where he managed a gym, training two bodybuilders who won Mr. Worcester titles.

As a child, Albanie "Bennie" Leblanc came from New Brunswick to New Bedford, joining other French-speaking Acadian families. As teenagers, he and his brothers worked menial jobs in the cotton mills. Leblanc married Anna Jaskolka, born in New Bedford of Polish parents. In the mid-1920s, after their first two children were born, they moved to New York City. There, despite vaudeville's waning years, they attempted a family act with their daughter, Stella, but it never caught on. Days, Leblanc ran elevators while his wife operated machinery in a factory. Their daughter stayed on the fringe of show business, working with the USO and later with Bob Hope for UNICEF benefits and on Miss World Pageants.

After the vaudeville era, New Bedford-born-and-raised Carol Haney made it big in show biz. She'd later reminisce that a Portuguese fortune-teller in New Bedford opened the way for her. When Haney was five, her mother visited a fortune-teller who foretold that her elder child would be a star. Her mother immediately enrolled her in every possible dance lesson. By the time she was 15, Haney had opened her own dance school. After graduating from high school, she moved to Hollywood to seek her fortune. In 1949, Gene Kelly hired her as his assistant choreographer for MGM musical films. Together, they worked on several memorable films including *On the Town, Summer Stock, An American in Paris, Singin' in the Rain* and *Invitation to the Dance*. She dubbed Kelly's taps in the title song "Singin' in the Rain" and danced with dancer-choreographer Bob Fosse in the film version of *Kiss Me, Kate*. Fosse pushed for her Broadway assignment, *The Pajama Game*. Her impressive performance earned her a Tony Award and two Donaldson awards, and she reprised her role in the film version of the play. Haney later concentrated on choreography and was nominated for three more Tony Awards for *Flower Drum Song, Bravo Giovanni* and, posthumously, *Funny Girl*.

Mayor Charles S. Ashley flanked by Senna brothers Clarence "Tony" (left) and Charles, 1932. *Mayor Ashley was the subject of the chorus in the song that Tony wrote on the 50th anniversary of his political career: "Keep Ashley there—right in that chair. Old New Bedford can't afford to lose him!"*

The Senna Brothers, Impromptu Composers

Clarence "Tony" Senna came from a theatrical family. His father, Manuel J. Senna, owned and managed the Pastime and Columbia Theaters where Tony played piano as a boy. At his 1912 marriage in New Bedford at the age of 18, he listed his profession as musician. His wife got an uncontested divorce four years later, maintaining he left her for vaudeville. Known as a songwriter and humorist, Tony divided his time between Tin Pan Alley in New York and performing on the road. Before 1920, he accompanied actress Lillian Fitzgerald on piano. In the 1920s and early 1930s, he teamed up with vaudevillian Ruby Norton, known as "Australia's Sweetheart." She sang and he played piano as they toured the world. In 1926, they came to New Bedford for an engagement at the Olympia Theatre. In 1928, Tony became the first person from New Bedford to record songs for phonographs. Colombia Records released a two-sided disc containing two of his short musical comedy routines. In 1932, he took on a new comedy partner, his brother Charles, a vaudeville performer with the Ziegfeld Follies. The Senna Brothers often returned to New Bedford, once even campaigning for Mayor Charles S. Ashley. Clarence took to the radio, and on Boston station WEEI as well as on stage, he became known as "The Impromptu Composer" for making up songs from the letters of a person's name. In 1935, he copyrighted the act as "Tunes Written from your Name." In the 1940s, Tony worked at cocktail bars, performing at Burt's Grille in New Bedford in 1948.

Alfred B. Delage as a youngster, circa 1929, and with wife Margaret, circa 1936. *At age 14, Delage was considered America's youngest professional magician. Also known as the "Duke of Deception," Delage featured Oscar the Baffling Bunny and Presto, a fox terrier, in his act.*

Alfred B. DeLage, America's Fastest Magician

In 1928, New Bedford-born Alfred B. DeLage first took his magic on stage at Normandin Junior High School. In 1930, at 16, he quit school to work as a cotton mill helper, but DeLage had ambitions. He began performing as an amateur illusionist, doing magic and sleight-of-hand for various city groups. In 1931, he met and impressed fortune teller and mind reader Prince Rajah Sigmund, in town to give séances at Acushnet Park. Prince Sigmund accepted DeLage as a new member of the show and they toured the country's vaudeville circuit. DeLage was billed as the youngest professional magician. By 1939, he was touted as "America's Fastest Magician" for his speed. DeLage transitioned to television as a featured performer on the *Milton Berle Show* in 1948, *To Tell the Truth* in 1960, the *Ed Sullivan Show* in 1963 and a special two-hour *Today Show* magic program in 1964. A prolific inventor, he developed several tricks, including a disappearing bouquet and flowerpot called "The Fastest Trick in the World." Woody Allen's biography mentions his fascination with another of his inventions, "Al DeLage's Sock Trick."

Eugenia Gramas

Born in New Bedford of Greek descent, Eugenia Gramas's family moved to Jacksonville, Florida when she was a "babe-in-arms." After completing two years at the Jacksonville College of Music, she sought the bright lights of New York where audiences came to know her as Jean Garry. After years of performing in nightclubs in New York and Long Island, she landed a spot in a vaudeville revue with Eddie Foy Jr.

The Jimmie Evans Revue

Jimmie Evans grew up on the mean streets of the South End in the early 1900s to become an accomplished renaissance man of his time. Forced to quit school and go work in a glass factory at 14 to help support his large family after his mother died, Evans had the grit to become a champion soccer player and the chutzpah to chase success on the vaudeville stage. After achieving theatrical fame, he became a well-loved diner owner and long-time Fairhaven postmaster.

Evans and the neighborhood toughs honed their soccer skills playing in the South End's empty lots, eventually forming a powerful team called the Defenders. Captained and managed by Evans, the team took multiple titles in the City League, which eventually expelled them for winning too much. Thereafter, a new generation of Defenders rose to the top of the US amateur soccer world, winning the 1926 National Amateur Cup.

Evans continued with soccer but also lucked into vaudeville. When he was 14, he and three friends were singing in a doorway when a passerby heard Evans fill the evening air with his fine Irish tenor. The next night he was singing at the New Bedford Theatre's *Passion Play*, earning $12 a week ($9 more than at the glass company). His father disapproved of theater, but when he saw the show, said, "Son, I didn't know you could sing like that." At age 19, when financially able, Evans "took his father out of the mill," his daughter Joanne Mee of Fairhaven would later say.

He went on the road singing background for silent films, then harmonizing with the New Bedford Village Four Quartet before joining a traveling vaudeville show. He joined a "girls and gags" show, where he fell in love with dancer Kitty "Kittens" Fraser, who later became his wife. "My mother was just as extraordinary [as my dad]," their daughter once said. "She, too, was motherless, and she grew up in a convent. A very good dancer, she was also a talented seamstress and we had a garage full of costumes. She was the first liberated woman, very stylish—she never wore house dresses."

Evans formed his own song-and-dance troupe, the Jimmie Evans Revue, with as many as 100 entertainers, whom he thought of as family. They performed to packed houses in Halifax and Canada's Maritime Provinces during their four-year run. Paramount Pictures bought the business, and in 1933, Evans came home to open the popular Jimmie Evans' Diner on Pleasant Street, which served home-cooked meals downtown for 24 years. In 1936, he embarked on another career as Fairhaven postmaster.

Evans left the stage in 1956. Before a large crowd at a testimonial dinner in his honor, he expressed gratitude for his life, his friends and family. As people were leaving, he collapsed, dying of a heart attack. He was almost 70.

Jimmie Evans Revue, circa 1925. *Seated are (from left) Jimmie Evans, Betty Shaw and Mickey Flynn. Those standing are identified as Dorothy, unknown, Florence Cunha, Phil, Mitzi, Ella, Chet Griffin, Evelyn Parr, "Dainty" Dora Davis, Peggy Cunha, unknown, Sammie Ford, Jackie Elwin and unknown.*

The Zeitz Theaters

New Bedford's 20th-century movie mogul family, the Zeitzes, arrived in the United States from Russia in 1888. Kopel and Fannie Zeitz emigrated with two sons, Phillip and Barney, and the family grew, with four sons and a daughter born in the US. As adults, the sons tried different professions. Frank was a bottler in the family soda factory. Phillip worked in a cotton mill and as a pawnbroker. In 1905, Barney started a demolition and salvage firm dealing in second-hand soda fountains, later expanding into private loans, jewelry and the Winchester hardware store on Union Street. His various activities employed brothers Fisher, Harry and Morton. Among other demolitions, he removed machinery from the Atlas Tack and New Bedford Copper companies.

The movie business started with the wreck of the freighter *Port Hunter* on November 2, 1918. Struck by a tug carrying war supplies for the American Mission fighting in France, *Port Hunter* sank at Hedge Fence Shoal off Martha's Vineyard. Barney's firm, the Mercantile Wrecking Company, earned a $300,000 profit from the salvage and invested in real estate.

In August 1921, he purchased property on the northwest corner of Sixth and Union Streets, later known as the Zeitz Building. In 1922, he incorporated Zeiterion Realty Corporation, naming Morton as treasurer and Fisher as clerk. Its first project was to build a grand vaudeville theater on Purchase Street—the Zeiterion Theater. It featured an Italian marble lobby and a massive Czechoslovakian crystal chandelier. It opened on April 2, 1923 with *Troubles of 1923*, a stage show starring George Jessel. Within months it was renamed the State Theater and began showing silent films.

In New Bedford, the Zeitz theater empire expanded to include the State, Empire, Capital, Olympia and New Bedford Theaters, which showed first-run films. The brothers also owned Academy Theater in Fall River, Paramount in Newport, Rhode Island, and Civic in Portland, Maine.

Brothers Harry (left) and Morton Zeitz outside the State Theater, 1931. *The marquee lists the 10th in a series of classic golfing featurettes:* How I Play Golf, by Bobby Jones No. 10: "Trouble Shots" *starring Joe E. Brown, Edward G. Robinson and Douglas Fairbanks Jr.*

"It's Alive! It's Alive!" *Moviegoers stand in the rain to see* Frankenstein *with Colin Clive, Mae Clarke and Boris Karloff at the Olympia Theatre, 1931.*

***Gold Diggers of 1933* at the State Theater.** *During the Depression, viewers flocked to movie houses, seeking to lift their spirits. The price for a first-run movie at a Zeitz theater in 1933 was 15¢. The Gold Diggers movie was one of the top-grossing films in 1933.*

Sound picture run-off, Olympia Theatre projection booth, 1934. *From left to right, Walter England operates the Simplex projector while viewing the screen below for possible flaws. Albert Jason checks the next reel before inserting it in the film drum to continue the screen drama. Wilfred Robideau rewinds the replaced reel and Thomas Maloney adjusts the timing. Visible at top center is the "phone," which broadcasts the sound to the audience.*

Standard-Times-sponsored cooking class, New Bedford Theatre, 1934. *Hundreds of women from Greater New Bedford turned out for the opening session of a four-day course taught by Margaret King of the DeBoth Cooking and Home Makers School of Wisconsin. The photograph, taken from the stage, shows a packed theater with the audience filling even the uppermost balcony. The lectures covered topics from nutrition, food preparation, menu planning, interior design, cleaning, laundry and budgeting. The DeBoth course travelled throughout the nation and King was a popular lecturer.*

Radio Heads

In the interwar years, radio swept New Bedford and the nation. Commercial radio began broadcasting in 1920 from station KDKA in Pittsburgh, Pennsylvania. Newspapers, catering to the upsurge of interest in radio, published articles on how to build "oatmeal box" radios or one- and two-tube radio sets. In 1930, 37 percent of New Bedford households had a radio; by 1939, 94 percent had one, and the city had four stores specializing in them.

Before commercial radio, however, amateurs ruled the air. In 1911, William W. Squires was New Bedford's only amateur radio operator. By 1915, seven amateurs broadcast here, growing to fifteen in 1920. During the 1920s, amateur Lester I. Jenkins wrote a radio column for the *Evening Standard*. In 1922, science teacher Dana Sanborn organized a radio club and an amateur radio station at New Bedford High School. In 1929, some devotees began the New Bedford Transmitting Association to train novices to pass the amateur radio examination. In 1930, they formed the New Bedford Amateur Radio Club. The name changed successively to the New Bedford Shortwave Radio Club in 1932 and the New Bedford Amateur Radio Association in 1935.

One early amateur pioneer was Irving Vermilya, known as "King of the Hams." Born in Mt. Vernon, New York in 1890, he was fascinated by wireless communication and learned how to build his own wireless equipment. He met one of his heroes, Guglielmo Marconi, who encouraged him. When the government began licensing ham radio operators in December 1912, Vermilya was the first in the nation to apply for one. He received License #1 from the Brooklyn Navy Yard. He honed his skill during WW I as a US Navy radio operator in Massachusetts. After the war, he worked in Marion at the RCA commercial wireless station. He operated his own ham radio station with call letters IZE (later WI-ZE).

Large companies owned the first commercial radio stations, but smaller companies wanted a piece of the action. In 1922, the owners of Slocum & Kilburn on Water Street asked Vermilya to help them open a new station and manage their radio department. New Bedford's first station, WDAU, began broadcasting in 1922 from a specially built studio on the third floor of Slocum & Kilburn. In 1924, the company pulled the plug because of costs. Vermilya opened his own commercial station, WBBG, at his Mattapoisett home.

In November 1925, Vermilya's next project, WNBH, went on the air. The 100-watt radio station began broadcasting from studios at the New Bedford Hotel, which inspired the station's call letters. Mayor Edward R. Hathaway offered opening remarks, followed by entertainment from local performers. Vermilya owned and managed the station, assisted by engineer Armando Lopez. By the late 1920s, it had 250 watts. WNBH became known for music and information—local news, talks by political candidates, religious services and local sports.

In 1933, Vermilya built and installed a police radio station, WFBN. It had a studio at police headquarters and a transmitter at the Atlas Tack Company. It allowed the police to communicate with each other and to disseminate emergency messages.

In May 1934, Vermilya sold WNBH to E. Anthony & Sons, owners of the *Standard-Times*. He remained the station's general manager and continued to promote ham radio. By this time, WNBH studios had moved from the hotel to the New Bedford Theatre building on Union Street, where they remained through the 1930s.

New Bedford High School Radio Station, 1934. *Roland Deschaine (seated) and Walter Mitchell at receiving board at station W1HUM.*

Irving Vermilya in his home studio in Mattapoisett, circa 1951.

Radio Hours

In 1940, WNBH moved to **Crow Island**, building a 375-foot transmitting tower described as "an impressive landmark from sea, sky and shore." Station manager Irving Vermilya said the tower made WNBH the nation's most efficient station of its size and power. The station's **Kiddie Revue** program provided a stage for talented local children. In the middle photo, a group of youngsters surround studio pianist Gladys Sylvia at an audition.

John Collier took the photograph while working for the Farm Security Administration. One of Collier's assignments focused on documenting the living conditions of a Portuguese American family. He chose the **Mauricia family**—Manuel, Lillian and daughter Juliette—and photographed Manuel painting houses, Lillian shopping and Juliette at school. He also took two pictures of the entire family together—one at the dinner table and this one sitting in front of the radio.

Domestic evenings often centered around the radio, although many immigrant families did not have radios. In 1930, the lowest radio densities occurred in immigrant-rich Wards 1 and 6. Many ethnic families preferred speaking their own language at home. However, for those who did have radios, listening to English-language programs helped with assimilation. Many immigrants also enjoyed foreign-language radio programs. For about one hour a week, New Bedford's WNBH aired foreign-language programming. It also broadcast regular religious programs in Portuguese.

During the 1920s, Joseph H. Brodeur became one of the nation's first French Canadians to initiate French-language radio programming. After he retired, Wilfrid Couture's "Franco-American Radio Hour" took over, playing Quebec artists such as singer Mary Rose-Anna Bolduc and showcasing local artists such as singers Oscar A. Joncas, Edgar Lemenager and Ephrem G. Gauthier and pianist Marguerite Boutin. The show featured skits written and read by Jeannette LeBlanc and Adrien S. Guillet.

WNBH also offered ethnic radio shows, with Francisco Oliveira's "Hora Portuguesa," which ran from 1932 to 1975, and the "Polish Hour," retransmitting Father Justyn Figas' New York-based Rosary Hour.

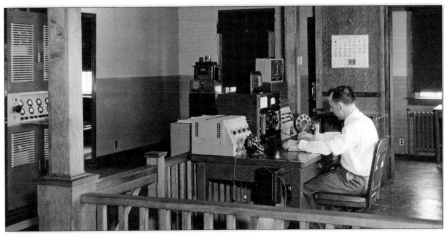
WNBH Crow Island studio, June 1941.

Kiddie Revue at WNBH, March 1939.

The Mauricia family relaxes to the sounds of radio at home in Presidential Heights, 1942.

Foreign Language Press

As foreign-speaking immigrant groups grew, they opened newspapers in their own language. The city had French, Polish and Portuguese newspapers.

French

Established in 1887, New Bedford's earliest French-language daily newspaper, *L'Ami du Peuple* (*The People's Friend*), was a short-lived local edition of Fall River's weekly *Protecteur Canadien* (*Canadian Protector*). In 1894, *L'Echo du Soir* (*The Night Echo*) began as a local version of Fall River's daily *L'Indépendant*. Bureau Chief Joseph Adelard Caron quickly rose to editor and manager. He left in 1901 to become secretary general of Union Saint-Jean-Baptiste d'Amérique, which became the nation's largest French-based fraternal and mutual aid society.

In 1904, Jean-Baptiste Archambeault founded *L'Echo de la Presse*, a local news-and-advertising supplement for subscribers of Montreal's *La Presse*, which covered international and national news. In 1910, Archambeault cut ties to the Canadian paper, took the New Bedford paper daily, renamed it *L'Echo* and printed it locally.

In 1910, New Bedford businessmen tied to Fall River's *L'Indépendant* opened a competing daily *Le Journal*, with French-born Gustave Hurel as editor. He also edited the weekly *Le Petit Journal* started the year before. Printed on the presses of its Fall River parent, *Le Journal* carried local content, advertising and special reports. By 1913, Hurel had left to edit Woonsocket's French-language newspaper.

From 1910 to 1913, New Bedford was the only US city with two competing French-language daily newspapers, *L'Echo* and *Le Journal*. Price hikes in postal rates between the United States and Canada helped bring that about. In 1907, second-class postage for Canadian newspapers mailed to the US quadrupled from one cent per pound to one cent per four ounces. With the increase, imports of Canadian newspapers fell and demand rose for locally printed ones.

In 1927, a group of New Bedford businessmen began publishing *Le Messager* (*The Messenger*), the city's longest running French-language newspaper. Under Editor Joseph Arthur Desaulniers, the weekly continued until 1953, by which time readership had dropped as older French speakers died and younger ones increasingly assimilated.

Linotype machines at *L'Echo*, 101 Kenyon Street, circa 1912. *Arthur J.H. Messier, printer for L'Echo Publishing Company, stands beside two Mergenthaler linotype machines that cast an entire line of metal type at once. Messier ran the presses at L'Echo for several years before leaving New Bedford in 1916 to fight in France during World War I.*

Polish

The *Trybuna Polish Weekly News* (*Tribune*) billed itself as "The only Polish newspaper in Southeastern Massachusetts." Polish-born Emil Szubzda began it in 1925 as an adjunct to his Liberty Press. It reported on local Polish American matters including lodge meetings, obituaries, personal items, sketches, pictures of baseball and football stars and—after 1941—local Polish Americans in the armed forces. During World War II, it examined implications of postwar links between Poland and Russia. *Trybuna* folded in 1952.

In January 1916, some 20 months into World War I, *L'Echo de New Bedford* headlined how Britain's National Labor Party opposed conscription.

Portuguese

In 1884, Pico-born Manuel das Neves Xavier moved from Boston to New Bedford. He entered into a partnership with Garcia Monteiro to publish *O Novo Mundo* (*The New World*), the city's first Portuguese-language newspaper. The partnership dissolved and the paper was discontinued. In 1895, Xavier started another newspaper—the *Correio Portuguez* (*Portuguese Mail*).

Francisco Caetano Borges da Silva, an evangelical pastor born in São Miguel, had a long career in newspapers. He edited *Progresso*, called the *Portuguese Baptist Journal*, beginning in 1898. By 1915, he was editor and publisher of *A Alvorada* (*The Awakening*), a Portuguese-language weekly.

In 1897, Alipio C. Bartholo and Rev. Antonio C. Vieira began *O Independente*, which lasted into the 1940s. As so many other newspapers had folded before it, they billed *O Independente* as "The oldest Portuguese newspaper in New England."

After Portugal's monarchy was overthrown in 1910, partisans took up the cause. New Bedford's *Centro Monarchico Portuguez* published the semi-monthly *O Thalassa* (*The Monarchist*) in 1923 and 1924, followed by *A Restauração* (*The Restoration*). Both advocated King Manuel II's return to the throne.

The *Diario de Noticias*, known as the "Portuguese Daily News," began as *Alvorada Diária* (*Daily Awakening*) in 1919, when Guilherme Luiz purchased *A Alvorada*. In 1919, it went daily and in 1927, the name was changed to *Diário de Notícias*. João R. Rocha bought half ownership in 1940, and took it over in 1943. The paper enjoyed great success and a regional circulation of up to 10,000. It also had a national readership wherever Portuguese had settled since the 19th century, and a limited circulation in Portugal. It ceased publication when Rocha retired in 1973. Its local successors are the *Portuguese Times* and *O Jornal*, which date from 1971 and 1975 respectively.

Manuel das Neves Xavier

The short-lived *O Novo Mundo* circulated throughout New England, 1891.

Diário de Notícias led with photos of the commemoration marking the discovery of Cape Verde held on May 20, 1928.

A History of Music in New Bedford ~ 1800s-1942

Overcoming the early Quaker settlers' aversion to music, New Bedford built a vibrant musical tradition, layering on the influences of the city's ever-changing immigrant communities. City musicians shared their music locally and beyond, carrying their New Bedford sound throughout the country and the world.

Marching Bands

From the 1800s, brass bands belted out New Bedford's early popular music at events ranging from musters, parades and picnics to concerts, funerals and fancy dress balls. They also performed in other cities and nearby states. Early groups included the New Bedford Brass Band, Hill's New Bedford Band, Sullivan's Band, French Band, Union Cornet Band and Reiter's Band. Various ethnic groups formed marching bands, pleasing onlookers as they paraded down city streets.

In the 1860s, New Bedford's musician-soldiers marched off to war. During the Civil War, 10 members of the New Bedford Guards Brass Band, including bandleader Israel Smith who organized the band in 1847, joined the 33rd Regiment of the Massachusetts Volunteer Infantry. In 1863, after the Battle of Lookout Mountain near Chattanooga, Tennessee opened the way to the South, Smith led the band to the mountaintop to triumphantly play the "Star Spangled Banner." Earning the position of top band in the Union Army, the regimental band played for President Abraham Lincoln at his 1863 review of the Army of the Potomac. The group also accompanied General William T. Sherman, performing concerts at the Atlanta Athenaeum and later accompanying the general on his infamous "March to the Sea."

Hill's New Bedford Band at Framingham, 1879. *Bandmaster George Hill wears the tall bearskin hat with striped plume. He and band members pose for this portrait taken at the September 1879 militia encampment. Among those identified behind Hill are, front row, left to right: Reuben Dunbar, Manuel Cayton and Joshua P. Dunbar; second row: William A. Dunbar, William H. Heap, Charles T. Searle, James Lilley and Jonathan Hawes; third row: David Wilkinson, Sydney Chace, Samuel Perry, James Omerod, George D. Richards, Drum Master Hathaway of Fall River, John Swift, Joseph Lord, Edward Gifford, Lorin Hayes and Fred Allen.*

Meanwhile, two short-lived brass bands played at home in New Bedford during the Civil War. The first, made up of African Americans, began in December 1864 with photographer Jonathan Hawes providing musical and drilling instruction. Charles Spooner led the second, a 19-member band formed in 1865 in the city's North End.

Following the war, the soldier-musicians came home and several continued playing together in New Bedford. In 1873, to honor the fire department, Smith introduced the "Fireman's Polka," which broke out with the sound of a fire alarm and signed off with three cheers for firemen who put out the fire.

After Smith left New Bedford later that year, band members called on Bavarian-born George Hill to lead a new group named Hill's New Bedford Band. Hill, who had arrived in America just a year before becoming bandleader, came from a musical family; his father was a bandleader and his brother played a variety of instruments. As a child, Hill learned the cornet and at age 14, attended a Munich music conservatory, where he studied band music. While a student, he was chosen bandmaster of the sixth regiment, a crack German army band. After military service during the Franco-Prussian war, he came to the United States and settled in New Bedford.

Hill led his namesake band for the next several decades until retiring in 1912. Dubbed "The Best Band this Side of Boston," it performed at military, political, fraternal and social events throughout southern New England. Hill composed or arranged quick steps and marches, including ones honoring nearly every fraternal order in the city. In 1879, Hill wrote "Onward March," a stirring patriotic piece.

The critically acclaimed band also served as band for the Third Massachusetts Regiment and appeared at annual encampments of the Massachusetts Volunteer Militia and the Grand Army of the Republic. In 1876, it went to Philadelphia for one week to play during the centennial of the nation's independence. Hill also led other bands and orchestras, including the Azores Band and Smith's New Bedford Quadrille Band, furnishing dance music for large parties, including clambakes at Otis Sisson's Sylvan Grove. Following his death, Hill's New Bedford Band remained with the Third Massachusetts Regiment.

In 1901, yet another reorganization returned the unit's name to New Bedford Band, this time with a more martial playlist, under the leadership of James Ogden Heap, with his brother William H. Heap as treasurer. William immigrated to New Bedford from Britain in the late 1860s, first working in the cotton mills and then as a cornet player; James came in 1901. For a short time in 1885, William served as bandmaster of the French Band, which was later known as the Union National Band under Flavien Casavant, a Quebec-born shoe repairer.

George Hill's nephew, German-born John W. Reiter, led a 23-piece marching band, which in 1899 performed Portuguese national airs in Boston during the state celebration of the 400th anniversary of Vasco da Gama's discovery of India. The *Sunday Herald* labeled the group "The Portuguese Band of New Bedford."

One-time city barber Henry Asa Gray and music storeowner Daniel J. Sullivan joined forces to form Gray and Sullivan's Orchestra, a popular group

Rare tintype of Gray's Band and Orchestra at Lincoln Park, 1900. Standing are Henry C. Gray, Leonard Gray, Edward Gray. Seated are Henry A Gray, Edward Alexander and Michael S. Robinson.

at the turn of the century. Gray arrived in New Bedford as a toddler and went whaling on the bark *Vigilant* as a teenager, later becoming a barber by trade. An amateur drummer, he traded his scissors for musical scores and in 1886 sold his combined barbershop-and-billiard-room to devote himself to music. Gray worked with Daniel J. Sullivan's Band and in 1888 partnered with Sullivan, who started the band as an adjunct to his Purchase Street music store. Having both band and orchestra allowed them to offer a wide range of popular music to the region. In 1902, they split. Gray formed a dance group, Gray's Band and Orchestra, with his son Edward. For 21 years, Gray provided the music for Dartmouth's Lincoln Park Ballroom and other regional amusement park venues. His was the first organized orchestra in New Bedford. He served as president of the musician's union, and developed a prosperous music supply business specializing in drums. Gray passed Gray's Band to his son Edward and Gray's Orchestra to another son, Henry C. Gray. A grandson, Leonard C. Gray, formed his own jazz band, Len Gray's Orchestra, and founded a music publishing company promoting local composers.

From the 1870s to the 1930s, more ethnic bands appeared as new migrants gathered to play music from their homelands. At one point, New Bedford had so many ethnic marching bands that it earned the nickname "City of Bands."

German-born Gustavus Rau led the Union Cornet Band, which played locally to mark the country's centennial celebration in 1876. Rau served as a musician during the Civil War with the Second Regiment of the District of Columbia Infantry. In 1874, St. Lawrence Martyr Church launched its Temperance

The New Bedford Reel. *Music for the "New Bedford Reel" first appeared in William Bradbury Ryan's 1883 collection of music for traditional fiddle players—Ryan's Mammoth Collection—one of several of his Boston-regional compilations. Stylistically, this type of traditional dance music dates to a much earlier era. Reels were popular in the folk music of South West England. The genre crossed the Atlantic with Irish and British immigrants, entering local musical tradition wherever they settled. The two-part reel (A and B) follows the AABB structure of most reels, with each eight-bar part repeated twice.*

Band also under Gustavus Rau. Seeking to keep the male parishioners from imbibing alcohol, the church organized alternate activities such as music groups and a soccer team. In September 1917, the *Boston Herald* noted the band "played with spirit" when saluting New Bedford and Fall River men leaving for military service overseas.

In the late 1890s, Arthur J. Parry, a Lakeville-born violin teacher, and Dennis Haworth, a Lancashire-born weaver-turned-musician, formed Parry & Haworth's Orchestra. It became Parry's Orchestra after Haworth left to sell pianos and other instruments. Parry became a straightener at Morse Twist Drill and by 1910 the orchestra had folded.

Franc Tireurs Marching Band, 1920s, at Mount Pleasant Reservoir. *In 1907, the largest French Canadian mutual benefit society called the Franc Tireurs, also known as the Sharpshooters Club, formed its own uniformed drill company, which merged with the Chevaliers of St. Louis. In 1933, the drill company expanded to become the Sharpshooters Drum and Bugle Corps, one of the most successful of its type in the country. It played during parades and drills and won the championship of the Union of Franco American Guards of New England from 1927 through 1931, and again in 1933 and in 1948. In 1938, Captain Prudent Coderre was chosen most popular captain in the New England Garde Drill Championships in Lowell, returning to the city with a large trophy cup. The fraternal group helped its members obtain citizenship, find jobs and pay funeral expenses.*

Music from Around the World

From Cape Verdean and Portuguese to Polish, English and French, ethnic traditions from many homelands took root in the city's music scene.

Shortly after 1900, Avila's Concert Band formed, drawing members from the Portuguese community and proudly featuring the coat of arms of the Kingdom of Portugal on its drums. The band boasted a concert group of strings and woodwinds and a marching group with a drum and bugle corps.

In 1920, the American Legion spun off an invitation-only honor organization for veterans called "La Société des Quarante Hommes et Huit Chevaux," French for "The Society of Forty Men and Eight Horses"—a reference to the boxcars that transported American soldiers to the front during World War I, which could hold forty men or eight horses. New Bedford's affiliate was called Voiture 577, French for Boxcar 577. It

Avila's Concert Band, circa 1900.

formed its own drum and bugle corps in 1931, winning the state championship of the American Legion's fife and drum corps contest on Boston Common for the next three years. Voiture 577's parade float sported a spouting black whale. Some city veterans and their wives later criticized the Society of 40 & 8 for barring black war veterans and their relatives.

Voiture 577 of The Forty Men and Eight Horses Drum Corps leading some Spanish-American War veterans in the city's Patriots Day Parade, 1940.

City of Bands

The City Band was founded in 1907 by Ernesto Santos, Lucindo Vieira, Jose Pacheco and Mariano Santos. Active for more than 60 years, it performed in parades, feasts and summer concerts. Its first director, Arbone Machado, was followed by Jorge Avilla. The band's clarinetist, Manuel C. Valerio, joined the Boston Symphony Orchestra, and its trombonist, John W. Coffey, later played with the Boston and Cleveland Symphony Orchestras, Radio City Music Hall and the Boston Opera Orchestra.

By 1900, veteran firemen's associations from 49 New England cities and towns paraded on civic occasions, each with distinctive uniforms. Around this time, the **New Bedford Veteran Firemen's Association Fife and Drum Corps** was organized to provide music for such occasions and association functions. Its members sported red flannel shirts. The florist Samuel J. Peckham served for many years as its drum major. The association disbanded around 1955.

Membership in the New Bedford Veteran Firemen's Association, which was organized in 1890, was open to anyone honorably discharged or entitled to honorable discharge from a fire department. To entertain the public, members participated in musters or tournaments, nostalgic contests pitting units against one another to "squirt" water the farthest from old, horse-drawn fire engines called "tubs." New Bedford's association competed with an old Columbian No. 5 engine built in 1855.

The city boasted one of the rare concertina bands outside the United Kingdom. In 1913, John Wright started the **New Bedford Concertina Band**, made up of Lancashire immigrant cotton mill workers who had brought their instruments (most purchased second-hand in England) when coming to America. The band, which lasted three years, played marches and popular tunes, with the bandleader teaching all arrangements by ear, since only three band members could read music.

City Band, circa 1910.

New Bedford Veteran Firemen's Association Fife & Drum Corps, Foster Street Station, 1920.

New Bedford Concertina Band on the steps of the Washington Club, circa 1930.

In 1920, Joseph M. Kavanaugh, a former New York-born salesman, founded Kavanaugh's Orchestra, known as the city's first swing band and dubbed "Prince Kavanaugh and his Orchestra." The band featured Kavanaugh on drums, Henry T. Hillman on trombone, George B. Krumbholz on violin, George Ramsden on piano, Frank Arruda on trumpet and Stanley Sterling Jr. on clarinet and saxophone. The orchestra's timing proved unlucky, as the Depression weakened what had been a widespread demand for music. By 1930, the orchestra had folded. Kavanaugh moved to his in-laws in Lynn and worked as a music company salesman. Hillman worked at Revere Copper and Brass. Krumbholz, an accountant trained at the New Bedford Vocational School, organized his own group called the Club Royal Orchestra and later worked as a traveling salesman for instrument suppliers. Ramsden became a mill man in Connecticut; Sterling, a representative for New Bedford Gas and Edison Light Company; and Arruda, a shipfitter at the Boston Navy Yard.

In the late 1930s and early 1940s, Jøzef Kulig led the Jøzef Kulig Warsaw Orchestra, one of the city's dance bands. He worked as a spinner in various mills to make ends meet. A son, Alfred Kulig, became a professional musician, playing saxophone and clarinet with a number of big bands nationwide.

The Depression proved tough on New Bedford's musicians as many bands in the city went silent. In response, in June

Kavanaugh's Orchestra, 1921. *Joseph M. Kavanaugh, drums; Henry T. Hillman, trombone; George B. Krumbholz, violin; George Ramsden, piano; Frank Arruda, trumpet; and Stanley Sterling Jr., clarinet and saxophone. The tune represented in the posed picture is "Alexander's Ragtime Band."*

1934, authorities created the E.R.A. Band with funds from the Emergency Relief Administration. Requirements for membership were need of a job and mastery of a band instrument. John B. Nelson, a British-born trainee of the British Army Conservatory, began organizing the band and veteran bandmaster of the Portuguese-American Band Joseph F. Cambra completed the task. Cambra molded its members, well-known players from city bands, into a crowd-pleasing civic organization that gave free concerts in municipal parks and performed for patients at the Sol-E-Mar Hospital, Sassaquin Sanitarium, St. Mary's Home and the City Infirmary.

Casino Band, circa 1923. *Most members of this short-lived musical group had recently immigrated from the Caribbean island of St. Eustatius in the Netherlands Antilles—an island one-third the size of New Bedford. Other band members came from the nearby islands of St. Vincent or St. Kitts. Most found unskilled or semi-skilled work in the city; two had their own businesses.*

Identified band members include: George Sprott, Robert Bennett, Edward Sprott, Garrison Oliver, John Bulgar, Henry Groebe, William 'Undertaker' Harris, Albert Houtman, Everett Timber, Edgar Henwood, Oswald Cuvilja, Alvin May, Edward Brown, Edmund Griffin, John Gibbs, Oliver Conward, George Miggins, Edwin Deshonge and George Groebe.

Joseph Hamel's Orchestra, circa 1920. *Made up of mill workers, Hamel's Orchestra played dance music at French Canadian weddings and parties. Loomfixer Pierre Messier stands with bass fiddle behind the drummer.*

O'Connor Orchestra, 1920. *Band members include: Jake Black, banjo; Bill Tinkham, trumpet; Henry Hillman, trombone; Tom O'Connor, piano; and Henry Johnston, vibes and percussion.*

Theater bands

Until Hollywood introduced talking movies in the 1920s, theater bands accompanied motion pictures, playing musical scores furnished by filmmakers with little room for improvisation or creativity. Theater bands also provided music for live performances at city theaters. Since each theater had its own small group, theater bands provided steady employment for a large number of musicians. Theater management occasionally allowed non-house bands to present a special program. In April 1917, when the United States entered into World War I, Olympia Theatre manager W. Maurice Tobin allowed the Masonic Band of New Bedford and the Azab Grotto Band of Fall River to give a concert of patriotic music.

Theater bands also provided fertile ground for recruitment by labor unions that likened in-house musicians to stagehands and electricians. In 1923, the Central Labor Union of New Bedford voted to extend moral support to the striking employees of Lowe's Theater and invited other labor organizations in the city to do the same. Later, the advent of talking pictures and the demise of vaudeville eliminated jobs for many theater musicians.

The State Band Club headquarters, Acushnet Avenue, circa 1938. *In 1920, renowned trombonist Manuel Vieira founded the State Band, later known under several different names. Vieira led the 20- to 25-piece band until 1937 and again from 1947 to 1970. His son, noted clarinet player Manuel Vieira Jr., took over for his father from 1937 to 1947 and from 1970 to 1981. The group performed for public and private parties and marched in civil and religious parades.*

In March 1937, the State Band Club moved into new headquarters at 100 Acushnet Avenue, the former site of the Luzitano Club. That August, with the name Broadcasting State Band displayed on the drum, the musicians performed at a huge picnic sponsored by the Centro Católico Português at Perry's Grove in North Dartmouth.

After World War II, Lincoln Park regularly featured the band. In 1952, as the Bay State Band, it won first prize in a four-band competition, one of many awards earned during its long existence. When it played at the 1964 World's Fair in New York, guest conductor Cardinal Richard J. Cushing of Boston led a march. Louis M. Borges led the band from 1981 to 1997. Currently, the Bay State Band boasts both a marching band that plays traditional military marches and a concert band that plays contemporary and standard selections.

Romaria da Camacha, Madeiran Folkloric Group, 1931.

Ernie's Venetians, circa 1932.

The Alvo Aristocratas and Camaradas Açorianos, 1935. *João Cordeiro Jr. is first left, middle row.*

A Taste of Portugal

As immigrants from Madeira Island arrived in New Bedford during the 1930s and 1940s, they formed folkloric groups that performed at local festas, parades and picnics, providing social and cultural familiarity. Popular groups of the era were the Romaria da Camacha, Grupo Santa Cruz, Saudades da Madeira and Recordações da Madeira.

The Madeiran group Romaria da Camacha was a small band formed in 1931 by members of the Baptista family led by José Baptiste. During the 1930s it performed Madeiran dances and music at festivals throughout the region. Family members made many of the instruments they carried and the costumes they wore, which were loosely based on those from the small parish of Camacha outside the capital city of Funchal, Madeira Island. Women wore brocaded, red vests over white blouses. Their white woolen skirts with stripes twirled to the music. Men wore white, linen trousers and shirts, blue berets and either belts or red sashes. From left to right, band members include: Manuel A. Pereira, Virginia Baptista, Frank Ornellas, Virginia Ornellas, Martins Baptista, Maria P. Baptista, Manuel Baptista, Josephina Baptista, Antonio Baptista, Maria Baptista and Frank Silva.

Born in São Miguel, Azores, Ernest Medeiros moved to New Bedford as a child. He worked as a second hand in the mills and later in the furniture business, but was well known during the 1930s as a musician and leader of his own orchestra, Ernie's Venetians. He was a noted pianist and violin player who composed many of the group's songs.

Also born in São Miguel, Azores, João Cordeiro Jr. arrived in New Bedford at 14. He owned Cordeiro's Variety Store on Allen Street. Active in the music scene of the 1930s, 1940s and 1950s as a guitarist, conductor and composer of traditional and popular Portuguese music, Cordeiro belonged to groups such as the Golden Star Serenaders and the Alvo Aristocratas. Cordeiro was featured on radio shows including the "Portuguese Hour" on WJAR-Providence and WNBH-New Bedford and the "Monte Pio Program Hour" on WSAR-Fall River. His sister Francelina Cordeiro also was a performer, and her son, Gilbert Travers (Tavares), played with Cordeiro. Cordeiro's two daughters, Vivian and Lillian, also performed.

Cape Verde Crioulo

At first, Cape Verdean immigrants to New Bedford largely continued their musical traditions at baptisms, weddings, funerals and holidays. On New Year's Eve, when groups went from house to house to sing, dance and play seasonal songs, householders gave them food and money. In 1917, a group of Cape Verdean businessmen, along with a mutual aid society called the Cape Verdean Beneficent Association, sponsored the Cape Verdean Ultramarine Band Club. It hosted popular bands, held weekly dances, sponsored fashion shows and served as a recreational facility. The Cape Verdean Ultramarine Band, for which the club was named, offered music education for families and youth. Members felt a duty to provide lessons to the community's children and teenagers. The band grew to more than 100 musicians in the mid-1930s, playing brass and percussion instruments. The military marching ensemble performed "street music"—a repertoire of American marches—in parades and at outdoor social events throughout New England.

Born in Cape Verde, Joaquim do Livramento immigrated to New Bedford in 1917 and was a charter member of the Cape Verdean Ultramarine Band Club. He was a composer, lyricist and musician, playing the French horn, piano, guitar and mandolin. Some of his compositions remained favorites of local Cape Verdeans for many years. His "Amor de Mia," inspired by a request from his son serving in the military during World War II, recounted the profound love for his mother.

The Star Orchestra, or B-29 Band, was popular in the 1920s and 1930s. Its Cape Verdean-born musicians included Manuel "Gelina" Silva, Manuel DaLuz, Frank Rogers, Jimmy Livramento,

Phil Edmonds Band at Wamsutta Club, 1939. *The horn section features Joseph Livramento, Armando Raposa and Paul Gonsalves. Tootsie Wright is on drums and Manuel Rose on bass. Seated at center is guitarist Jimmy Barros and at the piano are Mike Silva and Margie Araujo. Phil Edmonds leads.*

José DaGraça, Manny "Sheika" Britto, Epifano "Peefonte" Ramos and Pedro DaGraça. It played mostly Crioulo and some American dance music. Using string instruments (violins, guitars and mandolins) and occasionally a non-traditional drum, the Star Orchestra entertained at the New Bedford Hotel and New Bedford High School, as well as at cafes, clubs, dance halls and on radio. In the 1940s it merged with the Cape Verdean Ultramarine Band Club. During the same period, several other small bands also played similar music in the city. These included groups led by Boboy di Tai, Antonin "Boca" Andrade, João Britto and Jimmy Barros.

The Don Verdi Swing Band at Monte Pio Hall, Acushnet Avenue, circa 1938. *In 1937, at a talent contest held at Monte Pio, local favorite Don Verdi Orchestra went up against the Gonsalves Brothers trio and came in second. While the Verdi band featured talented clarinetist Joe Livramento (center), the victors showcased Livramento's best friend, saxophonist Paul Gonsalves.*

Bandleader Theophile "Tiffy" Viera, aka Don Verdi, stands at right; Roy Lomba is at the piano. In 1938, the Don Verdi Swing Band headlined the 478th anniversary celebration of the discovery of the Cape Verde Islands held at Monte Pio Hall. Organized by "Mingo" Gomes, the event featured a variety of musical and comedic acts. Attorney Alfred J. Gomes served as master of ceremonies.

Classical Music & Choral Traditions

From the early 1800s, choral and orchestral groups offered classical music. Although religious conservatives frowned on music as frivolity, these groups became popular entertainment. Among the earliest were the Gentlemen's Amateur Glee Club, Glee and Madrigal Association, Cecilia Ladies' Club and German Singing Society.

In 1834, the New Bedford Haydn Society's Ebenezer Harvey, master of the Sixth Street School, asked permission to teach singing to boys in school. In keeping with Quaker anti-music sentiment, the school committee refused, but allowed him to teach singing after school hours, marking the beginning of vocal instruction in the city school system. At year's end celebrations, the boys sang the popular tune "The Mellow Horn."

Meanwhile, noteworthy musicians offered private instruction. Clara Heronica Carney, daughter of Civil War hero Sergeant William H. Carney, was a popular music instructor. New Bedford High School's first female African American graduate was a professional pianist as well as a private violin and piano teacher. Helen Treot, a concert pianist in New York who performed with the Russian and New York Symphony Orchestras, left her music career and moved to New Bedford in 1923 after marrying local dentist Everett T. Waters. Until her death in 1967, she gave private lessons and private recitals.

As schools and instructors fostered young talent, many music groups formed. At the turn of the 20th century, the New Bedford Orchestral Club grew from the Amateur Orchestral Society and the YMCA orchestra, both founded by George Fox. Around the same time, two British musical groups held Saturday night performances at the Washington Social and Musical Club of the South End and the Workingmen's Club of the North End. After World War I began, they dedicated profits to British relief. In 1915, a 20-member, all-female group called The Treble Clef featured voices, instruments and a chorus guided by Addie Higgins (Ricketson) Covell, wife of Bristol Manufacturing executive William P. Covell.

Rodolphe Godreau raised the profile of the city's choral groups. He came to New Bedford to manage the advertising department of French-language newspaper *L'Echo de la Presse*. An amateur choirmaster with years of experience in Fall River, Godreau created *Le Cercle Gounod* in 1913 with French Canadians of the North End. He started with 10 close friends and initially expanded membership by invitation only. The group's first concert benefited Sargent Athletic Field. Within two years, it had earned a reputation of excellence and attracted non-French-speaking members as well. The chorus grew to 150, including many music teachers. The group's repertoire swelled to include operettas and musical comedies.

The Burleigh Club gave its first concert in June 1919 under Addie Covell. Throughout the country, local clubs promoted the music of Henry "Harry" Thacker Burleigh, an African American classical composer, arranger and professional baritone who developed characteristically American concert music and helped make African American spirituals available to classically trained artists.

Clarence M. Arey & the New Bedford Symphony Orchestra, 1942 ~ Rodolphe Godreau, 1918.

In 1913, Clarence M. Arey, supervisor of instrumental music for the school system, established the Philharmonic Orchestra for graduating high school students to showcase their musical talent. It performed in the auditorium, sometimes along with Le Cercle Gounod under Rodolphe Godreau, the school system's supervisor of vocal music. In 1913, Arey also created the state's first public high school orchestra. He went on to form the New Bedford Symphony Orchestra in 1915, and remained at its podium for 30 years. The NBSO celebrates its centenary in 2015. In his later years, Godreau directed the New Bedford Musical Association, the New Bedford Civic Chorus and the YWCA Glee Club.

L. J. Oscar Fontaine (left) with pianist and Masseuet Quartet, 1930.

Sheet music cover, circa 1914. *Edward McGarigle and Edward M. Sullivan lived in the Austin Street neighborhood. Both worked in factories but had show business ambitions. Sullivan wrote the words and music for two songs and the duo self-published them. They met with modest success for "Meet Me In my Home Town" when the Marr and Dwyer Sisters added the duo's 1914 piece to their vaudeville act of songs, dances and impersonations.*

From 1938 to 1942, the Unity Chorus grew from the local NAACP branch's revival activities. Walter Bonner, the first black male high school teacher appointed in New Bedford, founded the chorus of 30 male voices and 15 to 30 female voices. After the 1940s, the New Bedford Chamber Music Society, comprising 5 to 17 string musicians, performed in libraries and on college campuses.

Churches organized their own music groups. In the 1890s, British congregants at the South Primitive Methodist Church formed a choir of British-born mill workers and their descendants under choirmaster J. Frederick Griffith. The choir caroled on Christmas and New Year's Eves in the South End.

In 1910, Canadian-born L. J. Oscar Fontaine came to New Bedford as organist and choirmaster for St. Anthony of Padua Church after serving as organist at Notre Dame Church in Fall River. In the North End, he went from house to house seeking parishioners for his choir. He assembled 100, mostly working men and women. By 1913, their music had become so noteworthy that often more than half the 500 attendees at Sunday's 11 o'clock high mass came from outside the parish just to hear them sing. The men's choir had a repertoire of nine Latin masses, five of which Fontaine had composed. The women's choir that sang at the 10 o'clock mass featured solos and French-language songs.

Many of Fontaine's piano pieces were published in Boston by Thompson, in London by Leonard, in Montreal in the journal *La Lyre*, and in Philadelphia in the *Etude*. Le Cercle Gounod premiered Fontaine's march, "Our Boys in France." He also wrote songs, masses and motets. The Canadian encyclopedia noted that few Canadian-born composers of piano music had as wide an exposure as did Fontaine.

After 1910, Margaret M. Swift, the Universalist Church organist, formed a 16-member Girls' Vested Choir, which performed elaborate vespers services. When Robert Allen, organist at the North Congregational Church, organized a chorus of 20 singers in 1912, services became so popular that hundreds had to be turned away. Around 1915, another organist, Arnold F. Swift of the Trinitarian Congregational Church, organized a 40-voice chorus for young men and women while John P. Rooney, choirmaster at St. Lawrence Martyr Church, formed a 40-voice men's group, the Plymouth Glee Club, which sang secular and religious classical music, concert pieces and choruses from opera.

Copyrights

Through the years, city residents composed and copyrighted a wide range of original music. From 1907 to 1941, New Bedford residents received 366 copyrights for their compositions. The number surged from 1941 to mid-1946, with another 121 copyrights awarded in less than six years, largely during World War II.

Songs touched on topics such as love, heartache, work, recreation, patriotism, war, home and homeland. An early sampling included: "An Answered Prayer" by Olive A. Tranmer; "I Fell in Love" by J. O. Rock; "The Ball Game" by Nat A. England; "Uncle Sam is Calling" by William D. Wilson; "I'll Die like a True American" by Thomas C. McCauley; "Old Irish Legend" by Josephine T. Searle; and "Along the Shores of Old New Bedford" by Ellsworth A. Johnson.

Later, Billy Curtis composed a humorous anti-prohibition number, "Three Cheers for the Red, Wine and Brew," and in the depth of the Depression, Esther Wollison encouraged city residents to "Throw Your Troubles out the Window." In the days of World War II, Eva Rosetta Wyatt penned "To Fight for the Red, White, and Blue," and Antonio Rodriguez Alves wrote two versions of the same song in "Adeu Meu Filho" and "Goodbye My Son." With the end of the war, Betty Moore McGrath celebrated with "Back Home I'll Be Returning."

Immigration & Its Consequences, 1925~1950

Whaling's demise, the 1928 textile strike, the Great Depression and tighter immigration laws combined to slow immigration to New Bedford. From 1920 to 1950, the number of foreign-born residents living in the city fell by almost 25,000, or more than 50 percent.

Families still came from Portugal, Norway, Cape Verde, Canada's Maritime Provinces, Ireland, Central America and elsewhere, often attracted by the vibrant maritime economy. In addition, manufacturing's low-wage, unskilled jobs and service-sector work brought newcomers from Puerto Rico, the Dominican Republic, Eastern Europe, West Africa, Southeast Asia and the Middle East. Their influx, however, could not stem the post-1925 decline in the city's population.

Cape Verdeans

New Bedford has more residents claiming Cape Verdean heritage than any city or town outside Cape Verde.

Cape Verdeans arrived in large numbers through the 1910s and early 1920s. Ship manifests reveal that from 1921 to 1930, nearly 2,000 immigrants debarked in the port of New Bedford. Later arrival numbers dropped until after Cape Verdean independence in 1975. Beginning in the mid-19th century, several Azoreans and Cape Verdeans—including women—invested in ships. When the *Wanderer* sailed in 1924, its owners included New Bedford residents Captain Antone T. Edwards, John T. Edwards, Charles Mello and Sabina Gomes. Similarly, when the *John R. Manta* sailed in 1927, its owners included New Bedford residents Laura P. Mandly, Captain Antone J. Mandly, Antonio F. Dias and Henry Mandly, as well as Boston-based Leandro J. Costa and the estate of Manuel Costa.

With whaling's end, some Cape Verdeans bought barks and schooners and converted them to Brava packet ships that brought islanders to work in the city's textile mills or to toil in the Cape Cod cranberry bogs. These included the *Sunbeam, Carleton Bell, Bertha, Greyhound, A.M. Nicholson, William A. Graber, Margaret* and *John R. Manta*.

Whaling captains Antone T. Edwards and John Da Lomba, a Cape Verdean, helped drive the packet trade. Some mates on whaling ships later commanded packet ships, including Cape Verdean Isaac Azulay. However, with the tight immigration laws of the 1920s, annual island packet trips to New Bedford dropped from 15 or 20 down to only 3 or 4.

Bark *Coriolanus*, circa 1920. *By 1929, only two vessels sailed between New Bedford and the Cape Verde Islands—the bark* Coriolanus *and the Portuguese steamer* St. Vincent. *The latter also carried freight and passengers between the city, the Azores and Lisbon. The largest of the packet ships, the iron-hulled* Coriolanus, *carried up to 180 passengers. During Prohibition, US Customs seized and auctioned it off for $7,525. It was later bought by Abílio Monteiro de Macedo, mayor of Praia, Cape Verde. In 1931, he sold it to Arthur B. Cotnoir, noted French Canadian whaleman from New Bedford.*

Albanians

New Bedford once had the state's largest concentration of Albanians, who began coming with the breakup of the Ottoman Empire. The 1910 census included 58 Albanians, 50 of whom had arrived in 1909 and 1910. Census takers listed their birthplaces as either Turkey or Italy—but noted they spoke Albanian. All were men working unskilled jobs in the cotton mills. They lived together, cramped, 6 to 12 in an apartment, in the tiny neighborhood bounded by Granfield and Coggeshall Streets and Belleville Avenue. Some developed lung disease from breathing fine cotton dust at the mills. As soon as possible, they shifted to other jobs, often moving to other cities. They closely followed events in their homeland. In 1915, khaki-uniformed "Albanian Volunteers" from New Bedford went to Faneuil Hall to protest Italy's blockade of Albania. In 1920, the census showed 271 Albanians here; 250 had come after 1910. One in six was female; some families came with young children. Later, as mill jobs vanished, the Albanians left. The 1930 census noted only 53 in the city.

Sympathy for the KKK, 1925–27. *Wisconsin-born klansman Rev. Guy Willis Holmes' "unholy flirtation" with a local waitress scandalized the Methodist Episcopal Church into defrocking him. Ku Klux Klan members and sympathizers overflowed Holmes' Sunday evening "loyalty rallies" at the Pleasant Street Methodist Episcopal Church (right) until his ouster.*

Anti-immigrant Fervor and the Ku Klux Klan

Massive immigration to the United States at the turn of the 20th century at times fueled fear and resentments. Some individuals reacted by joining the Ku Klux Klan, whose ranks swelled during the 1920s.

New Bedford had a local chapter—Klan No. 13 of the Invisible Empire Knights of the Ku Klux Klan. Oral history recounts that members burned crosses on lawns of isolated immigrants' houses. However, speaking before a 1923 vote to condemn Klan activities, State Representative Andrew P. Doyle of the Eighth Bristol District stated that he and his fellow Roman Catholics had every confidence in their Protestant neighbors "to protect them to the full."

In 1927, Charles A. Briggs, the New Bedford Klan's secretary, or kligrapp, wrote to Governor Alvan T. Fuller on Klan stationery, urging the death penalty for Nicola Sacco and Bartolomeo Vanzetti, Italian-born immigrants convicted of committing murder while robbing a Braintree shoe factory.

One local figure attracted the nationwide Klan's vitriol. In 1926, the group launched a movement to deport evangelical Bishop Charles Manuel "Sweet Daddy" Grace. Klan officials claimed his activities roused local black populations to "fanatical frenzy." The deportation movement failed.

Beginning in 1925, Rev. Guy Willis Holmes, newly appointed pastor of the Pleasant Street Methodist Episcopal Church, held Sunday evening "loyalty rallies." He preached of racial purity and protestant patriotism. The meetings so boosted church attendance that hundreds had to be turned away. It was an open secret that the increased turnout came from the Ku Klux Klan. During the meetings, Holmes lit a fiery cross. He also tried to organize the church's Ladies' Aid Society into a Klan auxiliary. Holmes attended New Bedford Klan meetings and traveled elsewhere to lecture on "The American Ideal" before Klansmen in full regalia. Holmes' Klan activities so split the church that three of its four trustees, including the board president, resigned in protest. The New England Southern Conference of the Methodist Episcopal Church named a secret, special committee of 15 members to investigate complaints about Holmes. While it viewed his promotion of the Klan as heresy, the committee focused instead on his misconduct with a 19-year-old waitress, with whom he allegedly had a child. In April 1926, the Methodist Conference defrocked Holmes, finding him guilty of immorality and conduct unbecoming a minister.

In 1927, the local Klan "banished" Holmes for misappropriation of funds and for divulging the names of its members. Holmes moved to Rhode Island, where his wife and former Ku Klux Klan officials organized the American People's Church Inc., installing him as pastor. He pledged to continue the same policies he had implemented in New Bedford.

After several scandals during the late 1920s, Klan membership fell sharply, but New Bedford's chapter remained active. In 1937, New Bedford lawyer Ernest Laycock, Rev. Holmes' former attorney, testified before a special state house committee that he was trustee of a $1,000 bequest made to the Klan's still functioning New Bedford affiliate.

Norwegians

Norwegian immigrants came mainly during the 20th century. Some moved from the island of Karmøy on Norway's southwestern coast to New Bedford by way of Brooklyn during the 1920s and 1930s. Others joined the city's Norwegian Karmøy colony during the 1950s and 1960s.

Most were scallop fishermen. Scallop consumption boomed during the 1950s, and Norwegians contributed to the fishery's success. After a drop in scallop catches during the mid-1960s, many Norwegians moved to the West Coast to work in the salmon and Alaska king crab fisheries. Others returned to Norway, where oil discoveries opened new opportunities. Only a small community of Norwegian fishermen remained, largely based in Fairhaven. Tragedy often struck the local Norwegian seafaring community. During the 60 years from 1931 to 1990, it lost 57 lives and sustained countless injuries. A memorial located on Karmøy Island honors its fishermen lost at sea in America.

Rasmus Tonnessen came to the US at age 17. Unlike his fisherman father who visited in the 1880s, Rasmus could not go to sea—he got seasick. Instead, he and his wife founded New Bedford Ship Supply in 1935. By the late 1980s, it furnished groceries and equipment to half the city fleet. Tonnessen helped many fishermen by putting up bond money for their immigration and then extending credit until they got started. In 1994, the city named a waterfront park after him.

Norwegian fishermen on deck of the scalloper *Amelia*, circa 1950. *Seated in foreground, front to back are Jack Landsvik, Ingvald Frostad, Robert Landsvik and Sverre Haines. Sitting on the gunwhale are Selmer Fagerland and unidentified. Standing at center is Arne Edvardsen, Andrew Olden and Leslie Christensen are seated on the hatch, and Rasmus Vikre is behind them.*

***Nordlyset* (Northern Lights) Society of New Bedford, anniversary banquet at the New Bedford Hotel ballroom, 1941.** *The group met on St. Stephen's Day, which commemorates the first martyr, an official public holiday in Norway. As with other immigrant benefit societies, its objectives were to help Norwegians who did not speak English, to visit the sick and to provide financial help to members in need. Attendees include: Sig Midttun, Matias Bendiksen, Rasmus Tonnessen, Leif Mickelsen, Helena Mickelsen, Sally Tonnessen, Jack Simonsen, Pauline Simonsen, Kristine Jacobsen, Gellinore Arnold, Rasmus Jacobsen, Pete Jacobsen, Karl Larsen, Solveig Thompsen, Kristi Thompsen, Edith Gulbransen, Hans Davidsen, Toralf Midttun, Eddy Ostensen, Serine Davidsen, Peder Pedersen, Ralph Souza, Tom Larsen, Solveig Jacobsen, Solveig Thompsen, Hans Davidsen, Mikel Muse, David Arnold, Arne Edvardsen, Thelma Edvardsen, Gerda Olsen, Margit Thompsen, Ruth Hoines, John Hoines, Karl Hoines, Barbara Andrews, Theodore Pedersen, Ethel Pedersen, Serene Pedersen and Gunnar Pedersen.*

Wing Lee, flanked by children Mary (Toy Mee) and Charlie (Shee Yuen), January 1938. *The 15-year-old son and 13-year-old daughter reunite with their father after escaping Japanese-occupied China. The family operated Wing Lee & Sons Laundry on South Second Street. Although born in Boston, the children had lived with their grandparents in Canton since their mother's death. After the Japanese bombed Canton, they made their way to New Bedford via Hong Kong, Hawaii and Canada.*

Early Chinese Immigration

Tales of Chinese crew aboard whaling ships date to the 1840s. In the 1850s, the *Daily Mercury* reported on Chinese jugglers loitering on city streets and stowaway Chinese slaves in ships at port. The 1877-1878 city directory noted only one Chinese business—Kee Sam & Co.'s "Chinese California Laundry" at 119 Purchase Street. By 1887, the city had nine Chinese laundries, and by 1895, that number rose to 18. Early Chinese immigrants before 1900 often owned and operated laundries, while later arrivals frequently worked in Chinese restaurants. A few studied at the New Bedford Textile School.

The Chinese Exclusion Act of 1882 effectively halted Chinese immigration and prohibited Chinese immigrants from becoming US citizens. Some Chinese still entered via Canada and Mexico. Even after the law's repeal in 1943, when the US and China allied against imperial Japan, only 105 Chinese immigrants could enter per year. The 1920 census listed only 61 Chinese-born city residents.

The Sam Kee & Co. ad taken from the 1876 directory is the earliest listing of Chinese laundry establishments in city directories.

Charlie Wong (Chin Yow Doo) with wife Jade (Woo Shee Chin) and children, December 1933. *Eldest son Loy stands in the background. The children are left to right: Quen, May, Meline, Suey and Hoo Ying.*

One of New Bedford's best-known Chinese immigrants was Chin Yow Doo. Born in Canton, he came to the US in 1909, settling first in Boston and then in Fall River. He tried to enlist in the army in 1917, but was rejected as underweight. He later served in Company I of the 304th Infantry, 76th Division, and was preparing to go overseas when the armistice was signed. In 1926, he bought Charlie Wong's, a popular Chinese restaurant at 942 Purchase Street in New Bedford, and moved in upstairs. Crowds flocked to the restaurant for its hearty, five-cent chow-mein-and-noodle sandwich with gravy. After a fire destroyed it in 1939, it reopened a block away. Chin Yow Doo, who launched a second restaurant on Acushnet Avenue in the 1940s, became so well known as Charlie Wong that he petitioned the court in 1950 to officially change his name. That year, he bought the New York Sea Grill in Mattapoisett and remodeled it into the Cathay Temple. When Wong's health began to fail, his wife, Jade, the former Woo Shee Chin, managed the businesses.

Charlie Wong was the New Bedford American Legion's only Chinese World War I veteran.

Hing Whang Chinese Laundry, mid 1890s. *Hing opened his laundry around 1886 at 25 Pleasant Street, later moving to 14 Market Street, future site of the Boys Club building. He roomed upstairs.*

Donaghy Boys Club & Mary Ann Hayden

Many South End boys in the 1920s and 1930s considered Mary Ann Hayden their second mother. In 1920, she started a club for boys aged 10 to 16 at the Thomas Donaghy School on South Street between Acushnet Avenue and Purchase Street. In doing so she became the nation's first woman director of a Boys Club. In the evenings, boys could wrestle, box and tumble in the basement or play basketball in the cramped attic. They played quieter games such as ping-pong, parcheesi, checkers and chess on tables in the school corridors and auditorium. Serving as club superintendent for 18 years, Hayden focused her considerable efforts on building character, for which she received $5 a week.

While Hayden did not play chess, she found a good chess player willing to teach the boys. Chess soon became a leading activity. When the Great Depression ended the club's funding, she convinced individuals and service clubs to fund a volunteer organization that continued club activities in quarters near the Donaghy School. That arrangement lasted until 1938.

Later she served as a traveling supervisor at the city's seven playgrounds. At Hazelwood Park she organized a unique Human Chess Game where costumed children took the roles of different pieces.

A plaque honoring Hayden appears on a stone outside the John B. Devalles School on Orchard Street, where she first began

Pet show at the Donaghy Boys Club, circa 1930. *Donaghy boys show off their pet cats, dogs, pigeons and rabbits on the steps of the Thomas Donaghy School on South Street and Acushnet Avenue.*

working with children. At a ceremony, *Standard-Times* reporter Earle D. Wilson said, "Mrs. Hayden developed good men out of boys." After her death in 1946, her son Jim received a letter from Judge George Leighton, then living in Chicago. Leighton said Ms. Hayden made it possible for him to learn chess at the Donaghy Boys Club. In her memory he made a donation to the Chess Hall of Fame, where a bronze plaque now commemorates her accomplishments.

Donaghy Boys Club members playing chess in school corridor, circa 1930. *Founder Mary Ann Hayden stands in background, right.*

The YWCA and the Boys Club

The YWCA provided young women ample and safe opportunities for after-school recreation. Youth and teens could drop in to the convenient downtown location for exercise and gymnastics in the YWCA auditorium and swimming pool. When the high school moved to the outskirts of town in 1973, fewer had easy access to YWCA facilities, and attendance dropped.

The New Bedford Boys Club summer program at Camp Maxim on Blackmore Pond in Wareham made five days of low-cost camping available to the city's youth. Open to boys aged 7 to 14, the camp featured a private sandy beach and instruction in boating, swimming, archery, riflery, nature, arts and crafts, hiking and fishing as well as baseball. Additional parental incentives included free transportation to and from the camp, free medical and accident insurance, and free milk every day.

Skating and other winter sports, followed by indoor comforts before a big fireplace and an oil range, awaited these overjoyed lads at Camp Maxim. Carrying enough blankets to keep warm in the non-winterized cabin, they left to spend two days and a night at their favorite summer rendezvous. The group included James Palmer, Joe Souza, William Holmstrom, Leslie Taylor, Wilfred Garcia, James Daley, Harold Burrell, Frank Viera, Richard Herbert, Robert Pollitt, George Gracia and Benjamin Cohen.

The first Boy Scouts' charters in Massachusetts were granted to the Fall River and Fairhaven-New Bedford Councils in 1916. In 1935, state law required rechartering, and the Fairhaven-New Bedford Council became the Cachalot Council for the region. For nearly 30 years, the council used the Boys Club's Camp Maxim, but in 1945 the Boy Scouts purchased and constructed Camp Cachalot in Carver.

YWCA gymnastics group members show off their skills in forming a pyramid, 1938.

Baseball neophytes at New Bedford Boys Club Camp Maxim in Wareham, August 1938.

New Bedford Boys Club Boy Scouts, Troop 2, December 1936.

Schools in the Roaring '20s

During the 20th century, New Bedford's public schools suffered from earlier and continued miserly support for public education. In 1925, New Bedford ranked dead last of the state's 39 cities and 330th of Massachusetts' 355 cities and towns in spending from local taxation for schools. Lack of funds handicapped New Bedford's ability to educate its children.

Persistent illiteracy showed up from an early age. In 1921, only 5 percent of the city's five-year-olds attended school, compared to Fall River's 72 percent and Springfield's 79 percent. By 1927, the situation had improved only slightly; in that year, 442 of five- to seven-year-olds were not enrolled in school in New Bedford, while in Fall River, only 124 were not enrolled in school, and in Boston, with seven times the population of New Bedford, only 13 did not attend school. A late school start often resulted in a dropout.

Students in New Bedford's schools often fell behind and needed to repeat grades. In 1921, more than half of sixth-grade students had repeated a grade, and one-fifth of those had repeated grades three or more times.

Perhaps because New Bedford provided its children with such a poor education, many left school as soon as allowed by state law. Students could leave school at age 14 if they had completed sixth grade, or at age 16 regardless of grade completed. The majority of students left before graduating from high school; many left well before that. In 1927, for example, seventh-grade enrollment in New Bedford dropped 642 from the previous year's sixth-grade population. Meanwhile, Boston, with five times as many students, reported a smaller number leaving after sixth grade. Only 44 percent of those entering New Bedford High School in 1925 remained, going into senior year in 1928—and not all of those graduated.

If city schools failed in educating the general population of school-age children, they did even worse in educating immigrants' children. A consultant's report to the school committee pinpointed an ethnic link for many school dropouts. In the sixth grade, French Canadian and Portuguese students made up 46 percent of the students. Of every 100 French students in sixth grade, only five stayed to enter the freshman year of high school and only two graduated. Of every 100 Portuguese students, eleven entered freshman year, but only one graduated.

Howland School students in reading class with teacher Miss Irene Sadler, 1934.

New Bedford students lagged behind and often left school with less education than their counterparts in similar cities. For students at all ages, those in Fall River averaged one-half grade level higher than New Bedford students. The gap was greater when compared to Springfield. New Bedford's 13-year-olds were, on average, at sixth grade level while those in Springfield were at eighth grade level. Fall River and New Bedford had a similar ethnic mix, but Springfield had fewer non-English-speaking students. Part of the difference came from the earlier starts by students elsewhere; part came from forcing many non-English speakers to repeat grades.

Despite poor outcomes and low educational financing, New Bedford's teachers received high salaries. Only Holyoke paid its elementary teachers more, and 17 cities paid average elementary salaries that were less than New Bedford's minimum salary. In 1921, the city's female high school teachers received the highest average salary in the state. For all regular teaching positions, New Bedford offered the highest maximum salaries in the state, but because 70 percent of elementary school teachers and 96 percent of high school teachers already earned the maximum salary, they had no monetary incentives to improve.

With these high salaries and the best yearly advancement rate in the state, New Bedford should have been able to recruit the best and the brightest teachers of the day, but it did not. Instead, it recruited from normal schools and the city teacher-training program. Remarkably, in 1927, only eight of

Eighth-grade students at Parker Street School, 1930. *About half would not graduate from high school.*

its 517 public elementary school teachers had college degrees. By comparison, Lowell and Lynn's combined staffs counted 64 college-trained teachers among them.

New Bedford's school buildings also fell short. With the highest average class size in the state, New Bedford exceeded the average of 10 similar-sized Massachusetts cities by 30 percent. More than half the classes exceeded the nationally accepted norm of 42 students; one-fourth of classes had between 48 and 55 students. Desperately needing new classrooms, the city built three new elementary schools—Clarence A. Cook, Mount Pleasant and Charles S. Ashley.

Cooking class, 1938. *Parker Street School seventh graders dice vegetables for a beef stew in cooking class taught a mile away at Harrington School. Would-be cooks include Betty Southworth, Jane Ashley, Agnes Piva, Marilyn Pope, Pauline Baines, Alice West, Ruth Costa, Eunice Souza, Barbara Oman,*

Ruth Horne, Edna Geggatt, Vivian Chassey, Annie Robbins, Dorothy Baldwin, Josephine Ramos, Anastasia Gioiosa, Margherita Regis, Alice Honeyman, Dorothy Zolt, Barbara Shaw, June McAlpine, Eleanor Ledvina, Evelyn Miller, Lorraine Coon, Flora Dube and Jean Moore.

Normandin Junior High School, Tarkiln Hill Road, April 1927.

Roosevelt Junior High School, Brock Avenue, 1927.

The city's population fell by almost eight percent from 1925 to 1940, a period including the 1928 textile strike and the Great Depression. During this time, primary and middle school enrollment fell by 18 percent. In marked contrast, high school enrollment jumped by almost 30 percent, or 500 students. Overall, however, the number of students in the city's public schools fell. Faced with falling school enrollments, the city hired eight percent more teachers and supervisors.

In 1927, the school system introduced junior high schools. They helped alleviate overcrowding, but did little to stem the dropout rate. Many students left after junior high. In 1937, less than two-thirds of 1,316 ninth graders, or 868, continued on to New Bedford High School the following year. As a result of the 1928 textile strike, high school enrollment fell. From 1928 to 1929, more than 700 students left the classroom to help support their families. Later, the number of enrollees began to rise, but the high school did not reach its pre-strike size again until 1938. Dropouts persisted; only two-thirds of the 868 students mentioned above stayed in high school long enough to start their senior year in 1939. And not all of those graduated.

The strike and Depression had another effect on the system. As school-age workers were losing their jobs, some stayed in

First day of school, New Bedford High School, County Street, 1933. *Of the 818 new high school students in 1933, only 485 remained to begin senior year.*

John B. DeValles School, Orchard and Katherine Streets, 1927.

Fourth graders at Betsey B. Winlsow School, Allen Street, circa 1928.

school, although still less than half the unemployed youth remained. Before the Strike of 1928, two of every three children aged 14 to 16 worked. By 1939, only one in twelve had a job. Most of those who had gone to Continuation Schools for four hours per week after work moved into the public schools. Continuation School enrollment plummeted from an average of 1,400 between 1925 and 1927 to an average of 162 between 1938 and 1940.

In general, during the pre-war years, the city's lack of commitment to education barely changed. In 1938, New Bedford ranked 32nd of the state's 40 cities in tax effort per pupil. In 1940, although the city had increased the property tax levy to support schools, it only ranked 169th in the state on school financing from local sources.

After 1925, private schools continued to educate about one-fourth of the city's students.

Last day of class, Clarence Cook School, Summer and North Streets, June 23, 1938. *Almost one in ten sixth graders did not return to school.*

Eighth-grade graduates, St. Hyacinthe School, 1929. *George J. Thomas is third left, middle row. His cousin Arthur Thomas is fifth left, middle row.*

Bilingual Geography class at St. John the Baptist School, 1942.

Friends Academy had long provided quality education for a small, select student body. It remained in New Bedford until moving to Dartmouth in 1949. Many churches opened parochial schools, making up the bulk of the city's private schools. In addition to religious instruction, they taught pride in a strong ethnic identity among children of immigrants. In part, they responded to the New Bedford schools' refusal to recognize the needs of children who spoke a foreign language at home. Many parochial schools provided a bilingual education, often in French or Portuguese, with some instruction given in each language. After 1929, private school enrollment fell somewhat, but proportionately less than the school-age population or public school enrollment.

Two Catholic high schools, Holy Family High School and St. Anthony's High School, dated from 1883 and 1940 respectively. At St. Anthony's, all students took French one period per day.

Friends Academy, Morgan and County Streets, 1941.

Shrinking Enrollment

During the 1930s, the number of elementary and junior high students in New Bedford public schools plunged sharply. From 1927 to 1942, enrollment fell by 4,985 students. As workers lost their jobs, families—many with young children—left the city to look for jobs elsewhere.

Also, younger folks without jobs delayed marriage and starting new families, further reducing the school-age population. From the prosperous early 1920s to the depressed 1930s, the city's marriages fell by 40 percent. Marriages went from an average of 1,202 per year in the early 1920s to 725 in the early 1930s. In addition, births plunged 46 percent. New Bedford went from an average of 3,329 live births per year in the early 1920s to 1,793 per year in the early 1930s. Fewer new families and fewer births rapidly led to fewer children in the early grades. Kindergarten enrollment dropped 20 percent from 1929 to 1937.

The drop in enrollees had a positive effect on the school system, helping to reduce seriously overcrowded classrooms from earlier days of the city's rapid population growth. Smaller classes allowed teachers to give students more individualized attention.

Classroom instruction in an early grade at Rockdale School, Mount Pleasant Street, 1933.

Grade 7B students, Room 12, at Clarence A. Cook School, 1938. *Lucille Talmage, teacher.*

Students engage in morning schoolyard calisthenics, Thomas Donaghy School, 1930s.

Vocational School

Construction of Girls Vocational School, 1931.

New Bedford Vocational School welding class, 1941. Students practice joining pieces of scrap metal. Within a few months, demand for their skills skyrocketed to supply the nation's wartime allies with millions of miles of welded joints for ships, tanks, assault-planes, fighters, bombers, heavy guns, as well as bodies of mines, torpedoes and shells.

New Bedford paved the way for vocational education in Massachusetts. Created in 1907, its evening industrial program for men, daytime homemaking school for girls and evening practical art school were the first of their type in the state. Although not the first, its day industrial school for boys dated from November 1908, just one month after Framingham's Agricultural School opened. Enrollment in the vocational school's day programs more than tripled from 1925 to 1941, growing from 425 to 1,458 students. Most students came from New Bedford, and a few came from nearby towns, but non-residents dropped after 1934.

Boys' day programs included woodworking, electrical, automobile repair, machine and commercial. Those for girls comprised clothing, foods, millinery, secretarial and home nursing. In most years, demand for admission exceeded the available places and led to the creation of waiting lists. After 1934, a small number of girls, always less than a hundred, entered the boys' industrial day school. To better serve them, the school hired female teachers.

The evening industrial school for men grew more slowly than the day programs. It appealed to workers from nearby towns who, by 1941, made up 30 percent of the students. During the late 1920s, the evening practical art program formed the largest component of the vocational education system. In 1925, it enrolled 1,841 students. It provided similar instruction to that in the day programs for boys and girls. A drop in funding during the early 1930s brought enrollment down to 601 by 1935.

Kinyon Commercial School graduates, 1927. In 1911, William H. Kinyon opened a branch of his Pawtucket-based school in New Bedford. Known as Kinyon's Commercial and Short-Hand School, it taught business skills such as accounting, bookkeeping, shorthand, typing and penmanship. It provided students with practical, on-the-job training and employment contacts. Kinyon prided itself in training students for a position better than the one for which they applied, a practice that boosted the school's reputation among employers. It also gave graduates opportunities for rapid advancement after landing their first jobs. As a result, local commercial and manufacturing companies eagerly sought and hired Kinyon-trained staff.

Higher Education

Over the years, **Swain School of Design** directors worked to balance the fine arts and the commercial arts. In both areas, the school was nationally acclaimed. Using a limited endowment, the college provided free tuition for many years. It began charging fees in 1921—$60 for a full-time student and $20 for night school — although it still claimed to offer free tuition. That claim was dropped from catalogues in 1933. Students concentrated in fine arts, commercial arts and architecture. Limited funds hampered its expansion. To raise resources, it regularly sponsored faculty and student shows.

To complement the city's industries, the **New Bedford Textile School** specialized in cotton cloth. In 1923, it opened a new 59,600-square-foot, three-story building to house departments dealing with cotton yarn and cloth as well as for knitting hosiery and underwear. During the Depression, textile production and employment in New Bedford dropped by more than two-thirds. In the face of falling enrollments, the school raised revenue through fees for testing fabric, material, and machinery.

Swain School art class at Homer's Wharf, Nov. 2, 1939.

For a time, mill owners dominated the school's board, but by the end of the 1930s all had been replaced by second hands, overseers, designers, union leaders, doctors, dentists and a mortician. By 1940, more than 16,000 students had enrolled, but only 5,260 had graduated. Many skilled mill workers attended, although low proficiency in English or unfamiliarity with examinations kept them from completing course work. In the early 1940s, an expanding curriculum keyed the school's growth and survival, shifting focus from textile technology to engineering, science and modern technology.

Class prepares roving machinery in the spinning department at New Bedford Textile School, 1925.

Red Cross Chairman of Volunteer Services Alice (Tiffany) Knowles enlists Reserve Officers' Training Corps (ROTC) cadets in the annual roll call drive, Union and South Sixth Street, November 1941.

Chapter 2 ~ 1942–1960

War & Peace

Introduction: New Bedford during War Years

The Japanese attack on Pearl Harbor in December 1941 shocked America into officially going to war, and the country quickly got behind the effort. Even before the official declaration of war, New Bedford residents had begun preparing for the conflict. Many had already joined the military and others were mobilizing on the home front.

In 1940, M. Jennie Williams of New Bedford took the national stage, arguing in favor of a conscription bill. A former president of the American Gold Star Mothers, whose members had lost sons during World War I, Williams, at 70, went to Washington to lend her support. "If ever a woman had a right to hate war and dread its clutch on youth, this mother has. And does," wrote Elsie Robinson, a nationally syndicated columnist.

Yet Williams, despite having lost her son Ralph, who died of pneumonia after training as a radio electrician for the Navy, believed the country needed its men from 21 to 44 years old to enroll in one-year mandatory military training.

After the US entered World War II, New Bedford's home front switched quickly to a full-time war economy. With more men at war, women at home stepped in to work in factories, producing life rafts, gas masks and military fabric. Women also drove taxis, ran hot presses, learned how to weld and did whatever work needed doing. High school students were allowed out early to work factory shifts.

Remarkably, New Bedford contributed more than 2,000 tons to the war salvage campaign in a three-month period in

1943, using window cards placed in homes and businesses to alert junk collectors to stop in for collected paper, fats, cans, rubber, keys, rags, iron or mixed metals. Coordinated by the *Standard-Times*, the innovative window card campaign was the first of its kind in the country and became a model for other communities. Fats and oils left over from cooking were used to make explosives.

Children too gathered old newspapers, cans of fat, bottles, bits of rubber and rags. With the sudden demand for steel, young men combed the neighborhoods for scrap metal. Families bought war bonds and school children filled kits containing soap and toothpaste to send to Europe. Drivers slowed their cars to save gasoline and speed limits were lowered to encourage that effort.

Gold stars began turning up in windows, each alerting that a son or husband had died in the war. With reports of German submarines prowling the waters of Buzzards Bay and German planes flying over to spy on potential targets, the city was on alert. Fort Rodman geared up to full strength and air raid wardens held drills in city neighborhoods. When sirens went off, so did lights and residents retreated indoors.

Defense contracts created thousands of jobs in New Bedford as companies produced products ranging from gas masks to parachutes. In comparison to the anemic economy of the 1930s, New Bedford's wartime economy was robust, patriotic and prosperous.

Panoramic view looking north and east from the roof of the New Bedford Hotel, 1955.

The war ended in 1945. New Bedford commemorated the end of the war and celebrated the city's centennial in 1947 with a four-hour parade. Social organizations in the city proudly sponsored floats touting their war efforts and contributions.

The city sent thousands of men and women to World War II, of whom 280 died and 621 were wounded, the *Standard-Times* reported.

As men and women returned to New Bedford from the war, marriages went up and so did births, a reflection of the national Baby Boom. City schools continued to struggle with the peaks and valleys of immigration and demographics. More and more school-age children went to the region's private, often parochial, schools.

During these relatively upbeat years, New Bedford also made progress on the public health front, leading to an 80 percent drop in the city's infant mortality. In the 1920s, in a child's first year, there was an average of 90 deaths per 1,000 live births, a number that fell to 18.5 by 1960.

Korea—The Forgotten War

Sandwiched between World War II and the Vietnam War was a shorter military conflict, the Korean War, often referred to as the Forgotten War. A civil war between North and South Korea, the Korean War grew out of Cold War tensions following World War II. Intelligence of the Chinese and Soviets, who were backing North Korea, concluded that the United States would not intervene on behalf of its South Korean ally. On June 25, 1950, some 75,000 soldiers from the North Korean People's Army, streamed across the 38th parallel. President Harry S. Truman proved their assumptions wrong and the United States entered the war.

In early July, US forces sent troops to support the overwhelmed South Koreans. Within weeks, New Bedford mourned its first fatality. World War II veteran Sergeant Allen A. Sequin belonged to the 71st Medium Tank Battalion, 1st Cavalry Division. On July 24, 1950, he became the city's first citizen killed in action while fighting the enemy.

Baylies Square, Acushnet Avenue, 1948.

Sgt. William Carmo manning his 20mm anti-aircraft weapon in Taegu, South Korea, 1951. *An instrument specialist, William do Carmo (the military dropped the "do" from his name) was a gunner and in charge of navigation equipment. Out of 100 men in his squadron, 65 were killed, all pilots. Do Carmo grew up in the multicultural South Central neighborhood, which did not prepare him for the prejudice he experienced while serving in Korea. "As the military was being desegregated under President Truman, I ended up as the only "colored" guy in a unit with 100 white guys from the South. They treated me badly, taunted me, wouldn't sit with me in the cafeteria. I had no experience with that kind of thing and didn't understand it." In the end, do Carmo triumphed when he used the military training to become a skilled airplane mechanic. Back home, he earned three bachelor degrees and developed a career in building and architecture.*

In an event sponsored by the *Standard-Times* in celebration of the newspaper's 100th anniversary, the city buried a copper time capsule to be unearthed in 2050. It included a centennial edition of the paper, which featured a letter to the future citizens of New Bedford describing the concerns of the city at the time: "In the first place, we thought most about the atom bomb and that unknown factor, the H-bomb. We worried that the 1950 war in Korea would develop into World War III when World War II had been over but five years. But our faith in a happy ending was demonstrated by writing this letter and burying a time capsule in the common for you to open." So many locals were serving in the military in 1950

that the New Bedford Textile Institute would not field a football team in 1951.

Twenty-eight more New Bedford residents died in service and far more were wounded during the Korean War, which ended in 1953. In 1952, Private Rene G. Poitras of the 23rd Infantry Regiment, 2nd Infantry Division was killed by fragments of an enemy mortar shell one month before his wife gave birth to twin sons. Both sides took prisoners of war. Several from New Bedford joined 140 New Englanders who spent part of the war as "guests" of the North Koreans. They were freed after the signing of the armistice. They included Lieutenant Joseph A. Magnant, Sergeant Edward Fisher and Sergeant Roland O. Chartier.

City businesses did their part in supplying defense needs. During the war, a New Bedford firm garnered the most significant single defense contract in New England. New Bedford Defense Products (Chamberlain), a division of Firestone Tire and Rubber Co., won an $11 million contract for the delivery of 155mm artillery shells.

In 2000, fifty years after the start of the Forgotten War, New Bedford remembered the Korean War and dedicated a war memorial in Clasky Common Park. Ten years after that, a stretch of highway connecting Acushnet Avenue to Route 140 became the "Korean War Veterans' Memorial Roadway."

Industry

After World War II, government contracts dried up and New Bedford's economy stagnated once more. Despite repeated attempts to attract new business to locate in the city, New Bedford continued to lose jobs as mills and manufacturing moved south. Finding sea-based jobs was more promising. The fishing industry took off during the 1940s and the port became a major industry leader. By 1948, there were 1,400 fishermen working on 265 vessels, and 13 companies handled fish on the city docks. Some 27 filleting companies employed 550 people and there were six freezer companies, a fish auction, three fish canneries, four ice plants, eight fishing gear supply houses, five shipyards and six machine shops. The city was among the

Eastern-rigged vessels or side trawlers, 1940s. *At far left is the 65-foot fishing vessel* Four Sisters. *Built in Thomaston, Maine in 1926, the Four Sisters set out from New Bedford in March 1950, scalloping near Nantucket Shoal. On April 7, the boat contacted F/V* Dagny, *reporting that its hold held 700 gallons of scallops and that it was headed for Pollock Rip in order to make the Woods Hole market. Storm warnings for a northeaster 10 miles offshore had been issued over commercial radio stations.* Four Sisters *encountered winds up to 56 mph with gusts reaching 65 mph and 35-foot seas. The vessel was never heard from again. Neither its wreckage nor crew were found. The lost fishermen included Captain Gunnar Pederson, Martin Johnson, James Lopes Jr., Manuel Moniz Jr., Louis Boino, Victor Boino, James Morrison, George St. Clair, John Correia Jr. and Kenneth Dyer. The Coast Guard searched for days, covering more than 21,000 square miles. In a report, they declared the boat did not meet merchant vessel standards and was unsafe.*

nation's top 10 ports in 1946 and the fishing industry loomed large in New Bedford's economy. The greatest growth was in the scallop industry.

Down on the docks, longshoremen, many Cape Verdean, loaded and unloaded cargo vessels entering or leaving the port.

Transportation in New Bedford went from tracks to wheels. The city's trolley system gave way to buses and went entirely out of business by 1947. Commuter rail service to Boston ended in 1958. Auto traffic increased dramatically and put a strain on roads and bridges.

New Bedford's profitable steamship line to Martha's Vineyard and Nantucket collapsed when the legislature created a Steamship Authority that cut New Bedford out of the business, leaving it to Woods Hole, Martha's Vineyard and Nantucket. Officials are still debating what went wrong.

Air traffic was more promising. The city welcomed the building of an airfield, begun as a Works Progress Administration project in 1940, which stretched out over 400 acres in the northwestern part of the city. The airport was turned over to the federal government during World War II and returned to the city in 1947. Eleven years later, the Civil Aeronautics Administration took over the control tower, signifying air traffic had reached more than 26,000 yearly takeoffs and landings.

City Life

During these decades, downtown New Bedford provided a center for gathering, eating and socializing. Customers were greeted by the pungent smell of freshly ground coffee in Lorraine's Coffee Shop and the Bridge Diner on Pope's Island was known as the best place to take your date after a movie. Hurley's Lunch, Ralph's Lunch and Jimmy Evan's Flyer were popular eateries where people talked about work, weather and politics. The next best thing to a lunch counter was a bakery, which could be found everywhere in New Bedford—from Norwegian, Jewish, and Swedish to Portuguese, Scandinavian and American—Sig Midttun's on Union Street, Sunnyside's on Rockland Street, Worthington's on Acushnet Avenue, Kroudvird's on South Water Street and delightful Brenneke's in the West End—oh, the pies at Brenneke's.

Directory assistance, 1952. *The 20th century witnessed telephones' widespread growth and acceptance. First adopted as a business tool and then as a toy for the wealthy, the telephone soon became a family necessity and then a personal accessory. In 1905, two competing phone companies supplied less than 3,400 lines to New Bedford's business and residential customers. Switchboard operators manually connected callers. By 1960, more than 28,000 or 82 percent of residences had their own phones. Nearly all businesses used them. With the addition of numeric dials on newer phones, subscribers could call each other directly. Operators provided directory assistance, collect calls or overseas service. In this photograph, switchboard attendants from the city's largest companies visit the New Bedford office of New England Telephone and Telegraph as part of a joint effort to improve private exchange services.*

The Old West End charmed residents such as Joan Beaubian who remembers the warm, friendly African American community she grew up in, where "life revolved around school, neighborhood and church, especially church." Leonora Kydd Whyte, also a West Ender, was one of a small community from Bequia, an island in the Grenadines in British West Indies. The African Americans and black West Indians were one community and shared the same pews.

Standard-Times Publisher Basil Brewer estimated that in the early 1950s the city boasted "79 churches in an area ten miles by three, 53 Protestant, 23 Roman Catholic, and three synagogues."

In 1960, the biggest, grandest funeral ever held in New Bedford took place in the West End with locals and out-of-towners wiping away tears for Bishop "Daddy" Grace, a Cape Verdean immigrant who founded the House of Prayer for All People. Grace, a colorful, charismatic preacher with thousands of followers nationwide, believed God had recruited him to relieve the oppression of African Americans. Some thought him a charlatan and others were true believers of the bishop with his miracle cures, gold jewelry and fleet of cars.

The silver screen provided entertainment and a spotlight on the city. From 1948 to 1956, the city hosted at least five world premiere films, the most notable being *Down to the Sea in Ships* and *Moby Dick*, directed by John Huston who wrote the screenplay with science fiction, horror and fantasy writer Ray Bradbury. Of the three film versions of *Moby Dick* made between 1926 and 1956, Huston's stayed most faithful to Herman Melville's novel and kept its original ending. The city highlighted the premiere with several days of celebrations. Huston and the stars of *Moby Dick*, Gregory Peck and Friedrich von Ledebur, were gracious guests of the city. Residents joined in the fun and pageantry of it all.

In more infamous celebrity news, the city buzzed after the theft of the Amati Diamond. Three masked, armed men ambushed and robbed wealthy New Bedford printer Richard Coffin, owner of Coffin Press, and his wife, former Broadway showgirl Maria Patrice Amati in their palatial Dartmouth home. Her first husband was the author Damon Runyon. Two Rhode Island men served time for the crime, a third was charged but not convicted. The diamond, considered the 11th largest in the world, was never recovered.

Municipal Bathing Beach, West Rodney French Boulevard. *When New Bedford was hit by a heat wave on June 28, 1947, city dwellers cooled off in the waters of West Beach, one of the city's municipal beaches. In spite of sweltering temperatures, spirits ran high. The war was over, summer was here and the views from Clark's Cove were spectacular. In the background, the leafy trees of Hazelwood Park shaded the playground and picnic area. Visitors caught some shade in the pavilion, near the historic bathhouse built during the Depression by the WPA. Women's bathing suits were modest, mostly one-piece—not a bikini in sight—and bathing caps seemed to be mandatory. Shorter swim trunks for men were in fashion.*

During these decades, music beat deeply through the city and the lives of its people. During World War II and the post-war decades, the big band sound, jazz and popular music dominated New Bedford's music scenes from family gatherings to clubs and larger venues. Cape Verdean, Azorean, Madeiran, Portuguese, Polish and French influences found well-loved, unique musical blends and expressions. One of the favorite places to go was the Lincoln Park Ballroom just next door in Dartmouth, which featured star artists on special weekends, local bands other evenings. The ballroom was packed on dance night and many romances began and blossomed here—turning into long happy unions. Ask the old-timers in New Bedford and many will tell you their marriages began in Lincoln Park.

From 1944 to 1960, four major hurricanes slammed the city, destroying businesses and homes, swamping the fishing fleet and forcing the city to dig deep into its resiliency. Its people had to rebuild, again and again.

Hawthorn Street, looking east from Hawthorn Terrace, 1933. *In the heart of the West End's affluent neighborhood, Hawthorn Street featured large lots with splendid homes, many built by textile mill executives between 1880 and 1920. A canopy of elms shaded the thoroughfare in spring and summer until the 1944 hurricane's winds toppled most of them.*

Woodrow Wilson Hall, 1945. *Built around 1912 by the Fédération Franco Américaine, the building in 1932 was owned and sold by the Polish National Alliance to the Woodrow Wilson Club. The club operated a dance hall on the second floor between 1941 and the late 1960s. The venue regularly hosted boxing matches, concerts, theatrical performances and large functions. The International Sweethearts of Rhythm were the US's first integrated all-women band, playing swing and jazz on a national circuit. Originally composed of poor, orphaned and African American students from Piney Woods Country Life School in Mississippi, the band turned professional in 1941. On tours, especially in the South, members faced racial discrimination. After the war, it disbanded.*

Fort Rodman during WWII

Long before World War II, the US Army detected problems with existing harbor defenses. The harbor was vulnerable to aerial bombardment. Also, the seacoast guns, with their shorter range, proved no defense against naval bombardment. In 1923, the US War Department decided that the best national coastal defense would be a larger fleet or a much larger number of aircraft but that "the cheapest and most reliable defense appears to be guns and submarine mines." That year, the army decided to include Fort Rodman among the nation's permanent seacoast fortifications.

After reorganization in 1924, regular army units of Battery E, 10th Coast Artillery manned the fort's defenses. The fort continued to play a small, but important role. In the late 1920s, it hosted part of combined army and navy maneuvers to repulse a simulated enemy invasion. The defenders managed to save New England!

In 1931, in a cost-saving move, the war department abandoned several old forts, including many along the Potomac. However, it retained Fort Rodman and most others in New England. By 1934, the army faced shrinking troop rolls and neglected facilities. But in 1935, the quartermaster general undertook major repairs and improvements to Fort Rodman's buildings and grounds. The army continued to use Fort Rodman for training exercises, including monthly troop schools for reserve officers.

In September 1940, as war in Europe escalated, National Guard Coastal Artillery regiments and some regular Army Coast Artillery units were activated, and Fort Rodman received a complement of troops for the 23rd Coast Artillery. But, because the barracks and quarters were not yet completed, most enlisted men stayed in tents during the fall and early winter. In November 1940, the army constructed 24 barracks to house an additional 750 men.

Anti-aircraft gun practice, Fort Rodman, 1941. *The 23rd Coast Artillery Regiment practices loading one of the eight-inch rifles mounted on a "disappearing" retractable carriage at Battery Barton.*

During World War II, Fort Rodman acted as the linchpin in New Bedford's harbor defense. The army located supporting artillery batteries at Mishaum Point, Barneys Joy Point, Butlers Point, Cuttyhunk and Nashawena. In May 1942, as a preemptory move, Federal Bureau of Investigation agents raided the homes of 86 "enemy aliens" living near Fort Rodman. They arrested no one but confiscated shortwave radios, cameras, firearms, knives and swords, a telescope and a pair of binoculars. By mid-1942, with less need for small gun systems, the army removed most guns from the fort, leaving only Battery Milliken with two 12-inch rifles and two 155mm rifles. After the war, the 12-inch rifles were salvaged and the 155mm rifles were sent to Fort Banks in Winthrop, Massachusetts. On June 5, 1947, the army declared Fort Rodman as surplus.

In 1953, Massachusetts Maritime Academy considered, but later rejected, it as a site. As late as 1957, reserve officers of the US Army's General Command and Judge Advocate General Corps continued to take special training courses there.

Parade Drills, 23rd Coast Artillery Regiment, 1941. *Troops put on an exhibition for local residents and spectators. Beginning in March 1941, recruits held twice-weekly parade-ground demonstrations before a reviewing stand. Outside the fort, a long line of cars and spectators watch the maneuvers.*

*From **atop the southwest corner of Fort Rodman**, Privates Lucien Ouellette of Westport and Shepard Crane of Newton use flags to signal men on a nearby boat to release a target balloon.*

*In the right-hand photograph, a close-up look at a **parade drill** shows the Reserve Officers' Training Corps marching to the sound of the New Bedford High School Band and the Works Progress Administration Band. Clarence W. Arey, superintendent of music for the New Bedford school system, directed both bands.*

***The George N. Alden Ambulance Corps** crew stood by during 1943 summertime maneuvers of the State Guard. Members of Dartmouth and New Bedford Chapters of the American Red Cross served hot meals. During maneuvers, guard members learned concealment and camouflage, how to disarm an enemy and rudimentary judo. Left to right in front of the tables: Sgt. Adrian Cadieux, Joseph Ashenas, William Flood and Kip Des Ruiseau. Serving in the rear row: Mary Gifford, Ruth Babb, Florence Mosher, Estelle Oldfield, Rosalina Mello, Joseph J. Sylvia, Alouise Cheney, Oscar Braudy and Marion Viereck.*

*After troops moved into the completed quarters at the **Fort Rodman barracks** (at center of aerial photograph), abandoning their temporary winter tented quarters, garrison officers built an indoor pistol range, an outdoor rifle range and a set of baseball diamonds. Army officials also enlisted state and local governments and private groups, including the YMCA, to help provide recreational facilities for soldiers stationed at the fort.*

US Army training exercises, 1938.

Parading troops at the fort, May 1941.

George N. Alden Ambulance Corps, June 1943.

Newly-built 63-man barracks and support structures at Fort Rodman, post-June 1941.

Salvage for Victory

Scrap collection on the homefront allowed civilians to join the war effort. In October 1942, they had a chance to prove their patriotic devotion when newspapers spearheaded a nationwide metal scrap salvage campaign. The New Bedford Salvage Committee oversaw local efforts through its Permanent Salvage Campaign, the nation's first and only such program.

To motivate scrap collection, the New Bedford *Standard-Times*, *Cape Cod Standard-Times* and radio station WNBH offered cash prizes totaling $2,000 for the greatest weight of scrap metal collected by a group or a person.

Old street car rails, medals, trophies, political insignia, oil tanks, obsolete industrial equipment, scrap automobiles, steam radiators, bedsteads and iron fencing all went into the scrap heap. Boy Scouts, school children, Junior Chamber of Commerce members and other volunteers manned trucks to move the scrap. School children removed labels from old tin cans, opened them at both ends, washed them out, and jumped on them to flatten them. Post-collection processing removed the tin coating from the steel before reusing both metals.

The committee gave families donating scrap a window poster with two slogans: "We are Cooperating" and "Salvage for Victory." It wanted each household to display a poster. Families also used window cards, like those for the milkman or iceman, to tell passing junk collectors what was available.

Fire Chief Edward F. Dahill offered three old horse-drawn fire engines weighing 7,000 pounds each. The city council saved historic Cornelius Howland Steam Engine No. 4 at the request of the Veteran Firemen's Association. Students at New Bedford

Voke at work, October 1942. *New Bedford Vocational School students (from left) Norman Baron, Alfred Ramos, Arthur Burgo and Stephen Theberge dismantle obsolete steam fire engines donated by the fire department to the city scrap drive. Reclaimed brass and iron from La France-built engine No. 8 (left) and Amoskeag-built engine No. 7 (right) greatly aided the nation's war effort.*

Vocational School dismantled the other two into scrap. Other scrapped specialty items included a vintage *Standard-Times* printing press and the New Bedford jail fence.

The *Standard-Times* organized a Victory Key Campaign to recover old keys in the city and surrounding towns. The salvaged nickel and silver went into guns and gun fittings for the army and navy. Newsboys collected the keys while collecting for newspapers.

Other specialized scrap campaigns targeted surplus fats, paper, newspapers, cardboard, rags, tires and inner tubes. Junk collectors played a pivotal role in the scrap campaign. With equipment to weigh scrap and space to sort it, the junk man's job took on a newfound importance. Tire and filling stations handled rubber items.

Scrap entrepreneurs, 1943. *Licensed official scrap collector Frank Alves delivers 1 ton of paper, 150 pounds of fat, 300 pounds of rags and assorted iron to junkman Samuel H. Mirsky (with cigar). Atop the wagon, Joseph Silva hands Mirsky an iron bed rail.*

Collectors from Saint Anne's School, 1942. *Students display bed frames, tubs and a sled alongside their Brock Avenue school. In the group are Lois Almeida, Alice Laferriere, Vasco Santos, Raymond Laberge, Arthur Cadieux, Albert Aubut, Philip Roberts, Roland Choquette and Wilfred Spoor.*

A young woman with an attitude chalks *"New Bedford's Gift to the Unholy 3"* on the side of a railroad car. During wartime, the phrase "unholy three" often referred to Hitler, Mussolini and Hirohito. Typically, collectors chalked a favored destination and use for the metal gathered in the local drive. Every pound collected meant added production of airplanes, tanks, guns, ammunition and warships. During a one-day harvest in September 1942, city households contributed 28 tons of tin cans.

The **Austin Street Salvagers** proudly display opened, unlabeled and flattened tin cans. Members of the group include Eugene and Ralph Bisaillon; Sheila, Joan and Arlene Harrington; Barbara, John, Shirley and Milton Jacques; Fernanda, Hope and Natalia Sousa; William and Elizabeth Smith; Pauline, Lorraine, Paul and Donald LaJoie; Martin, Donald, Carl, Muriel and Shirley Fitchenmeyer; Philip and William Taylor; Josephine, Robert and Theodore Devlin; Raymond and Albert Sykes; George Hawkins, Bernard DePasquale, Ronald Foley, Theresa Kelly, Claire Moore, Francis Donovan, Mary Hodgins and Ronald Fisher. Raymond H. Wilcox served as adviser. For their efforts in the Standard-Times-WNBH scrap metal drive, the salvagers received War Bonds.

Members of Boy Scout Troop 1 at Saint Lawrence Martyr Church and **students of Holy Family School** load waste newspaper and cardboard. In the background stand John J. McKenna, Ernest LeTendre and Scoutmaster Edward Meaney.

"New Bedford's Gift to the Unholy 3," July 1942.

Austin Street Salvagers, September 1942.

Students of Holy Family Grammar School, July 1944.

The Home Front

With its heavy reliance on textiles and needle trades, prewar New Bedford already had one of the nation's highest rates of female labor force participation. As men went into military service and demand for war production mounted, even more women stepped in to keep New Bedford factories running. The US Employment Service appealed to them with the slogan: "This war is your war—this war is a woman's war." The state's first voluntary registration found 1,200 New Bedford women, without minor children, willing and able to work. Factories eagerly accepted these young workers with nimble fingers, but still they needed more.

From Sunday pulpits, ministers urged women parishioners to go to work. To attract mothers with small children to defense jobs, the WPA started its first Massachusetts day nursery in New Bedford. Other nurseries opened in schools and community centers.

New Bedford Vocational School offered employment training. By mid-1943, women formed more than half the city's employed. They worked on assembly lines in the city's war production factories making barrage balloons, life rafts, gas and oxygen masks, radio and electrical components, tire cords and military fabric ranging from mosquito netting to winter uniforms. As more men took higher paying jobs in the defense industry or went to war, women replaced them as taxi and truck drivers, meat cutters, fish processors, store clerks and garage mechanics.

Red Cross volunteers, 1943. *Members of the Red Cross work group of the auxiliary of La Chambre de Commerce, one of the best producing units in the state, are shown at work in their quarters in the North End's Capital Building. Organized in October 1942, by February 1943, the group of 71 women had already made 22,651 surgical pads, more than 3,000 diapers, and many sweaters, toddler sets and mittens for men and children. Seated around the table from left to right are Hermindale Marquis, Mary Fredette, Delia Provost, Marianne Barton, Armanda Despres, Amozelie Devault, Leda Boisvert, Oglare Levesque, Laura Boucher, Cora Pepin, Palmelie Jabotte, Marie Nolin, Anna Thibodeau and Alice Poirier. Standing are Clemence Gentilhomme, the director, left, and Alice Boucher, her assistant.*

War bonds salesmen, October 1944. *Drivers of the Union Street Railway Company (below) pose in front of streetcar 601—a rolling solicitation to purchase war bonds and stamps. Built by the Osgood Bradley Car Company of Worcester, the 601 entered service in 1929. During the war, it was the only car repainted red, white and blue. After victory over Japan, painters restored the Pullman-green color of the Union Street Railway.*

Mostly Women

Before the war, only men ran the hot, noisy presses at the **Acushnet Process Company**. They put uncured rubber into precision-machined molds before subjecting them to high pressure and intense steam heat. The rubber flowed, filled the molds and then cured (vulcanized) into the finished article. When men left for war or better paying defense jobs, women took over. Here, Beatrice C. Waite (center) and Lillian Ferreira (right) make nose cups, the inner "works" of a gas mask. Both women had family members fighting in the war.

Members of **New Bedford Women's Defense Corps** were trained in first aid, convoy tactics, map work and chemical warfare. They remained on call as a semi-military organization in case of emergency. In Buttonwood Park, Second Lieutenant Sarah E. Berry supervised Privates 1st Class Dorothy L. Sylvia, Mable Brais, Yvette Pruneau and Norma Banks as they examine an auto engine in preparation for a practice convoy.

North End Precinct 1B Air Raid Warden George Chabotte, Assistant Wardens Homer Darcy and Claude Heys and other wardens and messengers pose before new quarters at 386 North Front Street, 1943. Rumors of high-flying German observation planes and of German U-boats lurking off the coast in Buzzards Bay and near Newport, Rhode Island called for vigilance. As part of passive wartime defense actions, coastal residents learned to avoid betraying their presence to the enemy. Blackout drills signaled by air raid sirens conditioned residents to retreat indoors and douse all lights until the all-clear signal sounded. During the drills, no cars moved and stores' outside lights were shut off. Neighborhood air raid wardens each watched over a sector of about 500 individuals.

Wearing outdated World War I helmets and white armbands marked with a blue disc with a triangle of seven alternate red and white diagonal stripes, they walked their sectors to ensure no flicker of light escaped. Boy Scouts often accompanied wardens on their rounds. Wardens and scouts were also trained to fight incendiary bombs, dousing them with mist pumps because too much water would spread the burning magnesium.

Operating curing presses at Acushnet Process Company, 1945.

Women's Defense Corps 1942.

Air Raid wardens, 1943.

Honor & Sacrifice

New Bedford's 1947 centennial celebration commemorated the allied victory over the Axis powers with a four-hour-long July 4th parade. Touting the theme of patriotism, almost every organized city social organization sponsored a float boasting of its role in winning the last war.

Throughout the city, memorials venerate city residents of different ethnic groups who gave their lives in World War II. Seaman First Class Stephen Walt Okolski was born in 1924 in New Bedford. In 1940, he lived on 8 Viall Street with his parents. His father owned a gas station and his mother worked in a cotton mill as a speeder tender. Stephen died on December 8, 1943, the first Polish American serviceman from New Bedford to die in World War II. He is buried with more than 7,500 other Americans in Sicily-Rome American Cemetery in Nettuno, Rome, Italy. Okolski Square was dedicated in his honor on Armistice Day in the presence of his father and uncle.

A Sherman tank stands at the intersection of Mount Pleasant Street and New Plainville Road. A bronze plaque dedicated by Post 1 of the American Legion on September 16, 1956 reads: "In Memory of Technician Fifth, Norbert A. Papineau, Company C, 703 Tank Destroyer Battalion. Born Feb. 28, 1923. Killed in action in Germany Feb. 27, 1945. For love of his country and flag." Papineau was awarded a Purple Heart with Oak Leaf Cluster. He is buried with more than 6,000 other Americans in the Henri-Chapelle American Cemetery and Memorial in Liège, Belgium. Attorney Clair F. Carpenter and Lucien J. Beauregard, commander of Post 1, American Legion, rode the tank from the railroad freight yard down Belleville Avenue past Sawyer Street. Clarence C. Papineau, a World War II tank driver and Norbert's brother, drove the tank.

The "Welcome" banner hanging across Acushnet Avenue in the North End (opposite page) greeted state delegates to the first annual state conclave of the Polish American Veterans of World War II, June 10-12, 1949. Mitchell S. Janiak of New Bedford, its state commander, appears third from right atop the unit's quarters. At the conclusion of that convention, Governor

Victory Parade along Union Street during Centennial Week celebrations, 1947.

Dedication of Okolski Square at Rodney French Boulevard and Cove Street, 1947.

Tank on delivery to Papineau Square, September 1956.

Paul A. Dever presented a charter to the group, which had two chapters in New Bedford. Elsewhere, Worcester, Springfield, Lowell, Lawrence and Fall River each had one chapter.

McGee's Photo Supply on Acushnet Avenue sold all types of photo supplies, services and equipment, including cameras, projectors, enlargers and lenses. During the war, civilian photographers lived with persistent shortages. After the war, to attract potential customers, McGee's hosted traveling exhibits such as "Graflex at War" or Popular Photography magazine's salons of prize-winning photographs. McGee's also sold sporting goods including handguns, long guns and accessories. From 1940 through the early 1960s, the New Bedford Revolver & Rifle Club had a downstairs range beneath the McGee Studio.

Returning to New Bedford after 32 months in the Army Nurse Corps, nurse Dorothy Shea could not find work until she found some white stockings. None were left in New Bedford. From the end of the war until December 31, 1945, nylon stocking manufacturers focused on making war goods and produced only about 2.5 million pairs of stockings, an insignificant amount compared to prewar consumption of 35 million pairs per month. It took months to fully stock the supply chain, causing "nylon riots" throughout the country, as frustrated customers waited in lines that stretched and stretched.

Polish-American War Veterans of World War II welcome state delegates, May 1949.

Grand Opening of McGee's Photo Supply, featuring "Graflex at War" exhibit, circa 1946.

"Nylon Riots" come to New Bedford, January 1946. *Eager customers wait in line to buy scarce nylon stockings outside Cleare Weave Hosiery Store, 569 Purchase Street.*

The Hurricanes of 1944, 1954 and 1960

Four major hurricanes slammed the city over 16 years. On September 14, 1944, the Great Atlantic Hurricane rode in on an ebb tide, arriving toward dark and blowing 100 miles per hour by midnight. It caused heavy property damage but little loss of life. The storm hit after 7:35 p.m. high tide, keeping casualties low. Newspapers and radio warned residents in low-lying areas to leave their homes in time for many to seek shelter. Winds and rain washed away buildings, wrecked boats, shattered windows and ripped out trees. In New Bedford alone, the storm destroyed more than 2,500 mature trees, many of them the venerable elms that had shaded city streets. Falling trees yanked down transmission lines and crashed cables, leading to heavy losses for utilities. Winds snapped the top 225 feet of the newly erected WNBH-WFMR radio tower at Crow Island, leaving a 120-foot stub at its base.

In 1954, two Category 3 hurricanes barreled through the area. Carol, the first hurricane to be given a person's name, packed a quick but devastating punch on the morning of August 31, 1954. Beginning as a tropical storm near the Bahamas, it moved through Long Island and Southern New England before ending in Canada. It arrived here shortly after high tide, bringing with it 1.91 inches of rain. The storm surge in the upper harbor exceeded 14 feet, swamped State Pier with seven feet of water and the New Bedford-Fairhaven Bridge with five. It cluttered the shoreline from Fort Rodman to the

F. W. Woolworth Co., Purchase Street, 1944.

Coggeshall Street Bridge with boat wrecks, upturned homes, summer cottages and the debris of mills, shops and boatsheds.

Boats battered against the Coggeshall Street Bridge, knocking it out of alignment. High water smashed its bridge railings and ripped up about 15 feet of flooring on the Fairhaven side. A 20-foot boat stranded in the intersection of Coggeshall Street and Belleville Avenue blocked traffic.

At Marine Park on Pope's Island, three draggers, a large cabin cruiser and ten smaller craft came to rest. Floating wreckage smashed the bridge railings.

Carol destroyed 18 large draggers and hundreds of small and large pleasure craft. It littered Pier 3 with wrecks, but the Wharfinger Building withstood a tide 10.5 feet above normal. Water deluged the L. S. Eldridge building on Pier 4 and banged

Hurricane Carol, 1954. *View of North Water Street looking north from the foot of High Street, corner of Bridge Park and Ark Lane.*

Fishing fleet awry, 1954. *Hurricane Carol devastated the area's fishing industry. Here, the Mary J. Landry, Julia K and J. Henry Smith are flotsam piled along the New Bedford-Fairhaven Bridge abutment in Fairhaven.*

Union and North Front Streets, 1954. *At the height of the storm, water stood waist deep at the intersection. The receding tide left behind streets littered with downed power lines and shattered fragments of property.*

several draggers against the pilings. Rooftop-level water buried 30 cars on State Pier. The hurricane damaged buildings on Homer's Wharf and carried away part of a rock-and-dirt pier. Winds, water and flotsam crashed into the wharves of the Gas & Electric Light Company and the Greene and Wood Company. The waterfront suffered an estimated $10 million in damages.

Mills and factories along the river sustained $50 million in losses. Allen Beam Company at Wood Street and the New Bedford Lumber Company suffered water damage to equipment and supplies. Much of their stock floated away in the river. Acushnet Process Company had prepared for a hurricane with permanent chains and hoists above machinery that allowed crews to raise electrical equipment above flood level in four hours. Despite eight feet of water in the building, it suffered minimal losses. At Aerovox, the entire first floor flooded, damaging assembly lines and ruining raw material. More than

Fishing boats awash on Crow Island, 1954. *The hurricane smashed a dragger into the WNBH-WFMR radio tower, causing it to buckle as the station went off the air. Station engineer Leo Brunette dramatically described the incoming boat before he had to be rescued. When the waters receded, three large fishing vessels remained aground on the island: the* Mary J. Hayes, *the* Fleetwing *and the* Vivian and Fay.

100 cars bobbed in the adjacent, watery parking lot. The first-floor tenants at Fairhaven Mills measured seven feet of water at the height of the storm. Colonial Textiles Manufacturing Corporation, Whale Furniture Mart, Allied Manufacturing Company, Freedman Shoe Company and Park Motors body repair shop all endured damages. Revere Copper & Brass suffered heavy losses when water destroyed wiring, froze metal in the furnaces and swept away engineering plans, blueprints and valuable paperwork. Wamsutta Mills suffered extensive roof damage, hundreds of broken windows and widespread water losses to finished goods ready for shipping. A large roof section at Hathaway Manufacturing Company tore away, and goods and equipment were damaged. The lower floor of the cotton division flooded, ravaging spinning, weaving and cotton carding machinery. Cornell Dubilier's basement took in eight feet of water, but suffered relatively minor losses.

Carol downed at least 125 of the city's largest, historic trees and draped city neighborhoods with fallen power lines. The hurricane blew away the south side of the men's dressing room at Municipal Beach, smashed storefronts throughout the city and washed more than dozens of homes in the Cove Road area from their foundations. The winds bent roof vents at the high school, and damaged roofs at Normandin Junior High School, Roosevelt Junior High School and the Wood School. Power outages caused food spoilage in home freezers and refrigerators. Governor Christian A. Herter suspended the Blue Laws, allowing food stores to open on Sunday and on Labor Day.

Inland, the hurricane ruined nearly 40 percent of the corn crop as it leveled many fields. It destroyed the trellised and staked tomato crops and pummeled the ground with ready-to-harvest apples and peaches.

Surveying the damage at Dan's Pavilion, 1954. Destroyed by hurricane for the third time, Dan Bauer would not rebuild his popular function hall.

The New Bedford scalloper *Redstart* was lost with 11 hands, all from New Bedford and Fairhaven. The *Friendship II* sank, its crew escaping death when the dragger *Jacintha* rescued them.

Red Cross Disaster Relief, Salvation Army, Civil Defense and National Guard combined aid efforts to help. The Navy sent salvage vessels and a harbor tug to assist the Coast Guard and commercial firms to clear the harbor of sunken, grounded or stranded craft. Eleven days later, the city was still reeling from Carol but had cleared out much of the debris and begun rebuilding, repairing, rewiring and reopening, when Hurricane Edna hit. This second Category 3 storm struck on September 11, 1954, arriving during a rising tide and producing another storm surge. The mills and factories that suffered from high water during Hurricane Carol faced the same problem again, but they were better prepared. Sandbags protected mill buildings; plywood and boards covered windows; crews moved machinery out of harm's way. The utility company welded

Fishing Vessel *Clinton* lunging onto State Pier, 1954.

Battling Carol on South Water Street, 1954.

its doors shut to keep out water. Fishermen removed boats to north of the New Bedford-Fairhaven Bridge. Homeowners took down television antennas.

New Bedford airport recorded wind gusts of up to 80 miles per hour and rainfall of 3.44 inches, exceeding Hurricane Carol. Hundreds more trees were uprooted.

Although hundreds of families had moved inland from beach and waterfront properties, these buildings fortunately sustained little damage except for water. Schools were ready to welcome refugees, Bishop Charles M. Grace opened the House of Prayer for All People for refugees, and the Red Cross shipped 800 cots and blankets to New Bedford. But Edna caused far less damage than feared.

After the season's double blow, dozens of fishermen left New Bedford for safer ports or gave up fishing entirely, reducing the fleet by more than a third. In the aftermath, Richard B. Young and representatives of 35 other industries located on the banks of the Acushnet River formed a Hurricane Committee. Helped by Senators Kennedy and Saltonstall, they lobbied the US Army Corps of Engineers to protect the city from future hurricanes. Completed In 1972, the hurricane dike stretched a 4,500-foot barrier across the harbor's entrance.

On September 12, 1960, Hurricane Donna struck. Having dropped to a Category 2 storm, it brought only 0.76 inches of rain, but came shortly after 5 p.m. with whipping winds exceeding 90 miles per hour. More than 650 people had already

South Water Street, 1960. *In the wake of Hurricane Donna, children improvise a new playground near the intersection with Grinnell Street.*

been evacuated to Red Cross shelters. By midafternoon, 15-foot waves crashed onto East Rodney French Boulevard. Fallen trees and live wires closed many streets, leaving thousands without power or telephones.

Donna tore off a large section of the wooden roof at the Kilburn Mill Building on West Rodney French Boulevard. The front of Mello's Market on Howland Street collapsed and crashed almost to the street, held up only by utility wires. Only a few people suffered minor injuries, however.

Private Hermano P. Vieira Square, Orchard Street and Cove Road, 1960.

Industry at Midcentury

World War II gave a badly needed boost to city firms, with defense contracts creating thousands of jobs. But by 1949, with the war boom over, New Bedford was again struggling to attract new industrial firms and the jobs they would bring.

The Industrial Development Legion and Industrial Development Division had neglected New Bedford's best interests, local politicians claimed, because their members feared competition and pressure to raise wages. On August 23, 1949, in a new initiative, the state legislature authorized the New Bedford Industrial Development Commission (IDC) to promote and develop industries. In 1952, when the commission failed to get a quorum, Mayor Edward C. Peirce took control. He appointed the city solicitor, assistant solicitor and two of his secretaries to the IDC and moved its headquarters to his office.

The business community tried to organize a rival group, the New Bedford Industrial Plan Inc., but with little support, the effort collapsed. After Mayor Peirce left office, the IDC returned to normal. It regularly issued glowing reports listing jobs created by the new firms it had attracted to the city and hinted at other planned relocations to New Bedford. The *Standard-Times* found the reports exaggerated, with half the firms having folded, others threatening to close and still others never having had any contact with the IDC. Although politicians claimed newspaper bias, the mayor reorganized the IDC.

In yet another effort to attract companies to the industrial park, the New Bedford Industrial Foundation was formed in 1955. Its executive committee and board of trustees comprised members with extensive professional and community service records. Gladys Reynolds Savoie joined the board in September 1955 as its first female member—all 170 others were men.

Tying coiled copper sheeting at Revere Copper & Brass, 1954.

The foundation appointed Boston real estate broker R. M. Bradley Co. as its exclusive agent. The industrial park had plots for modern, one-story facilities with easy access to roadways, and its far North End site was touted to be "45 minutes from Boston." By 1959, electrical machinery maker J. C. Mendes Company became the park's first occupant. The Trimount Plastics Company, a lamination firm, soon followed.

The foundation followed the model of the Massachusetts Development Corporation (MDC), organized in 1953 to promote the state's business prosperity. In 1955, the MDC

View of Berkshire Hathaway Mills along Griffin Street, 1957. *In the twentieth century, as the city's other mills closed or went south, Hathaway Mills kept investing to become a modern, state-of-the-art textile company. In 1955, Hathaway Manufacturing merged with Berkshire Fine Spinning Associates to become a conglomerate of New England mills that accounted for about 25 percent of the nation's fine cotton textile production. Headquartered in Providence, Berkshire held several Fall River subsidiaries including the King Philip, Border City, Bourne, Luther and Sagamore Mills. The new company, with 12,000 employees in 15 plants, became known as Berkshire Hathaway and moved its headquarters to Cove Street in New Bedford. Malcolm Chace Jr., a descendent of the founder of the Valley Falls Company, became general manager. Hathaway's Seabury Stanton became its president.*

brought the National Silver Company to New Bedford with a $600,000 loan to cover moving expenses from Muncie, Indiana. National Silver took over part of the Nashawena Mills.

Despite these efforts, the city lost 13 percent of its manufacturing jobs from 1950 to 1960. With the closure of the Wamsutta Mills and most North End cotton and silk mills, 4,278 jobs in textiles and apparel were lost. The repeated efforts to bring firms to New Bedford merely replaced lost jobs. In the 1960 census, the city counted only seven more manufacturing jobs than it had in 1940.

The city's oldest industrial neighborhood, formerly called Willis Point, now known as North Terminal, March 1957. *In August 1958, owners of Wamsutta Mills announced a shutdown to move operations to Lyman, South Carolina as a way to confront overseas competition. With Wamsutta's departure went 950 jobs despite an appeal by officials of the AFL-CIO Textile Workers Union of America to President Dwight Eisenhower asking him to intercede to keep the 110-year old mill in operation. Revere Copper & Brass appears at right.*

From Textiles to Apparel

After World War II, the city's traditional textile industry declined. As factories closed, few jobs remained in yarn and fabric mills or in dyeing and finishing woven textiles. From 1940 to 1960, combined employment in those sectors fell 70 percent from 12,950 workers to 3,857.

In contrast, the city's apparel industry provided a bright spot. Small manufacturers made dresses, shirts, pajamas and suits—many of them top of the line. Industrial development boosters had lured several companies from New York City and Pennsylvania, heralding low-cost mill space and low-wage, often non-unionized, workers. From 1940 to 1960, employment in the city's needle trades shot up 175 percent from 2,204 jobs to 6,063. While overall the city lost jobs, women's employment climbed with the shift from textiles to apparel. Traditionally, women made up less than half of textile laborers. From 1940 to 1960, however, women took 75 percent of the new jobs in needle trades.

Looms from Wamsutta Mills bound for the South, 1958. *In August 1954, Leon Lowenstein and Sons bought a controlling interest in the Wamsutta Mills. Less than four years later, it announced its closure. Much of its machinery and equipment went south to other Lowenstein operations.*

Berkshire Hathaway, 1945. *In preparing to weave cloth, the warping process takes place. Simply put, the warp tender properly fills and guides the correct number of threads onto the warp (or loom) beam. Warp and weft form a simple crisscross pattern. Each weft thread crosses over one warp thread, then under the next, and so on. As the warp is drawn from the beam, the weft is thrown across it by a means of a bobbin-filled shuttle. Warp tender Diolinda Baroa handles the warping process. To her left, large metal carriages called creels hold spools of yarn destined to become warp threads. A machine called the warper head aligns and guides those threads onto a warp beam that will go on the loom and gradually unroll during weaving.*

Apparel Industries

In 1949, Nathan Lissak, owner of Brockton shoe manufacturer **Lissak and Company**, sought to expand production. Frank Leary, head of the Industrial Development Division of the New Bedford Board of Commerce, helped him explore New Bedford options. Lissak planned to employ between 200 and 300 in his New Bedford plant, and the former Royal Shoe Company in the Fairhaven Mill on Sawyer Street suited his needs.

In 1950, **Cameo Curtains** opened a New Bedford subsidiary, in part to be closer to its main supplier of material, Hathaway Mills. Cameo, founded in New York in the mid-1920s by David Rosenberg, occupied an important niche in fabricated textiles. Company officials noted their product needed "a highly skilled and intelligent workforce," which New Bedford had in abundance.

Cameo installed a large, modern facility occupying 200,000 square feet of space in the Whitman Mills building, formerly occupied by Stokely Brothers and Company, on the riverfront between Manomet Street and Coffin Avenue. It repaired and reconditioned floors, plumbing and lighting and hired 500 workers. Less than a year later, business surged when Cameo—which already had a government contract to produce insect netting—received a defense contract to make cargo parachutes, creating 500 new jobs. In 1955, the company consolidated all of its manufacturing in New Bedford, and soon claimed that it was the nation's largest curtain and drapery manufacturer under one roof.

Sewing uppers at Lissak Shoe Co., 1953.

Hemming curtains at Cameo Curtains, 1958.

Shortly after World War I, Jacob Palestine joined Charles and Max Siegal to establish what became one of the largest boys' clothing makers in New York—**Monarch Wash Suit Company**. With help from Mark Duff, who had been lobbying New York manufacturers to come to New Bedford and rent vacant mill space for pennies per square foot, the Monarch partners moved their business into the Taylor Shoe Company building on North Water Street. Monarch specialized in men's and boys' clothing. In 1935, the Palestine and Siegal families split to form their own companies. The Siegals kept the Monarch name and moved into the Fairhaven Mills in 1930. In the late 1930s they relocated into the Nonquitt Mills on Belleville Avenue and were joined by Frank Anapol. In 1940, the company was renamed **Calvin Clothing** after Charles Siegal's teenage son.

Meanwhile, Lester and William Palestine opened Ethan Ames Mfg., makers of men's and boys' outerwear, in the National Spun Silk plant on Brook and Deane Streets. In 1948, they opened Arlans, one of the first factory outlets in New England. Arlans later evolved into a discount department store and became a national chain with more than 100 stores.

In 1951, Frank Anapol left Calvin to start Youth Craft—later renamed Cliftex Corporation.

Monarch Wash Suit Company, 1946. Josephine Kravates stitches facing on garment.

Home from the war. In January 1946, three veterans press boys' suits at Monarch Wash Suit Company. From left are Roger Chase, Ernest Pacheco and Alex Kalife, foreman.

Examining aviator oxygen masks, 1942.

George Amaral, Omer Breton and Roique De Cotis compound rubber sheets in mill room, 1953.

A press with open mold ready to remove cured rubber parts, 1955.

Acushnet Process Company

After purchasing its New Bedford factory, Acushnet Process immediately began equipping it to produce the gas masks and hoses the company developed in conjunction with the Chemical Warfare Service's Edgewood Arsenal. By 1942, the plant employed 2,300 people. It lacked the room and manpower to assemble the masks, so it concentrated on producing parts and the army contracted the assembly to others.

In addition to mask parts, Acushnet produced critical parts for aircraft engines made by the three significant pre-war manufacturers: Pratt & Whitney, Allison Engine and Wright Aeronautical. With Harvard Medical School, Acushnet developed a better oxygen mask for Allied fliers. The new masks replaced leaky, uncomfortable ones that prevented fliers from reaching higher altitudes than their German counterparts. Together with Polaroid, Acushnet also developed a goggle that solved a hazardous problem with earlier oxygen masks, which left space between the mask and the aviator's leather helmet, leading to injury or blindness should a plane's engine get shot and hot oil stream back.

By war's end, Acushnet had almost 3,000 employees. As government contracts slowed, the company returned to making high-end rubber products including rings, seals, gaskets, rubber suspensions and windshield wipers. Conversion proceeded slowly as new molds needed to be machined. It worked closely with automakers to supply rubber parts used in automobiles. Once the government released access to rubber sources, Acushnet also returned to making golf balls to meet a pent-up demand. In 1957, Acushnet expanded still more, opening a 60,000-square-foot addition to its New Bedford plant, the first industrial structure built in the city since the Depression. In 1959, it bought a three-story vacant building, the former Manomet Mills at Belleville and Riverside Avenues, from the Rayon Company.

Acushnet always bought additional space at low cost. According to Dick Young, President of the company from 1955 to 1978, "It makes more sense to me to spend money on people and equipment than on space."

Aerovox Corp. & Cornell Dubilier

The city helped retrain textile workers for Aerovox Corporation, the first electronics plant to relocate to New Bedford. Aerovox produced electronic capacitors and electrical components. By 1938, it was one of the top two US condenser suppliers. Its Brooklyn plant had just survived a prolonged strike when Industrial Development Legion representatives approached company management about moving operations to New Bedford. On learning of the move, local CIO organizers leafleted, accusing Aerovox of running away from the Brooklyn union.

The company bought the empty Nashawena Mill B on Belleville Avenue in the North End, where it set up its research and development, test lab, manufacturing, warehousing and customer service operations. It remained strike- and union-free here—perhaps, labor leaders complained, because labor organizers seeking jobs at Aerovox seemed to fail training courses or fall short of efficiency standards too often.

One electronics manufacturer in New Bedford attracted another. In 1940, Cornell Dubilier Electronics, already operating in New York, New Jersey and Washington State, opened a plant in part of the former Butler Mill on East Rodney French Boulevard. During the early 1940s, the company mobilized almost 4,000 employees to support the war effort, supplying capacitors and other electrical components to allied forces. By 1950, Cornell Dubilier was the nation's largest maker of alternating current, high-voltage, mica and aluminum electrolytic capacitors. In later years, keeping pace with technological changes, it pioneered products for television, computer, aerospace and utilities.

From the late 1940s until the 1970s, Aerovox and Cornell Dubilier used polychlorinated biphenyls (PCBs) as electric fluids in transformers and capacitors. During this time, accidental and illegal dumping of these long-lasting, toxic chemicals—banned by the US government in 1979—contaminated the plant sites and New Bedford Harbor, which is now a federal Superfund cleanup site.

Cornell Dubilier, 1960. *Helen Knowles inspects air conditioner capacitors on overhead conveyor.*

Cornell Dubilier, 1960. *Edith Jones on drawing press, drawing metal into varied size cans.*

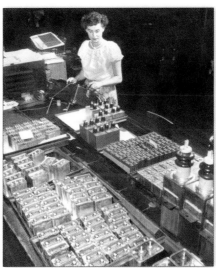

Aerovox Corporation, 1954. *Individually testing capacitors for shorts, opens and leakage.*

Aerovox Corporation, 1954. *Beverley deCosta gives a final check on capacitor prior to boxing.*

Aerovox Corporation, 1949. *Workers individually position elements on early circuit boards.*

Old and New Industries

Local industry stalled again after the initial World War II economic boost. Yet, in 1945, the reopened Fisk and **Firestone** tire factories could not find enough skilled workers and turned to the War Manpower Commission to draft textile workers from jobs making fine cotton to fill needed jobs in their tire fabric mills. When many older men and women draftees refused, claiming they lacked stamina for the heavy lifting job, the case went to adjudication. The Kilburn Mill offered its surplus capacity to produce the needed fabric, but the war board declined. Members of the War Manpower Commission later regretted having first used the civilian draft in heavily union-organized New Bedford.

Firestone closed in 1949, but in 1952, reopened its subsidiary **Firestone Defense Products**, which made 155mm artillery shells for self-propelled howitzers and field guns. During the Cold War, it alternated between periodic artillery contracts and plant mothballing under the Industrial Mobilization Planning Program.

During the war, **Goodyear** reopened its plant to make barrage balloons and life rafts. After World War II, it expanded into roofing products, rubberized fabrics and rubber sheet goods. Goodyear also promoted nylon-reinforced bicycle tires to newsboys in ads showing shiny new bikes with newspaper-filled baskets. It hyped the tires to the carriers—and their parents—by stressing that tough treads gave longer wear, a better grip and quicker, safer stops. During the war, it developed a puncture-sealant technology for bullet-proof gas tanks used in military vehicles and airplanes. The technology later evolved into the Goodyear Lifeguard Safety Inner Tube, which sealed its own punctures and protected against blowouts. In the early 1950s, Goodyear, claiming a 100,000-mile life for the self-sealing inner tubes, touted them as reusable. It urged buyers to take them out of worn-out tires and put them into new ones.

Meanwhile, the **New Bedford Cordage Company** continued to produce manila rope. Through the 1950s, it supplied the city's resurgent fishing industry and also filled occasional government contracts.

Worker stacking 155mm artillery casings at Firestone Defense Products Division, 1954.

William E. Costello lays uncured rubber in double bicycle tire mold, Goodyear, 1946.

Readying ovens to cure bullet-proof, self-sealing gas tanks, Goodyear Rubber Company, 1944.

Spinning fibers into yarn, step one in making rope, New Bedford Cordage Company, 1953.

With the push to diversify the city's industrial base, spinning and weaving cotton ceded ground to related industries. These included making silk, rayon and vinyl cloth, printing fabric and dyeing thread. However, all proved fleeting.

In 1939, George Joblon opened **Normandy Print Works** in Fall River. It hand-screened fabrics on small tables. With quality, reliability and Joblon's ingenuity, it became the nation's largest hand-screen printing company. In June 1941, enticed by the Industrial Development Legion, it expanded and relocated to East Rodney French Boulevard. During World War II, Normandy designed camouflage prints for the military and produced flags, draperies, scarves and women's apparel. Expanding into fabric dyeing and finishing during the 1950s, it bought roller-printing equipment and developed a special process to dye and print acetate knits. It closed in early 1959 and **Brittany Dyeing & Printing** later bought the business.

Coaters began in the early 1930s to make artificial leather for industrial and commercial use. After steady growth, it moved from its original location on Potter Street into part of the former Soule Mills located on Nash Road. It remained a relatively small operation.

In 1930, the **Kilburn Spinning Mill** closed No. 2 Mill to reduce costs and overhead. In 1931, the board authorized its sale, but an increased demand for combed cotton led them to electrify the mill instead and reopen it in 1934. Formerly, the steam-driven mill had generated its own electricity from the mill boilers. Electrification saved the cost of boiler operation for small power loads. During the early 1950s, Kilburn sold both mills, the office building, warehouse, machine shop, dye house and power houses and land, moving the machinery to a plant in the South. The new owners used the buildings to produce surgical dressing packages, sheets, pillowcases and other cotton goods.

At Normandy Print Works, workers mix and prepare dyes before printing, 1941.

Manuel C. Mello and Joseph Perry inspect rolls of vinyl cloth at Coaters, Inc., 1954.

Heat welding fiberglass screening at the Soule Mills, 1957.

Workers vat dye rolls of thread under high heat and pressure at Kilburn Spinning Mills, 1946.

Old, New and Renewed Industries

The city's efforts to relocate small industries in vacant mills brought **Cape Cod Ladder Manufacturing Company** to the Grinnell Mill building on North Front Street. The company made lightweight wooden extension ladders sold under the name Endura and carried a complete line of scaffolding. In 1940, owner Arnold E. Dahlberg patented an extension ladder locking mechanism.

In 1955, **National Silver** moved from Brooklyn, NY into the vast, single-story former Nashawena Mills weave shed. Attracted by lower wages and a loan of $600,000 from the Massachusetts Development Corporation, it planned to employ 1,000 to make stainless steel flatware and kitchenware. In the photo at top left, Carl Federico of Brooklyn supervises the installation of two blanking presses by Kenneth W. Allen and Arthur R. Phillips.

Founded in 1941, **Modern Venetian Blinds Company** set up shop in the former Booth Mill weave shed on East Rodney French Boulevard. It originally produced slatted, wooden Venetian blinds but over time became the nation's largest producer of steel and aluminum blinds. In 1951, it began rolling and selling its own strip steel. Charles W. Smith, a metallurgical research engineer, helped develop the rolling mill, which rolled metal to the thinness of gum wrapper foil. In 1952, Smith and the owners of Modern Venetian Blinds founded **Rodney Metals** to roll steel for the manufacture of Venetian blinds and also for use in the aircraft and electronic industries. In the mid-1950s, Rodney was the only rolling metal mill in the world capable of turning out mirror-bright, annealed, stainless steel in a wide thin format. By the late 1950s, Modern's blind business had fallen off, but Rodney Metals' metal producing division boomed.

By 1947, **Bay State Furniture Company** had moved into the Fairhaven Mills on Coggeshall Street. Domenico F. Russo, who came here from New York City, was president of the small family enterprise. The Russos, including Morris and Joseph, also operated Colonial Textile Manufacturing Company and Ideal Ladies Undergarment Company out of the Fairhaven Mills. All three companies lasted only a few years.

National Silver, 1955.

Cape Cod Ladder Company, 1956.

Rodney Metals, 1958.

Bay State Furniture Company 1948.

Several firms that had been owned by local families for generations continued their work in New Bedford. At top left, Herbert F. Pittsley of the **Weeden Manufacturing Company** assembles the company's signature toy steam engines. Founded in New Bedford by William M. Weeden in 1883, it initially produced various tinplate household items. In 1884 in the Youth's Companion magazine, it introduced the Weeden No. 1 Steam engine as "a new and great premium for boys." Weeden made more than a hundred models of toy steam engines until it ceased operations in 1952—a year the company produced more than 8,000 engines.

Chester Golas, tap thread grinder at **Morse Twist Drill**, performs a quality control check using an innovative machine developed there in 1955. It allowed for closer grinding tolerances. Called the Vectormatic Thread Grinder, it revolutionized the method of making taps, leading to smoother finishes, reduced friction and less binding.

Members of the extended Gundersen family came to New Bedford in the 1880s. Trained as glass blowers in their native Norway, several generations found ready employment at Pairpoint Company. During the Depression, Pairpoint's sales of fancy, handmade pieces tumbled, so in 1938, its buildings and equipment were liquidated. Isaac N. Babbit bought it and Robert Gundersen reorganized the company to produce handblown glassware under the name **Gundersen Glass Works** Inc. His nephew, Frederick Gundersen, uses a glass-blowing pipe to shape molten glass.

In 1954, **Continental Screw Company** celebrated its 50th anniversary. Founded in 1904 by Patrick Sweeney, it built a reputation for creative engineering and exceptional quality control. It expanded from a small plant near the waterfront to one that employed more than 1,000. It produced almost 2,000,000 different types and sizes of screws, bolts, rivets and special fasteners. Shown at right, Frank Wicherski watches flames shooting out from a gas-fed, heat-treating furnace into which screws will be loaded for hardening.

Weeden Manufacturing Company, 1952.

Morse Twist Drill Company, 1955.

Frederick Gundersen of Gundersen Glassworks, 1953.

Frank Wicherski at Continental Screw Company, 1954.

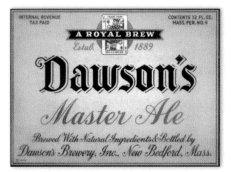
Bottle label, 1939.

Bottle label, 1933.

Home Brew

New Bedford's two breweries closed during Prohibition but reopened after March 22, 1933, when President Franklin Roosevelt signed the Cullen-Harrison Act into law. This law permitted the manufacture and sale of beer with a low alcoholic content of 3.2 percent. English-born Benjamin Dawson opened a small grocery store in 1868. It prospered, and by 1882, Dawson began selling wholesale and retail domestic and imported wines and spirits. In 1897, his son Joseph joined as partner in the newly renamed Benjamin Dawson & Son. Together, they built one of New England's largest breweries on Brook Street, producing and bottling beer, lager, ale, porter and cider under the Dawson brand. As Prohibition loomed, Dawson closed the brewery in 1919. He died shortly thereafter. His son continued making ice.

After Prohibition, hoping to satisfy a new, long unmet market for legal beer, Benjamin Rockman bought and reopened **Dawson's Brewery Inc**. It began shipping 3.2 percent beer on June 29 1933. After Prohibition's repeal in December 1933, Dawson's product line expanded. Rockman's nephew Samuel Brown managed the brewery for 35 years. It held out as the last independent Massachusetts brewery until 1978, when it was sold and then closed.

Filling and labeling bottles at Dawson Brewery, May 1954. Foreman Zygie Kwiatkowski checks the labeling process as Armand Mitchel and Wilfred Cote keep watch at their machines and Mitchell Stefanik packs the bottles into cases.

In the mid-1890s, brothers Joseph T. and James F. Smith opened a wholesale and retail distributor for whiskies, beers and ales on Purchase Street. Around 1903, they added a brewery located on Coggeshall Street at the railroad track as an adjunct to their liquor distribution business.

Forced to close by Prohibition, the brewery resumed operation in 1933 as **Smith Brothers Inc**. Until it closed in 1951, Smith Brothers produced several lines of beer, stout, ale, porter and bock. The brewery was razed after a fire in 1961.

Both breweries had a political edge. Ben Dawson, founder of Dawson's, served four terms on the city council and two terms on the board of aldermen. Jim Smith never held office but was active politically, usually on the opposite side of an issue from Dawson. People used a common question to determine political leanings: "What are you—Dawson or Smith Brothers?"

Smith Brothers Brewery, 1947. The brewery stood at the northeast corner of Coggeshall and Purchase Streets. In the foreground at the city's Purchase Street reservoir, firefighters and New Bedford Protecting Society members test pumps and hoses.

Old Colony Transportation Company, 1960. *George Vigeant Sr., left, company president and treasurer, chats with safety director Joseph Rita at the company terminal, 56 Prospect Street.*

Fish Transport Company, Pope's Island, circa 1960.

Transport Services

New Bedford once had a stalwart trucking industry. In 1940, three companies employed 310 as drivers, mechanics and schedulers. By 1982, all three companies were gone.

In 1936, Harvard Business School-trained George Vigeant Sr. bought the old New Bedford Transport Company. He continued acquiring regional transport firms, including Gurney Transport, Connors Transport, Foster Transport, Albany-Amsterdam Express, Lincoln Motor Express and J. J. Sullivan of Springfield. In 1944, Vigeant consolidated his holdings into the **Old Colony Transportation Company**. This new firm operated east-west, short-haul lines between New England and New York. By 1977, Old Colony had more than 750 employees and operated 150 trucks, 400 tractors and 700 trailers. Unfavorable economic conditions and two successive years of losses forced it to close in 1978.

Max Finkel founded the **Fish Transport Company** in 1934. His company trucked fish and cranberries from Massachusetts and Rhode Island to New York and Philadelphia. The Interstate Commerce Commission initially limited its return trips to carrying malt beverages but later authorized it to carry general commodities including wire, cables, meat and fishing supplies. The Fish Transport Company grew to employ 125 men in four states. In 1958, faced with an unauthorized strike, Finkel dissolved the firm.

In 1910, Irish immigrant Joseph Hemingway founded a transport company with two horse-drawn wagons. In 1913, the company acquired its first truck. By 1976, **Hemingway Brothers Interstate Trucking Company** had a fleet of 3,000 motor vehicles operating in nine states. The company, whose slogan was "A Whale of a Company," had 17 terminals strategically located across its service area, including a main terminal with 40 truck bays on Dartmouth Street. Shrinking freight markets coupled with a drivers' strike led to its closing in June 1982.

Hemingway Brothers Interstate Trucking Co., circa 1958. *The yard on Dartmouth Street near Rockdale Avenue is the current site of Stop & Shop.*

St. Luke's Hospital, 1942–1960

St. Luke's Hospital extended its community health care with funding from many sources. In 1943, the hospital trained 107 new nurses using a wartime grant from the United States public health service. In 1944, the Lumbard Volunteers, named for New Bedford philanthropist Anna M. Lumbard who helped establish the hospital at the turn of the century, opened a shop to raise funds. Proceeds improved the children's ward at the hospital with inhalators, resuscitators and oxygen tents for young patients with respiratory difficulties. In 1951, Henrietta Sylvia Ann Howland Green Wilks, daughter of financier Hetty Green, left a million dollars to St. Luke's Hospital in her will and the same amount to Massachusetts General Hospital.

During the polio epidemic that took 434 lives in the state, New Bedford lost seven residents from 1949 to 1960. The hospital saved many more afflicted with the illness using technologies such as the iron lung to assist breathing. Patients spent a week or more in the iron lung until lung paralysis abated.

In 1950, the health care industry in the city accounted for a mere 2.3 percent of the city's employment but that was soon to change as health care services continued to grow. In a preview of future developments, hospital employment alone grew by 44 percent during the next decade, while the city's overall employment fell by 4,645 jobs or more than 10 percent.

The delivery room. *At left, RN Lorraine Reed assists Dr. Gabriel Iskander, resident specialist in obstetrics and gynecology, in performing a Caesarean section, September 1956. At right, student nurse Jean Lowell holds a newborn at the nursery window while an anxious father looks on, November 1947.*

Volunteer soda jerks, Lumbard Shop, April 1948. *Lumbard board members Claire Izmirian and Caroline S. Goodwin serve ice cream to Shirley Lazarus of St. Luke's Hospital's Medical Social Service Department and student nurses Pauline Herbert (first year) and Dorothy Gracia (third year).*

Saint Luke's Hospital, 1946. *This southwest view of the hospital campus from above Hawthorn Street shows most of the original buildings and early additions. Many of these structures were removed during renovations in the 1950s, and most were gone by the mid 1960s. Two buildings that remain today are the horseshoe-shaped White House at center (though its wings have been clipped) and the outpatient building next door.*

In 1945, St. Luke's sent out its first complete **class of cadet graduates**. They are, first row left to right: Rose Languerand, Elena Rodrigues, Virginia Barney, Eileen Rett, Wanda Rymszewicz, Alma Nelson, Corrine Legg and Ruth Baxter. Second Row: Gladys Kirby, Ethel Viera, Bernice LaRocque, Catherine O'Neill, Florence Brady, Rita Romanowicz, Phyllis Seemenski and Helen Durant. Third Row: Margaret Tighe, Catherine Maguire, Patricia Clarke, Elinor McLeod, Marion Aseley, Lucille Andrews and Linda Payson. Fourth Row: Catherine Hartley, Louise Baldwin, Helen Tighe, Martha Winterbottom, Virginia Richmond, Supt. Annie Rogers, Mildred McCarthy, Mary Louise Sullivan and Lois Morgan.

As the number of polio cases in the city spiraled upward after World War II from one in 1945, to five in 1946, and ten in 1947, nurses and students felt the need to learn the particulars of the hospital's new **iron lung**. They are, standing left to right: Edythe Cormier, Marguerite Moore, Lois Mahan, Phyllis Madsen, Shirley Rhodes, Betsey Lord, Marie D'Alessandro, Elizabeth Muhlberger and Dorothy Poole. Seated left to right are: Beverly White, Gloria Michaud, Lois Hunter, Irene Park and Therese Farland.

Outpatients sitting or standing in the waiting room at St. Luke's represent a true cross section of the city's population. By 1938, it reported more than 40,000 patient visits. In this 1955 photo, the patients' composition clearly reflects the city's postwar baby boom.

First class of cadet nurses from St. Luke's Hospital School, May 1945.

Demonstration of iron lung to nursing students at St. Luke's Hospital, November 1947.

Waiting to be seen at Outpatient Services, May 1955.

New Bedford's Fishing Industry during World War II

Like most businesses during World War II, New Bedford's fishing fleet embraced a duty to support the war effort, which often strained its resources. It lost men as fishermen enlisted in the armed services, joined the Merchant Marine Reserve or took higher paying defense jobs. It lost ships as the navy requisitioned the port's largest trawlers to sweep for or to lay mines along the coast. Although boat owners sometimes complained of fishing crew shortages and of delays in buying and refitting replacement vessels caused by late payments from the navy, the fleet stood ready to aid the war effort.

Winnifred Martin, one of the few female boat owners in New Bedford at the time, told the *New York Times* that the port was "on call" as the nation readied for war:

> That ship has been sold to the government as a mine sweeper, as has another one that is now in drydock. More than 10 fishing boats have already been purchased, and our entire fleet of 24 large boats registered out of New Bedford is on call…. All of these vessels that are 10 years old or less are now recorded with the government for that purpose.

D. N. Kelley & Son and Peirce & Kilburn, two local shipyards, performed many of the conversions.

Maintenance suffered during the war, as ship owners could not readily get materials. High-grade manila nets from England became scarce due to the wartime danger of crossing the Atlantic. The war effort also monopolized copper and other metals needed for specialized paints used to protect boats. The navy also had priority on marine engines and parts, restricting repairs for fishing boats. And while commercial boats were given extra fuel, they had to deal with food rations for grub on fishing trips. In April 1945, when the Office of Price Administration (OPA) denied extra food rations, crews of nine fishing vessels refused to buy supplies for their trips on the black market and remained in port.

The navy refused to put guns on fishing boats. Captains were expected to radio in locations of German warships but were restricted from contacting shore regarding market conditions, navigation aids and weather updates. The OPA, which set ceiling prices for wholesale fish, favored New Bedford by setting prices for all ports based on Boston prices, the highest in New England. But fishermen clashed with fish buyers, at times claiming the buyers got the better part of profits. In 1943, to protest low OPA prices, fishermen in New York, Boston and New Bedford refused to go out. In July, New Bedford tied up 40 boats in port as another 30 were undergoing refitting and repairs.

The heart of New Bedford's fishing port, City Piers 3 and 4, circa 1958

Although somewhat restricted by rationing and price controls, the nation needed fish to feed soldiers and civilians. Both the quantity and the value of fish landed in New Bedford increased during the war. The prosperity that followed World War II pushed the port of New Bedford past Boston and Gloucester to become the East Coast's leading fishing port. With a spectacular rise in value, sea scallops brought in half the value of all seafood landings in New Bedford. The increases in yellowtail flounder landings and values pushed New Bedford over the top.

Good Fishing after the War

New Bedford's natural and man-made assets fostered its post-war success in fisheries. Its harbor, shaped by whaling over the previous 150 years, was the closest and best-equipped port for boats fishing on Georges Bank and in the Great South Channel between Nantucket and New York—two of the most productive fishing grounds in the world.

In the 1920s and 1930s, fishing industry pioneers developed and equipped New Bedford groundfish boats with the most advanced trawl net and winch system to catch cod, haddock and flounder Fishermen from Karmøy and other islands off

Fish processing. *Standing at a chute in the fillet house, workers sort the mixed lot of flounder, grouping them by size and species, 1949. At right, Danny Silva, a skilled fish cutter at Coastal Fisheries on South Second Street works his knife between skin and flesh, resulting in a boneless, skinless fillet, 1956.*

Norway who had settled in Brooklyn moved to New Bedford in the mid-1930s for closer access to the scallop grounds. When they found that trawl nets passed over most of the scallops on the ocean bottom, they developed a large dredge, 10 to 15 feet wide, to rake scallops into a chain bag. The New Bedford dredge, still used today, proved efficient at catching scallops and

Icing-up, 1941. *Crushed ice made in New Bedford is hosed directly into storage pens in the ship's hold. Shoreside industries such as ice manufacturing increased the port's importance as boats from smaller ports had to come to New Bedford to ice-up. Once here, they bought provisions.*

Gutting haddock aboard ship, 1945. *Gutting haddock without gloves was no fun. Bits of crushed shell and grit in the fish guts got between fingers and irritated the skin, a condition nicknamed "haddock rash."*

flounder that tended the bottom, especially yellowtail flounder, which New Bedford fishermen called "scallops with eyes."

The fishing industry took off, and by 1945, the port had become an industry leader. By 1948, there were 1,400 fishermen working on 265 vessels and 13 companies handling fish on the city docks. Some 27 filleting companies employed 550 people and there were 6 freezer companies, a fish auction, 3 fish canneries, 4 ice plants, 8 fishing gear supply houses, 5 shipyards and 6 machine shops. The city was among the top 10 ports in the nation in 1946.

Cooperation between fishermen and boat owners strengthened the port. In 1941, the Seafood Producers Association, representing the boat owners, and the Atlantic Fishermen's Union set up fish and scallop auctions in the city, which sold almost all of the fish landed in the port. Unlike the Boston auction where buyers bid on specific quantities of fish by species, New Bedford owners auctioned off entire boatloads. The auction was also limited by time. A bell rang 22 minutes into the auction, and the highest bidder at that time got the boatload. Bidding began leisurely and escalated just before the end, when a frenzy of bids filled the air as buyers shouted their offers.

Captains, many of whom were also boat owners, could belong to both organizations, which encouraged relatively harmonious contract negotiations. Captains often sat across from each other at the bargaining table. Union contracts limited quantities that could be landed per fishing trip, set minimums for time spent ashore between trips and forbade Sunday port departures. Seafood buyers saw these as a means of limiting supply to raise prices. They brought several anti-trust complaints against the union and owners, finally succeeding in winning a judgment against these practices in 1955. Both organizations were fined, and provisions restricting catch limits per trip and leaving port were stricken from the contract.

Little marketing was done in the early days of the fishing industry. But in the 1950s, New Bedford's Fishermen's Union and Seafood Producers started a marketing fund. Boats donated a small percentage of the catch to convince consumers to buy

Scallop fishermen returning home in New Bedford, circa 1958.

scallops. John Linehan, manager of the Seafood Producers in those days, recalled running a marketing campaign in Hartford. "We found out that the sale of scallops in the greater Hartford area increased, probably an 80 percent increase," he said. "So with those numbers, I was able to go back to our members and say, if we spend a little money here and there, we can expand our markets, and it took a lot of doing and all of this was voluntary. So we set up the Scallop Advertising Fund." In 1957, the Fishermen's Union too agreed to participate in funding scallop advertising. "Of course we had to change the name from Seafood Producers, so we came up with the name Seafood Council," said Linehan. "We had participation by boats, and this money was coming out of the gross stock so both the owners and the fishermen were participating… getting food editors together and showing them how to cook scallops. It was a very exciting time and, as a result, the population became aware of what scallops were and how to cook them."

To meet growing demand, the scallop catch increased from about 12 million pounds in 1950 to 19 million pounds in 1959.

The New Bedford Scallop Festival on Pope's Island followed soon after, providing great publicity. "The scallop festival that we developed was a real big thing for us," Howard Nickerson of the Fishermen's Union recalled. "Every boat would give a (50 pound) bag a trip, and many times, a boat might give as many as 10 or 12 bags. We also got help from the Department of Agriculture who gave us peas, canned peas, canned beans, string beans, potatoes. There was a surplus of potatoes around, and the Department of Agriculture couldn't get rid of them in the school system, so we took them."

The festival drew attention and attendance from across the country, landing stories in newspapers coast to coast. On August 7, 1960, the *Anderson Herald* of Indiana ran an article declaring, "Summertime is festival time all around the country. An especially interesting festival, held in New

Exchange Club volunteers prepare scallop dinners at the Third Annual Scallop Festival, 1960. *For over a decade, fishing families, the Exchange Club and the New Bedford Seafood Council organized an annual Scallop Festival. Their marketing skills helped make "New Bedford scallops" a name brand found on menus worldwide. While food was the Festival's main attraction—scallop plates at 99¢ for adults and 50¢ for children—there was entertainment, exhibits and mingling with Miss Scallop Festival Queen. At far right is Solveig Knutsen; third from right is Gail (Jacobsen) Isaksen.*

Bedford, Massachusetts, August 12-14, is one honoring the scallop.... While New Bedford won its fame as a whaling port, the fame now centers on the scallop, the New Bedford fishermen producing more than 80 percent of the country's supply." Published complete with a recipe for scallops au gratin, the article introduced cooks to scallops and was typical of those that ran during the time.

By the end of the 1950s, the port of New Bedford landed more value than Boston and Gloucester combined. Linehan recalled that, "for a period from the mid- to late-'50s, we were the only port in the nation that was increasing in economic value when all the others were going down."

Despite that, trouble loomed for New England fishing. During the summer of 1960, large foreign trawlers were spotted fishing for the first time on Georges Bank. In 1961, almost 100 fishing trawlers, most from the Soviet Union, fished there. Over the next two years, large numbers of trawlers from Great Britain, Poland, Norway and Spain joined the Soviet fleet in waters previously reserved for the US and Canada.

Aboard the scalloper *Noreen*, 1958. *Fishermen Eddie Harrington and Paul Dube haul the dredge on the* Noreen *under skipper Lou Henderson. The scalloper was built and launched from Fairhaven's Peirce & Kilburn Shipyard around 1950. In September 1957, the ship's crew reported seeing a grotesque sea creature off Pollock Rip that had a large seal-like body and the head of an alligator that rose 25 feet out of the water.*

The Longshoremen

City longshoremen unload and load cargo from vessels entering or leaving the port of New Bedford. Before 1936, they were known as dockworkers. A stevedore, who usually worked shipside and for the shipping company, would individually hire longshoremen, a term shortened from "men along the shore." Their day's labor determined the pay they received each night. They had neither benefits nor guarantees.

In 1936, dockworkers met in Liberty Hall with a union representative from Washington, DC, and formed a bargaining unit, Local 1413 and 1465 of the International Longshoremen's Association (ILA). Known as the Longshoremen, Warehousemen and Freight Handlers, most members came from the Cape Verdean community of the South Central neighborhood. Before organizing, they received 50 cents an hour, which rose to 70 cents after five p.m. Organizing strengthened their negotiating position, and with time, wages rose and they began to receive health and pension benefits.

Through the decades, the volume and nature of the port's traffic changed. Gone were the bales of cotton that used to line State Pier. Cocoa beans, lumber, steel, wool and cement began to come by road, especially with the growth of the Interstate Highway System. The number of unionized longshoremen fell, but they remained a potent voice of the local labor movement.

Unloading cotton bales on State Pier, 1936. *Winchman on the bridge and signmen on the deck coordinate the raising of several 500-pound bales of cotton from a freighter's hatch. There, they await sorting and consignment to New Bedford's remaining cotton mills.*

In the warehouse on State Pier, 1950s. *From left to right are: Hoxie Tavares, a company man counting and weighing his shipment of cocoa beans from Latin America, general foreman Antone Cabral, business agent Joseph Sylvia and on the forklift, Arthur Sylvia.*

Working the Boats

Union member **Julio J. Alves** began working in 1936 at age 19. In time he became a winch operator hoisting cargo out of holds. A coworker of 25 years said, "I can tell you he was one hell of a winch man." Alves moved from the docks to the office and then to business agent and secretary-treasurer of Local 1413 and 1465 of the ILA. He helped win the great victory of obtaining workers' health and pension benefits. A longshoreman by day, Alves turned musician by night. As a young man, he was a drummer with Joseph "Jedge Marita" Senna's orchestra before playing with the Skyliners.

Antone Cabral was the first union president and held the position for 25 years. He remembered vying for unloading privileges with the coal trimmers. "We waited until a ship came in and let them unload. They couldn't do it. That was the end of our problems with them. In fact, some of them joined our local. We really didn't have to do much dickering for wages. What New York got, we got."

George Baptista spent 40 years operating a forklift on the docks. "Most of all I remember unloading sisal from South America to make rope for the New Bedford ropeworks. I remember unloading cocoa beans, lumber, steel and wool from South America. The worst was cement. I would get rashes unloading cement."

John Rose worked as a hatch foreman. "At that time there were 21 men to a gang. Everything was loose. It used to take us two weeks to unload a lumber boat. We would grab one stick at a time. We worked 12 hours a day on lumber. Today it's all bundled. Take a couple million feet of lumber. You could unload a lumber boat in six hours today."

When Joe Ventor came to the docks, he worked as superintendent of maintenance at Arlans Department Stores. "We had to go down to the pier to get the sisal, which we put in our warehouses. I got friendly with the working men then. When Arlans went on the stock market, I quit—I was with them when they got poor and when they were rich. I remember how hard it was to unload frozen fish. We had to fight the cold—dress up real warm."

Four bales of wool weighing 3,200 pounds are hoisted onto State Pier, 1958. Stenciled on the burlap cover is the warning: "Use No Hooks."

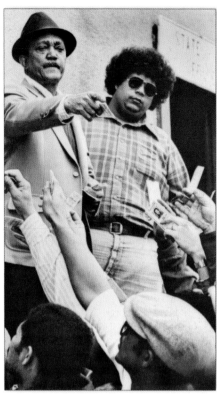

ILA President Julio Alves conducts a shape-up on State Pier. Shop steward Jack Tavares collects union cards, April 1979.

New Bedford longshoremen pose before going to work aboard an oil ship in Fall River, 1950s.
Front Row, left to right: John Lopes, Domingo Gomes, Antone Cabral, Joseph Fermino, Arthur Sylvia. Standing: Joseph "Cab" Rosario, Manuel Silva, Joseph Soares and Hannibal Montron.

Downtown New Bedford looking north from Walnut Street, 1945.

Transportation

Midcentury witnessed major changes in New Bedford's transportation networks. These mirrored profound changes taking place throughout the United States that reflected the triumph of individual over shared conveyances. As automobiles came to dominate personal transportation, they replaced collective transport systems that dated to the 19th century.

In 1947, the Union Street Railway Company removed all streetcars from city streets. Former passengers switched to buses, but bus ridership started a continuous decline. In 1958, the New York, New Haven and Hartford Railroad ended train service to and from New Bedford. An ever-decreasing number of commuters to Boston turned to intercity buses. In 1960, steamship service stopped. The newly created Woods Hole, Martha's Vineyard and Nantucket Steamship Authority no longer provided service to the city. To get to the islands, freight and passengers had to transit via Woods Hole.

The expanding auto ridership put a strain on local infrastructure, including bridges and roads. By 1960, the city closed the Coggeshall Street Bridge after a state report deemed it unsafe. As more cars used the New Bedford-Fairhaven Bridge, daily traffic streamed off the bridge after span openings and major traffic tie-ups occurred especially during peak summer vacation times.

Competing modes of transportation outside the terminal, Purchase Street, 1946. *Osgood-Bradley delivered Car 403 (center) to the Union Street Railway in 1917. It proudly ran until trolley service ended in 1947, when the company scrapped the remaining 400 series cars. Museum efforts to obtain at least one for preservation failed. The Queensboro Bridge Railway bought the 44-passenger Car 609 (right) after its decommissioning in 1947. Known popularly as an "Electromobile," it was built by Osgood-Bradley in 1929 and ran for many years on Route 1 between Lunds Corner and Fort Rodman.*

End of the Lines

In 1939, the Union Street Railway Company burned outmoded trolley cars on Pope's Island. The company removed the cars from service as it switched over to buses during its motorization push of the late 1930s.

The trolleys' supposed obsolescence proved premature. World War II's rationing limited access to raw materials including gasoline, rubber and many metals, and the Office of Defense Transportation directed companies to keep trolleys running. Union Street Railway put its motorization plans on hold. Remaining trolleys on the main north-south lines transported workers for the city's war industries. After the war's end and the closure of the Office of Defense Transportation, Union Street Railway resumed earlier plans to replace its rail vehicles, switching most lines over to buses in early 1946. The last remaining trolley lines were the Purchase Street Line and the depot branch. On May 3, 1947, city officials and Union Street Railway officers ceremonially rode the last car from the Weld Square car barn to Pope's Island, where the car was scrapped. After smashing the windows and removing the wheels, company workers burnt the discarded cars in the open air. Nearly 75 years after the New Bedford and Fairhaven Street Railway began serving New Bedford, the city's trolley service ended.

World War II provided a much-needed boost to the Union Street Railway Company's ridership—it doubled from 1941 to 1943 and remained high until 1947. However, as postwar prosperity set in, the number of fare-paying passengers fell 2.7 million, or 10 percent, from 1947 to 1949 and continued falling. The company retrenched, selling its Pope's Island prop-

Buses, trolleys and cars share Purchase Street near the Bristol Building, 1946.

On the city's last trolley run, May 3, 1947, veteran motorman Enoch Newsham bids adieu.

Flames consume two of six discarded trolley cars near the car barn on Pope's Island, 1939.

erty in 1949 and the car barn in 1962. It ended service to the airport in 1950 and to Providence in 1951. The railway increased fares in 1951, 1954, 1961 and 1963.

To provide jobs during the Depression and meet the needs of an increasing number of automobile drivers, the federal, state and local governments cobbled together a nationwide road network. Rail traffic suffered with the growing popularity of automobiles. In 1935, the Depression-weakened and insolvent New Haven Railway petitioned the US District Court of Connecticut for restructuring. In 1936, New Haven's bankruptcy trustees abrogated the long-standing lease with Old Colony Railroad to provide service to New Bedford. Their action first forced that line into bankruptcy and then into reorganization as a New Haven subsidiary.

The New Bedford service initially continued despite these financial troubles, but in 1937, New Haven discontinued the city's rail-island steamship link that served transiting vacationers. As a result, fewer passengers used the port. In a further blow to the city, New Haven closed the Weld Square train station in 1938.

World War II brought a brief resurgence in New Haven's passenger and freight traffic as rationing and war priorities reduced alternatives for moving people and goods. However, the revival faded after the war. Bus transportation continually cut into railroad passenger traffic. In addition, postwar growth in truck transport eroded the rail freight business that once formed a key part of the city's traffic. By 1949, New Bedford was left with only three daily round trip trains to Boston. The interstate highway system built after 1950 soon supplanted rail as the region's preferred means of travel. The New Haven Railroad planned to end passenger service on the Old Colony Line in 1958. An emergency subsidy from the state kept some Boston lines open for another year. But rail service from Boston to New Bedford finally ended on September 5, 1958. It had dwindled to only one round trip per day that served about 27 commuters. Old car 809 left Boston's South Station at 5:45 pm on its last run to New Bedford.

Largely empty excursion train car to Boston, 1949.

Empty trains as passenger service on the Old Colony Line halted, July 9, 1958. *Abandoning plans to take the morning train to Boston, 25 stranded commuters used buses or cars instead.*

Freight cars assembled in rail staging yard, March 23, 1948.

Boats & Bridges

Under emergency legislation in 1948, Massachusetts created the New Bedford, Woods Hole, Martha's Vineyard and Nantucket Steamship Authority "to provide adequate transportation of persons and necessaries of life" for Nantucket and Martha's Vineyard. One board member came from each of the four places, and a fifth came from Boston.

The Authority proved a disaster. Shortsighted directors acted to favor their fiefs, failing to act to benefit the overall mission of the Authority, its customers or other ports. As a result, costs rose, management suffered and investment bypassed New Bedford and went to the Cape and Islands. Under the authority, a once-profitable steamship line went into deficit. By 1960, the micromanaging board required upper management to clear all decisions in advance with each board member, and labor unions struck repeatedly. At the end of 1960, the legislature dissolved the Authority and replaced it with a new Woods Hole, Martha's Vineyard and Nantucket Steamship Authority, which ended steamship service to New Bedford.

SS *Nobska* leaving Steamship Pier, September 1962. Built in Bath, Maine, in 1925, the elegant 202' 5" SS Nobska was named for Nobska Point, Woods Hole. After the Steamship Authority dropped New Bedford as a port in 1960, the Nobska's days as a passenger ferry to the Islands ended. However, the ship found auxiliary uses as a freight and ice-breaking vessel. In this photograph, the Nobska participates in a "Spectator Fleet," part of America's Cup celebrations in Rhode Island. Scrapped in 2006, the Nobska was the nation's last surviving coastal steamer.

Cars wait in line to board passage to the islands at the New Bedford, Woods Hole, Martha's Vineyard and Nantucket Steamship Authority terminal and headquarters on Pier 9, March 1957.

Opened to horses and buggies in 1890 and completed in 1892, the **Coggeshall Street Bridge** encountered problems from the onset. Its funding raised hackles. Although begun as a Bristol County project, other cities and towns objected to paying for a bridge that benefited New Bedford and Fairhaven. In 1896, the bridge was raised because originally it had been built so close to the water that at high tide not even a rowboat could pass beneath it.

In 1936, a truck carrying five tons of steel girders plunged through the corroded bridge. Once the girders were recovered, builders used them to repair the bridge. After the 1954 hurricane, with the bridge already damaged and twisted by the 1938 and 1944 hurricanes, authorities banned trucks and buses from using it. In 1960, the state Department of Public Works declared it unsafe, and the mayor closed it for emergency repairs. After reopening, a sign warned users to pass at their own risk.

The **New Bedford-Fairhaven Bridge** had undergone its first major overhaul in 1931, a year after the state took over its mainte-

Coggeshall Street Bridge and Fairhaven shore from Fairhaven Mills in New Bedford, May 1945.

nance from county government. The state resurfaced sidewalks, repaired machinery and added concrete curbs. Between 1936 and 1961, the bridge received only minor repairs and improvements, including the addition of a house for bridge operators and removal of trolley lines.

From early days, river and road traffic competed with each other to get over or under the bridge between Fish Island and Pope's Island. Until 1947, boats had priority over road traffic, requiring immediate bridge openings. Increasing car traffic led to restrictions on openings during rush hours.

Route 6 westbound traffic coming from the bridge, High and North Second Streets, fall 1956.

New Bedford Regional Airport

On March 1, 1939, Henry Olden, then president of the New Bedford Aero Club, urged city and Works Project Administration (WPA) officials to build an airfield. A survey of sites identified the Plainville Road–Shawmut Avenue area as the best option. After acquiring land and securing funding, Mayor Leo E. J. Carney broke ground on April 9, 1940. When the Massachusetts Aeronautics Commission approved the city airport as a commercial landing field on April 28, 1942, it had two 3,500-foot paved runways with lighting systems.

After World War II started, the War Department requested the airport's use. On November 12, 1942, the city leased it to the Army Air Corps as a base for Atlantic Coast patrols. The corps extended both runways to 5,000 feet and added a hangar and auxiliary buildings. In April 1944, the US Navy took it over to provide advanced tactical training to naval aviation combat pilots and to support the Quonset Point, Rhode Island Air Station.

In 1946, the city council vested an Airport Commission with the "care, custody, control and management" of the airport. On October 10, 1947, the city recovered the airport without having to pay for wartime improvements. By year's end, Air Industries Flying School, Old Colony Aviation, Narragansett Airways and Hilton Air Service offered flight training. Hilton also had a photographic service. Northeast Airlines and New England Central Airways provided passenger service to Hyannis, the Islands, New York and Boston.

Clearing land for the new airport, 1941. Using WPA funds, crews cleared trees, brush and boulders from the site for the municipal airport. They also removed or demolished 77 buildings and built a new section of Plainville Road. The War Department coordinated with airport planners to incorporate military strategy needs in case of war. The airport terminal and runway extend into the Apponagansett Great Cedar Swamp, bounded by Old Plainville Road, Mt. Pleasant Street and Shawmut Avenue, seen in lower right portion of the aerial view below.

View of the airport runway looking northeast, circa 1954.

Under provisions of a Layout Plan approved in 1949, the airport's physical plant changed dramatically. Workers demolished 11 old military structures and relocated another four. The City Municipal Hangar was moved to make way for a new administrative building, completed in 1951. Also the US Naval Reserve discontinued its flight-training program.

In October 1952, the airport hosted a two-day air fair. A crowd of 50,000 people attended the professional air show, contests and demonstrations. Its success led to several more annual air fairs.

In 1958, the Civil Aeronautics Administration officially took over the control tower operation under federal provisions governing "Air Traffic of more than 26,000 yearly takeoffs and landings." Soon thereafter, major improvements took place including new approach lights, land clearing, the removal of trees and other potential hazards to planes, and a new radar hookup with Quonset Point, Rhode Island to better locate aircraft lost in bad weather.

In 1976, the terminal building, housing the control tower, offices and a restaurant, was renamed the Basil Brewer Administration Building after the long-serving publisher of the Standard-Times to honor his effort in helping restore the airport to city—rather than to federal—control. Brewer was a longstanding booster of aviation as the future of New Bedford and the principal investor in airport-based firms.

View at the Municipal Airport, looking toward the city hangar, 1948. Puddles mark the dirt parking areas, soon to be paved. Using war-trained pilots, Hilton Air Service in 1946 opened a flight school and photographic service. Old Colony Aviation Inc. began an air taxi and flight school in 1947. George's Grille served breakfast and lunch—including Sealtest Ice Cream—to hungry airport workers. At this time, Old Colony no longer occupied the building, which was without a tenant.

Administration Building, New Bedford Regional Airport, 1955. Massachusetts Air Industries offices and hangar appear in background.

Air Industries

Omega Aircraft made history in the summer of 1957 when it successfully tested the first-ever twin-engine helicopter. Working late at night at the municipal airport, pilots and mechanics labor to finish the tie-down testing phase for Civil Aviation Authority certification. From left to right are pilots Hillard L. Lubin, Charles Chase and David E. Frawley. Pilot Frank Sylvia and mechanic Arthur Tremblay check the engine.

In the **Massachusetts Air Industries hangar** at New Bedford Airport, Omega Aircraft personnel are shown working on different BS-12 helicopter models. The BS-12s were the world's first twin-engine utility helicopters. Designed for a wide variety of commercial uses, they carried loads behind the cabin at the helicopter's center of gravity. Local test pilot David E. Frawley first flew the prototype in December 1956. In 1960, Omega sought Federal Aviation Agency certification for the BS-12s and received it in April 1961. However, investors backing the Omega designs withdrew their support and ended any further development.

In 1948, **Air Industries Flying School** evolved into Massachusetts Air Industries, which offered training and charters. It also built a hangar and repair shop. In January 1949, Robert Hawes cofounded Massachusetts Airlines, which used war-trained pilots to fly to Boston, Nantucket and Martha's Vineyard. Publisher E. Anthony & Sons owned all of these companies, and Basil Brewer served as vice president and treasurer.

Testing the Omega helicopter at Municipal Airport, August 1957.

Building helicopters at Omega Aircraft Corporation, 1960.

Massachusetts Air Industries hangar, circa 1960.

 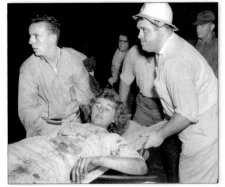 

Crash of Northeast Airlines Flight 285 near New Bedford Regional Airport, September 15, 1957. *During the mid-1950s, Northeast Airlines was beleaguered by several severe accidents, one of which occurred locally.*

On September 15, 1957, Northeast Flight 285 crashed on approach to New Bedford Airport, killing 12 of the 24 passengers and crew. The Douglas DC-3 went down in Apponagansett Great Cedar Swamp in heavy fog just a half-mile from the runway. It broke apart on impact. Rescuers worked through the night, at times thigh-deep in muck, to rescue survivors and recover the dead. A Civil Aeronautics Board inquiry blamed the crash on pilot errors.

Northeast Airlines

In 1933, aviation pioneers founded Boston and Maine Airways as a subsidiary of the Boston and Maine Railroad. Amelia Earhart, the first woman to fly solo across the Atlantic, was among its founders. From its Boston hub, the airline serviced Portland and Bangor, Maine; and later added White River Junction and Montpelier, Vermont and Concord, New Hampshire. In 1934, it added Montreal. In November 1940, it changed its name to Northeast Airlines. In 1939, the airline established one of the nation's first pilot training programs. Before World War II, at the request of the federal government, Northeast operated a national defense program to train advanced flight instructors. Many of those students later worked as civilian pilots in postwar commercial aviation.

During World War II, Northeast pilots, accustomed to frigid weather flying, made Air Transport Command flights to Labrador, Newfoundland, Greenland, Iceland and Scotland. After the war, these became the main commercial routes across the North Atlantic.

Northeast expanded rapidly during and after the war. In July 1944, it took over a route previously operated by Airline Feeder System, flying from Newark, New Jersey to Springfield, Massachusetts via New York City. In August 1944, Northeast acquired Mayflower Airlines and began serving Cape Cod, Nantucket and Martha's Vineyard. Northeast began flying to New York from Boston in 1945 and added an "Every Hour on the Hour" shuttle flight between both cities in 1946. On January 10, 1947, Northeast Airlines made its first commercial flight to New Bedford.

Northeast passenger plane Douglas DC-3 ready for take-off, circa 1958.

Lunch Counters, Diners and Cafés

At midcentury, downtown bustled with luncheonettes, cafés, taverns and restaurants. In 1939, residents could order up a grilled cheese sandwich at any of 42 lunch counters or sip a "Black Cow" ice cream float at one of 70 soda fountains in city drug stores. In the next decade during the wartime boom, the city's eateries multiplied, climbing by almost 40 percent. At **Ray and Joe's Delicatessen**, Elsie Tschaen stands at left. Her son Raymond Jr. stands next to his father, former City Councilor Raymond Tschaen Sr.

Prominent city pharmacist Harry Freeman ran **Freeman's Pharmacy**, located in the Olympia Theatre Building. He stands (second from right) in front of a sign advertising 15¢ milkshakes alongside three unidentified employees. A sign in the corner plugs 15¢ steak sandwiches. Harry's widow Ethel continued running the pharmacy and soda fountain after his death in 1956.

Ray and Joe's Delicatessen, 104 William Street, 1954.

Lunch counter and fountain at Freeman's Pharmacy, Purchase Street, 1954.

Irene and Bernard "Nino" Vercellone owned and operated the **Depot Café,** which specialized in spaghetti and meatballs. Regulars raved about the café's pizza and Italian dishes. Still others knew the Depot as a place to book a number or to socialize after basketball games.

Around 1897, English-born Frederick Lorraine opened **Lorraine's Coffee Company** selling teas and coffee at the southeast corner of Purchase and High Streets. It later moved, but kept the same atmosphere. The aroma of freshly ground coffee greeted several generations of customers as they entered the shop. Many came for coffee and donuts, while others preferred the coffee milkshakes.

Located at the eastern end of Pope's Island, the **Bridge Diner** welcomed families and business diners during the day. At night, it was a favorite date spot. Its location could prove precarious. During the 1938 hurricane, owner Antoine J. Viau and cook Edward Riendeau had to escape deep water sloshing through the building. After a boat struck the diner, they climbed aboard the rudderless vessel and rode it until it washed ashore in Fairhaven. Sixteen years later, during 1954's Hurricane Carol, high water again threatened the Bridge Diner but the restaurant remained standing.

Depot Café, Acushnet Avenue, 1951.

Lorraine's Coffee Co., Purchase Street, 1956.

Inside the Bridge Diner, Pope's Island, circa 1958.

Outside the Bridge Diner, Pope's Island, circa 1958.

Ringside Café, 94 Union Street below Second Street, 1949.

New Bedford residents enjoyed sitting at lunch counters, often combining a meal and conversation. At Harry Semiansky's **Ringside Café** on busy Union Street, longtime bartender Charles Mickelson presided over the regulars and served up much appreciated 5¢ beers. Seated at far left is Frank Neves, and beside him, Tony Silva.

During World War II, Raoul "Ralph" Payette converted a variety store and poolroom, formerly run by Albert Levesque, into a North End eatery known as **Ralph's Lunch**. Payette learned the trade working for many years as a cook in a nearby restaurant at 1546 Acushnet Avenue, owned by John Bousquet. At Ralph's, most breakfast choices cost a quarter or less, and included coffee. Luncheon sandwiches cost 35¢ or less. The 55¢ grilled pork chops was one of the menu's priciest dishes. During the summer, the restaurant featured Green Spot Orange-Ade, a noncarbonated drink free of artificial ingredients. Short-order cook Romeo Tremblay stands second from left while owner Payette stands at right, leaning on the counter.

Located in the building formerly occupied by Fire Station #1, the **Waldorf Cafeteria** was famous for its chicken pies and burgers. In 1955, German-born artist George Fliege painted a vivid mural on the north wall depicting whaling ships at sea. The cafeteria closed after serving customers for nearly half a century. In 1962, the Merchants National Bank bought the building and closed the eatery in order to expand its drive-in banking services.

Ralph's Lunch, 1421 Acushnet Avenue, 1944.

New mural at Waldorf Cafeteria, corner of Mechanics Lane and Purchase Street, 1955.

The **Paramount Restaurant** served food in a bright, Art Deco environment. Among its staff in 1940 were James Gulecas and Agnes (Kerns) Sullivan. By 1949, the Paramount was owned by Phillip Medeiros and Joseph Nogueira served as cook.

Jimmie Evans' daughter, Joanne Mee, remembers her father as a caring, kind man. "My father opened **Jimmie Evans' Flyer,** in part, so he could give people work, including performers from his own troupe. It was the Depression and that's where his heart was. It turned out that my mother actually ran the business. My father was a golfer and met lots of people. Through his many contacts, he met Senator David Walsh and through him, President Franklin Roosevelt. FDR was the one who put the final stamp on him becoming postmaster. My father loved the post office and worked hard to get people jobs through the WPA," she said.

Evans opened his first diner in Buzzards Bay in 1933 and moved it to downtown New Bedford, renaming it Jimmie Evans' Flyer. Open 24 hours a day, often with standing room only, the diner became a popular landmark on Pleasant and Middle Streets. In 1940, a new diner replaced the old one, but the Flyer kept its name and reputation. After Evans' death, his widow moved the 20-ton mobile Flyer to Route 6 in Fairhaven near Sconticut Neck Road. In the 1960s the diner found new ownership, a new name as Johnny's Diner, and a new location in Bourne. It was destroyed by fire in 2010.

Paramount Restaurant, Olympia Building, 894 Purchase Street, 1940.

Jimmie Evans (with tie) and cook inside the orginal Jimmie Evans Flyer, circa 1940.

The newer Jimmie Evans Flyer, Pleasant and Middle Streets, 1954.

City at Night, 1950

Only two buildings visible in this view taken from the top of the New Bedford Hotel on Pleasant Street still stand: the four-story Times Building at far right center, and the old Union Street Railway power plant (with smokestack) on the waterfront at upper right. Most of the other buildings were laid waste between 1969 and 1975—victims of the city's grand urban renewal experiment.

Bakeries by the Dozen

During early whaling days, wealthy New Bedford families relied on servants for their daily baked goods and patronized specialty bakers for fancy occasions only. Ordinary residents either baked their own bread and sweets at home or bought them from local bakeries.

Small bakeries supplied their immediate neighborhoods, while large operations specialized in ship's bread but also carried fresh rolls, breads, cakes, pies and pastries for walk-in customers. According to the 1849 city directory, New Bedford had 34 bakers, all men, roughly one for every 500 inhabitants. Twelve of those bakers owned small bakeries, and the rest worked in the larger establishments. Half were born in Massachusetts, and a quarter were born elsewhere in New England. The others came from Atlantic Coast states. Three of the bakers came from England, Ireland or Scotland.

As the city's immigrant population grew during the next half-century, so too did the market for ethnic breads. Working families had little time to regularly prepare specialty foods. Some immigrants recognized a niche and produced ethnic breads and pastries. According to the 1901 city directory, 160 bakers worked in 47 bakeries. Of those bakers, half were born abroad and many others were children of immigrants. The 40 French Canadians made up the largest group, while 39 came from England, Ireland and Scotland combined. The 20 Central European bakers hailed from Austria, Bavaria, Bohemia and

S. P. Richmond & Co. Bakery, circa 1890. *Owner Samuel P. Richmond began in the mid-19th century at 173 Union Street. By 1901, he operated three stores: 255 Union Street, 449 South Water Street and 861 Purchase Street. The fancy tissue-paper decorations hanging from the ceiling waved with every breeze; besides providing an ornamental value, they kept the flies moving!*

Germany. Only eight came from Portugal and the Azores. The rest were born of US-born parents. Five female bakers broke the male monopoly, owning and operating small home bakeries.

As time went on, buying habits for bread and baked goods shifted. Instead of buying fresh, rustic, handmade baked goods from small, local bakeries daily, families began shopping only once or twice a week and bought mass-produced bread and baked items made by large industrial bakeries that used automated machinery. By 1939, the city directory listed 68 retail bakeries. Many were small, and some—such as Edith A. Kasan's Home Bakery—were run by women from their own homes. Five had more than one retail storefront: Kroudvird's

Pie bakers at Giusti Baking Company, Purchase and Hazard Streets, 1939. *The new temperature- and humidity-controlled oven in the company's expanded quarters could bake up to 43,200 pounds of bread per day. In addition to white bread, it baked rye, crusty French, Vienna and twist loaves. The cake department made smaller quantities of pies, pastries and doughnuts. Staff bakers also specialized in designing elaborate wedding cakes.*

Central European bakeries, 1964-1967. *At the Old Home Bakery on Washburn Street, two bakers examine loaves of Polish pumpernickel bread, called* chleb. *In the late 1930s, during World War II, Kroudvird's Bakery on South Water Street stopped advertising "German" bread.*

Baking bread at Homlyke Bakery, Dartmouth Street, 1958. *Homlyke Bakery owner Joseph Moniz Jr. removes freshly baked breads from the oven. Bakers fed dozens of loaves daily, four to a paddle, into the interior of this oil-fired brick oven. With temperatures reaching more than 600°F, it would take about 20 minutes to produce a hot, crusty loaf. Only a few years earlier, Moniz used wood- and coal-fired ovens at his County Street location.*

Sanitary Bakery had four locations; Giusti Baking Company and Mercer Brothers each had three; New York Bakery and Wallner's Bakery each had two. Three wholesale bakeries operated in New Bedford—Loose-Wiles Biscuit Company, My Bread Baking Company and National Biscuit Company.

After the war, small retail bakeries continued to disappear. By 1949, their number had fallen to 51, dropping to 40 in 1959 and 32 in 1969. The number of large wholesale bakeries supplying greater New Bedford and Cape Cod stabilized. In 1969, there were seven: Brenneke's Pies, Continental Baking Co., Giusti Baking Co., My Bread Baking Co., My Bread Products Corp. (the thrift store), Sisson's Donuts and Table Talk Inc.

Below, personnel of the Millside Bakery line up along Dartmouth Street for a company portrait. Owners Joseph Moniz Jr. (first right) and Serafim E. Mello (fourth right) supplied a wide variety of Portuguese baked goods, proudly proclaiming to make the "Best Selling Sweet Bread in New England." In the late 1940s and early 1950s, the company delivered an assortment of breads to rural areas around New Bedford. Drivers maintained a system of logging deliveries into a book assigned to each family for later repayment. Easy credit terms allowed farmers to receive compensation for their own goods before paying the bakery tab. Moniz split with Mello in the late 1940s to become a poultry farmer. He re-entered the business in the early 1950s, opening Homlyke Bakery at 103 County Street. He later moved to 199 Bonney Street, before purchasing Millside from his former partner and renaming it Homlyke. Richard Moniz purchased the franchise from his father in the early 1970s, expanded it, and retired in 2008. The new owners closed it in 2013.

Millside Better Bakery Products, 319 Dartmouth Street, circa 1956.

Pie Makers

Born in Hanover, Germany in 1864, Martin Brenneke immigrated to the United States via Ellis Island in 1885. He and his wife, Martha, moved to New Bedford in 1890, where he worked as a chef at the Parker House Hotel until 1920.

In 1924, at age 60, Martin Brenneke began baking pies in his basement at 100 Parker Street. He sold them door-to-door, first in his own neighborhood and later around the rest of New Bedford. As the business grew, Martin Brenneke expanded by building a 20' by 40' cinder block addition to his house, where he baked, sold and distributed pies. In 1935, he sold the business to his son Rudolph and his son-in-law Henry Davenport.

They expanded the bakery, building another cinder block addition. They continued selling door-to-door, but also sold to pie resellers. During World War II, sugar and flour rationing limited Brenneke's pie production. After the war, Brenneke's expanded again, hiring five men, adding 10 pie-delivery routes and building two more cinder block additions to their Parker Street operation.

In 1961, they built a state-of-the-art baking facility at 447 Kempton Street, near Emerson Street. Two years later, Rudolph's son David, a graduate of the American Institute for Baking in Chicago, joined the family business to bake pies alongside his father, uncle and cousin. He eventually bought out their shares.

What made Brenneke's Pies so extraordinary? David Brenneke says the family used only the freshest ingredients—fresh unhomogenized whole milk and cream, farm-fresh eggs, locally grown blueberries, apples and peaches—which they combined into the most delectable pies. A Brenneke blueberry pie fairly oozed fresh fruit through its flaky crust.

In 1970, Worcester's Table Talk Pie Company purchased Brenneke's Pies. Table Talk had a local distributor since the mid-1950s. However, many local Brenneke pie enthusiasts did not readily accept the different taste and size of the pies and so never became loyal Table Talk customers.

Brenneke Pie Bakery, 1966. *At the Kempton Street bakery, Wesley Herron stacks dough balls as they leave the dough divider. A rack of squash pies cool down. Below, Albert "Al" Refuse puts the dough balls into the roller to flatten them. Billy Gonsalves (left) and Manny Dutra (right) put the flattened dough into pie plates. In the background, eventual owner David Brenneke unloads squash pies from the oven.*

Table Talk Bakery delivery fleet loading pies, circa 1958. *Table Talk's distribution center at 1000 Kempton Street handled pies baked in Worcester. There, a 120-foot-long oven turned out more than 300,000 apple pies per week plus seasonal pies of rhubarb, pineapple, cherry, blueberry or strawberry. It made cream pies and meringues for the restaurant trade and junior pies for a child's school lunchbox.*

Bakers by the Dozen

John Giusti started out small but dreamed big. He began by peddling bread door to door in a horse-drawn cart and eventually became the owner of New England's leading independent bakery.

Giusti had left his native Italy at age 16, arrived in New Bedford in 1902 and made his first $12 working for a baker. He liked the work enough to start a small basement bakery on South Water Street with his friend Cesare Giusti (no relation). They'd cook at night and turn out 300 loaves a day. They soon moved to expanded quarters on the same street and began producing 1,500 loaves daily. The pattern continued—expanding to a larger facility at Purchase and Pearl Streets, buying up other bakeries and hiring more workers. Eventually their one cart and four horses grew to a score of trucks.

Their biggest move took place in 1936, when they bought the old Wamsutta sheet mills at Purchase and Hazard Streets, transforming them into a scientifically equipped bakery. **Giusti Baking Company** now owned 40 trucks and employed 160 people, and its market went far beyond New Bedford. When the public toured the plant at the grand opening, they were dazzled by the white walls, white machinery, white uniforms of the workers and tons of pure white flour.

When John Giusti retired, Joseph Giusti, son of company cofounder Cesare Giusti, became president and CEO of the company. Upon his retirement, the business was sold to Nissen Bakery.

My Bread Baking Company also expanded in the 1920s and 1930s. Joseph P. Duchaine had taken the reins after his father Paul retired in 1923. In 1927, the company joined the Quality Bakers of America (QBA) Cooperative, a nationwide organization of independent bakeries that shared purchasing and advertising as well as research and development. In 1934, Duchaine initiated the first of four expansions that eventually culminated in the familiar four-story, white-brick building on Coffin Avenue that occupies almost an entire city block. Later, the facility baked a new QBA brand, Sunbeam Bread, for regional distribution. A fleet of trucks delivered breads, rolls and English muffins throughout southern New England.

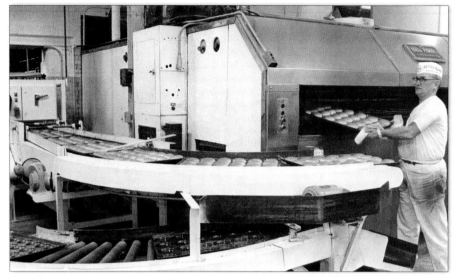

Giusti's Bakery, Purchase Street, January 1971. *Hank Spigliano baking hamburger rolls.*

Newly installed equipment at My Bread Baking Company, 1950s.

My Bread Baking Company, Coffin Avenue and North Front Street, 1950s.

The Old West End

Life in New Bedford's West End evolved around family, community and faith. Characterized by old houses, modest homes and active community centers, the neighborhood also brimmed with African American churches such as Douglass Memorial AME Zion, Bethel AME, Union Baptist Church and St. Ambrose Episcopal, a West Indian church serving many black families whose ancestors arrived through whaling.

Leonora Kydd Whyte, 1911–2013

Leonora Kydd Whyte lived in the neighborhood most of her 102 years. Her father William L. Kydd Sr. came here from Bequia, part of an emigre community from the Grenadines in the British West Indies. He was a whaler, as was his father. This group brought with them the particular flavor of the islands—music, food and sports, particularly cricket. (Intercity matches were held at Buttonwood and Victory Parks.) The neighborhood was one of the richest melting pots in the city with African Americans, Cape Verdeans, French Canadians, Italians, Native Americans and Portuguese as well as residents from the British West Indies, the Dutch and French West Indies.

She married William Darcey Whyte, and they raised four children. He was a Golden Gloves champion, originally from Panama where his father toiled on the Panama Canal. He trained boxers at the Boys Club, was serious about his portrait photography, and held many jobs including one as a custodian at the Standard-Times. Passionate about politics, Whyte never missed voting in an election. Just weeks before she died in 2013, she voted by absentee ballot.

At the Bethel AME Church, she devoted herself to the Martha D. Webb Missionary Society, helping those in need. She was active in the Martha Briggs Educational Club—Clara King, her mother, was one of the founders; the New Bedford Historical Society, the NAACP and the YWCA (Yvonne Drayton, her daughter, would one day become the executive director). Whyte also held many jobs, including one as the first director of the West End office of ONBOARD, an anti-poverty agency.

Another daughter, Linda Whyte (Toatley) Burrell, described growing up in the West End as a kind of paradise:

Leonora Kydd Whyte, holds a story about her grandfather, Civil War veteran Isaiah King, 1962.

> The West End was a small town with a mix of vibrant cultures and occupations, but we had great unity. We had fashion shows, dances, plays, church gatherings and picnics. We all knew each other and helped each other. It was wonderful.
>
> I remember the sounds of the neighborhood. The sound of the Miranda's door slamming. (They had a mid-century modern door.) The sound of my aunt's high heels on the sidewalk on her way to work. My friend's father said he could tell the time of day by how fast her heels were clicking. The sound of Mr. Timber's wagon creaking in the street, a handyman with a wooden cart full of tools. The sound of jazz coming from the clubs and music from the churches. The sound of my father's whistling and the sweet sound of my mother's voice.

West End Daily Vacation Bible School, First Baptist Church, Court and Cedar Streets, 1939.

Joan Henderson Beaubian

Joan Beaubian paints a lovely portrait of life in the old West End "before urban redevelopment tore the soul out of the community." The youngest of five, Beaubian was born in 1942. Her family was African American. Her father worked at Parson's Laundry, her mother at the West End Day Nursery. "We were poor but didn't know it," Beaubian said. "We were a family-oriented, mixed neighborhood. It was mostly black and everybody knew everybody."

Beaubian remembers Bible school and working at the Middle Street playground as a teenager: "The boys played basketball and I did arts and crafts with the girls, mostly making lanyards out of gimp—everyone loved gimp. Youngsters navigated the ins and outs of the neighborhood. We knew everybody's backyard, all the shortcuts, the mean old ladies," she said.

Beaubian attended nearby Cedar Street School and Cook School. She went to Roosevelt Junior High, taking a bus to the South End. "We got to meet the Cape Verdean kids for the first time, including some cute Cape Verdean boys. Our parents had not allowed us to associate with them, and their parents forbid them from associating with us," she said. "But our generation changed all that. We broke the barrier when the West End and South End girls became friends." Teenagers gathered at the "canteen," a youth center on Kempton and Cedar Streets. Adults listened to jazz bands, both black and white, at the West End Club. Summer evenings often found the Henderson family strolling to Buttonwood Park to enjoy a picnic under the shade trees.

Beaubian majored in education and household arts at the vocational high school, went on to Adelphi College and then a retail career in New York. "In the 1970s, I took a bus back to New Bedford and when I looked out the window, I asked, 'Where is New Bedford?'" she said. "Our neighborhood was gone…everyone scattered…we lost that sense of community."

Every five years or so, hundreds from the old neighborhood gather for a reunion, a way for the old West End to say, "Remember me."

The West End Youth Center, 1965. *The building housed the West End Branch Library and the Youth Center on the second floor, and the West End Police Station on the ground level.*

The West End Youth Center, 1949. *Joe Andrade serves Ray Williams (not visible) on the center's newly-rebuilt ping pong table.*

Cottage and Kempton Streets, 1941. *Looking north, Query's Drug Store and West End Public Market occupy the West End's busiest corner.*

WNBH and WBSM

During the war, WNBH moved to a new location on an expanded AM dial, and adapted its programming to a wartime audience. The station created a program called "Letters to Fighters." Listeners submitted names of their relatives fighting overseas, and the staff mailed out about 4,000 letters a month filled with news from the New Bedford home front. Local school children provided a grand assist in the effort.

WNBH also kept the public informed by providing local and national newscasts. When meat rationing began in April 1943, the station ran commercials for meat substitutes and served up tips and recipes for feeding the family. Patriotic music played over the airwaves and patriotic themes found their way into the plots of network soap operas. While listeners heard plenty of Sinatra and Crosby, they also sampled New Bedford voices, thanks to WNBH's own musical director who supervised live broadcasts by local talent. The station raised significant money for the war effort by sponsoring parades and concerts. One event, on Patriot's Day 1943, featured a whaleboat and brought in more than $47,000.

In the 1940s, WNBH owners were also readying for new technologies. In August 1944, E. Anthony & Sons applied for a television license as well as an FM station. Frequency Modulation, also referred to as "static-free radio," was still very new and few people had an FM receiver. WNBH nevertheless wanted to be ready, and in 1948 the station was finally able to put FM on the air. Getting a television station would take much longer.

WBSM-AM radio first aired on July 17, 1949, broadcasting from a studio in the old Browne's Drug Store on Union Street. Over time, the two New Bedford stations developed different programming styles with WNBH specializing in local and national sports and WBSM pioneering the talk show with long-term personality hosts.

WNBH radio personality Jim Gleason with recording artist Patti Page, 1951. *Patti Page's big hit that year was "The Tennessee Waltz." She sang it live at the station's inaugural celebration March 30, 1951.*

Inaugural celebration WNBH studio, 1951. *Hundreds wait in line to hear Patti Page perform and to mix with local celebrities and VIPs at the gala opening for the radio station's new studio at Union and County Streets, March 30, 1951.*

Participants celebrate the anniversary of the Franco-American Hour, March 1954. *Left to right are Doris LeBlanc, Edgar Viens, Robella Cloutier, organist Edmond H. Desrosiers, Emile LeMoine,. Imelda Grimshaw, Madelaine Rothberg, Marion Gauvin, Jose da Costa (seated at piano) and Adrien Guillet.*

Live at the WBSM studio, circa 1954. *Mingo Gomes leads his jazz orchestra during a live Music Week performance. Band members include Chick Boucher on drums, Michael Antunes on sax, Eddie Nunes on trumpet, vocalist Vera Hunt and Richard Haddocks on piano.*

Theodore A. Morde, Filmmaker

Theodore A. Morde was born in New Bedford where he attended public schools and graduated from New Bedford High School in 1929. As an adventurer and explorer, he wandered the globe for almost three decades. Shortly after graduating from Brown University in 1939, he went on an expedition to Honduras sponsored by the Museum of the American Indian. During the trip he was on the hunt for ruins of the Ciudad Blanca, a lost city first recorded by Spanish conquistador Hernán Cortés. According to Cortés' guides, natives of the city ate from plates of gold.

Later, as a war correspondent for Reader's Digest, Morde filed stories from behind British lines in North Africa. Under his reporter's cover, Morde worked for the OSS (Office of Strategic Services, a World War II precursor to the Central Intelligence Agency). In Istanbul, Morde tried to persuade the German ambassador to Turkey, former Chancellor Franz von Papen, to engineer a coup against Hitler. Such a plan, had it succeeded, would have ended the war in 1943. Later, as a lieutenant in the Naval Reserve, he earned a Bronze Star for making an intelligence survey of a Pacific island under heavy fire to prepare for a US landing. After the war, he made documentary films in more than 30 countries.

Morde was passionate about New Bedford. In 1953, he produced and directed A Rising Tide, a highly personal documentary about the city. It told the story of a New Bedford native who roamed the world and then returned there to make a film promoting his home city. He enlisted well-known scriptwriter Basil Beyea, photographer and film editor William C. Smith and also as narrator pioneering NBC radio and TV broadcaster William T. Cochran. The city's Industrial Development Commission (IDC) paid him $10,000 to cover the costs of the film. An enthusiastic Morde shot enough material for a three-hour presentation and he personally covered at least $2,000 in cost overruns. Morde delivered a 35-minute version to the client.

Lt. Theodore A. Morde in northern Italy, 1945. Morde was featured in "Who's Who in America" in 1954.

Premiered on December 16, 1953 at the New Bedford High School auditorium, the movie left its audience "Thrilled, proud, surprised and elated" wrote the Standard-Times. The film depicted city history from early whaling in 1767 to ongoing efforts to remake itself as a diversified industrial center after the collapse of the textile industry.

For television broadcast, the film needed to be cut to less than thirty minutes. The IDC wanted to cut material about the Standard-Times, its publisher Basil Brewer and its editor Charles J. Lewin, as well as footage of Mayor Francis J. Lawler handing out prizes at a local fishing tournament.

Resisting cuts ordered by the IDC as technically unsound, costly, and politically inspired, Morde resigned from the project. Despondent about the film and marital difficulties, two months later he committed suicide.

Filming a documentary, 1953. At left, Morde's crew films a scene at Revere Copper & Brass in New Bedford. At right, Morde (center) is assisted by Peter S. Grinnell (left) of South Dartmouth who was hired as location manager, and cameraman William C. Smith. "We'll tell New Bedford's story through its people because the ·people made New Bedford" said Morde. "It's a story which has needed telling on film for a long while and we're doing it." Also assisting Morde was teenage intern Ted Ellis, a New Bedford Vocational High School electrical student.

President Franklin Delano Roosevelt in New Bedford, October 1936. President Roosevelt addresses throngs of supporters from his car as it ambles along Pleasant Street in the New Bedford Common Park. Eleanor Roosevelt follows afoot holding a bouquet of roses. The press reported that the president's whirlwind tour of the state caused three heart attack deaths, 20 injuries and more than 100 "prostrations." Later the same day, in Boston, over 125,000 people mobbed Boston Common to hear the president speak for 10 minutes.

The Roosevelts in Fairhaven, 1936. After his speech at the New Bedford Common Park, the president and his family took time to visit the Delano family plot at Riverside Cemetery in Fairhaven. Sons Franklin Jr. and James flank their parents.

Three Octobers

President Franklin Delano Roosevelt gave a rousing speech to a large crowd in New Bedford on October 21, 1936, while campaigning for a second term on the Democratic ticket. Beginning his day in Providence, his cavalcade moved on to Fall River, then New Bedford. His motorcade crossed over the bridge to Fairhaven for lunch and to visit the Delano family plot at Riverside Cemetery.

FDR's maternal grandfather, Warren Delano II, grew up in Fairhaven. He married Catherine Lyman and they had many children, among them Sara Delano, the strong-willed mother of Franklin. In a solemn moment, the president visited Riverside Cemetery to pay his respects to his grandfather and other Delano family members. Prominent in the China trade and a town benefactor, Warren Delano II created beautiful Riverside Cemetery, designing its layout and leafy paths. He is buried in the Delano tomb with 20 other Delano descendants.

President Roosevelt, whose legs became paralyzed when he contracted polio at age 39, could not stand unaided and always kept a firm grip on the arm of his sons or aides, as seen here. He won a second term just two weeks after his visit and soon faced the morass and mayhem of World War II. This sunny day in October was his and Eleanor's last trip to New Bedford and the Delano homestead.

"City Hails Eisenhower," roared the headline in the Standard-Times on October 20, 1952 when the famed military leader and hero rolled into town in a 17-car Eisenhower special as he campaigned for president. General Dwight D. Eisenhower, a Republican, was greeted with a thunderous welcome by 80,000 people as he made his way through the city on Pearl, Purchase and Union Streets. He was all waves and smiles as workers in downtown office buildings stuck their heads out upstairs windows and sent confetti and streamers down into the streets to shouts of "We Like Ike."

Supporters raced alongside the convertible carrying Eisenhower and Senators Leverett Saltonstall and Henry Cabot Lodge Jr. The colorful red, white and blue cavalcade moved on to Buttonwood Park where thousands more waited for Ike to speak. Weeks later General Eisenhower became President Eisenhower, the 34th president of the United States.

Congressman John F. Kennedy, Democratic candidate for the US Senate, met most of New Bedford when he flew in for a daylong visit on a sunny morning in October 1952. Met at the airport by civic and labor leaders, Kennedy toured businesses, visited mills, greeted workers, walked the streets and shook hands with everyone he met. Later he spent time on the waterfront learning about the fishing industry.

On Pier 3, the Congressman inspected the L.S. Eldridge & Son, Inc. fish plant, one of the largest in the state, and boarded a dragger, where he saw how fish were unloaded, weighed and packed in ice. All the while, he was surrounded by fishermen loudly exclaiming, "You're our Man!" He is shown here talking with local fishermen and listening to their stories.

Rep. John F. Kennedy campaigns on the New Bedford waterfront, October 1952.

General Dwight D. Eisenhower greets an enthusiastic crowd along Union Street, October 1952.

Basil Brewer and the Standard-Times

Basil Brewer swept into town in 1931, quickly taking over the city's newspaper landscape and dominating the political scene with his forceful personality. The Missouri-born son of a Methodist circuit-riding preacher, Brewer first purchased a controlling interest in two of the city's three newspapers: the *Evening Standard* and the *Morning Mercury*. Both battled for readership and influence with the city's third newspaper, the *New Bedford Times*, but not for long. Two years after Brewer arrived, the *Evening Standard* and the *New Bedford Times* merged to become the *Standard-Times*. In 1942, the *Morning Mercury* ceased publication.

The *Standard-Times* Publishing Company increased its reach and holdings by acquiring the *Cape Cod Standard-Times* in Hyannis; two radio stations, local WNBH and West Yarmouth's WOCB; television station WTEV-6; and Massachusetts Air Industries airline. For the next three decades, Brewer ruled his tycoon kingdom, serving as president and treasurer as well as sometime editor, writer and

Composing room, *Evening Standard*, 1900. *Large windows and high ceilings maximized sunlight, making it easier for skilled compositors to spot and pick out the small individual letters. After compositors arranged letters into pages that were used to mold plates, each letter was returned to its case.*

Standard-Times building, Pleasant Street, circa 1952. *The original building (shown on p. 250 of Volume 1 of the* Picture History*) was extended south by 49 feet in 1911 when a fifth story was added. When Pleasant Street was widened between William and Union Streets in 1925, ten feet were truncated from the building's east side, a new façade erected and the building lost its distinctive diagonal corner entrance.*

grandstander of his newspaper. Active in local, national and international politics, he was an outspoken, passionate and fierce Republican who often veered to the extreme right. His commentary was not only prickly enough to jolt local readers, but it drew attention of newspapers nationwide. Few were neutral about Brewer. He had staunch defenders and won many awards. But he also had ferocious detractors. The *Harvard Crimson* once described him as "New Bedford's nevus" and *Time* magazine referred to him as the "Neanderthal Republican Publisher." In editorials, Brewer argued against FDR's "socialistic" New Deal and Social Security. He insinuated that opponents of Senator Joseph McCarthy's infamous "witch hunt" were themselves communist sympathizers. He balked at President Dwight D. Eisenhower's stand on school desegregation. However, Brewer was involved in multiple charities and dedicated to creating opportunities for young people. He was often praised for his outspokenness in his editorials, usually from afar rather than locally.

The year 1952 proved to be a particularly wild time for Brewer and politics when he headed the Taft-for-President state committee. Brewer's efforts were thwarted by Massachusetts Senator Henry Cabot Lodge Jr., another Republican, who instead urged General Dwight D. "Ike" Eisenhower to enter the race. Lodge believed candidate Robert A. Taft's right wing views were too far out of the mainstream to win a national election. Ike became the Republican candidate, going on to win the election.

In a fury, Brewer punished Lodge by brazenly backing Democrat John F. Kennedy to usurp Lodge's senate seat. Lodge,

John F. Kennedy and Basil Brewer *seated together at a United Fund of Greater New Bedford function, 1953.*

Newspaper librarians Alice L. Perry and Esther Cornell, 1950.

who lost to Kennedy in a close race, later revealed in a JFK Library oral history tape: "Brewer could make the difference of 35,000 votes. That's what he did. I was beaten by 70,000. If 35,000 had gone the other way, I could have been in the clear." Ironically, staunch, ultra-conservative Republican Brewer may have been instrumental in paving the way for liberal Democrat JFK to later take the White House. Brewer retired in 1963 and the local news world entered an unsettled period of mergers and buy-outs. In 1966, Ottoway Newspapers bought the *Standard-Times* Publishing Company and young James H. Ottaway Jr. took on the duties of publisher. Four years later, the company merged with Dow Jones and divested itself of the publishing company's non-newspaper holdings. The *Cape Cod Standard-Times*, an edition of the New Bedford paper, broke away to become the *Cape Cod Times*. Both papers are now owned by the Local Media Group.

Linotype operator Joe Kobak in the composing room, 1950. *At the 90-character keyboard, Kobak formed an entire line of metal type at once (a line-o'-type)—a significant improvement over manual, character-by-character composing that revolutionized typesetting and modernized newspaper publishing. Before the linotype, no newspaper had more than eight pages.*

News photographer Hal Nielson and reporter John J. Flanagan Jr., October 1947. *As Nielson takes notes on the back of his Speed Graphic 4" x 5" press camera, Flanagan takes hold of a Raytheon handset to make one of the city's first mobile telephone calls. Reporters early adopted the service that began in Ohio in 1946. In 1948, it served less than 100 cities and towns.*

Paperboy baseball excursion, October 1953.

Neither snow nor rain..., March 1960.

Hail Paperboys!

Generations of American paperboys—and later papergirls—had their first introduction to capitalism and work ethics through paper routes. Newspapers relied on them to distribute the paper and collect revenues. To help keep revenue streams steady, the companies tried to minimize employee turnover. They cultivated young paper carriers and convinced parents of the benefits to their children, including the chance to serve the community while earning regular incomes. Also, the seven-day-a-week job kept them busy and out of trouble, and taught them the importance of meeting deadlines and maintaining work discipline.

Some newspapers, including the Standard-Times, sought to promote the general welfare of paperboys by organizing recreational and educational activities, as shown on these pages. From a paperboy's perspective, a paper route provided money to buy the essentials that a pre-teen boy needed—Boy Scout paraphernalia, rock and roll records or a dime root beer at the soda fountain. The shift from an afternoon to a morning edition reduced the ranks of young paper carriers, few of whom could deliver daily newspapers before school or wanted to give up sleeping on weekends and during vacations.

The *Standard-Times* bus gets ready to roll on another field trip, 1952.

Newspaperboys Little League All-Stars baseball team, August 11, 1956.

Yellow Standard-Times' delivery vans threaded their way through the Southcoast region bringing stacks of newspapers to paperboys regardless of the weather. During a serious **snowstorm in March 1960**, a young paperboy on Pleasant Street in the South End seems about to collapse under the weight of the daily edition. The trucks also transported paperboys on outings such as a **trip to Marion in October 1953**.

The Standard-Times' **Newspaper Boys' Little League All-Stars** on August 11, 1956, before a night game with the Bourne Little League All-Stars at Sagamore Field to benefit the Jimmy Fund in supporting pediatric cancer care and research. Players include, left to right: Front Row: Robert Costa, Robert Newsham, Norris Walecka, William Hall, James Cook and Robert Clarkson; Middle Row: Manny Roderiques, Robert Trahan, Richard Begnoche, Stephen

Lopes and William DeSouza; Back Row: Barry Meunier, Daniel Conceição, Julio Alves, Dimas Roderiques, Paul Brodeur and Richard Monteiro.

The Standard-Times' **Newspaper Boys Band**, led by Joseph Cloutier, played at the State Theatre entrance before the opening of a new aviation film, Chain Lightning. The film starred Humphrey Bogart as a test pilot and former World War II flying ace; Raymond Massey as the owner of an aircraft company; and Eleanor Parker as the company's secretary and the Bogart character's former flame. The film drew from the short story "These Many Years," written by blacklisted writer Lester Cole, who wrote under the pseudonym J. Redmond Prior. At the time, many in the movie, television and radio industries were shunned or blacklisted from working on the basis of alleged political—usually Communist—beliefs and associations. The Writers Guild of America restored Cole's credit on the film in 1997. Hardcore Republican Basil Brewer was likely unaware of the film writer's true identity. If he had been, it is doubtful that the band supported by his newspaper would have performed at the occasion.

Standard-Times' delivery boys display posters on their bicycles in support of the **Greater New Bedford Community Chest** campaign. They pose on and in front of the steps of the Free Public Library with an indicator showing Community Chest funds raised hanging in the background. At this time, the Community Chest and three other Red Feather agencies occupied the Samuel Rodman House at the southeast corner of Spring and County Streets. Nationwide, Red Feather and Community Chest agencies evolved into the United Way of America in the 1960s.

During the 1950s, students in local junior high and high schools as well as members of service groups throughout the region raised funds under a unified appeal for seventeen local agencies; including, the Boy Scouts, Girl Scouts, Child and Family Services, YWCA, YMCA, St. Luke's Clinic and the West End Nursery. Contributors received stickers or signs bearing the Red Feather logo to place in their window. Organizers and participants in the annual campaign proudly displayed the Red Feather symbol throughout the area.

Standard-Times Newspaper Boys Band perform outside the State Theatre, April 2, 1950.

Greater New Bedford Community Chest paperboy supporters, 1959.

Sporting News

In 1949, junior **Bobby Watkins** scored 19 touchdowns to rank second in Bristol County. As a high school senior, several college coaches wooed him, including the soon-to-be legendary Woody Hayes of Ohio State. One of the first African American footballers at Ohio State, freshman Watkins played varsity. As a sophomore and junior, he led the team in scoring. In a rainy, mud-soaked 1955 Rose Bowl game, Watkins rushed for 67 yards on 16 carries, posted 3 receptions for 43 yards, and scored a touchdown. Ohio State won the national championship. Watkins made the All-Big 10 and All-Midwest teams and received honorable mention on the Associated Press, United Press and International News Service All-America teams.

In 1955, the Chicago Bears drafted Watkins in the second round. One of the Bears' first African American players, Watkins remained for four seasons before a knee injury ended his career.

After his football years, Watkins earned his bachelor's degree in business administration. In 2000, Watkins returned to this area in retirement and became involved with UMass Dartmouth. In 2007, he established the Bobby and Rillis Watkins Scholarship Fund, which helps high school football players receive an education at UMD.

Cawley Stadium's opening day featured a 15-lap, 5⅝-mile motorcycle race with 62 cyclists, including Virginia champion Johnny Butterfield and Canadian Leon Newall. Normand Lajoie built the stadium to honor his friend John J. Cawley who perished in World War II. The stadium formed part of the New England Midget Auto Racing Association circuit. The grandstands seated 3,000 and floodlights lit evening events. It was located east of Belleville Avenue between Washburn and Coggeshall Streets. Today, Interstate 195 runs directly through the site.

New Bedford High School champions, 1949. With a record of 9 and 1, the NBHS Whalers were Bristol County champs. Front row: Norman J. Poitras, Edmund Roberge, Harvey Mickelson, Captain Howard "Howie" Baptista, Robert A. Dias, William F. Moore and Anthony Figueiredo; Back row: Captain William F. "Billy" Taylor, Robert A. "Bobby" Watkins Jr., Richard "Dick" Belotti and Raymond "Rabbit" Letourneau.

Opening day, Cawley Stadium, April 19, 1948.

More Boxing Legends

Heavyweight Ted "Tiger" Lowry came close to rivaling the New Bedford greats of the 1920s. The war interrupted his boxing career, which began in 1939 in New Bedford. In the military, he served in the all-black 555th parachute battalion called the Triple Nickels. Training in Alabama, he faced Southern racial attitudes, including being relegated to the back of a city bus while white German prisoners of war sat in the front. His commander "volunteered" him for an exhibition fight with heavyweight champion Joe "The Brown Bomber" Louis, who told Lowry he had a future in boxing. Lowry returned to the ring in 1945. He was the only fighter to twice go the 10-round distance against legendary Rocky Marciano, nearly handing Marciano the only loss of his career. Some sportswriters actually thought Lowry bested Marciano in the first bout. Lowry was New England light heavyweight champion in 1949 and New England heavyweight champion in 1950. He left the ring with 70 wins, 68 losses and 10 draws.

During the 1950s and 1960s, New Bedford hosted many fine amateur boxers. Many got their start in the Southeastern New England Golden Gloves tournament that fed into the Lowell state championship. Others aimed at the New England Amateur Athletic Union (AAU) tournament. Some continued on to box professionally. Featherweight **Jimmy Connors** began amateur boxing while a student at New Bedford Vocational School, learning under the tutelage of school custodian Ozzie Bernard. Later, he joined the air force to escape a Continental Screw factory job. As an amateur, Connors became a National AAU Quarter-Finalist and All-Air Force World Wide Champion.

Connors turned pro in 1957 and fought boxers in Revere and Boston, compiling an impressive 14-0-1 record with eight early knockouts. Ring Magazine selected him as "Prospect for the Month." Connors won a 10-round decision against undefeated Bostonian Pat McCarthy, and was rewarded with a late December marquee matchup against future featherweight World Champion Willy Pep. The slugfest went the full 10 rounds and a unanimous decision declared Pep the winner. Connors considers it his career highlight. He compiled a professional record of 30-7-1. He never won a professional title but always remembered a coach's advice to save his money and invest it wisely. The day after his victory over McCarthy, Connors used his earnings to purchase a luncheonette in New Bedford. Several years later, and after more hard-fought battles, including wins over New England rivals Paddy Read (twice), Tommy Haden and Kid Chuck, Jimmy took out a mortgage to buy a downtown tavern—The Jimmy Connors Town Tavern on Pleasant Street. For many years, he ran a succession of successful downtown bars and restaurants, the last of which was Jimmy Connors Irish Pub.

Lightweight **Manuel "Manny" Burgo** was New England AAU Champion in 1953, 1954, 1956 and 1957. In addition, in 1957, he was New England Golden Glove Champion. In 1958, he turned professional. Burgo, called by sportswriters "one of the best club fighters in the country," boxed as a welterweight until he retired in 1963. He returned to the ring from 1967 to 1971, retired again, and came back for a final fight in 1977. For many years after retiring, he trained young amateur boxers at his "House of Champions." William "Smiley" Ramos won the US AAU Bantamweight Championship in 1954. He was the only New Bedfordite to hold that title since it began in 1888.

Jimmy Connors, Manny Burgo and friends. At left, Jimmy Connnors lands a left jab into the gut of Willy Pep in Boston in 1957. Pep, the future featherweight champ, defeated Connors in a unanimous decision. At right, trainer and former fighter Manuel J. "Manny" Costa demonstrates proper techniques during a Golden Gloves Tournament workout in 1955. The event was held at the Boys Club on Market Street. From left to right are Manny Burgo, his brother Delwin Burgo, Robert Graham, Manny Costa, Beaver Correa and trainer and former pro fighter Frankie Fay.

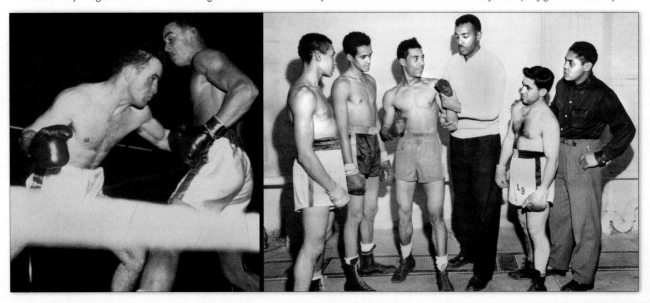

Now Showing: World Premieres

From 1948 to 1956, New Bedford hosted the world premieres for at least five films. Including *Moby Dick*, four dealt with whaling. *Harpoon* premiered at the Olympia Theater on October 20, 1948. The film recounted a multi-generational tale of revenge in the North Pacific whaling grounds. At the end, the hero married the heroine, a reformed saloon singer, after having saved an entire Eskimo village from starvation. It starred John Bromfield, who twice harpooned a whale while filming. The actor made a brief stage appearance at the premiere. A sentimental remake of *Down to the Sea in Ships* premiered on February 15, 1949. Lionel Barrymore as a crusty old whaling captain helps a young Dean Stockwell, who played his orphaned grandson, adjust to life at sea. Richard Widmark as first mate mentors the boy in modern whaling techniques. The ship collided with an iceberg before returning profitably to New Bedford. *All the Brothers Were Valiant* premiered at the State Theater on November 3, 1953. Robert Taylor and Stewart Granger starred as swashbuckling brothers and whalemen; Ann Blyth as the captain's wife at sea; and James Whitmore as a villainous pearl hunter. The hero and heroine survived diseases, kidnapping, mutiny and murders attempts. Ann Miller, a rising MGM dancing star, attended the premiere. She had a "whale of a time" and "especially enjoyed the big boat." Mayor Francis J. Lawler extended her the city's greetings.

Harpoon premiere at the Olympia Theatre, October 20, 1948

***Down to the Sea in Ships* premiere, February 15, 1949.** *The film opened on a sold-out triple premiere evening held at the State, Empire (below) and New Bedford theaters. Above, Caesar Romero, who was not in the cast, Richard Widmark and Mayor Arthur N. Harriman receive a police escort into the Empire. Later, the Wamsutta Club hosted a post-premiere chowder supper for reporters and studio guests. Many locals attended in period clothing and Mayor Harriman distributed plastic white whales as souvenirs.*

Moby Dick

The Moby Dick premiere on June 27, 1956 was New Bedford's social event of the century, featuring Hollywood star Gregory Peck, who played Captain Ahab, noted movie director John Huston and Austrian count Friedrich von Ledebur, who played chief harpooner Queequeg. City businessman Earl DeWalt, chairman of the event's executive committee, led the group's efforts to raise scholarship funds.

Senator John F. Kennedy bought the premiere's first ticket. Local artist Walter Owen and a Swain School design team produced a simulated Time magazine program about New Bedford. Dell Comics issued "Moby Dick" featuring Peck and the cast. A special $2 bill was valid tender in the city for 24½ hours. Downtown businesses decorated with whaling mementos and held special sales.

The Warner Brothers' delegation arrived on a plane newly rechristened the Moby Dick Special. About 10,000 people greeted the plane, thousands showing up at the airport four hours before its scheduled arrival. Local dignitaries met the guests and a crowd of 25,000 lined their motorcade route to the New Bedford Hotel. The next morning, Mayor Frank J. Lawler and the New Bedford City Council officially welcomed them, giving them keys to the city. Later they toured the Whaling Museum, Seamen's Bethel and Durant Sail Loft.

That evening, the delegation joined 400 attendees at a pre-gam party at the Wamsutta Club to which Peck escorted two of Herman Melville's granddaughters. A formal gam gathering followed at the Whaling Museum, where judges of the beard contest awarded Herbert Souza first prize. Meanwhile, a square dance on State Pier attracted 10,000 attendees.

The following day, the delegation visited Sol-E-Mar Children's Hospital and St. Mary's Home before presenting trophies to Moby Dick Regatta winners. They enjoyed a clambake lunch and ate Norwegian whale meat at Gaudette's Pavilion in Acushnet. Later, a seven-mile long parade showcased New Bedford. The film premiered simultaneously at three theaters: State, Empire and New Bedford. Peck and Huston appeared at all three venues. They left the next morning by train.

Miss New Bedford Carole Adams greets Gregory Peck at "Herman Melville Square."

Gregory Peck signs "Moby-Dick" comics for patients at Sol-E-Mar Children's Hospital in Dartmouth.

Mayor Francis J. Lawler hands keys to the city to director John Huston and Gregory Peck, 1956.

Orson Welles as Father Mapple, 1954. *The preacher addresses the faithful from the movie-set pulpit. In Moby-Dick, Herman Melville describes a prow-shaped pulpit, although the Seaman's Bethel did not have one at the time. After the movie, tourists expressed such disappointment when they did not find the prow pulpit, that in 1961 a bow-shaped pulpit was installed and remains today.*

Charles Manuel "Daddy" Grace, 1881–1960

Born Marcelino Manuel da Graça in Brava, Cape Verde, "Sweet Daddy Grace"—as he came to be known around the world—arrived in New Bedford as a young man. One of the city's most colorful characters, he became a larger-than-life religious leader revered by followers as the Black messiah, a faith healer and a prophet, and reviled by critics as a flamboyant cult leader, a charlatan and a cheat.

Once in America, da Graça changed his name to Charles Manuel Grace. After working as a cranberry picker, a railway cook and then a grocer, Grace heard his "calling," began addressing himself as "Bishop Grace" and started preaching. The story goes that in 1919, Grace built —by hand with rocks, salvaged wood and a meager $39—a church on County Road in West Wareham. He organized the United House of Prayer for All People, and in the early 1920s brought his ministry to New Bedford, preaching first on Kempton Street and then later at the former Ahavath Achim Synagogue on Howland Street. (Later, he built a new church at 419 Kempton Street.) From these beginnings grew a prosperous religious organization that continues today. At its height in the 1930s and 1940s, it had more than three million followers.

Similar to the growing Pentecostal movement of the time, Grace's religion was also very much his own creation. His teachings drew from many influences, including Catholic, Baptist and African traditions and rituals. Maintaining that God recruited him particularly to relieve the oppression of African Americans, he preached salvation and upward mobility. Detractors criticized his movement for not tackling widespread social reform. Still, he brought comfort to many a follower and they gratefully called him "Daddy," which he said was less formal than "Father." He often referred to himself as "boyfriend to the world." His parishioners showered him with gifts, tithes and riches, and he amassed a fortune.

In the early days in New Bedford, he sought to outdo other churches. He performed mass baptisms at Clark's Cove. Later, he became known for "watering" thousands at a time by fire hose. Tambourines and banjos, trance dancing and speaking in tongues enhanced his lively services, which sometimes went on until daybreak, to the irritation of neighbors. Believers saw him as similar to Noah, Moses and Jesus. As such, Grace said he could heal the sick, cast out devils and perform miracles. In 1923, he went abroad to further refine his philosophy. He soon opened churches in Egypt, Charlotte, Philadelphia, Newark, Washington DC and New York City.

In time, Grace's services became more elaborate, featuring shout bands and lively gospel music. In the late 1930s, Grace's interest in money and material goods grew as his church grew, and several collections were taken at each service, including special collections for the sale of his own line of anointed products—Grace soap, tea, coffee, facial creams and other items.

He dressed in a flamboyant manner, wore gaudy, expensive jewelry and flashed long red, white and blue fingernails. He eventually bought a fleet of cars and dozens of mansions around the country, including New Bedford's Nye mansion on County and Parker Streets. His personal life was complicated. Grace married and divorced twice and had three children.

Marie W. Dallum, author of Daddy Grace: A Celebrity Preacher and His House of Prayer, writes that Grace's church leadership was exceptionally innovative for the time and that "Grace should be considered among the most distinctive religious leaders of the 20th century." His attention-getting acquisitions were a symbol of power and achievement, not only for himself but for his congregations too.

His funeral in 1960 was the largest ever held in New Bedford, with thousands attending from all over the country. He pre-recorded his own eulogy, which was played at the service. Public viewing of Grace, in a $20,000 glass-topped coffin, lasted four days. He was laid to rest in Pine Grove Cemetery.

Bishop Grace, 1925 and 1953, and his 1960 funeral service at United House of Prayer for All People, Kempton Street. *Bishop Grace's lavish holdings included a farm in Cuba, a coffee plantation in Brazil and the world's tallest apartment building, the Eldorado, in New York City.*

Alfred J. "Lawyer" Gomes, 1897–1974

Born on the Cape Verdean Island of Brava in 1897, Alfred J. Gomes came to New Bedford with his family in 1904. He attended local schools and graduated from New Bedford High School as class valedictorian. During his high school years, he served as editor of the school newspaper, Alpha, and was president of the school's debating society. Gomes financed college by working part time at the old Public Market on Purchase Street. He graduated from Boston University in 1923 and was admitted to the Massachusetts Bar Association in October 1923, the same month he became a naturalized US citizen. He became one of the first Cape Verdean-born Americans to receive a law degree.

Gomes returned to New Bedford to practice law. He became one of the city's most prominent civic, church and community leaders, constantly seeking to promote the aspirations and betterment of Cape Verdean Americans. He was often referred to as "Lawyer Gomes."

Motivated by the collision of the liner SS Olympic with the Nantucket Lightship, he founded the Seamen's Memorial Scholarship fund. Of the seven lightship crewmen who perished in that tragedy, five hailed from New Bedford and four of those were Cape Verdean. The scholarship helped fund students of Cape Verdean descent wishing to further their educations.

In 1942, when Cape Verde experienced one of its periodic famines, Gomes organized the Cape Verdean Relief Fund to raise money for the stricken islanders. For his efforts, the Portuguese government awarded Gomes a Red Cross Order of Merit in May 1943.

In December 1962, Gomes became a trustee of the New Bedford Institute of Technology, which later became the University of Massachusetts Dartmouth. In May 1966, Bishop James L. Connolly named Gomes to the first religious-lay school board in the Fall River Diocese. In 1969, Gomes received the Marian Award for his charitable works.

Gomes was long interested in scouting. He organized the first Cape Verdean Boy Scout troop at the Cape Verdean Beneficent Association. He was awarded the Silver Beaver in October 1968. He also served on the board of directors of the New Bedford Boys Club for more than 40 years.

Additionally, he promoted Cape Verdeans in the arts, literature, music and dance. He sponsored them in exhibits and festivals. On the personal level, Gomes was a prolific historian and researcher of Cape Verdean history and culture.

He died on November 7, 1974. On June 16, 1975, the Commonwealth of Massachusetts honored him on Alfred Joseph Gomes Day.

Judge George N. Leighton, 1912–

George Leighton, a Cape Verdean boy from a large New Bedford family, grew up to become a famed civil rights lawyer and a US District Court judge in Illinois, appointed by US President Gerald R. Ford. As a youngster, he was forced to leave school before the seventh grade to help support his family during the Depression. In his childhood, Leighton (originally Leitão) spent his free time at the Donaghy Boys Club in the South End where he learned champion chess, a game he played throughout his life. Recalling days spent at the club, Judge Leighton spoke fondly of the club founder Mary Ann Hayden, and her decision that the club's underprivileged kids should learn to play chess: "No one has ever given me a greater gift than she did." He ended up working on an oil tanker in the Dutch West Indies. Later, he was employed locally in nearby cranberry bogs. Despite having had to drop out of school early, he studied and read widely and was later accepted to Howard University on the condition that he prove himself a good student. He did, and went on to Harvard Law School, graduating in 1946. He then settled in Chicago.

As a young attorney, Leighton was met with blatant and systemic racial discrimination. He was not allowed to join the American Bar Association or the Chicago Bar Association or even rent office space in many buildings in downtown Chicago. Yet he became an outstanding attorney and co-founder of one of the largest African American law firms in the US. As a defense attorney and a staunch civil rights advocate, he vigorously defended others who suffered discrimination. Later he became an eminent judge, a brilliant law professor, and a man honored for his lifelong service to the legal profession. As a judge, he said most Hispanics and African Americans assume the cards are stacked against them when they walk into a courtroom where everyone deciding their fate is white. But, he said, "They are relieved when they walk in and see a member of their race sitting on the bench."

One of his memorable quotes is, "The difference between God and prosecuting attorneys is that God doesn't think of himself as a prosecuting attorney."

New Bedford claims Judge Leighton, who celebrated his 100th birthday in 2012, as a favorite son and named its downtown US Post Office after him. Chicago also renamed its criminal court building after him.

Feeding bison, circa 1960.

The day after a February storm, zookeeper Arthur Knowles clears snow from trough for deer and llama to feed, 1942.

Buttonwood Park Zoo

The oldest continually operating zoo in Massachusetts and the twelfth oldest in the country, New Bedford's zoo opened in 1894 before the park was developed. In its early years, the park hosted a menagerie that held a small collection of native species such as black bears, foxes and deer. A little later, zookeepers added a monkey house. By 1900, the zoo also showcased foxes, raccoons, prairie dogs, squirrels, rabbits, owls, geese, ducks, guinea hens and guinea pigs.

In 1919, a small aviary was erected to shelter macaws, toucans, peafowl and ring-necked pheasants. By the mid 1920s, the zoo featured 35 different species of animals with additions of lions, eagles, coyotes, seals, leopards, elephants, elk and sheep.

During the Great Depression, a day at the zoo lifted spirits of children and adults. In 1935, Work Progress Administration workers completed major renovations to the park and zoo, building a new bear den, monkey house and a special petting zoo.

The first baby bison arrived at the zoo in 1954. To publicize the event, Mayor Edward F. Harrington held a contest to name the animal. The winner would receive a $10 prize awarded from the mayor's pocket. Taken from 250 entries, judges chose "Funelope" submitted by Paul Jason of Collette Street, who explained that the animal "is fun to watch and lopes all around."

Bears come out of hibernation from the bear den, April 1957.

Moby-Dick breaches at Storybook Land, Brooklawn Park, 1958.

F-94 Starfire jet touches down at Storybook Land, 1958.

Fantasy Lands

On opening day August 9, 1958, about 4,000 children entered the two oversized doors to the magical kingdom of **Storybook Land** in Brooklawn Park. A fantasy land, created by the city as a gift to its children, welcomed small guests with this inscription: "Through these portals pass the happiest children in the world, the future citizens of New Bedford." A colorful wall painted with circus animals and Mother Goose characters bordered the 48,000 square-foot area.

Children could climb on 17 large nursery rhyme exhibits, wander in a wooden maze, stumble around a crooked house, board the "Good Ship Lollypop," explore a little red schoolhouse, greet a spouting Moby Dick and pet small animals.

At the opening, Mayor Francis J. Lawler promised to add to the exhibits and he kept that promise. The most striking addition was not from Mother Goose but the real thing—a jet aircraft. With the help of Post 1 American Legion, Lawler acquired a F-94 Starfire interceptor jet from Otis Air Force Base. Children could climb into the cockpit and pretend to head into the wide blue yonder with companion "Steve Canyon," a popular comic book character of a mythical Air Force hero of the time whose name city workers painted onto the fuselage.

In 1967, Storybook Land was replaced by ball fields.

The **Festival of Lights** on Clasky Common Park on County and Pearl Streets highlights the holiday season for many families. This dazzling display of lights fills the seven-acre park, lighting up the nights during the holiday season. The common's centerpiece is a magnificent old tree, which is lit from below. The festival speaks to many religious traditions—Christmas, Chanukah, Three Kings Day and Kwanzaa.

With backing from the city, local folks each year create this winter wonderland, especially hard-working students from Greater New Bedford Regional Vocational Technical High School, who practice their trades as they invent the seasonal magic. Aided by city workers, electrical students string lights and engineering students get automated figures moving. Carpentry students build staging and paint figures—sleds, barns and reindeer. Fashion design students dress the elves and Santa, played by a jolly Voke Tech student who arrives with bells ringing. Parker Elementary School singers fill the air with song and everyone gets a welcome from the mayor.

The festival began in December 1952 and continues today, though the park remained dark for several years in the early 1970s due to vandalism. Upgraded security, watchful neighbors and fond memories brought back the celebration.

Choral display at Festival of Lights, Common Park, 1961.

Manger, chapel and other displays, Festival of Lights, 1957.

Education

Education in New Bedford saw major changes during and after the war years. From 1941 to 1942, public high school enrollment dropped 17 percent as some students left for ready jobs and high wages in defense industries. Others lied about their ages and enlisted in the armed services. Beginning in 1944, Mayor Arthur N. Harriman joined other state mayors to announce a "Back to School" movement that stressed the need for a high school education in the postwar environment.

Although the city's population fell by seven percent between 1940 and 1960, the number of students remained constant, in part due to the post-war Baby Boom and lower infant mortality. During and after the war, city marriage rates and subsequent birth rates skyrocketed. In 1940 the number of marriages in the city jumped to 1,291, almost 60 percent higher than in 1935, as folks anticipated enlisting or being drafted into military service. Marriages continued rising for the next two years. As a result, in 1942 the city's birth rate of 18.6 per thousand hit its highest mark since the city's 1928 strike.

After the war, many men and women returned to the city to marry, starting families whose children became part of the Baby Boom. In 1946, marriages jumped 80 percent higher than in 1944. In 1946, New Bedford's birth rate rose to 21 per thousand.

Better public health initiatives also contributed to school enrollment as more children lived to school age. The city's infant mortality rate dropped by a striking 80 percent from

Study at Normandin Junior High School, 1942. *Juliette Mauricia, daughter of an Azorean-born immigrant father, studies her English Grammar book,* Words: Their Spelling, Pronunciation, Definition and Application, *by Rupert SoRelle and Charles Kitt, published in 1903.*

an average 90 deaths for 1000 live births in the 1920s to 18.3 deaths per 1,000 live births by 1960.

In 1949, the House Un-American Activities Committee examined the city's school textbooks for Communist propaganda as part of a hunt through state schools and colleges. They found nothing of note in New Bedford's textbooks.

City schools stood at the forefront in the battle against polio. In April 1955, the city received its first shipment of the Salk vaccine. In May 1955, New Bedford students lined up to receive their doses as part of a statewide mass vaccination of first- and second-graders. The following year, the number of polio deaths in Massachusetts fell to five.

Allen F. Wood School, 1944. *Wood School fourth graders pledge allegiance in the first public school in the United States to fly the American flag. Students reciting the pledge on the first day of school include: First vertical row (closest to blackboard): Alice Sylvia, Benjamin Silva, Betty Ann Lopes and Leroy Oliveira. Second row: Eugene M. Pina, Laura Duarte and Herman Galvin. Third row: Genevieve DaLuz, Walter Lomba and Lucille Barros.*

Public and Private Schools

Midcentury saw an increasing number of children enrolling in the city's private, often parochial, schools. The change was most notable in the early grades: From 1940 to 1960, while the number of 5- to 7-year-olds in public school rose by a third, those in private schools jumped by 130 percent. Also, for the 7- to 16-year-olds, the number of students in public school fell by 1,350 or 11 percent, while those in private schools rose 5 percent. In addition, the 1959 opening of the regional, Catholic high school Bishop Stang, located just over the line in Dartmouth, gave New Bedford students a new alternative. The following year, New Bedford High School's freshman class size dropped by one-fifth.

In the photograph at top, **Holy Family Grammar School's** first grade class members include Jimmy Aylwood, Eleanor Bolger, Kenneth Burke, Danny Callahan, Jimmy Considine, Kathleen Curry, Annie David, Mary Lou Davis, Dick Flood, Winnifred Gifford, John Hanson, Margaret Hatton, Margaret Lynch, Frank Mahoney, John McKenna, Anne Marie Murphy, Jimmy Murphy, Winifred Murray, Peter Smith, Ann Smith and Kathleen Sylvia.

Saint Hyacinthe (at center), the tiny French parochial school on Rivet Street, contained just six rooms—a kindergarten, a cafeteria and four classrooms holding two grades in each. In the 1950s, the school enrolled between 80 and 90 students. First row from left, front to back: Rita Marshall, Lenora Hotte, Diane Brassard, Jeanne LePage and Lorraine Rocha. Second row, front to back: Anthony Thomas, John Marshall, Barry Sylvia, Jean Rousseau and Richard Zerbonne. Standing, front to back: Rolande Savaria, Marie LaChapelle, Peter Marshall, Robert Rousseau, Stephen Thomas, Carl Champagne and Sister Anne, SSD.

At bottom, kindergarten class (1958-59) at the **Clarence A. Cook School** on Summer and North Streets. Teacher Alice D. Silvia sits at her desk in the corner. Identified students include Frank Tolentino, Audrey Ollivierre, Russ Grace and Eva Henderson.

First grade class at Holy Family Grammar School, circa 1941.

Third and fourth grades, Saint Hyacinthe Grammar School, Rivet Street, 1958.

Kindergarten class, Clarence A. Cook School, 1959.

Massachusetts Air Industries class, 1949.

New Bedford Textile School, 1955.

Vocational Training

Armand F. Perry, chief mechanic for **Massachusetts Air Industries**, teaches students in the company's classroom facilities at the municipal airport. The program in aircraft and engines led to commercial licenses. Some pioneering young women students can be seen in this class.

At the **New Bedford Institute of Technology**, Jacqueline Oliveira, left, Barbara Amandoles, center, and Polly Field, work with materials in Evelyn Ramalhete's fashion design class. To learn pattern drafting and draping, each student had a personal dress form. She then had to design a garment, print the pattern on fabric, make and fit the dress, and model the finished garment.

Students in the general vocational department of the **Continuation School** learn home nursing. RN Beverly Burgo bandages a seated Ethel Rose. Anile Gonzales shakes down a mercury thermometer to take her temperature. Pauline V. Reis serves a meal to bed patient Evelyn Smith. The Continuation School provided an alternative to the high school diploma program,

New Bedford Vocational School Graduating Class, June 1960.

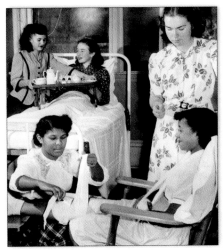

Continuation School, 1948.

Campbell Secretarial School, County & Campbell Streets, circa 1955.

teaching job skills to students 16 years old or older who ere at risk of not graduating. Its programs ended after the 1955-1956 school year.

Students at **Campbell Secretarial School** learn data entry on a variety of adding machines—without looking at the keyboard. One student at far right transcribes a dictation tape. Hector J.

Robitaille, the school's long-serving director, oversaw a program of business administration, secretarial science, accounting, civil service and office machines. Campbell merged with Kinyon's Commercial and Short-Hand School in 1969 to become the Kinyon-Campbell School, which closed in 1999 as more students attended Bristol Community College.

In Joan Beaubian's **1960 graduating class** from New Bedford Voke, young women in the front rows model their handmade gowns. "We created our own patterns and made the gowns, which we wore to the prom as well—a September to June project," Beaubian recalled. The public always turned out to see them, no two alike, as they lit up the courtyard.

St. Mary's Home

Raymond Rivard spent his teenage years at Saint Mary's Home and returned at 22 as its custodian, a post he held for the next 30 years. Rivard came from a family of eight children, five boys and three girls, and lived his early years in the Presidential Heights housing project. As with so many others, his family met rough times. When his world fell apart, St. Mary's sheltered him.

"The year was 1948. I was 13 and out caddying on the 15th hole at the New Bedford Country Club when my older sister told me I had to go with her. My parents had split up, and the next thing I knew, I was walking through the front doors of St. Mary's Home for Children," Rivard recalled. St. Mary's Children's Home on Kempton Street was established in 1894 to care for orphan children and the aged poor during the Whaling era. Run by the Diocese of Providence and the Sisters of St. Francis of Glenriddle, Pennsylvania, the home supported itself through fundraising and aid from local parishes and charities.

Troubled, Rivard's mother moved to California to live with a sister and his older siblings left home to fend for themselves. His father couldn't take care of Rivard, his five-year-old brother Bobby and seven-year-old sister Patricia."He had a good job as a sewing machine mechanic, repairing machinery at different

St. Mary's Home, facing Kempton Street, corner of Liberty, 1935.

factories, but he had drinking problems. So, he took us directly to St. Mary's Children's Home. I only saw him twice after that. Years later, I learned he had died when the funeral home called and asked who would be making the arrangements," Rivard said.

At the time, St. Mary's cared for 110 children. "I was afraid of the nuns at first because I had never seen one. All I saw were these big people standing there with white collars and all-black clothes. I wanted to run out the back door, but after a while we got along pretty good," he said. The children wore uniforms, and followed stringent rules and a strict routine. "We got up at 6:00 AM, went to mass at 6:30 and did our chores before

Youngsters surrounding Mayor Francis J. Lawler wave goodbye before leaving for their annual outing at Lincoln Park, 1956.

Dinner preparations, St. Mary's kitchen, 1949. *The young girl peeling potatoes is Eugenia Nascimento.*

The St. Mary's Home Boys Harmonica Orchestra, 1947. *The boys practice to perform at an event to raise money for the Catholic Charities Appeal fund, which provided instruments for the boys.*

breakfast. School went from 8:30 to 10:30 AM, then we went back to finish our chores. After lunch, we went to school again from 1 to 3:00 PM and had playground until 6:00 PM. From 6:30 to 9:30, we went back to school for study hour—a quiet time. So we went to school three times a day," Rivard said.

Discipline could be harsh. "The worst punishment came after the boys had a pillow fight in one of the bedrooms and a nun got in the middle of the fight and got hurt," Rivard said. "Our punishment was to sand down the chapel to its bare wood. It was made of dark oak, so it took a lot of work to sand it down. We would work two hours every evening, about five or six of us, and the whole thing took three or four months. After we finished, Father Thompson said, 'It looks all right, but I want it back the way it was.' So we had to stain it back."

Life could be painful for the children dealing with family upheaval, abandonment and loneliness. Yet there were lighter times as well: sitting around listening to Roy Rogers or the Green Hornet on the radio, building model airplanes, playing checkers, shuffleboard and hopscotch. The children also played sports such as baseball and soccer.

"We would go to a lot of theaters with the Sisters, the Olympia, the State and New Bedford theaters," Rivard remembered. "We had to walk down the street in single file, all 110 of us with two Sisters. We must have looked like a bunch of ants going down the road."

Chores were built into daily life. "We did a lot of work at St. Mary's. We made our own beds, and washed our own clothes. The laundry was a small brick building across the street and there were huge wooden washing machines. I was in charge of my own laundry, my brother's, and the laundry of a couple of the younger kids," Rivard said. "I did the sheets too, and we were in charge of our own ironing. I also washed the basement floor and did many other chores."

Soup and cheese were a staple at St. Mary's, although not always favorites. "At mealtimes, I was in charge of the kitchen area. I washed dishes for four years," Rivard said. "The children ate at big long tables with benches, with a captain in charge of each table. Sister would make soup in big Army pots; it would last for three or four days. There was cheese on everything and, to this day, I cannot eat cheese. I cannot eat bologna and hot dogs either. Our best meal was on Sunday when we'd have chicken, ham or turkey."

Rivard left St. Mary's when he was 17 with his younger siblings when his mother returned and took custody of them.

He worked as a sheet metal cutter for a time at Cornell Dubilier. "Until I got a call from Father Hogan, offering me the job of custodian at St. Mary's," Rivard recalled. "I took it. The year was 1958. I was 22, and I had the job for the next 29½ years."

In 1965, the Department of Social Services took over St. Mary's, which became a residential treatment center with social workers and a psychiatrist. The five remaining nuns left in 1983. During this time, the state's foster system grew and the state favored placing children in private homes rather than larger institutions. St. Mary's population dwindled and eventually it closed. The building became the home of the Bristol County Sheriff's Department and then the Eastern MA Correctional Alcoholic Center. Rivard gratefully remembers St. Mary's for giving him shelter, an education and a strong work ethic.

"I came from St. Mary's Home, and I ended up back here," he said. "I got married and had three children. My boys came to St. Mary's constantly when I was working there. I taught them what Father Thompson used to say: 'You're here; we're doing everything we can for you. But when you get beyond the two front doors, what you make of yourself, you do it.'"

New Bedford Day Nursery

When mothers and grandmothers who traditionally provided childcare began working long days in the industrial mills, young children were often left alone, or with siblings forced to stay home from school to babysit. Though nurseries had arrived in France and England, the idea was suspect in America in spite of an obvious need. Parents did not want strangers looking after their children in strange places.

But childcare became so haphazard that many worried about the welfare of young children. New York City opened its first day care center in 1850. In 1886, a group of concerned New Bedford women, ages 18 to 20, formed the New Bedford Day Nursery. Its first slate of officers included Bertha Mandell as president, Nella H. Gifford as vice president, Helen W. Prescott as secretary, and as treasurer Elizabeth S. (Holmes) Rugg, who held office for thirty-three years.

Determined fundraisers, the women collected donations, raised subscriptions and sponsored amateur shows. The first day nursery opened in 1887, in a small house on Pleasant Street in the North End. The South End New Bedford Day Nursery opened 15 years later on Howard Street, later moving to County Street, and finally settling on Cove Street, where it remained for 75 years.

Suspicious, many families were reluctant to enroll their youngsters. But eventually, parents warmed to reliable daycare, where children were fed and kept busy with books and toys for a rate of 10¢ a day. The organization became an active voice for child welfare. During the 1918 influenza epidemic, nursery officials argued to stay open round-the-clock to care for children whose parents had died or were too ill to care for them.

When the defense industry enlisted more women during World War II to work in factories turning out parachutes and ammunition, the federal government helped fund nurseries through the school department. Over the years, the nurseries struggled to stay open in the face of ongoing budget problems, mill strikes, outbreaks of diphtheria and polio, changes in daycare regulations, education trends, neighborhood safety issues and building maintenance costs. The New Bedford Day Nursery closed in 1997. It was the second longest-running daycare center in America.

In their History of the New Bedford Day Nursery, Ruth Nicolaci and Francine Weeks wrote that the organization's mission shifted to become a non-profit fund distributing grants to programs for children, especially in the South End. Today, reports Marguerite "Gig" Lang, recording secretary of the fund, the organization continues to distribute grants from its $800,000 endowment.

South End Day Nursery, 1904.

South End Day Nursery, Cove Road, 1933. *Caregiver Jeanette Morrow watches over a relaxed group of children. Despite the need for nursery centers, working mothers did not take advantage of the city's social services. During the Depression, three WPA nursery schools supplemented two community-supported nurseries. Yet only 70-75 children used the centers—a fraction of the number in need of care.*

Ruth B. McFadden

Born in Lincoln, Rhode Island, Ruth B. McFadden became the first female school superintendent in New Bedford and in Massachusetts. She started teaching primary grades in New Bedford's Abraham Lincoln School in 1920 and transferred in 1927 to Roosevelt Junior High School as a social science teacher. During the 1930s, she earned her bachelor's and master's degrees in education from Boston University. She moved to the high school in 1939.

By October 1955, McFadden was assistant superintendent for elementary education. She became acting superintendent upon the retirement of Kenneth Burke. The school board spent 10 weeks examining the credentials of 22 male applicants before discovering it already had a qualified candidate—McFadden. Although she had not applied or been consulted, the board named McFadden to the post. The job made her the city's top public wage earner with an annual salary of $10,000. During her tenure, McFadden advocated for many changes to the system. She pushed for new elementary schools allowing children to remain together from kindergarten until sixth grade instead of being shuffled into separate classes after third grade. She argued for cafeterias in all schools so students would be assured lunches. She repeatedly singled out the city's 50 percent dropout rate as the school system's worst problem and felt the high school should provide more courses for students not planning to attend college. She argued against a single, large high school in favor of two separate schools with a maximum enrollment of 1,500 students each. She also recommended longer classes and a longer school day.

McFadden stayed on the job for six years until her retirement in 1961. In 1975, the city named the Hayden-McFadden School to honor her and her successor, Dr. James R. Hayden.

Elnora M. Williams

Born in New Bedford and a city resident for her entire life, Elnora Williams spotted a problem and found a solution in the West End Day Nursery. In 1941, Williams noticed that as an increasing number of women were pressed to work in defense-related industries, more children were left without traditional daycare and were sometimes fending for themselves without supervision. Sponsored by the Martha Briggs Educational Club, Williams opened the nursery on Mill Street (later moving to Kempton Street) to provide that missing care and supervision for preschool youngsters.

Her legacy endures. The West End Day Nursery still operates today on Cedar Street. Almost 75 years later, the non-profit, charitable institution continues to provide the same types of family services including child development and basic education as well as programs centered on health, recreation and nutrition.

Williams came from a family of civil servants. For many years, her father Ira Joseph worked as a gardener in the city's public cemeteries and she too followed a similar civil service career path as a janitor in the city libraries. Her husband Moses H. Williams also became a gardener in the city cemeteries.

She remained active in community affairs all her life. Williams was a member and trustee of the Bethel AME Church, a board director of the New Bedford Home for the Aged, a member and past president of the Martha Briggs Educational Club, and a member of the Jane Jackson Circle of the Ladies of the Grand Army of the Republic.

Elnora M. Williams (right) and the West End Day Nursery, 1943. A total of 126 children ages 5–12 were enrolled for the noon meal, solving the problem of how to feed children of working mothers. Meals consisted of meat loaf, mashed potatoes, cabbage, carrot salad, wheat bread, tapioca cream and chocolate milk served at a charge of 10¢ per child. Parents paid what they could afford, while the Martha Briggs Educational Club paid the rest. Milk was provided daily by the Children's Aid Society and meats were sent once a month by two local markets.

A History of New Bedford Music, 1942–1960

From World War II through the post-war decades, the big band sound, jazz and popular music dominated New Bedford's music scene. The city's strong Cape Verdean, Azorean and Madeiran Portuguese influences found ready musical expression, as did those of Polish and French groups.

Musical venues proliferated as bebop sound generated heart-pounding rhythms and dance fever. The Lincoln Park Ballroom in Dartmouth topped the bill for local ensembles and marquee national bands. In New Bedford, neighborhood venues such as theaters, union halls and social clubs all provided stages for musicians who played to packed dance floors.

Lincoln Park Big Band Sound

Each week, a star artist or band would headline at Lincoln Park, which featured local bands the rest of the time. The park provided steady employment for the region's musicians, while the groups defined the park's dance and music entertainment styles. Noted local bandleaders included Gene Marshall, Ted Bettencourt, Al Rainone, Bob Hughes and Art Perry.

Gene Marshall's Band provided training and secure jobs for local musicians during the prewar years and after as soldier-players returned to civilian life. Marshall played regular gigs at Lincoln Park on Tuesday, Thursday and Saturday nights, and once a week the show was broadcast live on radio.

Joseph Perreira and his family came to the area from São Miguel, Azores, in 1901, and settled in New Bedford, where Perreira worked in the cotton mills and Americanized his name to Perry. Adept with the Portuguese guitar, Perreira passed his love of music on to his children. He taught his son Gus (Augustus Perreira) the mandolin. Gus in turn bought a violin for his musically inclined younger brother, Jackie (Antonio Pereira), who organized the first Perry Brothers Orchestra in 1922. Jackie led his brothers Joseph ("Joe"), Manuel ("Matt") and Francis at engagements in Chatham and the Nantucket Yacht Club. Jackie played violin, guitar, saxophone, banjo, clarinet, trumpet, accordion, piano and drums, and performed with the Paramount Theater Orchestra and Kavanaugh's Orchestra. The Perry Brothers Orchestra disbanded in 1924, when Jackie moved to Philadelphia and joined the Charlie Kerr Orchestra along with trombonist Lloyd Turner, drummer Edward Andre and bassist Stanley Soboski of New Bedford. In 1929, Arthur, the youngest Perry brother, reassembled the family orchestra. This time, it played for more than a decade before breaking up, as members joined the military during the war. It regrouped for a short time after the war but disbanded in 1947 as big band music slipped out of vogue. The brothers went on to form other bands, including the Matt Perry Band, originally made up of five brothers and four nephews, and the Art Perry Orchestra, nicknamed the Band of 1,000 Melodies.

In 1958, several Perry family musicians played at Lincoln Park for an anniversary show. The reunion band consisted of six brothers, ten nephews and a niece. At that time, nephews Leonard Rapoza (Lenny Rapp) and Louis Mendoza (Louis George) each headed their own bands.

During the late 1970s and 1980s, although dance music was in decline, Art Perry's orchestras and combos revived the oldies dances at Lincoln Park, regularly drawing 300 to 400 senior citizens a week.

The Matt Perry Orchestra at Moose Hall, Dartmouth Street, 1949. *From left to right: front row: Sylvia Ann (Rapoza) Sylvia, vocalist; Matt Perry (seated), piano; Manny Rapoza, sax; Lenny Rapoza, sax; Joe Mendoza, sax;* "Pee Wee" Perry, sax; and original band organizer Jackie Perry (standing). Back row: Gus Perry, bass; Eddie Rapoza, drums; Gus Rapoza, trombone; Tony Rapoza, trumpet; Art Perry, trumpet; and Louie Mendoza, trumpet.

Dance night at Lincoln Park, 1954. *Drummer's perspective shows bandleader Gene Marshall soloing to a packed crowd at the Lincoln Park Ballroom. The drummer, Teddy Bettencourt, was also a photographer.*

The Graylords, 1957. *Featuring Teddy Bettencourt, Jackie Coelho, Lionel Soares and Manuel Machado, the Graylords brought together four veteran musicians who sought to poke fun at their age and experience.*

Lionel Soares Orchestra, circa 1940. *Soares was a saxophonist, clarinetist, composer and music teacher who performed throughout the US, Canada and Europe. Left to right are Frank Dzedulevitz, accordion; Thatcher Chase, piano; Lionel Soares, saxophone; Albert Aston, trumpet; Hervey LaBonte, trombone; John Denault, bass violin; and Walter Piwowarczyk, drums.*

Teddy Bettencourt's quartet at Smith's Lounge, Union Street, 1950s. *Bettencourt spent the 1940s and 1950s playing drums in almost every jazz combo in the region, including his own. Smith's Lounge would later become the Picadilly Lounge and in the 1960s, Jimmy Connors Tavern.*

Skyliners, May 1959. *The horn section limbers up for a gig at Music Week's Dance Bands Festival in the High School auditorium. Left to right are Jimmie Costa, Eddie Pinto, Henry Houtman, George Macabello and Albert Fermino.*

Ed Roderiques Orchestra, 1955. *The band's horn section featured (left to right) Cab Rozario, Joe Ribeiro, Antone Costa, Ed Rodrigues and Gilly Ferro.*

The Legend of Paul Gonsalves

Some Cape Verdean musicians leveraged New Bedford beginnings into greatness. The son of Cape Verdean-born parents, tenor saxophonist Paul Gonsalves often came to New Bedford from Pawtucket, Rhode Island, to perform with his two brothers. Their father, John, an accomplished chef, taught them to play guitar. In 1936, Paul switched to saxophone. In 1937, the Gonsalves Brothers Trio entered—and won—a Creole talent contest at Monte Pio Hall. Hoping to make the most of the win, Paul began hitchhiking to New Bedford on his own to play with local musicians. He gigged and subbed with local groups until joining the Phil Edmond Band. The group played Creole music and swing on the Cape Verdean dance scene and the New England college circuit. With a steady job, Gonsalves moved to New Bedford, staying until he joined the army in 1942. After the war, he rejoined the Boston-based Sabby Lewis Band, with whom he had briefly played earlier. He later played saxophone with jazz music's three most exciting orchestras, beginning with Count Basie from 1946 to 1949. Then, for almost a year, he performed with the Dizzy Gillespie Band. He joined Duke Ellington in 1950. When Ellington performed in New Bedford in 1952, members of Local 214 American Federation of Musicians honored fellow member Gonsalves. In 1953, when Ellington was between record label contracts, Gonsalves did a short three-week stint with trombonist Tommy Dorsey.

At the 1956 Newport Jazz Festival, Gonsalves' long solo bridge between the opening and closing sections of Ellington's "Diminuendo and Crescendo in Blue" so energized the crowd that it led to a revival of the bandleader's career. While many considered it a milestone in jazz history, in some ways it put

Gonsalves blasts away with Louie Bellson in a city club, 1953. *An internationally known drummer, composer and bandleader, Louie Bellson is credited with pioneering the use of two bass drums. Bellson performed with Benny Goodman, Tommy Dorsey, Harry James and Duke Ellington. He is the drummer on Ellington's 1952 recording of "Take the A Train" with Paul Gonsalves on sax. At the far right on alto saxophone is Russell Procope.*

Gonzales in bondage. Everywhere the band went, audiences demanded a repeat of his legendary feat. Gonzales was obliged to play extended, up-tempo solos instead of the relaxed and thoughtful ballads he preferred. For the Ellington band's last 25 years, Gonsalves was its principal soloist. He died in London in 1974, a few days before Duke Ellington's death. Whenever he visited New Bedford, friends arranged after-hours gigs with the area's Cape Verdeans. He would also drop into local venues such as The Kettle in Acushnet, the Piccadilly Lounge, the Cape Verdean Band Club and the Sharpshooters Hall. Gonsalves said he preferred playing for New Bedford's Cape Verdean crowds over audiences in New York, whom he felt took musicians for granted.

Blue Room, 1949. *Paul Gonsalves is accompanied by Ted Bettencourt on drums (not visible), Manny Rose on bass and Mike Silva on piano. The Blue Room was on the second floor of the Band Club on Acushnet Avenue.*

Musicians Union honors Paul Gonsalves, 1952. *When Ellington (second right) performed in New Bedford in 1952, members of Local 214, American Federation of Musicians honored Gonsalves (center). At far left are Adolph "Doc" Coimbra and Louie Bellson. At far right is Joseph "Jedge Marita" Senna.*

Cape Verdean & Crioulo Big Band Sounds

Beginning in the 1920s, Cape Verdean orchestras led by younger musicians, including sons of Star Orchestra members, fused traditional Crioulo style with jazz. The new generation had grown up in the US and developed an appreciation for American music. Their new sound brought in brass horns, woodwinds, keyboard instruments, string bass and electric guitar.

Vocalist and dancer Isadore Oliveira, whose name became Americanized as Duke Oliver, led the Ultramarine Club's dance band called the Skyliners. Oliver had previously headed up the Creole Vagabonds, also known as Duke Oliver's Orchestra. The Skyliners performed at local dances and at a namesake nightclub on Acushnet Avenue, where many Cape Verdean bands played. They specialized in swing music in the Duke Ellington style. Joseph "Jedge Marita" Senna managed the group before branching out with his own orchestra, which played arrangements by pianist Raymond "Ray" Lomba, Alvaro Duarte and others. Felix "Phil Edmund" Barboza, Don Verdi and Jimmy Lomba each led medium-sized jazz bands, mainly playing popular American music with a Crioulo edge.

On weekend nights, Cape Verdean bands with violin, guitar, Portuguese viola, reeds and horns performed at local clubs including United Social Club and the Crystal Café as well as the Cape Verdean Ultramarine Band Club. The audience listened and danced to music that embodied a heritage shared between generations.

In 1947, the Cape Verdean All-Stars formed a touring orchestra, with many of New Bedford's leading musicians: Joe Ramos; Manual Britto; saxophonist Jimmy, pianist Ray and violinist Johnny Lomba; and vocalist "Joli" Gonsalves. It toured the East Coast, Midwest and California.

Brothers Frank C. "Chico" Monteiro and Pedro Monteiro made their mark on New Bedford's music scene. Their father worked in the mills and an older brother Antonio was a fisherman. Frank and Pedro also worked but followed their musical passion—Frank played bass and Pedro played trombone. In the late 1930s, they were with Duke Oliver. Later, Pedro took over the leadership of the Cape Verdean Ultramarine Band and Skyliners Orchestra. Frank succeeded his brother and led the orchestra for many years. He served as president of the local branch of the American Federation of Musicians Local 214.

Others who fused a Crioulo sound to American songs found a ready audience outside the Cape Verdean community. Trumpet player Joe Livramento grew up in New Bedford and got a start with the Cape Verdean Ultramarine Band Club. In the late 1930s, he joined the Don Verdi Orchestra. In 1954, he toured Venezuela with the Machito Orchestra. On returning to the US, he played the Apollo Theater, Birdland, the Palladium

Duke Oliver's Orchestra, circa 1942. *Left to right: Phil Edmund Barboza, Peter Monteiro, Alvaro Duarte, Julio "July" Alves, Mike Sanchez, Raymond Lomba, Duke Oliver, "Snubby" Almeida, Frank Monteiro, Albert "Burt" Fermino and Jimmy Lomba.*

The Ultramarine Band Club, 1955. Members celebrate a Memorial Day Parade performance at the "Band Club" on Acushnet Avenue. From left to right are: Henry Sylvia, Mike Sanchez, Baboi Soares, Jiwe Galvin, John Santos, July Alves, Cab Rozario, Manuel Rose Jr. and Frank Monteiro.

Jimmy Lomba on sax at the Blue Room, upstairs in the Band Club, 1945. From left to right are: Mike Sanchez, Bill Britto, Jimmy Lomba, Chick Boucher on drums and Ray Lomba on keyboard.

and the Audubon and Savoy Ballrooms. At the Roseland, he played with the Ramon Argueso Orchestra.

Jimmy Lomba parlayed his job playing saxophone with local Cape Verdean bands into a music career that took him all over the world. Born in New Bedford to Brava-born parents, he bought his first saxophone at age 19 using savings from a textile mill job. From 1940 to 1950, he had a 12-piece band that played cafeteria lunchtimes at the Cornell Dubilier plant, where employees eagerly awaited his shows. He also played with Duke Oliver's Orchestra. After moving to San Francisco in the 1950s, he backed up legendary artists including Motown's The Temptations and Smokey Robinson, blues singer Dinah Washington, comedians Bill Cosby and Bob Hope, and movie icons Sammy Davis Jr. and Ginger Rogers. Later, he formed his own band, Jimmy Lomba's Orchestra, which interpreted Duke Ellington's music. After returning east in 1972, he turned to education, teaching music theory and improvisational techniques. He also taught woodwinds, clarinet and saxophone for the Old Rochester Regional school system. Jimmy's brother, pianist Ray Lomba, performed locally. He led his own Latin-American Combo in the mid-1950s.

During the early 1930s, Columbia Records made an effort to preserve some of the European mazurkas and polkas that formed part of the classic Cape Verdean repertoire. Columbia recorded the orchestra of Candido "Notias" Almeida, who owned a music shop on Walnut Street; Johnny Perry's instrumental Crioulo trio; the Cape Verde Serenaders, which featured the legendary fiddler Boboy de Tai; and the Portuguese Instrumental Trio led by Fogo-born violinist Augusto Abreu.

Some Cape Verdean musicians clung to their roots. Orchestras under John "Johnny" Duarte and Henry Silva played traditional music with guitar, violin and viola at Cape Verdean community dances. Duarte, interested in music from age five, first learned the saxophone and later the violin.

Phil Edmund Orchestra at Lincoln Park 1942. At far left are saxophonists Paul Gonsalves and Joe Livramento; Tootsie Wright is on drums; Phil Edmund Barboza stands front and center blowing the trumpet; Manny Rose is on upright bass; Mac on piano; and vocalist Helen Watkins is seated.

Traditional combo, 1960s. *Johnny Lomba (on violin) had his own orchestra, which occasionally performed traditional tunes at the Band Club. In addition to Lomba, it included violist Al Lopes, guitarist Joe Rogers, saxophonist Avelino "Boboi" Soares, bassist John Grace and guitarist Joe Andrade.*

Ray Lomba's Latin-American Combo, 1955. *Players include, left to right, Frank Monteiro on bass, Julio Alves on drums, Roland Roy on sax, Manuel Piva on percussion, pianist Ray Lomba and Cab Rozario on trumpet.*

He joined Henry Silva's band in 1946 and took it over from 1952 to 1961. After an eight-year hiatus, he joined Freddie Silva before forming his own band, which regularly played at the New Bedford Hotel Ballroom. In 1970, he joined the Creole Sextet while working at Chamberlain Manufacturing. Members of the Creole Sextet periodically reunited; in 1991, they did so at a retirement party for Manny and Julie Cabral. Violist Henry Silva learned to sing and play by listening to his father repeat the music that he had learned in Cape Verde. Silva formed his first band in 1941 to play original Cape Verdean songs sung in Crioulo. Even as band members died or left, demand for such music remained high. Into the 1980s, Silva and friends performed nearly every weekend in local clubs to increasingly older audiences.

The 1940s saw new instruments brought into Cape Verdean music. The Al Lopes Orchestra had Frank "Pawpaw" Pontes on maracas and Domingo "Mingo" Pina on accordion. Until the 1950s, Lopes recorded music on his own record label, "Verda-Tones." He sold records through his shop in the Grace Building at the corner of Acushnet Avenue and Wing Street.

During the 1950s and 1960s, other small bands kept Cape Verdean traditional music alive. One of these was the Four Kings, originally a brass band that later added drums and maracas. Guitarist John C. Rogers Sr., also known as "Johnny DeMarguida," played for the Four Kings and for his own group called Johnny Rogers and His Band. Well known for his guitar solos, he received numerous awards for his Cape Verdean music.

The Skyliners Orchestra, Dance Bands Music Festival, NBHS Auditorium, 1950. *Front row seated: Charles Gonsalves and Vick Viera. Second row, from left to right: Henry Houtman, José Ferro, Burt Fermino, Jedge Senna and Eddie Pinto. Third row: Egidlio Mello and Jonny Trobonae. Fourth row: Peter Monterio, Sonny Rodrigues, Alvaro Duarte, Cab Rozario. At right: pianist Mike Silva, drummer July Alves and bassist Frank Monteiro.*

Fado ~ Portuguese Blues

Fado, a wistful music, evokes life. Well-known local singer José Vinagre goes even further, claiming, "Fado is life." Whether it deals with themes ranging from politics to love, he notes, "Fado is about people, heritage and roots, so no matter where you are and you hear it, it reminds you, [that] you are always Portuguese." The emotional core of the fado is *saudade*, an indefinable yearning for love, times past or a lost home.

One early fado singer made New Bedford her home for some years. Emília Moraes was born in Yonkers, New York. Her family returned to mainland Portugal during the Depression. At the end of World War II, she took a freighter back to the US and lived in New Bedford where she worked in the factories. After a short-lived marriage, she left for New York City where she took voice lessons and performed at Portuguese clubs. Moraes returned to New Bedford in the early 1960s and played the local Massachusetts and Rhode Island circuit. Her fans called her Little Amalia because her voice reminded them of the icon of fado, Amalia Rodrigues. She remarried in New Bedford, but her new husband did not support her singing career. One of her last appearances was at a benefit concert in the Immaculate Conception school in 1963. On that same bill were local performers José Pereira de Melo, Teresa Ana Cabral, Lucília Mota Rioux, Kevin Rodrigues and Maria Gimong, known as the Portuguese Sophie Tucker.

Manuel Hilario was another early fado singer. Born in Algarve, Portugal, he served as a sailor in the Portuguese Navy. There, others noticed his talent for singing fado. After leaving the navy, Hilario became a professional singer performing at fado houses throughout Portugal. In the 1970s, he came to the United States and settled in the New Bedford area, readily finding work as a fisherman. He also sang at restaurants and Portuguese clubs throughout New England and occasionally performed on the West Coast.

Maria (Fernandes) Alves was widely recognized as the first American-born fado singer. Born in Cambridge, she was raised in Acushnet. Her husband, John Alves, grew up in New Bedford. She began her singing career at age 13, performing frequently in New Bedford and throughout the Northeast, and traveling to Lisbon, Rio de Janeiro and Canada. She sang some fado music in English, which endeared her to non-Portuguese speakers, but she also sang traditional classics appreciated by an older generation of listeners. A recurring theme to her music was the particular loss felt by immigrants and their strong yearning for home in the old country. She was honored by the governors of Connecticut and Rhode Island for her continuing work with Portuguese communities.

João Cordeiro and Natalia Costa perform fado at the Aliança Liberal Portuguesa, 1940s. Natalia also sang live on the Ferreira-Mendes show.

More Luso Performers

One of New England's finest baritone horn players, New Bedford native Joseph S. Lopes, performed from the 1930s to 1970s with marching and symphonic bands in Southeastern New England. The son of Azorean-born parents, he was the youngest conductor of The Green Front Band that later became the Portuguese American Band. He also worked in Wamsutta Mills' accounting offices where he excelled in the new field of computers and data processing. He later managed data processing at Morse Cutting Tools before moving to the Bristol County courts system.

New Bedford-born Milton Ferreira founded and directed the Portuguese American Band. Of Azorean-descent, he also imported and distributed Sagres Beer, a well-known Portuguese brand. He was a founder of the Prince Henry Society, a community service organization of business and professional men of Portuguese descent. An ardent clarinet player, he played solos for Fort Sam's Own Band, the 323rd Army Band at Fort Sam Houston in San Antonio, Texas. After his return, he was president of Local 214, the New Bedford affiliate of the American Federation of Musicians.

With the reorganization of the State Guard in 1943, the 28th Infantry at the State Armory was authorized to form a band. Bandmaster Alipio C. Bartholo was placed in charge of recruiting. The son of an Azorean-born father, Bartholo graduated from New Bedford High School. A trumpeter with the New Bedford Symphony, he also taught music in Fairhaven, Dartmouth and Westport schools.

Luso Big Band Sounds

In 1932, Francisco Oliviera began the **"Hora Portuguesa" or Portuguese Hour.** He continued it for the next 43 years. It mixed music and short dramatic presentations that featured local amateur singers and players. Members of Oliviera's troupe also performed at society and church benefits in Massachusetts and Rhode Island.

Born in New Bedford, **the Ferro brothers** traced their love of music to their father Jacintho A. Ferro, a clarinetist from the village of Santa Cruz in Madeira. After arriving in the US in 1919, Ferro joined the Camacha Folkloric Group. He took his sons to local feasts to listen to bands, and at home he taught them to read music. After dinner and evening chores, the boys would take turns cranking the Victrola while the family listened to the marching music of John Phillip Sousa, Ferro's favorite. The boys learned to play guitar and mandolin at Tuna União Portuguesa. They also learned to play other string, reed, keyboard and horn instruments from their maternal uncle Antonio Piedade. Early on, the four brothers played with the marching band **Portugal-America Band**. Later, Jesse Ferro played with The German Band and served as president of the local musicians' union. Anibal Ferro led a group called the Village Combo and played with the Skyliners and Art Perry Orchestra. In the 1960s, the brothers became founding members of the **Tri County Symphonic Orchestra** and Joe and Gilly Ferro played for the New Bedford Symphony Orchestra.

Gilly Ferro was perhaps the most accomplished brother. After returning home from World War II naval service in Brunswick, Maine—where he played for the Brunswick Blue Jackets dance band—Gilly played with the Gene Marshall Band, the Four Kings brass quartet and two marching bands called the Bay State Band and the Portuguese America Band. In 1958, he started his own five-piece combo, Gilly Ferro's Orchestra, which included brother Joe. They stayed together for 15 years until failing health forced Gilly to retire in 1973. One of the most popular local band leaders of his time, Gilly played for President Dwight D. Eisenhower when he toured New Bedford and also for Sen. John F. Kennedy before he was elected president.

The Portuguese Hour Orchestra, 1939. *Led by host and moderator Francisco Oliveira (far left), the orchestra included string musicians (seated from left) Mac Fazendero, Tony Braga, Joe Ferro and others.*

The Portugal America Band, Stackhouse Street 1939. *This early marching band boasts four Ferro brothers. Jesse is at left in fourth row holding the tuba. Gilly is sixth from left, fourth row, with trombone. Anibal and Joe are in the second row, fourth and fifth from left, saxophones in hand.*

The Ferro Brothers Tri-County Symphonic Orchestra, 1963. *Founding members of the orchestra were Jesse (Jacintho) on tuba, Anibal on clarinet, Gilly (Gilbert) on trombone, and Joe (José) on bass.*

Mixed Bag

As a young boy growing up on the South End's Jouvette Street, Johnny Duke dreamed of owning his own violin, but his Azorean-born parents could not afford one with four children in the family. He got his first instrument, a saxophone, when he was 16 or 17. Despite a childhood bout of polio, he worked as a roving boy in a cotton mill when he left school. In his 20s, he left the city to study clarinet at the New England Conservatory of Music in Boston. He played dances and clubs on weekends. At 28, he left classical music and went to New York, where he formed the Johnny Duke Orchestra. The band signed with the Music Corporation of America, playing dance music in upscale hotels and clubs. He played and performed into his late 70s, having been to every major American city and 10 countries during his career. Then, he stumbled into a new career when a sore knee hampered his dancing at a senior citizen social. A would-be dance partner told him "to eat nine raisins and drink some gin" to cure the knee, prompting him to write his first story, "Raisins and Gin," and launching a writing career.

Trombonist Robert E. "Bobby" Pring also left his New Bedford roots to make it on the national music scene. From a musical family, he received his first trombone from an uncle. He joined the union in 1941 and played at local venues, including a live radio show. On graduation from high school in 1942, he joined Gene Marshall's band at Lincoln Park. During the war, Pring served as an Air Force band member in Greensboro, North Carolina. After the war, he traveled with the Glenn Miller Orchestra under the direction of saxophonist and bandleader Tex Beneke, and later with Beneke's own orchestra. He joined Les Brown in 1950. Much later, after settling in Los Angeles, he did movie soundtracks, studio work and short stints with the best bands of the day, including Benny Goodman, Bob Crosby, Frank Sinatra, Charlie Barnet, Bob Florence, the Commanders and David Rose. He also fronted his own group for several years. In 1977, he moved to New York, where he worked with Max Kaminsky at Jimmy Ryan's. Still later, he worked with Buck Clayton, Marty Grosz, Dick Meldonian, Ken Peplowski, Loren Schoenberg, Bobby Short and the American Jazz Orchestra, led by Gary Giddins. Critics described Pring's trombone playing as "smooth as satin." Fellow musicians noted he had "not a wrong note in his horn."

Edmond B. Ames was known professionally as "Eddie Stack." A former naval officer who worked for New Bedford as a project manager in the model cities program, he developed an innovative free genetics testing program that tested New Bedford's students and residents for Tay-Sachs disease and

Johnny Duke, 1977.   **Eddie Stack at Newport, 1967.**

sickle cell anemia. He was a noted local bandleader, composer, arranger, lyricist and a celebrated tenor saxophone player. He was the first Newport-born player to appear at the Newport Jazz Festival in Rhode Island. He and his quartet opened the event in 1954, and he appeared two other times. Barbara J. (Oliveira) Rose sang with his quartet.

Ralph Saxon also came from a musical family. His sister Lillian James earned her living as a musician. After a stint as a bootblack, Ralph was valet and tailor at the New Bedford Hotel. He played piano and organ in his free hours and put together a group called Ralph Saxon's Orchestra, playing evening engagements at the New Bedford Hotel and venues as far away as Newport. Ralph also played organ at the Skipper Restaurant.

Madeira-born Richard Freitas grew up in New Bedford and then moved to the Bronx. An expert violinist, he headed the music department at the Horace Mann School, then affiliated with Columbia University. He played violin with the NBC Symphony Orchestra. During World War II, General "Vinegar Joe" Stillwell persuaded him to lead the Official Ground Forces Orchestra on a 265-concert national tour that included two concerts in New Bedford. After the war, Freitas kept the nucleus of the orchestra together as a chamber music group. He formed the Paulric Artists Bureau in New York to handle the group's bookings and recordings. Two of those early songs had interesting histories: his wife wrote the lyrics for "Tiny Cowboy Lullaby" to boost the confidence of their five-year-old son, Richard Jr., on his first day of school; then, the couple wrote lively song "Pagliacco" for their three-year-old son. Richard Jr. became a prolific composer and musician, writing and producing 1,200 songs. He performed with artists such as Tony Bennett, Rosemary Clooney, Patti Austin and Nell Carter. His music garnered three Emmy nominations, two Grammy nominations, and seven International Telly Awards.

Young New Bedford native John C. Grady hadn't planned on a music career; he didn't play an instrument and never studied music. However, he had written poetry since he was a young child, winning his first award in the eighth grade at St. Mary's School. The *Saturday Evening Post* published a few of his poems. When he served with the 101st Field Artillery of the Massachusetts National Guard, he kept his poems a secret, saying, "You can imagine the riding I'd have taken if they knew I wrote poetry." After the war, Grady worked at Cambridge's Air Force research laboratory, but a rainstorm changed his career path. Water had soaked through Grady's apartment ceiling, and when he went to confront the upstairs tenant about his bathtub overflow, he was met by William Leavitt (who, it turned out, was bemoaning his own leaking ceiling, caused by rain coming through the roof). Leavitt taught musical composition at Schillinger House, the precursor to the Berklee College of Music. Impressed with Grady's poetry, Leavitt set "My Baby's Comin' Home" to music for singer Dixie Brandon. Others loved the song. Les Paul and Mary Ford recorded it, and the initial pressing reached 250,000 records; Billboard selected it as a "tune of the week." Grady and Leavitt left their day jobs to concentrate on music and met with modest success.

Concert pianist Edward J. Brown, the son of West Indian immigrants, was born in New Bedford in 1920. Harboring a deep love for classical music, he studied locally with Aldemard P. Langlois and then under one of Leonard Bernstein's teachers, Heinrich Gebhard. In the late 1940s, on three occasions, he won the National Music Week Auditions for the Young Musicians Music Festival. Until the 1960s, he combined playing piano professionally with working as a purchasing agent at Cornell Dubilier.

Edward J. Brown, 1947. **Bill Britto, 1950.**

Bassist William "Bill" Britto was born and raised in New Bedford. In Boston, he studied at Schillinger House, the precursor to the Berklee College of Music. He also worked with Phil Napoleon (born Filippo Napoli), an early jazz trumpeter and bandleader. Although an acclaimed soloist, he thought that the bass in jazz combos should furnish only a firm rhythmic foundation. Most often, he played in modern jazz trios composed of a pianist, bassist and drummer. His musical career took him to Toronto, where he married noted jazz pianist, Carol (Whitney) Britto. They played together for years as part of the Carol Britto Trio. In Toronto, Marian McPartland, another noted jazz pianist, hired him for her trio, noting that he had a big sound and a solid sense of swing. The years with McPartland proved the highlight of his career.

Harrie Johnston directing the New Bedford Symphony Orchestra, New Bedford High School Auditorium, 1952.

Sweet Harmony

Four-part harmony barbershop music swept the nation in a burst of nostalgia. The Society for the Preservation and Encouragement of Barber Shop Quartet Singing in America, or SPEBSQSA, was founded in 1938 for men only. The female counterpart, Sweet Adelines International (SAI), began in 1945. Both started out as whites-only organizations but later opened their membership. SPEBSQSA deliberately chose a long name whose convoluted acronym would lampoon the short ones of President Franklin D. Roosevelt's New Deal agencies.

New Bedford had affiliates of each. The Harpoon Harmonizers, founded in 1946, was first directed by George Arkwell, a professional choir and chorus director. As membership grew, quartets spun off including the Bell-Chords, Four Sharp Edges, Four Smoothies, Helmsmen, Oarsmen, The Jolly Whalers and The Neptuners. Some went on to compete internationally. The local Sweet Adelines organized shortly after. Both did much charitable work singing at benefits and church or civic functions. The Harpoon Harmonizers won the regional championships in 1950 and 1961 and the group is still going strong with some of the sons of its early members. In 2011, the group took first place in the Patriot Division Small Chorus Competition. It has also organized a youth chorus called G20. It remains one of the oldest barbershop affiliates in the nation.

During the 1950s, The Harpoon Harmonizers and Sweet Adelines shared the same director, Eldridge Everett "Ev" Wood, who also directed the award-winning Providence chorus. Admirers called Wood "a chorus director supreme" and joked that he had spread more barbershop seeds throughout New England than Johnny Appleseed had scattered apple seeds.

The Oarsmen outside the Fulton Supply Co. chandlery, Front and Hamilton Streets, 1949. *The group would appear that night at a dinner for out-of-town press and radio and screen celebrities, held at the Wamsutta Club by the* Standard-Times *in conjunction with the world premiere of Down to the Sea in Ships in New Bedford. Kneeling in front is director Everett Wood. Standing, front row, left to right: Gerald Pelletier, Kenneth Bastien, Albert Pollard, Joseph Hamburges, Albert Morse and John Gonsalves; second row, Albert Whittaker, Melvin Burnham, John Briden and Luther Pease.*

Three of the Four Sharp Edges actually also held the title of barber. Peter Pumilia, tenor, Antone Rocha, lead, and Silvio H. Leblanc, baritone, cut hair at the Hotel Harvey Barber Shop on Pleasant Street. One day, truck driver Joseph Camara, bass, came in for a shave. He heard one of the barbers humming a popular song, joined in and was joined by the other two barbers. The unusual barbers' barbershop quartet was born. Camara's death, following a car crash in Acushnet in 1956, broke up the group.

The Harpoon Harmonizers, April 1951. *Standing left to right are Joseph Hamburges, George J. Law, Charles R. Adam and William Hemmings. Seated is Edward J. Stetson.*

The Four Sharp Edges, 1949. *At Silvio's Barber Shop on Pleasant Street, from left to right, are Peter Pumilia, tenor; Joseph Camara, bass; Antone Rocha, lead; and Sylvio H. Leblanc, baritone and proprietor of the shop.*

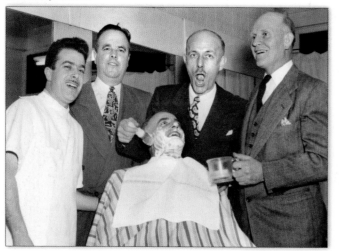

Marching Bands

The Whalers Drum & Bugle Corps grew from the Société l'Assomption Bugle & Drum Corps founded by the mutual aid society in the late 1930s. Corps members were overwhelmingly of Acadian French extraction, who differed from the region's migrants of Quebec origin. In 1950, it was judged the most outstanding drum and bugle corps in New England. In 1955, members traveled by Almeida Bus to Moncton, New Brunswick and performed at the Bicentenary of the 1755 Acadian Deportation. They also played at local civic activities and Franco-American festivities. About 1959, during an effort to expand, members realized many potential recruits did not have the sought after ethnic descent. As a result, all but six members, deciding that expansion was more important than ethnic purity, split to form a separate corps. They included all majorettes, the color guard and strutters. They called themselves the Jolly Whalers.

The new band initially had an all-girl color guard, but in 1961, the corps became all male and changed its name to the Whalers Drum & Bugle Corps. The group won awards at the All-American Circuit Championships in 1962, the Northeastern Circuit Senior Drum Corps Championships in 1963 and the Massachusetts American Legion Championships in 1967. They were the All-American Drum and Bugle Corps Senior Champions in 1965. The corps went inactive in 1969 and ceased operations in 1972.

The US Boy Couriers, 1942. *The group was founded by Leopoldo and Anterio Burgo and Manuel Rose in 1939 for Cape Verdean youngsters aged 6 to 16. They drilled several times weekly seeking to instill the ideals of patriotism and good citizenship. It folded after the start of World War II.*

In the postwar years, a number of short-lived Cape Verdean drum and bugle corps appeared. The Golden Clovers of the Verdean Vets was an award-winning organization in the 1960s, competing on the American International Contest Circuit. Later, the Varkeros drum and bugle corps represented the Verdean Vets. In 1993, the Dream Warriors junior drum and bugle corps emerged from a youth organization at the Cape Verdean Memorial Hall. Its members ranged in age from 10 to 19 years old. It won the Eastern Massachusetts Class C Drum Corps Championship in 1995 and 1996. After a short life, each group became inactive. Of the more than 500 junior corps active in the 1970s, fewer than 30 remain active today.

The Jolly Whaler Drum and Bugle Corps play for a festival audience, August 1961. *Early in 1961, the Jolly Whalers made national news when the band members refused to represent Massachusetts at the meeting of the national Junior Chamber of Commerce scheduled in Atlanta, Georgia. In segregated Atlanta, the corps would have been required to use separate accommodations for its white and non-white members. The non-white members decided not to go, but the Whalers' white members opted to "throw a harpoon at bigotry" and unanimously turned down the invitation.*

Music Week

"Good music is a joy!," announced Mayor Walter H. B. Remington to mark America's first National Music Week in 1924. New Bedford joined 452 cities and towns nationwide to celebrate the occasion. Sponsored by the National Federation of Music Clubs, President Calvin Coolidge designated the first full week in May as Music Week to increase public awareness of music's importance in all aspects of life and to create joy and receive pleasure from music in the home, community, nation and the world. "The love of good music may be cultivated," stated Mayor Remington "that all the people may find enjoyment and that the performers may add to their enthusiasm and culture…"

Rodolphe Godreau was New Bedford Music Week's first chairman. The opening program featured the Joseph M. Kavanaugh swing orchestra along with traditional ethnic performances honoring the city's Belgians, English, French, Germans, Hebrews, Irish, Italians, Polish, Portuguese, Russians and Scots. At the day's finale, the audience sang Samuel Francis Smith's "America."

One of the highlights was the Steiger-Dudgeon Company's chorus of 200 employees. The store threw open its doors for half an hour every morning to let crowds rush in to listen. Saxophonist Anthony J. Perry and pianist Anne Pittle led the singers. In the South End, 900 people packed the DeValles School Hall to enjoy Portuguese folk and dance music. At the Sharpshooters Club on Hicks Street, organizers turned away more than 300 people from the packed concert hall. They had come to hear young baritone Clovis Fecteau intone Gregorian hymns. The 35-member Whitman Mill band, organized by overseer Max Erlbect and led by Josef Bazzar and drum major Fred Swanson, played and marched along Acushnet Avenue in Saturday's Boys Loyalty Day parade. At the program's closing, the mayor proclaimed the weeklong event a great success, which would bring increasing joy and enthusiasm to listeners and

Music Week, 1957. *Festivities launched with a Pleasant Street parade followed by a concert on the steps of the New Bedford Free Public Library. Five city bands participated: Art Perry's Orchestra, Bay State Band, National Band, Portuguese-American Band and Ultramarine Band. New Bedford and Fairhaven high school majorettes led the bands and the Fairhaven High School color guard escorted them. With 2,000 in attendance, the Bay State Band, led by Manuel Viera, opened with a number that featured a trumpet solo by high school student John Taber.*

Music Week in the 1950s. *Clockwise from left, The Five Bellhops (1956); Chick Boucher and his Cotton Pickers (1956); Songs of Norway Singers (1958) with Svanhild Bendiksen, Bonnie Wilhelmsen, Marian Isaksen, Jane Isaksen and Kirsten Berg; The Sal Pelli Trio (1952) with Sal Pelli, bass violin, Joe Peters, accordion, and Joe Pelli, guitar; and The Vagabonds (1955) with Manuel Laboa, bass, Gil Travers, mandolin, Joseph Correia, guitar, and José Ferro, guitar.*

performers with each passing day just "as a rolling snowball grows." He described the enthusiastic community spirit as "good Americanism."

New Bedford observed National Music Week well into the 1970s, with a wartime pause in the mid-1940s. In 1968, the festival's main venues were the high school and junior high school auditoriums. the *Standard-Times*, Frank Gallant, the Massachusetts Council on the Arts and Humanities and the American Federation of Musicians Local 214 sponsored the event. It had music for all ages, including symphonic, choral, jazz, rock and roll, folk and marching bands as well as folkloric dancing, children's concerts and Battles of the Bands.

Music Week, 1955. *The String Ensemble performing at the high school auditorium includes: Susan Leach, Mildred Majorka, Rosemary Murphy, Susan Murphy, Barbara Padelfor, Avis Shapiro, Frank Tamits, Vivian White, Teresa Belcher, Holly Davenport, Jocelyn Kinney, Anne Sherman and David Brenneke.*

Chapter 3 1960-1980
Winds of Change

Two old-timers survey the handiwork of the New Bedford Redevelopment Authority on Acushnet Avenue between Kenyon and Washburn Streets, 1965. The area is being cleared to make room for Interstate 195.

Introduction: New Bedford in Transition

The old port and mill city of New Bedford saw the closing of several chapters during the 1960s and 1970s. Evangelical legend "Sweet Daddy Grace" died, Nye Oil Co. sold off the last drops of commercially legal whale oil and iconic glassware maker Pairpoint Manufacturing Company burned to the ground, ending eras long-woven into the city's tapestry.

Turning to the future, in the early 1960s the city rode the wave of celebration that greeted John F. Kennedy, the youngest president ever elected to office. Devastated, residents joined the nation in mourning three years later as JFK became the youngest president to leave office when he was assassinated in Dallas in 1963. The city caught its breath again in grief and disbelief when civil rights leader Martin Luther King Jr. was gunned down in 1968. With the rest of the country, New Bedford experienced the turmoil of the times as it struggled to provide its children with education, its youth with answers and its residents with food, housing and jobs.

The heyday of traditional textiles disappeared, giving way for a time to a busy apparel industry that provided one-third of manufacturing jobs. But by the late 1970s, even as city and business leaders worked to stanch the losses, mill after mill echoed empty and the once vibrant textile and apparel industries faded.

The 1960s and 1970s also saw beginnings of events that would haunt the city for decades to come: urban renewal, race riots and the discovery of dangerous pollutants in the harbor. From these ashes also rose movements for historic preservation, civil and political rights and environmental responsibility that still are hard at work in the city today.

Confronting the persistent problem of replacing lost jobs, successive mayors aimed to steer New Bedford away from relying too heavily on a single industry by courting diverse groups of manufacturers such as electronics assembly, toolmaking and rubber manufacturing. Mayor Francis J. Lawler

Downtown New Bedford, 1946. *The old mill city changed little physically between 1925 and 1965. Few buildings, streets or vacant lots were developed in the city center. In the North, South and West Ends, the most active construction came in the form of federal housing projects. Ambitious business leaders, politicians and civic-minded residents aimed to change that through aggressive revitalization plans.*

embraced the development of the Industrial Park and the hurricane dike. Mayor Edward F. Harrington seized on urban renewal, supported by the city's Redevelopment Authority and Industrial Development Commission as well as federal money. New Bedford received more federal funds per capita for urban renewal than any other American city.

Begun with the best of intentions, urban renewal grew out of the federal government's concern over the nation's post-war housing shortage and the blight of rundown urban housing. Its mission was to tear down and rebuild. For many years, much of New Bedford's center appeared to have been bombed. People, especially old-timers, craved for the downtown they remembered—the lunch counter in Star Store's basement, the soda fountain at Woolworth's, the smell of roasted peanuts from Mr. Peanut and the bookstore upstairs in Saltmarsh's—but their time had passed, not just here but in cities across the nation.

Visionaries, 1966. *New Bedford Redevelopment Authority Chief Howard Baptiste (right) points out his vision of the city's harbor development to Senator Edward M. Kennedy (center) and Mayor Edward F. Harrington.*

Downtown New Bedford and the North Terminal, 1974. *In the frenzy of urban renewal, city leaders planned on razing more than 100 acres downtown, most of it in the designated North Terminal area, north of Route 6. The Whaling Museum and much of what eventually became the New Bedford Whaling National Historical Park stood in the original proposed path of Route 18. Fortunately, museum officials, WHALE members and history-minded citizens protested and successfully convinced planners into looping the highway east of the historic district, thus sparing one of the city's most valuable assets. Most of the area visible here was rebuilt with highways Route 6 and Route 18.*

Several waterfront renewal projects represented a large-scale investment in the fishing industry. During the 1960s and 1970s, with its high-revenue catches of sea scallops and yellowtail flounder, the city's fishing industry secured New Bedford's place among the world's top fishing ports. With urban renewal, new piers and bulkheads were built. Waterfront property was freed up so fishing-related industries could now be located in one area. While a boon to the fishing industry, it gutted neighborhoods of housing for the poor as well as demolished many irreplaceable historic buildings. The city lost more than 150 blocks of homes, buildings and businesses with the highway construction of Routes 195 and 18.

A few farsighted citizens realized the city could lose its history, lose the buildings that told New Bedford's story as the

whaling capital of the world. By reaching out to the community, their group multiplied and became WHALE (Waterfront Historic Area LeaguE.) Working together they managed to save dozens of historic buildings, and the Waterfront Historic District won a place on the National Register, an important stepping-stone on the journey to become the New Bedford Whaling National Historical Park.

The building of a hurricane dike ensured that the city would retain its fishing and waterfront industries. The harbor had been subjected to destructive hurricanes and storm surges throughout its history, threatening the very life of the commercial fishery. But the barrier, completed in 1966, gave the city one of the safest ports and waterfronts on the East Coast.

New Bedford waterfront and downtown, 1962. *State Pier appears at center with Union Street running west. To the right are City Piers 3 and 4 and to the left of State Pier are the Steamship Pier, Homer's Wharf and Leonard's Wharf (formerly P & R Wharf). Berthed on the right side of State Pier is the Coast Guard cutter W380 or Yakutat, which served in World War II and the Vietnam War.*

While progressive change rocked the urban landscape, social unrest shook the streets.

The civil rights movement hit home in the 1970s when a black man was arrested in the West End for a minor violation and the African American community began protesting a decades-long pattern of systematic harassment. This was followed by the tragic death of Lester Lima, a black teenager killed by a drive-by white shooter. Rioting began. For many nights, chaos ruled the streets with looting and burning of stores and an occasional tenement. Senator Edward Brooke, the state's first black senator, arrived to negotiate and address grievances, which included lack of job opportunity and inadequate housing. The simmering turmoil in New Bedford was worsened by the controversy of war, which affected its citizens directly.

Throughout the late 1960s and early 1970s, the Vietnam War hung over the nation and touched many. New Bedford sent dozens of young men to the war, and some lost their lives. Residents rallied behind the troops at Veteran's Day parades, but also protested the war. Local educators, clergy and citizens became involved as early as 1967 and formed a The Greater New Bedford Committee to End the War in Vietnam. The group was small but created a stir. They took out ads in the *Standard-Times*, set up debates in local coffee houses and opened a Draft Information Center on Union Street. Counselors

Action on North Front and Kenyon Streets, 1967. *Urban renewal became a spectator sport for many. Old and young alike spent hours curb-side—on lawn chairs, strolling or on bicycle— watching the giant cranes dismantle the old neighborhoods.*

received guidance and training from the American Friends Service Committee. Through it all, New Bedford played and made its music: jazz, soul, fado, folk and rock 'n roll.

On the music scene, Duke Ellington performed at New Bedford High School. Local rhythm & blues band Chubby and the Turnpikes released the record "I Know the Inside Story," and later, the group, now known as Tavares, came out with

West End under siege, 1970. *Heavily armed riot police raided Black Panther headquarters on Kempton Street, arresting 21 people.*

the hit, "Heaven Must Be Missing an Angel." Folk singer Paul Clayton began recording local sea chanties. Tryworks Coffee House opened, a gathering place for young musicians, poets, artists and playwrights.

On August 2, 1975, New Bedford hit a record temperature of 107 degrees Fahrenheit. Three years later, the Great Blizzard of 1978 buried the city in a cold, deep freeze that created snowdrifts as high as 15 feet.

The hurricane dike protected the port from storms but from the 1940s to the 1970s another danger quietly threatened the harbor. For years, electrical component manufacturers released toxic polychlorinated biphenyls (PCBs) and heavy metal pollutants into the water, creating a hazardous Superfund waste site that has been the focus of federal clean up efforts for decades.

As the 1970s closed, the Vietnam War had ended but its aftershocks would be felt for decades to come. Some of the counter-cultural revolution remained, pushing forward the agenda of the civil rights movement. The city worked to heal and rebuild after the upheaval of urban renewal and the race riots that tore apart the city. But a national recession was brewing for the 1980s, and New Bedford would be hit hard again.

The Blizzard of 1978. *On Monday, February 6, most of New England was put at a standstill while a "winter hurricane" dumped nearly three feet of snow in one of the most intense blizzards on record. County Street became a scene of confusion, catching many off guard as they left school and work. Up to 10,000 cars, school buses and trucks were stranded in their tracks by midafternoon. Many vehicles disappeared under the heavy wet snow, while hurricane force winds gusted up to 115 MPH. After a state of emergency was declared, the National Guard deployed 5,000 troops to assist in rescue and recovery operations.*

Sagres visits New Bedford, 1964. *This view from Fort Phoenix shows the Portuguese training ship, the three-masted Sagres, moored in the harbor alongside coffer dams being used in construction of the hurricane barrier. The ship arrived in July for a three-day visit, attracting thousands of visitors. Sailing under the Portuguese flag since 1962, the Sagres takes its name from the port town where Prince Henry the Navigator founded his navigation school.*

View of New Bedford Harbor under protection of the Hurricane Barrier, extending from the foot of Griffin Street to Fort Phoenix in Fairhaven, 1966.

Hurricane Protection

Over the years, New Bedford had suffered colossal losses, financial and psychological, after having been in the path of several brutal hurricanes. Each major storm required the city to build and rebuild again. Rather than live with such uncertainly, officials decided to build a hurricane barrier. Construction began in October 1962 and the US Army Corps of Engineers completed it in January 1966 at a cost of $18.6 million. The project involved modifications to electric, water, sewer and drainage facilities and the acquisition of property. At the time, the project was considered the most expensive federal public works project since the Tennessee Valley Authority (TVA) electric project.

Though it has not been severely tested, the Hurricane Barrier makes the harbor one of the best-protected ports on the Atlantic seaboard. Built in four main sections, the hurricane protection includes the dike that crosses the harbor, measuring about 4,500 feet in length with a 150-foot-wide gate; an extension barrier of 4,600 feet that runs along East Rodney French Boulevard; a Clark's Cove section of 5,800 feet that protects the land around the cove; and a Fairhaven section that runs 3,100 feet. All told, the barrier stretches for three-and-a-half miles and averages about 21 feet in height. It is constructed of earth fill with granite slope protection.

The Army Corps of Engineers determined that the best source for gravel and stone was a quarry consisting of massive granitic gneiss in South Dartmouth, just six miles southwest of Cove Road. The stone was trucked to the site in an unending parade of trucks barreling over city streets for five years.

The 800-ton steel center gates close when mean tides rise above three feet, coinciding with a south or southwest wind. The dike has given great confidence to the fishing industry, manufacturers and homeowners along the shore. Considered to be the first structure in the Western Hemisphere to close off an entire harbor and protect the surrounding area from hurricane damage, it was nominated by the American Society of Civil Engineers in 1965 as an outstanding feat of civil engineering.

In its 50-year lifetime, the rock-faced dike has proven to be impermeable. An Army Corps inspector wrote in 2007: "The stone workmanship is among the finest ever seen in a coastal structure outside of Italy."

Gate and dike construction from inside the cofferdam visible at top left, 1964.

In the inner harbor, the dike and concrete gate structure rest on a foundation of rock ledge. During construction, the site was isolated with cofferdams and dewatered, so the US Army Corps of Engineers could excavate to the rock floor. A temporary channel was constructed to the east to allow ships to pass during construction and was filled in after completion. If future harbor traffic should require larger ships with deeper drafts, the gates would have to be entirely rebuilt, an endeavor made more difficult since the east channel opening no longer exists to reroute vessels.

Information on the environmental impact of the hurricane protection project is scarce. Research has found that sediment is accumulating faster in some areas of the harbor inside the barrier, and less water is being exchanged between the inner and outer harbors. A 1972 Final Environmental Statement determined that the opening and closing of the gates had no detrimental effects on marine life. Since the early 2000s, the federal government has studied water circulation and water quality and monitored possible problems related to the hurricane barrier, although no major findings have been released.

Much of the 890,000 tons of granite was harvested from a single quarry located just off Rock O'Dundee Road, not far from Russell's Mills Village in South Dartmouth. At the start, general contractor Perini Construction targeted the ledge beneath the Medeiros family farm as a source for the granite. According to neighbors, for some years the farm had not been a lucrative enterprise, owing in part to the ledge that made it difficult to till. A contractor offered to buy the farm, but the farmer refused, agreeing instead to sell the granite for about $1 per truckload (less than 5¢ per ton), so that he could leave the land to his heirs. In the end, the five-year project involved a legion of trucks hauling millions of tons of Dartmouth granite across the town and city. Shortly thereafter, the farmer retired and moved to Florida.

Gate construction, 1964.

Fishing vessels exit the inner harbor, 1980. Since its construction the barrier has yet to be challenged by a storm creating a tide or surge anywhere near its peak design height. The draft of the channel passing through the gates is 30 feet and the 800-ton steel gates open to a width of 150 feet.

The South Terminal Urban Renewal

In 1965, the New Bedford Redevelopment Authority (NBRA) sent a pamphlet to residents of the South Central neighborhood:

Dear Fellow Citizen,

The city of New Bedford, through the Redevelopment Authority, plans a waterfront industrial area between the Fairhaven Bridge and Potomska Street. As a result of this program, nearly all the structures in the project area will be acquired. The people living in the area will be relocated to other housing.

The South Terminal Urban Renewal Project demolished a waterfront neighborhood and transformed it into an industrial area to serve the fishing industry. This sweeping project, carried out with gut-wrenching efficiency and a minimum of citizen input, continues to generate critical assessment and emotion.

Urban renewal grew out of the federal government's concern over the nation's housing shortage in the mid-20th century. With the return of soldiers from World War II, the country needed to focus on the home front and deal with a national housing shortage and an excess of substandard housing.

The Housing Act of 1949 became the law of the land but it was amended, clarified and extended throughout the 1950s. Eventually slum clearance and urban renewal became its twin goals, to be carried out by local public bodies. The policy relied mainly on private business to meet as much of the total need as it could and government would assist in doing so. Thus began the long and tangled process of "revitalizing" urban areas and building affordable housing.

By 1965 urban development had become big business. As the revitalization of cities became a national purpose, the Department of Housing and Urban Development (HUD) was created. That same year the New Bedford City Council voted unanimously to approve the plans for the South Terminal Project. Mayor Edward F. Harrington and the *Standard-Times* also supported it. Though the legislation was originally intended to serve the urban poor, it later grew to encompass industrial development. This significant change in direction led New Bedford to consider a large-scale investment in the city's fishing industry. It is ironic that the legislative intent of the Housing Act of 1949 became a vehicle for the destruction of the homes of the poor who lived in the South Terminal area.

The neighborhood in the project's targeted area, historically referred to as "the marsh," covered an area bordered to the east by the Acushnet River, to the north by the New Bedford-Fairhaven Bridge, to the south by Potomska Street and to the west by First Street, Second Street and Acushnet Avenue. Once the hub of the world's whaling industry, it later became home to workers employed by factories, marine industries and utility companies along the harbor front and within the neighborhood. By the 1960s, it had become a mixed neighborhood of working poor—a dominant culture of Portuguese and Cape Verdeans and a sprinkling of other minority groups. Many businesses, large and small, lined the streets. Kids played sports on the empty lots. People felt a sense of community.

True, much of the housing was over 75 years old. Many homes had been kept up by proud owners. Some houses were substandard or derelict, but some could have been rehabilitated. The neighborhood had a place in the economic hierarchy of the

Greek Revival apartment house on South Water Street, circa 1960. Among its more recent denizens were families named Lopes, Pina, Ferreira and Sylvia. Next door—in the former grocery store building of Alfredo Fernandes—is the storefront occupied by Our Lady of Fatima Youth Services. Both buildings were demolished.

The Irish House, South Water Street, circa 1960. This historic duplex rooming house dating back to the mid-19th century was once home to itinerant whalers, cranberry bog workers, stevedores and immigrants from Europe and Cape Verde Islands. It was among the first casualties of the urban renewal onslaught of the 1960s.

city, providing new immigrants and others who were at a disadvantage with the opportunity to be self-sufficient. Fishing was the number one industry in New Bedford, and a major goal of the project focused on relocating fishing-related industry to one area—the South Terminal. The plan would involve "removing a large, blighted, decadent slum area in the waterfront," according to the NBRA. This "slum clearance" would free up adequate land for the expansion of the fish processing industries and the service needs of the fishing fleet. The plan entailed building a highway that would slice through the doomed neighborhood, giving trucks easy access to the fish processing plants, with a direct connector to Route 195. It would also connect the North and South Ends of New Bedford, from Coggeshall to Cove Street. In addition to the loss of the neighborhood, another huge negative loomed over the highway project. It would separate the city from its working waterfront physically and psychologically. At the time, few understood the profound loss that would come with such progress.

As for "citizen participation," a concept that was mandated in urban renewal legislation, only two public hearings were held.

View of a section of the South Central district just before highway construction, 1965. *Many homes had already been razed, vacated or shuttered in the South Central district. The mills at top left face Prospect Street. Parallel to Prospect, left to right, are South Front, South Water, South First and South Second Streets. The area lies between Howland (bottom) and Potomska Streets. The Pairpoint factory at far left is being razed following a destructive fire. At top center, on Prospect and South Streets, is the old Quisset cotton mill.*

The plan was developed, boundary lines drawn and properties selected for demolition well before any public meeting. The timing of the second meeting, one month before demolition was slated to occur, suggests that citizen input held little sway. Even an enormous outpouring of opposition at that juncture could not have halted the inevitable. New Bedford did little to give voice to neighborhood residents.

As the formal eviction process went into effect, two qualified local men appraised the properties and residents were offered compensation for their loss. "I believe the compensation was fair…maybe two percent were not satisfied," said NBRA Relocation Director Roy E. Shimizu. "We used eminent domain when we were unable to come to an agreed price. They got more than they would under normal circumstances.… I had to educate both the tenant and the fishing industry. Most fish processing plants were over on Homer's Wharf and it was tough to get the first one to move over to the new dock area.… In one case, a fish processing plant was located next to the bus station and another was in a house that had put on an addition. We gave relocation money to residents to move out and for fish houses to move in."

In the end, the NBRA overwhelmingly succeeded in centralizing the fishing industry's shore-side support sector. The agency listed its accomplishments in a 2004 report: In total, the project opened up 197 acres of land. It was the largest, most expensive urban renewal project in New Bedford's history and created the most jobs. It increased the tax base, added housing for low- and moderate-income residents, disposed of dilapidated housing, created a highway system and reconstructed piers and wharfs. It was a success—but at what cost? What was lost?

Announcing urban renewal to the South Central neighborhood, 1965. *Youngsters photographed at the corner of Walnut and South Second Streets are unaware of the chaos, disruption and devastation that five years of urban renewal would exact on their neighborhood.*

Monetarily, the project cost the federal government $18 million and the city $2 million. But there were other costs. Displaced residents suffered the loss of homes and neighborhood. Some 317 buildings, many of architectural significance, were demolished. These included 203 dwellings and 114 businesses. About 247 families were displaced, 783 people were moved out of their homes and 103 families or 41 percent of the displaced families were removed from private housing, whether owned or rented, and put into public housing.

Questions linger as to whether all structures in the project area had to be demolished. Certainly there were other options including rehabilitation and preservation, relocation of historically and architecturally significant buildings, more inclusive

Howland Street, east of South Second Street, 1966. *One of the city's oldest streets, Howland Street was completely obliterated to make way for Route 18. Among the 19th-century homes and rooming houses is the former House of Prayer (third from left), home of Bishop Charles "Sweet Daddy" Grace's first New Bedford parish; until the 1940s, the same building held Ahavath Achim Synagogue. The United Social Club is the last building visible on the left.*

planning and a better design and realignment of the highway. Instead, none of this happened. The neighborhood was simply squashed, powerless, in the face of the planned highway that would serve the fishing industry, and it had to go.

In the 1960s the preservation movement was in its infancy but became more active. The South Terminal project showed New Bedford residents how quickly history, culture and connection could be demolished. Historic districts and the Office of Neighborhoods and Preservation were created. When the West End Urban Renewal Project began the process of expanding the supply of low- and moderate-income housing, citizens were better represented. A Model Cities Planning Council was established to oversee the various projects, with members elected by the residents of the renewal areas. But the old South Central neighborhood was lost forever. As one man lamented, "We don't have that place to go back to. This place is gone. We had left our land in Cape Verde and the one place we had here was taken away from us."

Last home standing, 1966. *Rear view of a house facing South Water Street taken from South First Street between Howland and Grinnell Streets. In the background are vacant buildings of the Pairpoint Corporation. The narrow block once held more than 35 residential dwellings. "I offered one woman three houses," said Relocation Director Roy Shimizu. "One she turned down because she said she didn't want to live in the North End and the other two she said she didn't want because of ethnic reasons. Now she's dissatisfied because she had to find her own place. I had another who turned down seven apartments. We do all we can, but we can't do enough for some people."*

First home razed during South Terminal urban renewal, June 27, 1966. *John J. Duane Company's wrecking team razes the roof of the urban renewal project's first victim. The home was located on South Water Street between South and Potomska Streets. Property owner Frank Lopes, 71, said he had been living in the house since 1912. According to Redevelopment Authority officials, at least 200 families and 25 businesses were earmarked for relocation from an area one mile long (Potomska to Middle Streets) and 2,000 feet wide (encompassing all streets east of South Second). The NBRA purchased the land, evaluated it, notified tenants, and paid them $200 per family in moving assistance. Businesses were paid $25,000 for their companies.*

Neighborhood Lost ~ South Central

In the path of development, these houses were purchased from property owners by the New Bedford Redevelopment Authority and razed. Clockwise from top left: Wild Root Barbershop and Tiny's Lunch occupy the whaling-era, Greek Revival-style building at 46 Howland Street, corner of South First, 1967; a two-family home and garden at 87 Potomska Street between South First and South Second Streets; construction workers lay underground infrastructure and foundation work for the new highway along what was once South Water and Grinnell Streets (now Conway Street), 1968; and three- and two-family homes at the northeast corner of South Front and South Streets, 1967. Below, a view looking south from the foot of Howland Street, 1967, shows a recently demolished and almost fully cleared South Water Street.

The End of South Water Street

It took about 15 years (1966-1980) to obliterate one of New Bedford's busiest and most historic thoroughfares—South Water Street—and transform it into a six-lane highway. Clockwise from top left: The eerily desolate west side of South Water just north of Cove Street, already marked for destruction, 1965; in a wide-angle view of the same area, taken in 1980, commercial buildings at the corner of Cove Street are taken down; razing buildings on the east side of South Water Street near Delano Street, July 1967; and a building at 924 South Water Street that collapsed on its first-story storefront— former home of the Silver Star Cafe—1967. Below, a view looking south from Boa Vista tower on South Second Street shows the South Terminal before completion of the highway, terminal streets and buildings, November 1970.

The North Terminal

Since whaling's demise, New Bedford has looked to unleash the potential of cargo port development with limited success. The port accounts for less than one tenth of one percent of New England's ocean freight shipments.

In the 1960s, planners linked development of the maritime terminal north of Route 6 to an ambitious urban renewal agenda. Originally the North Terminal's major commercial objective was to provide suitable land for development of a retail shopping center to compete with suburban malls. That did not happen. The plan was somewhat more successful with its industrial goals, constructing bulkheads north of the bridge for maritime industries and clearing land for expansion.

The North Terminal is bounded by Middle Street on the south, Wamsutta Street on the north, the river on the east, and a western border alternating between Acushnet Avenue and Pleasant Street. Of its 120 acres, 40 were consumed by asphalt and roadway belonging to Routes 6 and 18. The remaining area was slated for a complete makeover, replacing existing homes and businesses with a wharf, industries,

Quaker Oats facility expansion, North Terminal waterfront, 1964. *The city developed maritime terminals to attract industry to the waterfront. In 1958, Quaker Oats opened a pilot plant, becoming the first tenant. Later, the company built a large waterfront plant at the North Terminal to process fish for the company's various pet food lines. Quaker ceased city operations in 1976, falling victim to rising fish prices and increased popularity of dry pet foods over the canned ones made in New Bedford.*

housing for the elderly and middle-income groups to be built over a parking lot. It also included a large commercial center, a replacement bridge over the Acushnet River and a widening of Route 6 to Rockdale Avenue. After individuals, families and businesses were forced to relocate and their old buildings razed, most of these objectives were never realized.

Looking west from the Acushnet River into North Terminal area, 1967. *The terminal's southern border, Middle Street, runs adjacent to the Route 6 on-ramp at lower left. It runs west to Pleasant Street where the city's tallest building, the New Bedford Hotel, stands. The perimeter runs north along Pleasant, turns east at Hillman, north on Acushnet Avenue and then continues to Wamsutta Street—several streets beyond the right edge of the photograph—an area consisting mostly of railroad yard and part of the neighborhood east of Purchase Street.*

Looking north from atop the Times Building at Purchase and Middle Streets, 1968. *Early in North Terminal's land clearance, boarded-up buildings stand on blocks between Purchase Street and Acushnet Avenue, bulkheads have been graded and some land for Route 18 has been cleared.*

As part of the downtown renovation and highway development, workers built the Elm Street Parking Garage, Melville Towers—a 320-unit apartment complex for the elderly—and a downtown traffic interchange, nicknamed "The Octopus." The project installed new streetlights, utilities, and water and sewer lines, but omitted the addition of retail space. Six lanes of highway replaced the old brick and wooden mills, factories and warehouses along North Second and North Water Streets and Acushnet Avenue. East of the highway and railroad tracks, new deep water docking areas and new waterfront bulkheads provided expansion space for maritime industries and fish processing firms to proliferate.

Looking northeast from the Post Office, corner of Pleasant and Middle Streets, 1973. *It took just five years to completely flatten the North Terminal area. In this view, at center, remnants of the Hotel Harvey hint at the structures that once filled this 120-acre swath of downtown New Bedford. The sidewalk, visible at bottom left, runs in front of the former New Bedford Hotel (transformed into an elderly housing facility). With no hotel and no bus terminal, "Destination New Bedford" sputtered. It would take more than a decade to replace the bus terminal; two decades to build highways, a bank and two subsidized housing towers; and three decades to attract a hotel to the waterfront. Downtown still has no hotel.*

Downtown Destruction

*U*rban renewal advocates gnawed at the edges of their respective areas, enabling them to reach deep into New Bedford's supposedly sacrosanct historic center. Renewal authorities gerrymandered the South Terminal Renewal Area to include two blocks on the south side of Union Street. That allowed them to raze a row of historic three-story buildings that ran from Acushnet Avenue to South Water Street and to replace them with parking lots.

They engineered the North Terminal Renewal Area to extend to the south side of Pleasant Street. That enabled them to raze the Chapman Building and Olympia Theatre across the street from the US Post Office. The buildings were replaced with a high-rise office building and associated parking lot.

Renewal authorities also manipulated the West End Renewal Area to include the north side of William Street from County Street to Sixth Street. That allowed them to demolish the iconic YMCA building to build a parking lot for city hall.

Razing the south side of Union Street, July 1968. A crane knocks down Sher's furniture store and Sher's Company Auction Sales Room between Acushnet Avenue and South Second Street. The Redevelopment Authority designated the site for parking. Later, Compass Bank purchased the lot and the historic police headquarters in the background to build a five-story bank building. Overall, urban renewal pockmarked downtown with "parking craters" that destroyed the historic center's diverse character and weakened its ability to generate revenue.

South side of Union Street between South Second and the waterfront, 1965. On a sleepy Sunday morning, Union Street is quiet. The 1965 Mustang parked in front of Colonial Restaurant Supply Co. enjoys free downtown parking, an amenity soon to become just a fond memory along with this historic neighborhood. In a few months, demolition crews would raze these blocks of old stone, brick and wood buildings that housed eateries, fruit and produce vendors, cabinet makers, barber shops, tobacconists and taverns.

*Two views of the **Chapman Building on Pleasant Street** between Elm and Middle Streets. Home of Paragon Travel and various businesses and professional offices, the Chapman Building also housed Cornell Hall, a popular venue for music, dance and small functions. Looming behind the building is the rear side of the Olympia Theatre, New Bedford's largest-capacity indoor entertainment venue. Below, the city's venerable **YMCA building** meets the wrecker. The oldest active YMCA building in the US at the time, it was occupied and in good condition up until its day of reckoning. Today the lot is still vacant and is used by city hall officials for parking. While urban renewal cleared space for a handful of high-rise housing and commercial buildings, the loss of early 20th-century, industrial-style commercial structures, such as the Chapman Building and Olympia Theater, and 19th-century Queen Anne-style buildings, such as the YMCA, is immeasurable.*

Highway Development

In 1947, officials began planning a new road to replace old Route 6. On technical grounds, they wanted a substitute for Route 6's poor alignment and narrow bridges. On safety grounds, a controlled-access roadway without Route 6's intersecting streets would have lower accident rates. On efficiency grounds, a new route would end Route 6's long and costly delays in Fall River and New Bedford caused by severe summer traffic congestion.

Called the "Cape Cod Expressway" when unveiled in 1954 by an interstate study committee, the spur from Route 95 became known as Route 95E when construction of the western end began in 1958. Eventually, the name changed to Interstate 195.

Its planned path quickly found enemies. Mayor Francis J. Lawler wanted it moved slightly north to avoid taking homes in the Elmwood Housing Development. City council members complained of being kept in the dark. Councilor William Saltzman peppered newspapers with letters opposing the costly route that would deprive the city of tax revenue; he favored a more northern course. Homeowners in the roadway's path feared for their future.

Department of Public Works (DPW) officials used a road-count survey to justify siting the highway closer to the city center because 90 percent of traffic surveyed had the city as origin and/or destination. The DPW plan had the road from Fall River extending to the Acushnet River. If the city did

Pathway for the Route 18 downtown connector to I-195, June 1966. *This view looks south from the railroad bridge near Wamsutta Street into what was once the heart of the city's Holy Acre neighborhood. At left is Acushnet Avenue. At right are the rears of properties facing Purchase Street.*

not accept the routing, the road would end at the Dartmouth line. The city accepted the plan. The federal government paid for 90 percent of the highway through New Bedford to the Acushnet River, and 50 percent of the cost of continuing the road to Cape Cod.

By 1962, plans had advanced enough that the city set up a Relocation Agency to aid the roughly 650 families and 125 businesses forced to move. Interstate 195 also resulted in the demolition of Chesed Shel Emes Synagogue and properties of the Protestant and Catholic churches. With so many of its parishioners displaced, the diocese closed Holy Rosary Church on Acushnet Avenue between Hicks and Logan Streets. As households moved from the path of I-195, two-thirds of

Weld Square, May 1965. *In this view taken from the railroad embankment near Purchase and Logan Streets, North End Police Station 5 stands alone in what remains of Weld Square. In foreground center is debris from the Weld Square Gulf Station. Three cars traveling on Weld Street cross the intersection with Ashley Boulevard, heading north. On the empty lot to the right of the Boulevard stood an Esso gas station on the former site of the Weld Square Hotel. Acushnet Avenue enters the square at distant right, where it is met by Hicks Street and continues north.*

Cedar Grove neighborhood under siege, August 1963. *Summertime activity for Myrtle Street residents (background) was the daily spectacle of a controlled blaze fed by wreckage of once stolid three-decker apartment houses that were cleared for Interstate 195.*

Grading the path for I-195, April 1965. *Telephoto view from the fire training tower shows the highway's path between Penniman (left) and Cedar Grove Streets, west of County Street. The area had been densely populated with wooden three-decker tenements and two-family homes.*

families that had rented moved to other rental property, mostly in New Bedford. However, one in six renters bought or built a home. Only a few moved into public housing. Half of the former homeowners bought or built a new home; almost one-fourth moved their old home to a new location in the city; another fourth, most of whom were over 65 years of age, moved into rental housing.

While the city lost millions in taxable residential and business property, assessors held out the hope that property values would surge near the intersections with Route 140 and Coggeshall Street within two years. When the new yet unfinished road opened for the July 4th weekend in 1967, it put New Bedford within four hours of New York City on a route with no traffic lights. City planners claimed that trucks would easily speed the city's industrial production to their destinations. Those planners also asserted that many vacationers on their way to Cape Cod would stop in New Bedford, even though the road it replaced traveled right through the center. Work continued on a downtown connector that opened in September 1968.

Weld Square, August 1966. *In this view taken from the Fire Department Training Tower near the corner of Purchase and Cedar Grove Streets, highway stanchions fill acres of land once occupied by 15 city blocks.*

Taking land by eminent domain in the Weld Square neighborhood shown here—from County Street east to the river and Cedar Grove south to Pearl Street—involved relocating 70 to 80 businesses and 450 families.

WHALE ~ The Waterfront Historical Area LeaguE

One of the scrappiest street fights this city has ever seen took place in the 1960s and 1970s between urban renewal and an upstart preservation group called WHALE. Still a fledgling movement, preservation had yet to become a valued concept in most communities. Urban renewal, however, promised progress. To tear down the old and build something new—this was the future.

WHALE had to get ahead of that kind of future to save the kind of past it wanted to preserve. "What happened in New Bedford was the most interesting process I'd ever watched in my whole life," said Providence's revered preservationist Antoinette Downing. "New Bedford saved more of its architectural past and made it work perhaps better than any other city in the US."

The city's beautiful Whaling Museum stood in the midst of a blighted area full of neglected and derelict buildings that held important New Bedford heritage: sail lofts, counting houses, whaling-era homes and buildings. Urban renewal bulldozers were beginning to tear down structures, and a handful of people saw danger—a city about to lose its history. George Perkins, Peter Grinnell and Stephen Delano stepped up to form the Historic Area Committee with the goal of saving what was left of the heart of the city—the 10-acre turf where New Bedford began.

In an unusual twist, city planner Richard Wengraf urged them apply for urban renewal funds—not to wipe out the old neighborhood but to find a way to preserve the district. The committee brought in Downing, an expert in historic preservation, to assess what was salvageable. She concluded that more than half the buildings were treasures waiting to be uncovered—a natural focus for telling the city's story. With that assessment to back their plan, the committee began reaching out to the community. The committee's working name became WHALE—Waterfront Historic Area LeaguE.

WHALE was officially incorporated on July 20, 1962 and soon had 25 members, $44.50 in its treasury and $64.72 in debts. Though support was growing, Perkins said the group constantly met with resistance from many of the city's movers and shakers—"You people are nuts. You're all dreamers."

A WHALE research team pored over old deeds, tracing each building's history. Grinnell, a photographer, climbed up buildings Spiderman-style, taking 300 individual, overlapping photographs, which, laid together, formed streetscapes. The committee won its grant, laying the foundation for something much bigger: federal designation of the Waterfront Historic District as a National Historic Landmark.

Sarah Delano took over as president of WHALE in 1966, serving with courage and a sense of adventure for the next 16

John K. Bullard and Sarah Delano, circa 1975.

years. Although a coup, the historic landmark designation did not automatically protect the district and its buildings. Urban renewal was leveling the South Terminal area to make room for an expanded fishing industry and new highway. Many of the historic buildings in the district stood in the way. WHALE was usually just one step ahead of the bulldozers, and sometimes behind. In desperation, WHALE members sometimes emptied their own pockets to buy, restore and sell buildings to people who promised to live or work in the district. Some buildings had to be relocated within the district to avoid "urban removal," as some called urban renewal.

John K. Bullard, who would later be mayor, became the agent for the district. A multi-talented point man, he got diverse groups from the Whaling Museum to the Bedford Landing Taxpayers to work together in support of renovation plans. Richard Pline, head of city Community Development, pleaded WHALE's cause with the city administration. Mayor John A. Markey came through with a $1.3 million grant for the Waterfront Historic District, a magnificent decision that would save the city's heart and go down in the city's history.

Work began in the district in the fall of 1975—cobblestone streets, period lighting fixtures, landscaping. Tony Souza, director of city Historic Preservation, said, "It seemed like such a blur, there was so much going on.... I thought that forever, for the rest of my life, New Bedford would be on a high about preservation."

WHALE saved 20 buildings, and the district won a place on the National Register—an important steppingstone on its incredible journey to become the New Bedford Whaling National Historical Park.

WHALE has expanded its mission to rescue and restore properties throughout the city. "If you bulldoze your heritage, you become just anywhere," said the late Sarah Delano as she reflected on WHALE's grand achievement.

Among the Many Saved Buildings

The granite-block Benjamin Rodman House on Second Street, built from 1825 to 1830, stood on its original foundations, but commercial storefronts masked its four façades. A then-anonymous donor, later revealed to be Catherine Crapo Bullard, bought the house and gave it to WHALE along with funds for restoration. In October 1965, WHALE stripped away the storefronts to reveal a building hidden for more than 75 years. With the help of Donald Rex, the preservation group replaced more than 100 granite blocks. Stone quarried for building the hurricane dike was trucked to Vermont, cut to size with old-fashioned saws, trucked back and then installed. WHALE also reinstated shutters and four tall brick chimneys, restoring the house close to its original condition. A mid-19th-century northern addition almost half the width of the house and a large foyer fronting on Second Street were not restored.

WHALE's most dramatic project was relocating the 550-ton Robeson House. The group purchased the house and the adjacent Bourne Warehouse in 1975. The latter was to become the new home of Pairpoint Glass, but the Robeson House was in the way. It had once dominated the block, showing off a Federal brick façade with marble lintels, French glass and fine detailing. As the neighborhood changed, the warehouse was built in the mansion's front yard, obscuring it. The city and WHALE decided to move the Robeson House to the old Reynolds/Mercury building site half a block away. So began a circus of events that will live forever in New Bedford history. The plan was to bring the house south through a parking lot onto William Street and then turn it 90 degrees. But the building started to sink into the parking lot. As movers solved this problem, another developed. The mansion couldn't be turned and had to travel William Street as it was, barely squeezing between the Pequod Lounge and the Custom House. The first contractor defaulted, and the house sat in the middle of William Street. After the Blizzard of 1978, the building sat stranded for weeks.

When the snows cleared, the Robeson House continued to its new home and was restored to its former glory.

Benjamin Rodman House, North Second Street, before restoration, 1950s.

Restored Benjamin Rodman House as the New Bedford Glass Museum, 1980.

Andrew Robeson House being moved to new location, 1978.

Andrew Robeson House, William and North Second Streets, after restoration, 1980s.

Buildings Lost

Rotch Counting House demolition, September 1972.

Hetty Green's Counting House, 1967.

WHALE had hoped to get the Rotch Counting House safely relocated to Centre and Front Streets before the highway broke ground in the waterfront district. This required an enormous fundraising effort, and WHALE was unable to get the money in time. Before a court order to cease operations could be executed, the New Bedford Redevelopment Authority (NBRA) went in and demolished the counting house. Constructed around 1785 by William Rotch Jr., it was one of New Bedford's oldest commercial buildings and had been placed on the National Register of Historic Places.

Located at the foot of Commercial Street and bounded by Front, Union and Prospect Streets, the massive stone and brick structures were known as Hetty Green's Counting House.

Lacking any architectural ornament, the simple buildings initially formed the offices of Isaac Howland Jr. & Company and his successor, Edward Mott Robinson, the father of Hetty Green. The other floors housed sailmakers, chandlers, outfitters, agents, Old Colony Railroad offices and various maritime services. They, too, were lost to Route 18.

Often forgotten are the many old houses and small commercial buildings that once lined Purchase Street between downtown and the North End; most of the one-mile strip vanished. The distinctive Plymouth Hotel, located at the northeast corner of Purchase and Mill Streets, is one such building. In its day, the hotel provided long-term rooming for craftsmen from various European countries.

The Plymouth Hotel, Purchase and Mill Streets, 1967.

Buildings Saved

The Rodman Candleworks before restoration, 1965.

The Double Bank Building, 1966.

Samuel Rodman's Candleworks, built about 1815, was one of the first factories in New Bedford to produce spermaceti candles. Later, it housed a number of businesses, such as a warehouse and a bakery. In the late 1960s, after damage by fire, it was abandoned. In 1976, the NBRA transferred ownership to the Candleworks Associates for restoration. John K. Bullard and Andy Burnes developed a "creative" financing plan—wooing chef Maurice Jospé to open the Candleworks Restaurant on the lower level, a bank on the street level and a law firm above. The $650,000 restoration project was stunningly successful and the pale-pink building, elegant in its simplicity, would soon become a model for public/private partnerships throughout the country.

The 1831 Double Bank Building designed by Russell Warren originally housed the Mechanics Bank and Merchant's National Bank. By the early 1960s, it had lost a highly visible column—an indication of the interior's poor condition—and was in danger of being lost. Skilled craftsmen rebuilt the missing column and completely restored the building's interior and exterior.

Looking south, several blocks of smaller buildings on the east side of North Water Street escaped the wrecker's ball as political pressure forced the path of Route 18 to swerve around the heart of old New Bedford and pass closer to the waterfront. Businesses on the tiny waterfront blocks defined by Hamilton and Centre Streets and Rose Alley had all supplied essential services to whaling activities.

The east side of North Water Street from the foot of William Street, 1980.

Kempton Street blockade during curfew, July 9. Police in riot gear facing west line up shoulder to shoulder across Kempton Street between Cottage and Cedar. WBSM newsman Manny Simmons walks toward the police line.

Confrontation at city hall, July 10. At a meeting held in Mayor George Rogers' office two days before the shooting, United Front Chairman Donald Gomes confronts City Councilor William Saltzman.

Hot Town, Summer 1970

In mid-1970, New Bedford resembled a powder keg awaiting a spark. At 28.3 percent, it had the nation's second-highest unemployment rate. In "pockets of poverty," including parts of the West End, that rate reached 35 percent. It was Massachusetts' only city labeled by the federal Department of Labor as having "persistent and substantial unemployment." Official estimates set the number of unemployed at 5,400, but that number would worsen in July with the apparel industry's traditional "layoff" month to take inventory.

After highway and urban renewal programs destroyed 1,200 housing units, overcrowding plagued the West End. Affordable replacement housing lagged. Local youth had few recreational facilities other than two small, unlit basketball courts that were unusable at night. A community proposal to build "People's Parks" remained unfunded. Attitudes of mutual antipathy and distrust marked relations between the community and the city's police department. To top it off, daily temperatures hovered in the mid-to-high 80s with excessive humidity and no cooling rain.

Citizen frustration, July 12, 1970. *West Enders wait to speak at a meeting in city council chambers to address housing and policing issues in their neighborhood. When councilors arrived late, community members occupied their seats and refused to give them up, criticizing the councilors for their tardiness and apathy. After a short speech, everyone walked out, exacerbating tensions that led to rioting over the next few days. Among those present are Duncan Dottin, Mary Barros, Jamie Lopes, Jeanne Costa, Marlene Tavares, Charlie Perry Sr., John and Albert Ribeiro, Albert Fortes, Kenny Houtman, Lloyd Haddocks, John Monteiro, Michele E. Merolla, David R. Nelson, David and Bobby Andrade, John Duarte, Ronnie Lomba, Ray Baptiste, Paul Alves and Lolita Neves.*

Restlessness gave way to violence during three hours on Wednesday, July 8, as several hundred youths threw rocks causing minor injuries to four police officers and a fireman. They also burned a car and threw barricades across Kempton Street, later cleared by police in riot gear.

On Thursday, police arrested Warren Houtman for allegedly driving with a defective headlight. A rock-throwing and bottle-breaking crowd quickly gathered. Police eventually cleared the area and arrested three. Twenty-three were injured. Two major fires destroyed the Model Cities office and the Masonic Temple in the West End, which had been frequented by upwardly mobile blacks. On Friday, with three officers to a car, police patrolled the West End with riot gear and extra tear gas. They arrested three white Fall River residents who had the makings of Molotov cocktails, including gasoline, bottles and wicks. A US mail truck outside the post office on Elm Street was burned.

On Saturday, violence escalated as whites from Acushnet and Fairhaven fired shotgun blasts from a moving sedan into a crowd at the corner of Cedar and Kempton Streets. They struck and killed Lester Lima, a black teenager, and injured three others. Mayor George Rogers clamped a curfew on the city.

Senator Edward W. Brooke and Representative Hastings Keith met on Monday, July 13, with the mayor, city officials and black and Puerto Rican leaders in an effort to ease tensions. They agreed on the basics of a peace plan. Two days later, Mayor Rogers lifted the curfew.

Grieving for a slain son, July 15. *Family and friends of 17-year-old Lester Lima, killed in a drive-by shooting on Saturday night, July 12, leave the funeral service at Colonial Funeral Home on South Sixth Street. Rose Lima (right), Lester's mother, is consoled by Charlie do Carmo (center). At far left, a young man assists Lester's godmother, Dorothy Spinner. Lester's sister Marie (with shawl) and Rose Lima's sister, Elizabeth Rose, are behind do Carmo. Funeral director Eddie Silveira is at bottom right, assisting Rose Lima.*

Fire at Burns Electronic Supply Co., 349 Kempton Street, July 13. *Manning the hoses are West Enders Jeff Baptista, Peter Almeida, Karl Hall, Clyde Ribeiro and others. Looters had broken into and emptied the store on Saturday, July 11. A spray-painted "KILL THE PIG" defaced the front of the building. Two days later, it burned. Firefighters are noticeably missing from the photo. Concerned for their safety, they deferred the matter to the locals.*

More Heat

On July 31, 1971, police raided the former Pieraccini's Variety Store in the West End, which served as the headquarters of the New Bedford Chapter of the National Committee to Combat Fascism, the Black Panther Party's organizing and fundraising arm. Police, saying they had seized a small arsenal, arrested 21. Authorities charged the "New Bedford 21" under the Sedition Act with conspiracy to commit anarchy, conspiracy to commit murder, inciting to riot and unlawful assembly. At least two of the arrested were serving on Senator Edward W. Brooke's ad hoc community committee at the time and had come to the scene in connection with their duties. Others found themselves in custody merely for being nearby. All pleaded innocent but were sent to jails throughout the state. After languishing more than six months behind bars, most of the New Bedford 21 were released and all major charges dropped. Three stayed in custody on minor charges, including Robert M. Stevens, a Vietnam veteran who was president of the Black Student Union and a student trustee of Southeastern Massachusetts University. Stevens had been accused of carrying a gun in his car during the riots, but the Supreme Judicial Court later threw out his six-month conviction because police obtained evidence using an illegal search warrant.

The three white youths accused of murdering Lester Lima and wounding three others remained mostly free while awaiting trial. On Tuesday, May 18, 1971, an all-white jury acquitted them of all charges after only 45 minutes of deliberation. Three black jury pool members had asked to be excused. Four black witnesses summoned by the prosecution failed to appear.

The verdict set off more arson, looting and stoning of police and fire officials. On Tuesday, an abandoned cottage on Kempton Street burned. Police in riot gear protected fire crews from rock throwers. On South Water Street, a vacant hardware store burned while looters targeted a hardware store and a jeweler, but the city did not erupt.

Raid on Black Panther Headquarters, Kempton Street, July 31.

Looted Pieraccini's Variety Store, Kempton Street, July 12.

Silva's Market, South Water and Blackmer Streets after rioting and looting, July 30.

Looking south on South Water Street over rioting and looting debris, July 30.

West End Development

The New Bedford Redevelopment Authority (NBRA) put aside demolition in the historic downtown area and turned to the West End to meet the needs of the underserved black community. NBRA's signature accomplishment was a 200-unit community, the United Front Homes, built using funds from the non-profit United Fund Development Corporation (UFDC) combined with a $4 million loan from the Massachusetts Housing Finance Agency and federal aid. The homes, built on an 11.5-acre site acquired by NBRA and conveyed to UFDC, provided low- and moderate-income housing in the West End Urban Renewal Area. The complex opened in August 1974. Most tenants were law abiding, but the project suffered from the actions of a few young males involved in gang activity. Police were frequently called to the area. Shortages of maintenance funds left the homes looking shabby.

Federal and state monies combined with support from several partnerships funded the project's $42 million rehabilitation in 2011. It more closely connected the homes to the surrounding neighborhood, and the authority more strictly screened tenants. The eye-catching, pastel-colored homes took on a new name, Temple Landing, in honor of Louis Temple, a black man whose innovative harpoon transformed the whaling industry.

Senator Edward W. Brooke (center) tours the scene of weekend rioting, July 13.

Crippled buildings near Panther headquarters, south side of Kempton Street, east of Cedar.

Demolition makes way for high-rise apartments, County and Kempton Streets, April 1972.

Vietnam

New Bedford sent men, women and a ship to the Vietnam War. For many, coming home after the war proved difficult. Vietnam veterans suffered from high unemployment, homelessness and battled with post-traumatic stress syndrome. They struggled with war injuries and the lingering toxic effects of exposure to Agent Orange, as well as antiwar sentiment.

Many did not return. In July 1965, Edward C. Almeida, 18, became the first city resident to die in the war. Altogether, 26 young men from New Bedford died; their average age was 20. Most were single, leaving behind their loves and fiancés. Five left widows. In honor of those who died and served in Vietnam, New Bedford erected several monuments throughout the city.

It took a long time for some to return home. Navy Lieutenant Commander Frederick R. Purrington spent six years as a prisoner of war after his attack bomber was shot down in 1966. While in captivity, his mother died in 1971, followed by his father just months before his return in 1973. Family members withheld the news until he came home.

When taken prisoner in 1968 during the Tet Offensive, Thomas Rushton was working in Huê as a civilian employee of Pacific Architects & Engineers, a government contractor. He was held for five years, before being released in 1973.

The New Bedford-based Coast Guard Cutter *Yakutat* left for Vietnam in 1967, carrying 160 seamen, many of them local. It spent nine months patrolling the Vietnam coast to deter the Vietcong from smuggling arms and supplies. When it returned, a crowd of 2,500 greeted the ship. After its second tour in 1970, the *Yakutat* was turned over to South Vietnam, where it did duty as a warship and was renamed *Tran Nhat Duat*. When South Vietnam fell at the end of the war, its officers filled the ship with refugees and sailed to the Philippines. The US later transferred it to the Philippine navy, which used it for spare parts.

At the Selective Service office on William Street, March 1964. Clerk Helen Nollette writes up boarding passes for the bus to Boston where draftees will take their physicals. From left are John J. Belli, George A. Maudsley III, John J. Bourque, unknown, Paul A. Langlois, Manuel Rose and Paul A. Dauteuil.

Saying goodbye, May 1968. On May 13, 1968, following the seizure of the USS Pueblo and the Tet Offensive in Vietnam, President Lyndon B. Johnson activated the 1st Battalion 211th Field Artillery. It was Massachusetts' only Army National Guard unit mobilized during the Vietnam War. The army called up 284 soldiers from New Bedford, Fall River, Middleboro and Falmouth. Some were sent to "training" at Fort Benning, Georgia. Guardsmen complained that the army kept them on housekeeping duties—restoring barracks, policing the base and maintaining equipment—instead of practicing artillery fire to prepare them for Vietnam. Following a congressional investigation, the army announced that it would only call up individuals from the unit with badly needed skills. In September 1969, 50 of those in-country members got together at Long Binh, Vietnam.

City industries received multi-million dollar contracts to supply the war effort. From July 1965 through July 1966, New Bedford companies won 114 major contracts totaling more than $20 million. Local contractors included Acushnet Process, Aerovox, Bristol Electronics, Cornell Dubilier, Firestone Tire & Rubber, Raytheon and Revere Copper & Brass. As the war wound down, the contracts fell off. The city's unemployment rate jumped from an average of 7.2 percent in 1973 to 13.8 percent in 1975.

The controversial Vietnam War brought out patriotism and support for the troops, even as it also stirred peace rallies and antiwar protest.

On October 15, 1969, in support of National Peace Day, Holy Family students released a dove of peace after mass at St. Lawrence Martyr Church. Two Franciscan brothers led about 260 Swain School students to Clasky Common to listen to readings on peace. A peace rally at nearby SMU drew about 300 students. The day culminated locally with a two-hour rally at the steps of the public library, drawing a crowd of 1,000. Mayor Edward F. Harrington called the deaths in Vietnam "a shame of American democracy." Speaker Michael S. Dukakis characterized the war as "pouring $30 billion annually down a rat hole 9,000 miles from here."

However, students at Voke hung banners in front of the school in support of President Nixon's policies. On November 16, 1969, an antiwar silent peace vigil on the steps of the public library drew only 50 persons. One sign said: "Support Our Boys in Vietnam. Bring Them Home."

Many veterans spoke out against the war and fought to end it. A group called New England Resistance spoke in local high schools including New Bedford. Others channeled their resistance to more militant groups. Frank "Parky" Grace was a controversial, highly visible Vietnam veteran and antiwar protester. Grace traced his radicalism to his Vietnam experiences during a 1967 tour of duty. In the spring of 1970, he helped found the New Bedford chapter of the Black Panthers. Grace, who said he was framed for his radical activism, served nearly 11 years of a life sentence for a 1972 murder before a judge overturned the conviction when another man confessed to the shooting.

At top right, **Caroline A. Arruda** (left) is sworn in and commissioned a second lieutenant in the US Army Nurse Corp by Captain Sue Pinkerton. The event took place at the Pleasant Street recruiting office. Duty in South Vietnam was "simply something I had to do," she explained. Miss Aruda began thinking about service overseas after listening to St. Luke's, staff surgeon Dr. John Greer McBratney, talk about his time in Vietnam treating civilians. "That started me thinking of the need there for nurses." The graphic portrayals of suffering, combat and wounded Americans on nightly newscasts were the catalysts that solidified her decision.

Other New Bedford women served in Vietnam as nurses, caring for wounded soldiers. Lieutenant Colonel Mary Donovan was chief nurse in the Army's 85th Evacuation Hospital in Qui Nhon. The Army awarded her the Legion of Merit. Air Force Lieutenant Colonel Mary M. Clark received the Bronze Star for exceptional duty while attached to a dispensary near the front. During free time, many nurses volunteered in the surrounding communities. Lieutenant Adrienne Papazian taught sanitary procedures such as the use of surgical gloves to Vietnamese midwives. As a result of her work, death rates dropped for Vietnamese mothers and children.

At right, two scenes **at the Draft Board** (or Selective Service offices) in the Cummings Building on William Street: Inside, young men stand in line, and outside, loved ones bid adieu to a young man.

Below, activists Mark and Marilynn Dworkin (center) lead a **demonstration** along Purchase Street in support of the Black Panther Party and against the Vietnam War.

Nurse Caroline A. Arruda, March 1968.

In line at the Draft Board, November 1965.

Outside the Draft Board, December 1965.

Downtown demonstration, 1969.

Protests, Rallies & Marches

After US forces invaded Cambodia, protests erupted on campuses nationwide. When the National Guard shot and killed four students demonstrating at Ohio's Kent State University, protests intensified. SMU's Student Senate voted for an indefinite strike. After an on-campus rally in Dartmouth, some 600 **students and faculty marched** down Route 6 to New Bedford City Hall. They stopped at Bishop Stang High School in Dartmouth where the principal threatened to suspend any students joining the march. Marchers passed by the Selective Service office on Purchase Street in New Bedford before reaching city hall where, at the marchers' request, staff lowered the American Flag to half-mast in mourning for the slain Kent State students. Students and faculty addressed the group for about an hour before the group dispersed.

Following the Attica riot, **prisoners elsewhere demonstrated**. New Bedford proved no exception, except in the patience, confidence and humor shown by prison authorities. Sheriff Edward K. Dabrowski circulated at the peaceful protest in the prison yard and promised no reprisals against demonstrators and complete amnesty. The event began with Chaplain Fr. William Norton's memorial mass for the 42 prisoners and guards who died at Attica. Later, waving signs hand lettered on cardboard squares, prisoners circulated in the prison yard. Their grievances centered on better medical care, better facilities, better training for guards and inmates and repeal of the law prohibiting parole for certain inmates. Eight elected spokesmen spoke to the press and the sheriff.

In June 1980, **New Bedford fishermen**, led by mostly Portuguese fishermen and their families, became so outraged over fish auction prices that they staged an organized port-wide tie-up. While fishermen received auction prices as low as 10¢ a pound for cod, haddock and yellowtail, the fish sold for up to $3.00 in the retail markets.

The tie-up brought redress to economic problems facing the industry and fishermen agreed to limit sending out boats, to decrease the glut of fish on the market.

Students at city hall, May 1970.

Prisoners demonstrating at the Bristol County House of Corrections, 1971.

Fishermen and the families lead a demonstration up Union Street, 1980.

Opportunity Knocks

The **Rodman Job Corps Center** opened in New Bedford's South End in August 1965 as part of the federal Office of Economic Opportunity's War on Poverty program. The residential program helped teen dropouts develop academic and job skills. The IBM-run program offered training for computer programming and offset printing. Clashes between corpsmen and city youth led to dozens of corpsmen being arrested and the city council voting to kick the program out of town in its first year. But officials worked to better integrate the program into the community and the Job Corps stayed open to assist more than 1,000 teenagers, many of them black youth from the South. About 75 percent of the corpsmen found jobs, joined the military and continued their educations.

Reverend Wallen Bean, the program's counseling director, said that despite problems, the program did much good work.

"I was never so proud as the day Ennis Bowie, the first graduate, received his certificate. He was immediately hired by IBM. The fact is, IBM hired many boys who had taken computer programming, and others went back to their ghettos and languished," Bean said. On March 1, 1968, the Rodman Job Corps closed.

ONBOARD (Organized New Bedford Opportunity And Resource Development) was the city's community action project agency. Through it, the federal Office of Economic Opportunity channeled grants for city programs that were administered by local neighborhood centers. The grants provided education, employment and recreation opportunities for minority groups, the underprivileged and the poor. However, in some eyes the programs fell short.

First Job Corps training group at work on the Wharfinger Building, March 1965.

Occupying ONBOARD's Union Street office, 1970. *United Front president and spokesperson for the black community, Donald Gomes, addresses ONBOARD's Steering Committee with 22 demands on issues such as the lack of blacks in key posts and the nature of ONBOARD's supervision of the local government programs that it funded. Others in attendance are Ronnie Cruz, Jim Magnett, Bill do Carmo, Jim Bargasse, John Monteiro, Zoe Fabio, Charlie do Carmo, Arthur Lopes, Marlene Tavares, Julio Alves, Bumby Lopes, Regina Henderson and Rose Tavares Pinto.*

Model Cities

New Bedford was one of 151 cities in the US federal Model Cities Program, a project intended to mitigate the debilitating effects of prejudice and neglect on urban communities. Funded in 1968, Model Cities embraced a democratic structure with power shared among three groups—citizens, the city and the program's professional staff.

One of the program's most successful initiatives focused on the public schools. To address a serious racial imbalance in four of seven city schools, the program recommended a new, bigger school that would draw from a larger area. The Alfred J. Gomes Elementary School became the model for three future schools. Model Cities brought in teachers' aides and established a curriculum development and training center. It started breakfast and lunch programs, which later grew to be citywide.

To address the urgent need for public housing, the program bought a highly deteriorated, three-acre commercial strip along South Water Street. Model Cities relocated the residents, leveled the area and turned the land over to the Housing Authority, which developed 58 units of public housing in two years. The housing was well maintained and became a source of community pride. Model Cities also worked to better relations between police and community groups. The program allocated $90,000 to renovate and reopen the South End Police Station. Director Richard Pline emphasized the importance of the Model Cities Program as it grew into the Community Development Block Grant Program. "Model Cities was a transition away from urban renewal," he said. "It was a quiet revolution."

Model Cities Success Story

Jan Baptist credits the Model Cities program for helping her become a self-supporting woman with a rewarding career, delivering her from hopelessness to success. She grew up in a North End tenement and left high school during her senior year to work in a pajama factory. "I had walking pneumonia and missed a lot of school. I told my mother I wanted to quit and she said okay—she did not have high expectations for me," Baptist said. She graduated, married at 19, and jumped from one job to another: nurse's aide, waitress or Tupperware salesperson.

"Then something life-changing happened at one of my Tupperware parties," Baptist said. "A woman named Pat Mello was there and she worked for Model Cities. After my presentation, she came up to me and said, 'You know, you'd make a great teacher. The way you organized your ideas. The way you spoke. I think you could do this teacher aide job at Model Cities.'"

Baptist was struggling at the time, in the middle of a divorce and at a loss regarding what direction her life should take. Model Cities sparked her hopes and fueled her dreams. She worked as a Model Cities teacher's aide, then went on to earn her associate's degree at Bristol Community College, her bachelor's at UMass Dartmouth and her master's at Cambridge College. She was selected by Smith College to be an Ada Comstock Scholar, a program for non-traditional students.

She went on to buy a home in New Bedford, and for 40 years has enjoyed a career at Bristol Community College as an educator, administrator and consultant.

Construction of the Alfred J. Gomes Elementary School, 1977. *Model Cities vigorously lobbied city hall to help people struggling in the wake of urban renewal. Bill do Carmo, former Model Cities president, recalled how Duncan Dottin, Jack Custodio and he worked tirelessly to buy NBRA land, plan housing developments and secure construction funds. "People needed something. They were desperate and hopeless. Their lives were uprooted, neighborhoods torn apart. We met with Mayor Harrington on Sunday mornings and convinced him that he would be acknowledged as a hero, enhance his legacy, if he did something for the people in need. He said, 'Yes. What can I do?' And that's one way we were successful in building housing developments such as United Front and Boa Vista."*

Claremont Companies

The Claremont Companies started small and grew to become one of the largest and most respected real estate development and management firms in New England. Cofounder Claire T. Carney grew up in New Bedford and graduated from New Bedford High School in 1940. Her father was a drop forger at the New Bedford Shuttle Company and her mother was a skilled seamstress working out of the home. After high school, Carney worked at Morse Twist Drill, her college dreams financially out of reach at the time, but not forever. In 1944, she married Hugh Carney. While he served overseas during World War II, she performed war-related office work at Otis Air Force Base, the US Naval Hospital and the Internal Revenue Service. Tragedy struck in 1962, when her husband did not recover from surgery and she was widowed with four children—ages 10, 12, 13 and 15. Carney returned to work at Morse Twist Drill, raised her children and sent them to college. She earned her real estate license, as did her oldest son Patrick. The two went into business together while he was still in college.

Pat Carney recalled that in the 1960s, urban renewal had demolished many residences and New Bedford had a housing shortage. The mother-and-son team invested in real estate rehabilitation, first buying three dilapidated but structurally sound three-decker houses on Clark Street to fix up and rent out to families. That was the beginning of the Claremont Companies. Three tenements became five, and five tenements became thirty rehabbed apartments. They were in business. It was then that Carney decided to take on her biggest dream and enrolled in college, majoring in English at Southeastern Massachusetts University. In 1973, she earned her college degree at 50. Claremont Companies built, rehabbed and developed many complexes in the region, including Buttonwood Acres, Hidden Brook, Solemar and Hidden Bay. By the 1980s, the business was doing so much work in the Boston area that it moved its offices in between to Bridgewater. It also expanded into other regions of the country.

Clarkwood Apartments. For its first housing development, Claremont Company converted five three-decker tenements into low- to moderate-income apartments on Clark Street. It was one of the first such developments financed through the Massachusetts Housing Finance Agency.

One of the most admired of its New Bedford projects was the transformation of the Car Barn. The large two-story brick building dates back to 1910 when it housed the cars and repair shop of the Union Street Railway. While maintaining the historic integrity of the building, Claremont renovated the property and turned it into 114 rent-assisted units for seniors.

Claremont Companies has established a Carney Family Foundation, run by Patrick Carney's daughter Kate, with education its primary focus. One of Claire Carney's greatest investments is the UMass Dartmouth Library, which recently underwent a major renovation to become the centerpiece of the university. "The most important thing is to teach young people how to think," she said. The Claire T. Carney University Library is named in her honor.

The Car Barn at Purchase and Weld Streets, shortly after renovation, 1982.

Immigration 1950–1980

The nation's anti-immigrant sentiment softened in 1957 and 1958 when the 13-month long eruption of the Capelinhos volcano on Faial with hundreds of associated earthquakes elicited concern for refugees. The Azorean Refugee Acts of 1958-1960 allowed many to enter the US and scores ended up in New Bedford, home to an Azorean community since whaling days.

Later, the Immigration and Nationality Act of 1965, sponsored by Senator Edward M. Kennedy, abolished national quotas and promoted family reunification as the basis for immigration. Would-be Portuguese immigrants suffered under the earlier quotas. Under the new law, Portuguese and Cape Verdean immigrants flocked to New Bedford joining family members already here. By 1969, Portugal had become the nation's seventh most important source of newcomers. At the 1980 census, 65 percent of foreign-born Portuguese speakers in Southeastern Massachusetts had come to the US after 1965. The influx helped offset the almost 10 percent drop in the city's population from 1960 to 2000. That short-lived immigrant surge dropped to a trickle following the 1974 military coup that ended both the dictatorship and colonial wars. It slowed even more after Portugal joined the European Union in 1986, improving job prospects.

Newer Portuguese-speaking immigrants often had low educational levels. Only a third had completed six years of grammar school. Many arrived knowing little English. Adults had few job choices other than low-skill factory work, or jobs requiring little education or language ability. Some worked in construction or grounds maintenance. Their children had a major impact on city schools. While some succeeded, overall fewer finished high school than did students of other ethnic groups. While time saw improvement, Portuguese-speakers still fare worse than other ethnicities in the city.

Learning English, 1968. Portuguese boys studying English at classes held at the Thompson Street School try reading the local newspaper. Beginning in 1966, New Bedford's schools scrambled to adjust to the flood of non-English speaking students. School authorities discussed opening summer school programs to accommodate the immigration influx. By May 1967, 508 youngsters had enrolled in non-English speaking classes.

The Immigrant Assistance Center

In 1969, Manuel F. Neto was elected chairman of the board of the New Bedford Migrant Education Project, a federally funded program to help migrant workers in Southeastern Massachusetts, particularly cranberry bog workers. When the program lost funding in 1971, volunteer members such as Neto and Paul Andrade helped establish the Immigrant Assistance Center to help newly arriving immigrants. First located in a space donated by the Faial Club on Orchard Street, the program secured a Community Development Grant of $5 million from Mayor George Rogers' administration to restore the Thompson Street School, one of several schools earmarked for razing. The center partnered with the Luzo American Soccer Association (LASA) and the Casa da Saudade, the first Portuguese library in North America.

Councilor Manuel F. Neto, election celebration, 1971.

Refugees from the 1958 Faial volcano eruptions arrive in New Bedford, 1960. *After a difficult and long-delayed trip, the Avila family of five reunited with their American relatives. Maria Luisa Andrade, wearing a shawl, arrived with one of her daughters, Albertina Avila (third left, third row) and her husband José (first left, fourth row) and their two children, Fatima, 10 (first left, second row), and Francisco, 6 (second left, first row). Others in the picture are Andrade's four daughters, their husbands and children. They include: Augusto and Clementina Jesus Almeida, Manuel and Aldina Bettencourt, João and Filomena Neto and John and Maria Paiva. Children include George and Manuel Bettencourt and John Neto. Young Manuel F. Neto (third right, third row), future Ward 5 City Councilor, is in the third row, second from right.*

Puerto Rican Migration

From the 1940s, Puerto Ricans came to work in the region's farms, bogs, orchards and nurseries. Often, they went home in the winter to cut sugar cane. In time, with available housing, city amenities and abundant year-round, low-skill jobs, many stayed on at the end of the growing season and settled in New Bedford. The city had the reputation as a place where one could integrate without friction or racial bias.

Puerto Rican-born residents were the city's first Spanish-speaking residents. Initially, they settled in two small enclaves, one in the North End and the other in the South End. By the 1970 census, they totaled 643. Later, those settlements disappeared to make way for the path of Route 195 and the extension of Route 18.

The city's Puerto Rican community grew as more friends and relatives arrived. It reached 4,532 in 1990 and 9,761 in 2010. Most came chasing the American dream, but they often encountered obstacles. Language barriers and employer prejudice made it difficult for some of them to land jobs. It was not uncommon for these newcomers to apply for 60 or 70 jobs in a year. Some found jobs as fish cutters or in the packing houses. Some became assistants to plumbers or carpenters. Others worked in factories as stitchers, pressers and cloth cutters.

In some cases, relocation led to spiritual dislocation. Nominal Roman Catholics felt abandoned through the 1950s when few priests in New Bedford spoke Spanish. Many turned to storefront Pentecostal Churches for services in their own language.

Children speaking only Spanish at home went to school unable to communicate with teachers or fellow students. New Bedford's schools lagged in providing classes for students learning English as a second language. For years, community leaders raised their education concerns to political and school leaders—and repeatedly judged their responses inadequate.

Young Spanish-speaking residents receive First Communion in the chapel of Regina Pacis Center, 1961. *The First Communion highlighted the Puerto Rican community's celebration of the Feast of Saint John the Baptist—their first large religious and social event in New Bedford. Diocese head Bishop James L. Connolly addressed the gathering in Spanish and the choir of Our Lady of Assumption Church sang during the Mass and for Benediction. Regina Pacis Center was established by the Diocese in March of 1961 as a Hispanic mission to administer catechetical instruction and to provide orientation to life in the United States. In 1961, according the Standard-Times, an estimated 1,300 Puerto Ricans resided in New Bedford.*

Hispanic Development Center, Potomska Street, 1978. *Members of the center review documents. Frank Baez is at left.*

Regina Pacis Center summer program, South First and Rivet Streets, 1968. *Rev. Coleman Conley (standing left), director at the center, works with volunteer assistant Gloria (Xifaras) Clark (seated left).*

Meat & Noodles

Each wave of new arrivals brought new foods to New Bedford.

At **Amaral's Linguiça**, workers stuff mixed ground, spiced meat into casings. They hang them on "smoke sticks" before placing them on the rack (in background) and carting them to the smokehouse. Taking part in the effort are Constantino Salvador, Jose Valentin, owner Antonio Rodrigues, John Demello and Mr. Souza.

Azorean immigrants José and Maria Amaral started Lisbon Sausage Company in 1928. The 1938 hurricane wiped out its building located near the junction of Rockdale Avenue and Cove Road, but the Amaral's rebuilt a few years later, buying out Gouveia Linguiça on South Second Street. Daughter Hilda took over in 1955 and when she died in 1960, Antonio Rodrigues bought and expanded the company, renaming it Amaral's. He still operates it with daughters Joan and Nina. Antonio, born in mainland Portugal, explains that Azorean islanders prefer a spicier sausage, called chouriça. Thus, Lisbon sausage-makers have adapted, creating a hotter style to serve their largely Azorean clientele. The Rodrigues still make linguiça the old-fashioned way—by hand mixing all spices, blending them with meat, stuffing the casing and smoking the sausage in one of their three hardwood-fired ovens.

Shortly after 1900, grocer **James Davidson** began specializing in cooked meats. He initially marketed to fellow Englishmen who enjoyed his McGregor brand Scotch hams, Piccadilly breakfast sausage and bacon. Much later, women preparing traditional summer clambakes simply chose Davidson's as "the best sausage there is." With time, Davidson's began adapting to changing tastes and began producing its own linguiça. Here Manuel Medeiros, left, and John Paiva prepare to put the meat into a converter which will mix and finely chop the meat to the correct consistency for filling the casings.

Oodles of egg noodles drop from the machinery in New Bedford's Chinese noodle factory. Supervising the operation are, from left, Don, William and Dick Leung of the **China Clipper restaurant** on Purchase Street where the factory is located downstairs.

Amaral's Linguiça Company, South Second Street, 1976.

Davidson's Meat Market, South Second Street, 1962.

Making noodles at China Clipper Restaurant, 1961.

Fernandes Supermarket, Rockdale Avenue, 1971. *Madeira-born Joseph E. Fernandes founded Fernandes Supermarkets, a chain of stores throughout Southeastern Massachusetts and Rhode Island. The chain grew to 37 supermarkets employing more than 2,700 people. Fernandes was active in Portuguese civic affairs. Among others, he was president of the* Portuguese Times *and the Portuguese cable channel, which served more than 65 local communities. He helped develop the TV show, "Portuguese Around Us," that aired on New Bedford's WTEV.*

Vegetable shopping at the Brockton Public Market, 1978. *In 1899, Maynard Davis, born in Poland, Maine, bought a small grocery store in Brockton and called it Brockton Public Market (BPM). In 1914, he opened a branch store in New Bedford. It stocked all of a household's needs under one roof. In 1918, Davis purchased Maine-based George Shaw Company and ran the two chains independently. After his son, Stanton Davis, joined the family business, both companies merged under the name Shaw's. New Bedford's BPM closed on May 5, 1973.*

The Brockton Public Market, Purchase and Spring Streets, 1967.

Chef Joseph A. Pires and the Spouter Inn Restaurant (right) at the New Bedford Hotel, 1968. *Cape-Verde born Chef Pires spent more than two decades cooking for guests at the New Bedford Hotel. From the hotel kitchen, he supplied food to the hotel's three whaling-themed eateries—the Moby Dick Restaurant, the Jolly Whaler and the Spouter Inn. Items on the menus included broiled filet mignon wrapped in bacon with mushroom caps and broiled lobster à la Moby Dick stuffed with scallops. Each dish cost $4, and was served with vegetables, salad and coffee.*

Howdy Beefburgers drive-in restaurant, Purchase Street, 1967. *Howdy's introduced New Bedford to the 15¢ hamburger, 18¢ cheeseburger, 12¢ fries, 5¢ coke and 5¢ apple pie. A truly "happy" meal, dad could feed the family on pocket change. Jane (Galligan) Thomas and Susan Grace both worked at Howdy's around this time, when servers were required to say, "Howdy sir, can I help you?" and follow up after an order with, "Would you like an apple pie with that?" When a Howdy inspector dropped by pretending to be a customer, Thomas spouted the chain greeting and earned a reward of $5. Grace remembers burning her arm daily on the deep-fryer bulb: "We were always in a rush, always getting burned."*

Maxie's Delicatessen, Pleasant Street, 1978. *A favorite luncheon take-out for downtown workers, Maxie's was operated by Tom and Marilyn Poulos and daughters Leslie, Lisa and Linda.*

Willow Tree Restaurant, Rockdale Avenue, circa 1965. *Owned and managed by the Ferro family known for their musical prowess. Staff includes Robert Botelho, Jesse Ferro, Richard Medeiros, Elsie Ferro and Wayne Vieira.*

Ma Raffa's Restaurant, North Water and Maxfield Streets, 1967.

Poulos Pharmacy fountain, Union Street, 1979.

John C on Pier 3, 1966. *"Johnny C's" was a popular breakfast joint for fishermen, especially after the auction.*

Industrial Park and the Acushnet Cedar Swamp

The New Bedford Industrial Park (now the New Bedford Business Park) initially included 550 acres in the city's far North End, bordered by Freetown to the north, Route 140 to the east, Acushnet Cedar Swamp to the south and Dartmouth to the west. In 1955, local businessmen funded the Greater New Bedford Industrial Foundation to develop a park-like setting to welcome new companies. The park officially opened in 1961.

Located in an environmentally sensitive region and bordering the ecologically fragile Acushnet Cedar Swamp State Reservation, the business park grew to cover 1,300 acres and house 45 firms employing about 5,000 workers.

The Acushnet Cedar Swamp

Massachusetts bought the Acushnet Cedar Swamp State Reservation—one of the largest, wildest and most impenetrable such swamps in the state—from the Acushnet Saw Mill Co. in 1972. It encompasses over 1,800 acres in New Bedford and Dartmouth. The fragrant and durable Atlantic White Cedar was harvested for centuries for shingles, furniture and boats but today harvesting is limited for the health of the swamps. Most trees live to 200 years, although some grow as old as 1,000. Mature trees grow to 80 feet in height and four feet in diameter.

Managed by the state Department of Environmental Management, the reservation was designated a National Natural Landmark by the National Parks Service in 1972, one of only eleven such landmarks in the state. Unique and delicate ecosystems, white cedar swamps are sensitive to commercial and residential development. Although somewhat protected by wetlands and conservation laws, environmentalists fear construction and expansion proposals at the nearby New Bedford Airport, Industrial Park and rail service could encroach on the sensitive swamplands.

The swamp is home to many unusual, rare and threatened creatures including Ringed Boghaunter Dragonflies, Pale Green Pinion Moths, Eastern Box Turtles and the Hessel's Hairstreak butterflies, which feed exclusively on Atlantic White Cedar. The reservation features quaking bogs and some of the state's most pristine stands of the tree, which grow in a narrow coastal belt from Maine to Mississippi.

Archaeologists believe the Acushnet Cedar Swamp formed an important part of the Native American cultural landscape. Excavations at a site in the southern section of the Industrial Park revealed signs of Native American occupation during the Middle and Late Archaic Periods 3,000 to 7,500 years ago. The presence of worked quartz show that the inhabitants made tools there and harvested the swamp's resources.

Industrial Park and the Acushnet Cedar Swamp, 1962. This view looks south with the railroad running diagonally across center and Church Street at left. In the foreground, the park is under construction and Duchaine Boulevard (the oval roadway) and the Braley Road connector to Church Street are being built. At upper right, beyond a mostly undisturbed portion of the forest, the Municipal Airport is visible.

Early Tenants at Industrial Park

By 1963, the city had invested more than $2 million toward development, water, sewer and utilities for the industrial park, and several firms had relocated there. In 1967, **Schaefer Equipment Company** of Pittsburgh opened a division called Schaefer Marine. It made lightweight, weather-resistant hardware for large sailboats. That same year, it bought out Whaling City Marine, a New Bedford-based specialist in small sailboat hardware. Schaefer built a 17,000-square-foot plant in the park to house both operations.

At center left, Mayor George Rogers meets with workers at **Polaroid** during an open house in January 1971. The 128-acre property included manufacturing buildings, a power plant, a wastewater treatment plant, asphalt parking areas, undeveloped wooded and wetland areas and a pond. Polaroid operated a high-resolution media manufacturing division and a photographic negative manufacturing division until 2006, when MultiLayer Coating Technologies (formerly Polaroid Contract Coating) was established. In 2008, Konarka Technologies Inc. acquired the property for the manufacture of thin-film photovoltaic material.

At center right, Antonio Leite uses a binocular stereo microscope to make final adjustments on micro titanium forceps at **Codman Shurtleff, Inc**. The company, the oldest manufacturer of medical products in the world, dated from 1838, when Benjamin S. Codman founded it in Boston. It specialized in surgical instruments and later became a subsidiary of Johnson & Johnson.

Sophisticated equipment on the can line at the **Canada Dry Bottling** plant produces private-label or store-brand cola for Somerville-based Finast Supermarkets. Inspectors watch every step as sanitized cans with tops on, but no bottoms, are fed upside down onto a conveyor belt. At the filling station a supply line under constant pressure fills them with a precise amount of cola at a canning temperature of 36 degrees. After filling, a bottom is put on. A sealing device spins the can and crimps the bottom to seal it. The filled-and-sealed can is then brought back to room temperature. Rinsed and dried cans are weighed in a quality control check before being packed into boxes for shipment.

Land (or swamp) is cleared for one of the Park's first tenants, Shaefer Equipment Co., 1967.

Open house, Polaroid Corporation, 1971.

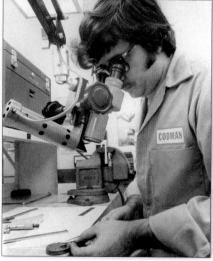

Making forceps, Codman Shurtleff, 1979.

Canada Dry Bottling Company, 1964.

Owner Henry R. Keene poses before a sample of **Edson Corporation** output. After buying Edson in 1956, Keene updated the product line by emphasizing lightweight materials, such as aluminum castings. The company, manufacturers of pumps and marine steering gear since 1859, moved from the Boston waterfront to New Bedford in 1949 and to the Industrial Park in 1965.

The oldest printed circuit board production company in North America, **Electralab Printed Electronic Corp.**, began in 1952 when Electralab and Printed Electronics Corp. merged. It remained strongly connected to the development of the printed circuit board for the electronics industry, computers and spacecraft. In 1969, it provided printed circuit boards for the Apollo 11 spaceflight, which landed the first humans, Neil Armstrong and Edwin "Buzz" Aldrin Jr., on the moon.

J. C. Rhodes, founded in Whitman in 1868, moved to New Bedford in 1891. Rhodes built its reputation as the nation's premier shoe eyelet manufacturer. Later, it made eyelets for the electronics industries and snaps for nine-volt batteries. As the footwear industry globalized and the US imported ever more shoes, the domestic market petered out, and demand for Rhodes eyelets steadily dropped. In 1996, Scovill Fasteners bought J.C. Rhodes. Despite local opposition and a firestorm protesting job loss, Scovill rejected a local buyout and instead closed the plant and moved operations to Clarkesville, Georgia, to economize.

In 1960, **Nu-Era Gear Corporation** of Rochester, Michigan, moved its production facilities to New Bedford. Its 250 employees made gears for automatic automobile transmissions in a 51,000-square-foot building, situated on a 12-acre site in the Industrial Park. In 1964, truck and auto parts maker Northwest Automotive Products Co. bought it out. In 1970, Borg-Warner, a specialist in automobile parts that had diversified into chemicals, plastics, industrial products and armored cars, purchased it. Borg-Warner introduced an improved transmission called the Model 45 and delocalized much of the production to Australia and South Wales.

Edson Corporation, 1971.

Electralab Printed Electronic Corp., 1964.

J. C. Rhodes workers Raymond Peel, Edmund Rose and William Crabtree, 1968.

Nu-Era Gear, 1961.

Dartmouth Finishing Corporation, 1964.   Daisy Cup Corporation, 1964.

Seven-Up Bottling Company, 1961.   Hancock Industries, 1963.

Coyne Industrial Laundry Inc., 1983.

Other Industry

After the Great Depression and largely due to the efforts of several city-promoting groups, New Bedford assembled a varied group of industries producing items ranging from consumer goods such as soft drinks and disposable cups to intermediate goods such as finished cloth for the clothing industries and steel sinks for construction. They also provided services such as laundry for hotels, hospitals and factories.

Dartmouth Finishing opened in 1946 in the former Dartmouth Mills weave shed to bleach, print, dye and finish cotton cloth. It later expanded operations since it did not have to treat the already low-mineral-content tap water. In 1951, the company installed a mercerizing plant, which strengthened cotton cloth using a caustic soda solution containing sodium hydroxide, increasing the luster of the dye.

Daisy Cup Corporation employed a specially designed automatic cup-forming machine to make its six-ounce disposable paper cups for hot beverages. It cut sides from a wide roll of stock, rolled them and glued them to bottoms punched from a narrow stock roll. Another machine sprayed the finished cups with waterproof lacquer and dried them in an oven. As business picked up during the mid-1960s, the company added another line.

In the bottle washing and inspections department of **Seven-Up Bottling Company**, Charles Evans on the right and production manager Richard Luke inspect the cleanliness of the large, heavy one-pint, twelve-ounce returnable glass bottles before they can be refilled, capped and placed in wooden crates.

At **Hancock Industries**, press operator Jack Offley carefully stretches a protective plastic cover over a stainless steel sheet. Installed in 1963 and seen in the rear, a Galton double-action hydraulic press applied 700 tons of pressure to form the combined plastic and steel sheet into the shape of a stainless steel sink. The shaped metal was then trimmed and fitted with holes, and its edges were rimmed and polished.

Robert E. Rudd, chief of maintenance at **Coyne** headquarters in Syracuse, tests one of two four-module giant washers newly installed at Coyne Industrial Laundry. The machines washed large quantities of soiled cloth and extracted as much water as possible to reduce energy costs of drying. The washers' weight required specially poured foundations.

#

Acushnet Company, Rubber Division, 1967. *The Pangborn deflasher machine removed rubber waste edge, or flash, formed during molding. Liquid nitrogen made the flash brittle, and it would break off during tumbling. In 1960, Acushnet set up a corporate research and development division in a former Aerovox building. In 1968, to modernize its image, the company changed its name to Acushnet Company with a stylized "A" logo.*

Aerovox Corporation, 1972. *After 1960, Aerovox had years of irregular net income, declining sales, losses and legal troubles. It closed unprofitable product lines. In 1972, it sold its non-ceramic capacitor plant and name to Belleville Industries. Former Aerovox executive Clifford H. Tuttle Jr. headed the new firm and continued production. In September 1976, authorities announced finding high levels of cancer-causing PCBs in clams from the Acushnet River. Aerovox's new troubles had just begun.*

Chamberlain Manufacturing Corporation, 1962. *The subsidiary of an Iowa firm, Chamberlain was New Bedford's leading defense contractor. In November 1967, it purchased the operation previously run by New Bedford Defense Products, a Firestone subsidiary in the old Manomet Mill #4. The company made 155mm artillery shells. As such, more than any other city firm, its fortunes waxed during military buildups or waned during defense cuts.*

Depending on US foreign policy and security needs, Chamberlain's contracts for ammunition alternated with plant mothballing. Ammunition contracts showed greater volatility than did multi-year contracts on R&D, aircraft, missiles and electronics. Over time, because artillery shells were not high-tech, their importance in the defense budget dropped. In July 1991, shortly after the end of the first Gulf War, Chamberlain closed its New Bedford plant.

John I. Paulding Company, 1977.

Goodyear Rubber Company, 1966.

Columbia Electronics, Inc., 1972.

Morse Twist Drills, 1965.

American Flexible Conduit Company, 1967.

Teledyne Rodney Metals, 1971.

Job erosion took place quietly in postwar New Bedford. Outside interests increasingly bought local firms, exposing city jobs to national market forces. As a consequence, manufacturing employment fell by more than 10,000 jobs, or roughly a third, from a high of 31,736 jobs in 1947 to 21,300 in 1982. Even traditionally steady employers that remained in the city could not provide large-scale job creation and sometimes sent jobs elsewhere.

After Revere Copper & Brass bought **John I. Paulding** in 1964, the subsidiary encountered problems. In 1977, the Consumer Product Safety Commission said Paulding's aluminum electrical wiring, widely installed in homes between 1965 and 1973, constituted a fire safety hazard. Later, Paulding was one of eight firms convicted of conspiring to fix the prices of electrical switches and power outlets. James B. Buckley, its former president, was sentenced to jail time and paid a hefty fine. In 1978 and 1979, a series of federal and state cases against Paulding and its co-conspirators sought to recover damages resulting from their conspiracies.

At top right, **Frank Netinho** builds up press blankets used in offset printing by pouring a liquid synthetic rubber called "dough" on 50 feet of blanket as it slowly passes through a spreader at **Goodyear Tire and Rubber**. During an eight-hour period, he successively applied as many as 100 thin rubber dough layers to a fabric base to gradually build up its surface to its final thickness of 2/100 inches. In 1976, during a long strike by the United Rubber Workers, Goodyear ended production of bicycle tires and tubes, eliminating almost 300 New Bedford jobs.

At center left, **Alice Costa** removes molded plugs on dryer cords from the injection-molding machine operated by **Altinho Carvalho** at **Columbia Electronics**.

Morse Twist Drills, center right, had been a subsidiary of Van Norman Industries since the 1940s. Universal American Corp. bought both of them in 1962. In 1967, it began negotiating for a plant in Mexico City to manufacture drills.

Manuel Carvalho Jr., bottom left, coils armored cable, one of three product lines, at **American Flexible Conduit Company**. Nortek, a diversified manufacturer of industrial and consumer products from Rhode Island, bought American Flexible Conduit in 1969.

In 1967, Teledyne Inc. bought **Rodney Metals,** bottom right, in a stock exchange. Rodney had perfected the rolling of thin metal stock that had been used in a prototype strategic bomber called the XB-70A.

Hospitals

During the second half of the century, local hospitals grew in size and consolidated. Advances in medical technology, costlier diagnostic equipment and new treatments such as antibiotics drove changes in health care.

Built in 1910, **Sassaquin Sanatorium** served patients suffering from tuberculosis, the dreaded disease that devastated many mill workers. Dr. João Carlos da Silva Pitta, a New Bedford doctor who emigrated from the Azores, felt great sympathy for this stricken population. He founded the Portuguese League of Assistance to Consumptives, which built the sanatorium. It offered treatment with extended rest in fresh air and sunshine. With advances in treatment, such as the introduction of streptomycin after World War II, the spread of the disease slowed significantly. From 1915 to 1955, New Bedford's new tuberculosis cases plummeted by 90 percent from 423 to 42 and the number of tuberculosis deaths fell from 139 to nine. In 1956, the sanatorium changed its name to Sassaquin Hospital. With the continued drop in tuberculosis, in July 1963, Sassaquin Hospital closed. The remaining 25 patients went to other hospitals or rest homes in New Bedford. Today it serves as the Mediplex Rehabilitation Hospital.

Union Hospital (top left and center) outgrew its obsolete facilities at the corner of Pleasant and Willis Streets. In 1915, Dr. J. Conrad Ross founded Union as a small, 36-bed general hospital in what had formerly been a private residence.

In 1964, Union bought the closed **Sassaquin Hospital**, invested $1.2 million in renovations, doubled its capacity and converted it to a 135-bed general facility with modern diagnostic equipment (top right). In 1980, Park Healthcare bought Union, which had been losing patients and doctors to St. Luke's Hospital. Park proposed converting it into a psychiatric facility, but dropped the idea in the face of community opposition. In 1954, a couple converted Union's old Pleasant Street facility into a nursing and convalescent home. In 1967, a group called Doctors Chronic Hospital converted it again, this time to care for chronically ill patients.

At bottom, hard-hatted Robert Mortenson, engineer for Volpe Construction Co., surveys the **site for St. Luke's addition** with the assistance of college student Peter Tallman of Fairhaven. The $6.5 million, four-story addition would contain administrative and medical staff offices, a visitor's lobby, a gift shop, 130-seat conference room, 100 beds for medical and surgical patients, a pediatric division with separate facilities for teenage patients, an intensive care unit, an x-ray unit, laboratories and an emergency room suite.

Union Hospital, 1074 Pleasant Street, 1957.

Sassaquin Hospital, Acushnet Avenue, 1962.

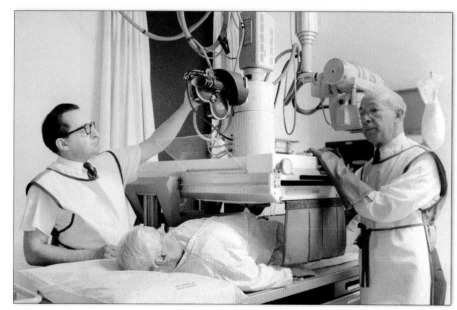

Union Hospital, 1966. Lab technician Jesse Oliveira (left) and radiologist Samuel L. Poplack (right) demonstrate the new diagnostic fluoroscope that simultaneously projected moving X-ray images on a television screen and made reference movies of them.

Planned expansion of St. Luke's Hospital, 1965.

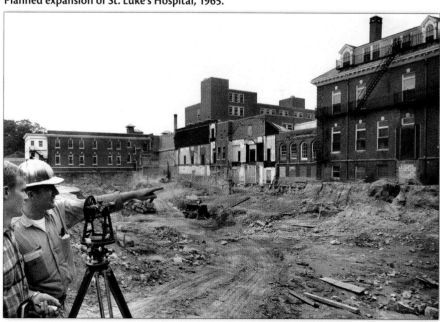

New Bedford Needle Trades

As textiles left, New Bedford leaders looked towards New York to attract related industry to fill empty mills. The city offered deals on city-owned mill space taken for back taxes to entice apparel and home furnishing producers. Special offers included breaks on rent, taxes and utilities if firms guaranteed certain employment levels.

At its height in this area during the 1970s, between 15,000 and 20,000 people worked in the stitching shops.

"They weren't sweatshops," said Cindy Rodrigues, President of the New Bedford Labor Council and a former stitcher. "I earned $60 a day as a stitcher in 1975. That's like $100 now."

Dick Early, who worked at the *Standard-Times* from 1946 to 1976, the last 10 years as editor, remembered this industrial revival of New Bedford. "When I came here in 1945, there was a constant drive for industrial diversification. The business leaders didn't want to repeat the mistake of relying too much on one industry. New Bedford developed the reputation as a place where people would take menial jobs and work hard at them."

However, diversification remained elusive, leaving the city's economy vulnerable.

Foreign competition, new technology and shifting demand for goods eroded the city's foothold in the needle trades. From 1967 to 1977, Massachusetts lost one-fourth of its apparel jobs to overseas or Southern competition. By 1977, New Bedford's remaining 8,139 apparel jobs accounted for 34 percent of the city's almost 24,000 manufacturing jobs.

In an effort to stabilize the apparel trade, in June 1985, the Needle Trades Action Project brought together employers, unions and community representatives. The region formed the nation's third largest center of apparel production. The project wanted to upgrade equipment with low-interest loans, offer firms technical services and develop worker-training programs. But the organization suffered from mistrust between its constituent groups and the project soon disbanded.

Despite attempts to reverse the trend, from 1977 to 2002, New Bedford hemorrhaged 91 percent of its apparel employment, losing roughly 7,400 apparel trade jobs.

While most area shops have since moved out of the country, a few remain today, including Joseph Abboud, maker of high-end men's suits and clothing.

States Nitewear, 1965. *A supervisor shows off current models. The non-union firm produced pajamas, snap coats, shift gowns and quilt robes at its Healey Street plant in the Nashawena Mills.*

Stitcher at work, Cliftex Corporation, Brook Street, 1966. *At this time, Cliftex was owned and managed by Frank Anapol and his sons Joel and Walter, and Nicolaci brothers Domenick and John.*

Top of the Line Shops

Izaura Walker, long-time employee at **Cameo Curtains**, uses a special attachment to rough sew the hems of gingham curtain panels. Cameo was one of the largest curtain manufacturers in the US.

Cape Cod Sportswear specialized in boys' and men's sports jackets. Before packaging goods, quality control inspectors examine finished items to ensure that the product is flawless. At right, Eva Demers and Alex Kalife Jr. scrutinize and touch up sleeves on finished goods. The company occupied a niche of filling small orders that did not interest larger manufactures. It regularly employed from 20 to 50 workers.

Frank Anapol and Pasquale Nicolaci both worked for Calvin Clothing in the 1940s before teaming up in 1951 to start their own apparel firm, Youth Craft, in the Grinnell Mill on North Front Street. By the late 1950s, they renamed the company **Cliftex Corporation**—makers of boys' and young men's clothing—and relocated to Brook and Deane Streets. Finally, in the late 1960s, they purchased Manomet Mills Nos. 1 & 2 on Riverside Avenue. By this time, two sets of brothers, Joel and Walter Anapol and Domenick and John Nicolaci, were running the company. In 1969, they sold it to the National Student Marketing Corp. (NSM). The following year, after major losses, NSM reversed the stock exchange used in the buyout and Cliftex became independent again. By 1979, it employed 1,800 workers.

At **Calvin Clothing**, workers trim the facing on men's sport coats. Facing fabric is applied to garments' inside edges to provide contrast, decoration or strength. Facing gives the garment a clean look by hiding raw edges. By the 1960s Calvin Clothing, led by Calvin Siegal, built a niche market making boys' and young men's tailored suits. In 1968, the company merged with Palm Beach Corporation and became pioneers in the use of designer labels—a practice that would become New Bedford's calling card in the world of clothing manufacture. The company produced for Pierre Cardin, John Weitz, Ralph Lauren and others well into the 1970s. Soon, other companies boasted similar high-end designer labels and the "Made in New Bedford" moniker was proudly displayed in windows along NYC's Fashion Avenue.

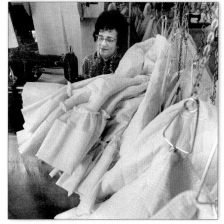

Cameo Curtains, Riverside Avenue, 1973.

Cape Cod Sportswear, 1972.

Cliftex Corporation, 1976.

Calvin Clothing, 1980. Workers trim the facing on men's sport coats. Facing applied to garment edges provides contrast, decoration or strength. It gives the garment a clean look, hiding raw edges.

Outlet Stores

One popular stop for shoppers was the old Kay Windsor Factory Outlet Store in the North End, where bargain hunters rummaged through racks filled with hundreds of ready-to-wear frocks. Whereas earlier Kay Windsor collections of the 1950s were focused on secretarial and housewife themes, later they sought to elevate the "cotton house dress to charming chic." The concept worked until the growing popularity of women's pants suits in the 1980s cut into the dress business.

Anderson-Little Clothing, maker of fine men's clothing, pioneered the concept "direct from the factory to you," and took great pride in its specialty, the traditional blue-black blazer. Founded in 1933 by Morris R. Anderson, the company began in Fall River. By the early 1950s, outlets had opened in New Bedford and 10 other New England cities. The New Bedford outlet was located on Water Street and Ark Lane, at the foot of the Fairhaven Bridge. The business grew to 100 stores under the ownership of F. W. Woolworth Co. In 1992, most Anderson-Little stores were closed, and the remaining seven were sold to Cliftex Manufacturing. In 2008, Stuart Anderson (Morris's grandson) and his son Scott reclaimed the trademark rights, and today Anderson-Little maintains an online company based in Miami. The Classic Blue Blazer remains its signature product.

Worleybeds on Pope's Island remains true to the authentic factory outlet intent. Many so-called factory outlets no longer sell seconds or overstock factory items directly to the consumer, instead selling products specially manufactured for sale at these stores. But Worleybeds continues the "direct from the factory to the consumer" tradition. The family-owned and -operated business manufactures and sells custom-made mattresses

Kay Windsor Frocks, Inc., 1966. *Stitchers manufacture dresses at Kay Windsor's Brook Street plant. In a 1961 public stock offering, Kay Windsor described itself as a company "engaged in the design, manufacture and sale of a nationally advertised line of medium-priced dresses and suit dresses for women and girls of all ages and sizes."*

and box springs for homes, RVs, boats and even antique beds. John L. Worley Sr. started making his own brand of bedding in 1954 in the old Taylor Shoe manufacturing building on Acushnet Avenue. He later moved to 139 North Second Street, a two-story brick building that once served as the Post Office garage and, later, a Chrysler-Plymouth dealership. According to John Worley Jr., the Worleys pride themselves on making mattresses the old-fashioned way, using only American-made (mostly local) materials and padding both sides. "Most national brands create a product padded on one side. That's like selling a cheeseburger with one slice of bread," he says. He and his wife, Martha, took over the business in 1973 and have since turned over stewardship to their son Patrick. "When a customer calls, a Worley answers," Worley says.

Anderson-Little Clothing, North Water Street and Ark Lane, 1963.

Worley Bedding and Furniture Factory, Inc., 139 No. Second Street.

Discount Department Stores

Arlans was New Bedford's first discount department store. Brothers Lester and Herbert Palestine and their associate, Hyman Feinstein, founded it in 1948. Arlans initially served as a factory outlet for boy's clothing made by the Monarch Clothing Company, which they also owned. From a modest beginning at the corner of Brook and Deane Streets, it expanded rapidly into a nationwide chain store selling general retail merchandise; by 1970 it had 119 stores, most of them located in the Northeast and Midwest. During that year, it began to suffer from a recession that saw unemployment reach one million nationwide. As sales fell, Arlans experienced heavy losses. From 1970 to 1973, it lost $65 million despite closing 40 percent of its stores and laying off more than 4,000 employees. The situation worsened, and by the 1974 Christmas season, only 10 stores remained. In 1975, those, too, were liquidated as part of the company bankruptcy proceedings.

Mars Bargainland was a small chain of full-range discount stores headquartered in New Bedford. Most of its stores were located in eastern Massachusetts and southern New Hampshire. Matthew Tatelbaum opened the first Mars Bargainland in August 1962; it was located on Riverside Avenue in the former Building No. 1 of Whitman Mills. Other stores soon followed, including one in South Dartmouth. By 1971, Tatelbaum's 16-store chain had expanded into western Massachusetts. However, the economic recession of the early 1970s led to five straight years of losses. The chain managed to survive by either closing or selling nine stores and reducing inventory in the others. The respite was short-lived. Mars Bargainland was liquidated in 1990. Only the Dartmouth store, renamed and transformed into Big Value, survives as a Tatelbaum family holding.

The Page Mill Discount Center opened in 1956 at the corner of Cove and Bonney Streets. It provided space to independent specialized merchants who offered a wide range of low-cost merchandise. Shortly thereafter,  after having been renamed the Cove Discount Center, it began to aim at a wider public. When Louis Queen and James Falk bought it in 1972, they used their retail experience, gained at New Bedford's Arlans and at Mars Bargainland, to expand the store. They stressed meeting customers' needs with items not readily found elsewhere; for example, immigrant families, often unaccustomed to washing machines, could buy washboards there. Cove Discount served its mostly South End customers until 1998, when building problems including a leaking roof, spotty heating system and derelict air conditioning forced it to close. An extended going-out-of-business sale ended in November 1998. The building was demolished in 2000.

Cove Discount Center, 1960. **Mars Bargainland, 1962.**

Arlans Department Store, 1966.

Fishing Industry 1960–1980

From 1960 to 1980, sea scallops and yellowtail flounder secured New Bedford's place among the world's major fishing ports. As New England's other ports languished during and after World War II, these two fisheries propelled the value of landings in New Bedford. It rose from fourth among the nation's ports in 1950, to second in 1959 and to first in 1983 after the US extended its exclusive economic zone to 200 nautical miles.

The long post-war rise in New Bedford scallop landings peaked in 1961, after which landings declined steadily until 1973, to only 60 percent of their wartime average. Increased fishing by Canadian scallopers on Georges Bank led to the decline in New Bedford's scallop landings. By 1965, the Canadian scallop fleet caught three times more scallops on Georges Bank than the entire US fleet. New Bedford scallopers reacted by shifting the fishery to mid-Atlantic grounds and caught three-fourths of 1965s landings from these grounds. Sea scallop revenues varied far less than did landings; rising prices softened the blow of lower catch just as falling prices had restricted revenue when landings rose.

Fishermen unload bluefin tuna at Homer's Wharf, 1964. *New England's commercial bluefin tuna fishery was carried out mostly by small and medium-sized purse seiners. Landings rose to about 1,630 metric tons in 1962, and then fell to 607 metric tons in 1964. At this time, most bluefin landings came into New Bedford where handling, storage and transportation costs were less than they would be going to canneries outside New England. In the 1970s, increased prices caused yearly landings to rise slightly until stricter quotas were enacted in the 1980s. As tuna migrations began, local seiners off-loaded in New Jersey.*

Homer's Wharf, 1960. *By the 1960s, fish buyers and processing companies such as Sea View Fillet, Aiello Brothers and Parisi Fillet occupied both sides of Homer's Wharf. Other tenants include ice makers, storage facilities and Louis Giusti's Wharf Diner, later called Louie's on the Wharf. Before the end of the decade, all of the structures would be razed and the wharf rebuilt. In the meantime, buyers and fillet houses relocated to the modern, pre-fabricated, highway-friendly facilities of the new South Terminal a few blocks away. Today, Homer's Wharf is lined with new fillet houses and fish companies.*

Rising yellowtail flounder catch took up the slack left by the decline in scallop landings. Due to high prices and the abundance of yellowtail, some scallopers targeted yellowtail instead, and some draggers switched from cod and haddock to yellowtail. In 1961, the 30 million tons landed in the city accounted for 75 percent of total yellowtail landings. By 1965, yellowtail flounders brought almost as much value to the port as did the higher-priced scallops.

By 1960, the port's physical structure had changed little since whaling times although offshore draggers, scallopers and inshore boats had long replaced whaleships at the docks and new fishing-related businesses occupied the whaling-built structures. By the end of that decade, three major investments transformed the port's physical character: the Hurricane Barrier, the South Terminal and the highway linking the waterfront to interstate highways. All three improvements resulted from the cooperation between the New Bedford Fishermen's Union, the Seafood Producers and the Seafood Dealers Association working with local and state political leaders.

First proposed in 1948 as protection from hurricanes for New Bedford and Fairhaven waterfront businesses, the "largest Hurricane Barrier in the world" was built by the US Army Corps of Engineers between 1962 and 1966 using almost one

Unloading yellowtail flounder, 1966. *Although landings fell by 20 percent to 24,000 metric tons, value reached an all-time high of $6.8 million. Concerned scientists proposed conservation measures, including using larger mesh sizes, closing fishing grounds and enacting size limits on fish.*

Aboard the dragger *Christina J*, 1980. *Fishermen Paul Hirth (left), Dennis Sherman (at winch) and Billy Sherman prepare to set the trawl for a tow on Nantucket Shoal. On this trip the catch was mostly yellowtail flounder. Skipper Herman Bruce mans the wheelhouse. In May 1985, under a different crew, high seas flooded the 67-foot dragger's engine room about 20 miles off Nantucket, knocking out power. In freezing seas, the crew abandoned ship, which sank within 15 minutes. Adrift on a raft for 42 hours, the crew survived on 5 bags of chocolate chip cookies and 12 ounces of water. After being rescued seven miles off Nantucket, Captain João Medeiros declared, "Without God, and the supply of cookies, I don't think we would have made it."*

million tons of Dartmouth-quarried granite and steel gates weighing 400 tons each. Since then, it has protected boats, homes and businesses lining the harbor.

The New Bedford Redevelopment Authority supplied Urban Renewal funds to dredge the area within the Hurricane Barrier and to use the dredge material to create bulkheads for processing plants. It completed the South Terminal in 1968 and sold the land and docks, where fish and scallops could be unloaded directly to the processing plant to fish processors. These moved in almost immediately, building modern, efficient processing plants. The Redevelopment Authority also funded the John F. Kennedy Memorial Highway connecting the waterfront and South Terminal to recently completed Interstate 195. "(New Bedford) is the only place where you can leave a pier and you can put your driver behind the wheel and you drive on a state highway wherever you want to go: NY, Boston, Provincetown," said Howard Nickerson, chairman of the Redevelopment Authority at the time and later a spokesman for the fishing industry. Large year classes of small scallops appeared on Georges Bank during the mid-1970s. New Bedford scallopers fishing off New Jersey returned to Georges Bank. In addition, the federal government's vessel subsidy programs, created in response to complaints about the foreign factory ships taking all of the fish, added many new scallop vessels to the fleet.

The 1973-1974 oil embargo raised fuel prices. While scallop prices kept pace with inflation, oil prices rose faster. Diesel fuel prices tripled between 1973 and 1980, cutting into fishermen's shares and boat owners' profits with repercussions on processing and other shore-side businesses. Trips to the northern edge of

Unloading swordfish from the *Sanson Joy*, August 1966. *Two men wrest a 200-pounder to the platform at Ell Vee Dee, Inc. The firm unloaded 200 fish this day, bringing a weekly total of 310, with another 51 expected next day. As a result, wholesale prices dropped to 33¢ per pound. Annual landings rose to 222 metric tons..*

Georges Bank and to the scallop grounds off New Jersey proved too costly.

Foreign factory trawling fleets also vexed New England fishermen. The Soviet Union tripled its vessels from 100 in 1961 to 300 in 1963. Including Canadian landings, foreign fishermen took twice as much fish from Georges Bank as did the US. By 1972, they took three times as much fish from Georges. According to Congressman Hastings Keith, the Soviet fleet "looked like a Navy task force or the great echelons of combines we see pictured in Kansas wheatfields."

Dragger *West Wind II* trawls for yellowtail on Nantucket Shoal, 1980. *Two draggers visible in the distance mean fish aplenty along this run.*

Boston, Gloucester and Maine drove the political movement to exclude foreign fleets from Georges Bank because of foreign fishing's effect on the cod, haddock and herring landed there. New Bedford's scallop and flounder catch suffered less as foreign fleets did not target these species. Even with political support from both the East Coast and West Coast fisheries, and from the US petroleum industry that wanted rights to offshore oil and gas, extending the exclusive economic zone to 200 miles wasn't a simple solution. As a major trading nation, the US had long supported freedom of the seas. After Iceland declared a 200-mile exclusive fisheries limit in 1975, followed by other fishing nations, pressure grew on the US Congress.

The federal government found a political solution that focused on the management of fish stocks instead of excluding foreign fishing vessels. In 1976, the law extending an exclusive economic zone to 200 miles was labeled the Fishery Conservation and Management Act, which established Federal control over fish stocks. It empowered regional fishery management councils under the National Marine Fishery Service, a Federal agency, to create fishery management plans charged with maintaining fish stocks by controlling catch by species.

Unloading scallops, South Terminal, 1976. *Lumpers hustle to unload bags of scallops from the New Bedford scalloper* Blue Surf, *part of a record haul that saw 4,321 metric tons of shellfish worth $17.5 million landed here during the year.*

New Bedford's landings of fish and scallops surged along with landings in other ports immediately after the law's passage. This boom proved short-lived, however, as both scallop and groundfish landings declined within a few years, starting a new chapter in the history of the New Bedford's fishing industry.

Fishing vessel American Hope, 1980. *Steel-hulled stern trawlers such as* American Hope *began replacing wooden side-trawlers or eastern-rigs in the late 1970s. Before the end of the 1980s, nearly half the fleet's vessels were steel hulled. By 2010, a wooden offshore fishing vessel was hard to find.*

New Bedford Schools, 1960–1980

Beginning in 1950, New Bedford's school population grew, as baby boom children began entering kindergarten. By 1967, when baby boomers filled every primary and secondary class, school attendance was 45 percent higher than it had been in 1950. However, the need to educate ever-increasing numbers of pupils did not guarantee that city fathers would provide adequate resources for the school system. New Bedford's education expenditures remained low. In 1967, the city's school spending per pupil from local sources ranked a dismal 336th of the state's 351 cities and towns.

Perhaps reflecting those budgetary constraints, at the elementary level New Bedford relied heavily on teachers who had not finished college. In 1964, 45 percent of the city's public school elementary teachers lacked degrees. Other cities did a better job of hiring teachers with degrees; that year, 35 percent of teachers in Fall River and only 18 percent of teachers in Boston lacked degrees. During the mid-1960s, city school administrators adopted a policy to recruit teachers with better credentials. By 1967, only 32 percent of New Bedford's elementary teachers had no degree.

New Bedford Vocational High School students making graduation gowns, 1965. *Under the watchful eye of Margaret E. Cameron, longtime sewing instructor for the school's second- and fourth-year students, New Bedford Voke seniors make and fit their graduation gowns. They could choose any fabric, provided it was white. Instructors judged the results and recognized the winner. During the 1971-1972 academic year, students in the senior girls' sewing class completed new stage curtains for the Little Theater Group of the New Bedford YWCA.*

Automotive students, New Bedford Vocational High School, 1972. *Students trace transmission problems and do engine tune-ups. In the foreground, left to right, are Ricardo Cruz, Mike Enos, Dennis Desroisiers, Mike Baptiste, Jude Couto, Manny DaSilva and instructor Stanley Boelher. The three men in background are unidentified, but barely visible in the distance is instructor Ed Kocur. Students are using a new Sun 1120 Electronic Engine Tester. Introduced in 1969, the tester was designed to diagnose the condition of an automobile engine in the shortest possible time. Since many garages adopted them, Voke students carefully honed their skills with the new engine tester to improve their job marketability.*

Machine shop at Keith Junior High School, 1966. *Instructor Ernest Bourgeois in foreground instructs students about the safe use of bench lathes. The industrial arts program, begun as a summer program for educationally deprived boys, proved so successful that it was adopted into the regular school curriculum. Similar programs were later adopted for girls.*

Upholstery making, 1964. *Under a state program, New Bedford Vocational High School provided 75 practical arts evening classes ranging from upholstery to clothing and tailoring. Classes were open to anyone over 16 not attending school. Students provided their own tools and materials; there was no fee. In the foreground, instructor Harry Siegel gives a helping hand to one of the students.*

New Bedford High School Graduation, Olympia Theatre 1969. *Wearing maroon caps and gowns, some with gold honor cords, the 718 graduates marched in a light rain down William Street to the theater. Some whistled the theme song from "The Bridge on the River Kwai." Commencement speaker Dana M. Cotton, dean of the Harvard Graduate School of Education, and Mayor Edward F. Harrington both warned students of the turmoil facing them in the world on leaving high school. Students observed a moment of silence to mark the recent death of NBHS principal John F. Gracia.*

City schools continued to face the long-standing problem of excessive high school dropouts. Only half the members of the 1959 cohort from the city's ninth-grade public school class began their senior year in 1962; more than 500 students had already left school. Moreover, not all the seniors graduated. While the retention rate gradually improved during the rest of the decade, roughly 30 percent of students left after one year of high school; more dropped out before entering their senior year. Sadly, the dropout problem began earlier, in junior high school. Despite the introduction of a vocational component to provide job skills, each year an average of 10 percent of public junior high students left school.

Elementary school authorities regularly raised the problem of over-aged, oversized pupils in Grade 6. Some students repeated grades so many times that they no longer fit in socially—and they could not be promoted to junior high school. In 1966, sixth-graders ranged in age from 10 to 16 years. Once the law no longer required their attendance, many older students dropped out, discouraged and overwhelmed.

Parents increasingly turned to private schools to educate their children. From 1960 to 1967, the number of students in the city's private schools increased by almost 850. During the 1960s, private schools educated almost 30 percent of city students.

Fewer New Bedfordites attended vocational school during the 1960s than before World War II. City enrollees in the day industrial programs for boys and in the evening industrial program for men fell by 50 percent; those in household arts program for girls fell by one-third. Only enrollment in the evening practical arts school grew by a mere 10 percent. In sharp contrast, non-resident enrollment in all programs rose by at least 35 percent.

Out with the old, January 1966. *Parker Street School students trudge east through fresh snow carrying their books to the newly built and renamed John Avery Parker School before participating in the flag raising and inauguration.*

Music class at Ellen R. Hathaway School, May 1967. *Programs to teach instrumental music remained starved for funds. In 1966, all city elementary schools combined spent $135 for instrumental music, while devoting $2,529 for physical education.*

Grade 4 enrichment class, Charles S. Ashley School, December 1972. *During the 1970s, Massachusetts schools tried out many innovations, often with the help of volunteer resource persons from the community. These aimed to improve the school environment and increase student involvement. Standing with models they made of city buildings are (clockwise from lower left) Doreen Reis, Alfred Vieira, Kristina Jardin, Denise Cloutier, Scott Verissimo, Michael Alpert, Karen Metivier, Lori Washington, Donna Lyonnais, Harry Ainsworth, Matthew Picard, Wendy Rogers, Matthew Labarge, Randall Souza and Duane Brown. Among the buildings they modeled are: the main Post Office, the Free Public Library, the Whaling Museum, the Standard-Times, Superior Court, Saint Anthony's Church, Police Headquarters, the First National Bank Building and the Municipal Building.*

During this period, the city's physical educational structures changed dramatically. Old schools were demolished to do away with "antiquated" facilities and replaced by modern buildings. After a fire at the Henry F. Harrington Memorial School on Court Street in 1960, the historic Romanesque-style structure designed by noted architect Edgar B. Hammond was taken down at a cost of $6,000. The city council had quashed premiums for fire insurance that would have paid for its restoration. The Ellen R. Hathaway School, erected across the street at Court and Liberty Streets, replaced it in 1962.

Two up-to-date high schools appeared. The city council took the Parker Street Dump and additional land by eminent domain. Some councilors worried that subsurface conditions would lead to additional costs, but construction proceeded nonetheless. The school opened in 1972. The Greater New Bedford Regional Vocational Technical High School was built on land on Ashley Boulevard across from Pine Grove Cemetery. Dartmouth, New Bedford and Fairhaven issued bonds to pay for construction. It opened in 1977.

Two 1,000-student public grammar schools launched in 1975: Hayden-McFadden and Casimir Pulaski. Two other large grammar schools started in 1977: Carney Academy and Alfred J. Gomes. Three older elementary schools closed: the Clark Street, John H. Clifford and Thompson Street schools built in 1897, 1901 and 1884 respectively.

Henry F. Harrington Memorial School, 1960.

Holy Family Grammar School, September 1977

Greater New Bedford Regional Vocational-Technical High School construction, September 1976.

Aerial view of New Bedford High School under construction, May 1971.

New Bedford High School Class of 1963. *Engaged in a lively class discussion are, from left to right: Joanne Morrison, Joyce Sylvia, Janet Shepley, Georgette Biscari, Sue Bellotti, Scott Gatenby, Rodney DeRego, Lorraine LeBlanc, unknown, Anthony Zimon and Patricia McNally.*

Latin Class, New Bedford High School, 1963. *Formed that year, club members read Latin newspapers and discussed Latin's application to the modern world. Seated foreground are: Lisa Golub, Jan Aillery and Phyllis Geller. Rear, left to right: Abigail Leaming, Joyce Sylvia, Richard Jaslow, Janice Twarog, Betsy Schuster, Carol Topolewski, Eileen Alderson and Michael Lague.*

Smiles all around at the end of the first day's classes, September 1963. *New Bedford High School enrollment had grown to approximately 2,650, a rise of about 150 students from the previous year's total. Of the roughly 1,200 entering freshmen students, 35 percent would leave school before the first day of their sophomore year. Less than 700 of them remained to begin the cohort's senior year in 1965 despite rises in school enrollment.*

Lunch time, Normandin Junior High School cafeteria, 1965.

New Bedford Voke students ready to serve lunch, October 1965.

Bus Stop, Purchase and William Streets, 1970. *High school students congregate downtown after school. Students heading north or to Fairhaven waited in front of Cherry's; students going south are across the street, near Sears Court. Some Catholic school girls rolled up the waists of their modest uniform skirts. Walking at center are Holy Family High School girls Theresa Sadek Brum (with glasses), Maureen Berry Costa (to her left) and Lynn Riley Stanton at far left. At far right is Shelly Brooker. Gary Nielson is in background center. David Green holds a copy of "We Bombed in New Haven," a recently published anti-war play by Joseph Heller, the author of Catch-22. No one carries a smartphone!*

Film, Television and Radio, 1960–1980

New Bedford lept into the media age, trumpeting three major radio stations (WNBH, WBSM, WJFD), a network-affiliated television station (WTEV) and a local Cable TV channel that provided news, talk shows and entertainment in two languages.

Several nationally known personalities came from the New Bedford, including Brian Healy, producer for CBS News and 60 Minutes, and Curt Worden, cinematographer and two-time national Emmy-winning broadcast journalist.

A Rising Tide, 1963

On October 13, 1964, television station WTEV-6 premiered a New Bedford promotional film, *A Rising Tide*. Narrated by Chet Huntley, co-anchor of NBC evening news, it told the story of a city on the mend. Huntley described an air of progress and optimism, job creation and new housing as well as newfound purchasing power. The film drew its title from slain President John F. Kennedy's favorite sailor's maxim: "A rising tide lifts all the boats."

The US Department of Commerce's Area Redevelopment Administration (ARA) funded the $40,000 film. ARA had already pumped $1.9 million into twelve local projects meant to generate 1,070 jobs. With the film, the ARA wanted to show New Bedford as a model of what cities could do if they considered "problems as stepping stones and not stumbling blocks."

Noted documentary filmmaker Jack Glenn directed the film and Gordon Knox, famous for his documentaries, produced it. At a post-premiere celebratory dinner held at the Wamsutta Club, ARA Administrator William L. Batt, Jr. expressed pride in the city. He noted that the film accurately portrayed New Bedford's battle for economic survival and its efforts to diversify industry.

WNBH, 1978. Jazz DJ "Sunkiss" Derek Rose spins an eclectic contemporary jazz sound on his Sunday morning show at the County and Locust Street studio. His playlist was on the cutting edge of contemporary jazz. WNBH ran a music format of mostly old-time, big-band jazz and dance music. Local sports and public affairs were also part of the station's repertoire.

WBSM–AM 1420

Listeners calling WBSM's Open Line show in the mid-50s spoke to Hal Peterson. Beginning in the 1960s, callers would reach Stan Lipp who manned the phones for three decades. Beginning in 1973, Jim Phillips spent four decades in radio and TV, much of that as WBSM's news director. Phillips recalled earlier, long-gone radio days when people worked hard but life seemed more relaxed, when half the city sat around the breakfast table, sipping coffee and opining on Open Line. He remembered Peterson as "a man for all seasons and a jack-of-all-trades," who could host music, sports and talk radio. He started the charity Quarters for Christmas. Lipp too made his mark in the city.

Still frames from the documentary film, A Rising Tide, 1963. As the camera pans the harbor front and fishing fleet, film titles and credits cover the Cuttyhunk ferry, Alert, berthed at Pier 3. At center, slasher tenders and other textile workers are portrayed at Berkshire Hathaway. At right, Z. Walter Janiak, Director of New Bedford Vocational School, assists individuals interested in technical training and adult education programs.

Whaling City Cable TV, circa 1982. *Editing videotape at the studio are Program Director Jim Donnelly and News Director Ana Cabrera.*

Romper Room set at the WTEV studio, 1971. *Romper Room was a rare franchised and syndicated series. Before 1981, all local shows used the same script with local children. WTEV's Miss Kris opened each program with a greeting and the Pledge of Allegiance. An oversized bumblebee, Mr. Do-Bee, helped teach the children proper deportment.*

"Stan Lipp, a unique human being," Phillips said. He treated everyone with respect including some difficult listeners. He was a great communicator, a cantor at the synagogue, a man deeply involved in the community. And nobody did a commercial like Stan. He adlibbed. He went out in the streets into the auto shops and carpet stores, and talked to the owners. When customers showed up to buy, they always said—Stan sent us."

WJFD–Portuguese Radio

Portuguese radio in New Bedford grew into a powerhouse. From 1950 to 1972, it was WBSM's first FM station, briefly called WGCY. After 1975, it became WJFD-FM (97.3) with 50,000 watts. "We are the link that connects all the Portuguese communities and the only radio station that broadcasts in Portuguese 24 hours a day," said co-owner Paulina Arruda. "Listeners can hear Portuguese music and world music, traditional and new music—we even have a Brazilian DJ—and we have huge collections of Portuguese music, including LPs and singles. We broadcast soccer games from Portugal and deliver the news from Portugal every hour."

In 1975, Edmund Dinis, local prosecutor and politician, bought the station and remained until his death in 2010. Dinis found radio a perfect vehicle to air the Portuguese community's social, economic and political concerns.

WTEV ~ Channel 6

New Bedford's first television station, WTEV (Channel 6), began broadcasting on January 1, 1963. Viewers loved the quirky staff and its focus on the local scene but they often had difficulty receiving it through their rooftop antennas. E. Anthony & Sons, publishers of the Standard-Times, founded the station to serve the New Bedford/Providence areas with local programming and the ABC network.

Children thrilled at making their first communion in front of cameras, singing in local talent shows or appearing on "Bozo the Clown" or "Romper Room."

Adults relied on news from Truman Taylor and watched cooking shows and specials about the Portuguese community.

When Pulitzer Publishing bought the station in 1979, the company moved it to Providence, changed its call name to WLNE and lost the flavor and excitement of local New Bedford participation.

Whaling City Cable TV

Jim Donnelly arrived at Whaling City Cable TV in 1976 and stayed for 33 years, moving up from production assistant, to program director and senior producer, while the station's ownership changed—from Colony Communications to Media One to AT&T Broadband to Comcast. Donnelly got in on the ground floor of the new cable technology that stressed: "Local news, local sports, local festivals."

Joe Langhan was the company's director of programming and chief idea man. His nightly newscasts drew in half of all subscribers. Langhan also created the Portuguese channel, and he cooked up a national 24-hour food network. He became executive producer of the Food Network and created "Emeril Live!" as its signature program.

Sounds of New Bedford

After the 1950s, Cape Verdean musicians began to merge into mainstream American music. Tavares, a group of five brothers with strong musical roots who grew up in New Bedford, performed rhythm and blues. Their father, Fox Point-born Feliciano "Flash Vierra" Tavares, was a noted singer and guitar player. Self-taught, he got his first real guitar at the age of seven from the Salvation Army. During the 1940s, he toured New England and New York with a succession of bands. Flash later moved to New Bedford to play guitar in the Jimmy Barros band. His sister, Providence-based Vickie Tavares Vieira, sang lead vocals with groups that performed both traditional Cape Verdean music and American jazz. Critics hailed her as "the premier female American Cape Verdean singer."

Flash's sons went on to become one of the most famous musical phenomena ever to come out of New Bedford. Beginning in 1962, the group went through many personnel and name changes. Eldest brother John Tavares formed The Del Rios, a male doo-wop group with himself and his three brothers, Antone "Chubby," Arthur "Pooch," and Ralph Vierra Tavares. When John left, another brother, Feliciano "Butch" Tavares took his place. When Pooch had surgery, yet another brother, Perry Lee "Tiny" Tavares, subbed in for him. When Pooch returned, they turned the quartet into a quintet. They also changed their name successively to Chubby & the Realities, Chubby & the Turnpikes and then just The Turnpikes before finally settling on the name Tavares.

Tavares sang rhythm & blues, funk, disco and soul music. They scored their first rhythm & blues top 10 hit in 1973 with "Check It Out." Other hits included a gold record, "Heaven must be Missing An Angel." In their honor, Governor Michael S. Dukakis declared September 12, 1976 as Tavares Day. To commemorate the occasion, Tavares appeared at the New Bedford High School Auditorium, bringing their father to the stage to honor him. He played and wowed the audience.

Tavares appeared in concert with the Jacksons and the Bee Gees. In 1978, they contributed to the "Saturday Night Fever" soundtrack, singing "More Than a Woman" which won them a Grammy. After Ralph left in 1984 and Tiny in the mid-1990s, the remaining brothers continued touring. In 2009, Tiny rejoined the group. The family's musical tradition continues: Two of Tiny's grandchildren, Anthony Paul Verville and Lorae Tavares, have performed with him.

Playing and Teaching

Born in New Bedford of Azorean-born parents, Antonio "Tony" Pacheco attended New Bedford schools and graduated from Swain School of Design. Pacheco drew and painted as a child, continuing all his life. During World War II, he painted the noses of bombers before they took off for Germany. An accomplished guitar player, he is said to have toured Europe as a teenager playing with jazz legend Django Reinhardt. From 1952 to 1980, Pacheco owned and operated the Tony Pacheco Guitar Studio and Music Store, where he taught music and painting. An avid Django fan, in 1966 he recorded the album,

Tavares on stage during a televised performance in the 1970s.

"I'll Remember Reinhardt." He played New England solo or with a group of students called the Tony Pacheco Folk Minstrels.

Three of Tony's children followed in his musical footsteps. Daughter Patty (Pacheco) Sanders worked for 30 years as a professional musician performing vocals and flute. An audio engineer and producer, Patty has played and recorded music ranging in style from jazz to fusion, rock and country. Son Tom Pacheco is a country and folk singer/songwriter whose songs have been covered by Jefferson Starship, The Band, Ritchie Havens, John Hall and dozens of European artists. In 1966, Tony's sons Paul and Tom formed The Raggamuffins in Greenwich Village. The legendary band played with rock legends Jimi Hendrix, Randy California and John Hall, and opened in rock clubs for the Doors, Orleans, Spirit and others.

The Tony Trio, 1947. From left are Bill Britto on bass, Tony Pacheco on guitar and Eddie Cheetham on organ.

Dan Fortier, a student of Pacheco, learned guitar from him as a school student. Dan initially played rock, folk, urban and country blues. However, after buying a Martin guitar in 1975, he began playing the bluegrass styles of Doc Watson, Dan Crary and Tony Rice. By the late 1980s, he focused mostly on flat-picking guitar and bluegrass music. He plays rhythm & lead guitars with Crab Grass, Cape Cod's "premier Bluegrass band."

Pacheco introduced another New Bedford student, Brian Mello, to flamenco guitar, which had fascinated him since working with a Spanish group in the 1960s. Mello later studied with noted flamenco guitarist Roberto Ríos, absorbing flamenco music's cultural roots, the product of a unique mingling of Jewish, Christian and Moorish cultures. He claims familiarity with at least 40 of the 60 different styles in flamenco music. Cultural foundations support Mello's work in explaining the origins and history of flamenco music.

Local drummer Laurier "Chick" Boucher was an anomaly. He came from French Canadian descent at a time when most local jazz musicians were of Cape Verdean extraction. Boucher grew up in New Bedford and started playing drums when he was 12. During a wartime stint in the Navy, he played the big band sound, appearing with top entertainers. He studied at the New England Conservatory and toured with small bands throughout the US and Canada. Later, he played mostly local venues, including the Cape Verdean Social Club, but sometimes Boston and New York. An influential music teacher and mentor, through the Joseph DeMello School in Dartmouth and his own studio, Boucher trained generations of drummers. After the 1950s, his House of Drums music store was a magnet for local talent who would spend hours jamming there in his enthusiastic presence. Some of his students went on to national and regional fame such as Mike Curran, Manny Santos, John Borges, Wayne Ferreira, Leo Dumas, Paul Nunes, Bobby Carreiro, Rick Cormier and Jackie Santos. Boucher died in 1999.

Throughout his school years, Jack Gomes played in the New Bedford school bands. Later, he traveled as a trumpet soloist with the Air Force Band of The East. He performed for President Richard Nixon's return from Russia in 1972 and at the 1973 World Series. Still later, he played trumpet on the road with The Tommy Dorsey Orchestra and Tavares. While he remains active in the jazz and club circuit throughout New England, he also puts his studies at Berklee College of Music and his degree in music education from UMass-Dartmouth to use teaching music in the New Bedford schools.

Folk Minstrels perform at New Bedford High School Auditorium, May 1965. *Paul Pacheco is at far left on upright bass.*

New Bedford Folk Revival

In 1967, New Bedford acquired a venue for its growing group of folk music performers. Inspired by the national folk revival, Rev. John DeSousa, minister of the United Pilgrim Church, and Rev. Richard Kellaway, pastor at First Unitarian Church, proposed a coffeehouse to help get neighborhood kids off the streets and into a drug-free environment. Tryworks, a New Bedford coffeehouse, opened in May 1967. Irish-born Maggi Kerr Peirce took the helm of Tryworks and firmly enforced the no drug policy, adhering to the coffeehouse's original mission. When Tryworks first opened in 1967, admission was 50 cents; in 1971, it was raised to $1.00.

In 1971, it needed a new home. Rev. David Rankin proposed the First Unitarian Church hall and there it remained until 2002 when it closed. By then, Tryworks had become the nation's second-oldest continuously-running coffeehouse.

For 35 years, Tryworks attracted generations of New Bedford youth. Its shows ranged from folk music and blues to storytelling and poetry readings; they drew as many as 160 people a night. During her 20 years as manager, Maggi Peirce ensured that Tryworks remained a healthy, creative environment. "Those were tough times for New Bedford—the late sixties and early seventies—with drugs and people getting shot and stabbed. But we had zero tolerance for drugs. This was a place for local kids to go on a Saturday night. The performers were mostly unknown and they could express themselves however they liked, including a cappella soloists, which we introduced to the area."

When Peirce resigned in 1987, Jody Heck took over as director and held the position until 2002. She introduced concerts to the Tryworks playbill. This opened opportunities for budding local musicians and poets and exposed audiences to touring performers. One local player who shone at Tryworks was New Bedford-born Jim Couza, who later gained fame as a hammered dulcimer player. Early on, however, he appeared at Tryworks with a well-used Gibson guitar and a banjo, playing and singing mostly British Isles music in his distinctive voice. In the early 1970s he began playing the hammered dulcimer and in 1982, moved to England where he became a favorite with British audiences. He worked both as a solo performer and with the D'Uberville Ramblers.

Young duo playing at Tryworks, early 1960s.

Mark Roberts, an Irish flute, banjo, bouzouki and guitar player, regularly appears at local functions. As a teenager, he recalls often going to Tryworks with his sister. "I'd sit in the back with my penny whistle. It was great training. It allowed me to learn tons of music." Having played Irish music for almost thirty years, he has recorded and toured extensively, both as a solo musician and as a member of several bands including The Clayfoot Strutters, The Sevens, The Red Clay Ramblers, the Childsplay music group and Touchstone, which he helped found. He has played in the US and Europe for Broadway shows, movie soundtracks, festival crowds, contra dancers, in theaters and at small house concerts.

Art Tebbetts was another Tryworks regular where he began playing while a student at UMass-Dartmouth in the late 1960s. He performed under the moniker "Dr. Jazz." From there, he went on to become a fixture on the local folk music scene. Known as New Bedford's troubadour, Tebbetts began a long tenure as the Main Stage host at Summerfest and later the New Bedford Folk Festival. He has also hosted the popular Open Mic nights on Thursdays at Café Arpeggio with a trademark conversational style. He would also occasionally sit in with the Pearly Baker Band. Fans note that wherever there's music, Tebbetts can be found playing, emceeing or both.

Other local artists got their start at Tryworks. Fairhavenite Paul "Truck" Croteau wowed his audiences with guitar, mandolin and bouzouki. He later toured with ClanJamfrey and often served as back-up musician with Folk Legacy. After a stint with Calaban, a seven-voice a cappella group specializing in Celtic songs, he met his current singing and performing partner, Mary Beth Soares.

Guitar player Tony Medeiros grew up in Fall River but loved performing at Tryworks. He went on to play and tour with various members of The Band over the years, including Rick Danko, Garth Hudson, Levon Helm and Robbie Robertson. He played with them in 1989 when they were inducted into the Canadian Music Hall of Fame. He is best known for a New Orleans style funky/bluesy style.

Maggi Peirce's favorite folk, blues and jazz artists include Paul Jeremiah, Martin Grosswendt, Barbara Carns, Joan LaFerriere Akin and Jack Radcliffe, all of whom continued to play in New Bedford for many years.

The Tavern Door Singers perform at the Tryworks, circa 1969.
Left to right are: Bob Amaral, Jill Simmons, Cheryl Jeffries, Paula Bragg and Larry Jackson. In 1968, the group opened for the Lovin' Spoonful when they played at the Olympia Theatre.

Paul Clayton ~ Folk Legend

Born Paul Clayton Worthington in New Bedford, he went by his first and middle names, Paul Clayton. Clayton was a key figure in the mid-1950s rise of folk music to media popularity. He became fascinated as a young man with whaling songs learned from his grandfather, Charles Hardy, a whaling outfitter. During high school, Clayton hosted a short radio program singing and playing traditional music on his guitar. He was first heard on WFMR (precursor of WCTK) and later on WBSM. His program initially occupied a 15-minute slot, but the station expanded it to an hour. Always on the hunt for new folk music, Clayton pored through logbooks at the Whaling Museum and public library searching for original manuscripts of seafaring songs.

At the University of Virginia, Clayton studied with folklore specialists. He focused on discovering the traditional songs of North Carolina, Kentucky and Virginia, financing his field trips by performing at colleges, schools, bars and coffeehouses. He also hosted weekly programs on local radio stations. Through his recording and collecting, he brought hundreds of obscure folksongs to the mainstream radio and music market. He recorded many of them for the Virginia Folklore Society and the Library of Congress.

Clayton's first album, Whaling Songs & Ballads, was released in cooperation with the New Bedford Whaling Museum. This compilation of occupational folksongs earned him a unique place among contemporary folksingers. He later issued other records of whaling and sailing songs on different labels. In 1956, Folkways released his album, Bay State Ballads, with some of his grandfather's landlubber ballads and sea chanties. The Premiere Committee chose him to entertain at the 1956 New Bedford opening of John Huston's Moby Dick. Among his almost 20 full-length albums, in 1965, Clayton recorded the first version of Woody Guthrie's "This Land Is Your Land" to make the national charts.

Paul Clayton performs at the 1963 Newport Folk Festival.

In early 1960s Greenwich Village, Clayton acted as a mentor to Bob Dylan, recently arrived in New York. Beginning in 1963, they and two other friends traveled cross-country. Along the way, they visited poet Carl Sandburg in North Carolina, attended Mardi Gras in New Orleans, retraced the presidential motorcade route in Dallas three months after the Kennedy assassination and then headed west to meet Joan Baez in California. Dylan acknowledged borrowing from Clayton for both "Don't Think Twice, It's Alright" and "Percy's Song."

A closeted gay man in a milieu that strongly disapproved of gays, Clayton tragically took his own life in 1967. He is buried in Oak Grove Cemetery.

Fado in New Bedford

Thirty years ago, some speculated that fado had died. They associated its melancholy lyrics and soulful delivery with the fascist regimes of António de Oliveira Salazar and Marcelo Caetano that together held power for half a century. When the 1974 coup toppled the Caetano government, young Portuguese repudiated fado as being too bourgeois and too somber. But instead, fado was reinvented. New artists experimented with the fado style, added new touches and helped revive the genre. New Bedford has been home to some of those new, contemporary fado singers.

Ana Vinagre, 1978.

Born in the fishing village of Buarcos, Portugal, Ana and José Vinagre settled in New Bedford in the 1970s. Ana began singing fado in Portugal, following in the footsteps of her sister, mother and grandmother. At the insistence of friends, Ana started singing fado at New England Portuguese restaurants and social clubs. She and José have also appeared in regional folk festivals. During 2001 they consulted for the movie Passionada, set in New Bedford, teaching actress Sofia Milos the essence of fado. In 2003 and 2004, Ana received a Massachusetts Arts Council Grant to teach fado to young singers.

Another well-known Portuguese-born fado singer now from New Bedford, Madalena Pata notes that in the US, fado is often background music, while in Portugal the music is featured at Casas de Fado, Houses of Fado, where people go just to listen. Fado singers agree that attentive silence is essential to properly perform and appreciate fado. Both Pata and Vinagre say they have had greater commercial success singing for non-Portuguese groups that see fado as exotic than for Portuguese American audiences. As a result, Pata has sung at far more venues out of New Bedford than in the city. She also featured prominently in Heaven's Mirror: A Portuguese Voyage, a documentary by filmmaker Joshua Dylan Mellars that constitutes his love song to fado music.

Catarina Avelar was born in New Bedford of San Miguel, Azores-born parents. She dismisses naysayers who say only those born in Lisbon can truly sing fado. As a young girl, she sang in the choir of St. John the Baptist Church, at other churches and at social or charitable events. On the Day of Portugal 2005, she sang at the official residence of the Minister of the Republic to the Azores, charming audience members with her youth and mesmerizing them with her singing.

The Zeiterion regularly showcases Portuguese or Luzo-American fado singers, following the trend whereby large concert venues replace the small, intimate rooms in which fado originated.

Jazz, Rock and Rythym & Blues

Savannah, Georgia-raised saxophonist Bobby Greene occupied a major place on the local and New England jazz scene for a quarter-century, first playing with The Seven Blends. After studying at the New England Conservatory of Music and Southeastern Massachusetts University, he taught jazz and rock-and-roll courses at UMass Dartmouth and the New England Conservatory. He hosted a jazz and gospel program on UMD radio station WSMU-FM. He played saxophone with Coleus, a band he founded in the early 1970s. One critic called Greene a "jazz giant" and another described his playing as "a study in dynamics, intonation and improvisation." Greene directed the New Bedford Arts Center and played with the New Bedford Musical Ensemble and the New Bedford All Stars. He also composed and his "City Suite" premiered at Boston's Jordan Hall. Greene died of cancer December 30, 1991, in Boston. Coleus played its traditional First Night engagement the following evening according to his wishes. In 1992, UMass Dartmouth awarded him an honorary doctorate and Savannah's Coastal Jazz Society inducted him into its Jazz Hall of Fame.

Jazz drummer Herbert "Herbie" King claimed to be a musician first and a teacher second, but many of his friends disputed that order. Also born in Savannah, he played as a teenager in Florida resort hotels backing different groups. He moved north, attended the New England Conservatory of Music and worked with big bands and small ensembles. He taught drums, at times at Tufts University and UMass Dartmouth, and also loved teaching younger students. He called the new generation "youngbloods" and wanted to cultivate, foster and mentor them. Every winter, King, vocalist Semenya McCord and stand-up bassist Dave Zinno played three or four concerts a day in elementary schools. King taught drumming at Symphony Music Shop, encouraging new players and working with professional drummers. He played with local and national jazz, blues, funk and soul musicians including Dave Brubeck, Bob Greene and Chick Corea. In 1982, he and McCord established an annual musical tribute to Martin Luther King Jr. called "Journey Into A Dream."

Jazz saxophonist Richard A. "Rick" Britto exclaimed, "Music was the family business!" He came from an impressive list of relatives, including distant cousin Paul Gonsalves, uncle Joe Livramento and great-uncles Frank "Chico" Monteiro and Pedro Monteiro. Britto began playing clarinet at age 5. By 12, he played tenor saxophone, piano and organ. At 14, he performed professionally with The Skyliners Big Band. During his career, he performed nationally and locally with such jazz notables as Ray Brown, Monty Alexander, Rosemary Clooney, Dick Johnson, Dave McKenna, The Artie Shaw Band, The Buddy Rich Band and Count Basie's Orchestra. He also played with The Drifters, The Tuneweavers, Tavares and Queen Latifah. A graduate of Berklee College of Music, Britto taught at UMass

Bobby Greene at the Unitarian Church, New Bedford, 1980. *At small venues, Bobby Greene characteristically approached listeners and played directly to them as though speaking in conservation. In this scene, Greene serenades young Christopher Harrison, nephew of pianist John Harrison III (left). Seated in the pew at right is the pianist's father, John Harrison Jr. At right are members of Coleus in the mid 1970s. Clockwise from left are Danny Schwartz, percussion; Richie Haddocks, vocals; John Harrison, keyboards; Herbie King, drums; Bill Britto, bass; and Bobby Greene.*

Frank Monteiro, President of Local Chapter of AFM Union, 1978.   *Rick Britto performs at Bobby Greene's memorial tribute, 1991.*   *Jackie Santos.*   *Michael Antunes.*

Dartmouth and Wheaton College. He also gave private lessons for saxophone and jazz piano and directed music ensembles. Britto owned Saurus Studio, which produced and recorded many local artists for radio and television. He died in 2012.

Saxophonist Michael "Tunes" Antunes of New Bedford came from a family noted for Crioulo music. He learned saxophone in a school music program. His grandfather Joaquin Antunes was a noted violinist and his father Peter J. Antunes was a well-known local musician who played bass, guitar, violin, saxophone and organ. For 17 years, Antunes played with world famous John Cafferty and the Beaver Brown Band. In the 1983 hit rock-n-roll movie Eddie and the Cruisers he played the bandleader's best friend, saxophonist Wendell Newton. A special benefit movie showing at the Zeiterion raised scholarship funds. Antunes endowed scholarships, named in honor of his father, to further musical education of promising students. He also played Cape Verdean music with local groups including Joseph Silva, the Henry Silva Band and the Tavares rhythm section.

Drummer Joaquim "Jackie" Santos' father sang at Lincoln Park and his godfather Freddie Silva played Crioulo-style guitar. Santos began his musical training with local drummer Laurier "Chic" Boucher. His big break came as a 14-year-old during a show in Peabody. Santos was twirling some broken drumsticks just as jazzman Buddy Rich came on stage. When Rich gave Santos the chance to use the sticks, the teenager so surprised Rich with his knowledge of the performer's songs and arrangements that the performer offered him a drum solo. The crowd responded with a standing ovation. After graduating high school in 1972, Santos toured with local rock band The Bedfords before joining The Australians, a Texas-based show band from Australia. In 1977, Santos joined Tavares and toured with them for 12 years. During his career, he shared the stage with Michael Jackson, Marvin Gaye, Lou Rawls and Aretha Franklin. Named "Most Influential Drummer of the '80s and '90s" by Commandments of Rhythm and Blues Drumming, Santos also played with the jazz group Armsted Christian and Peaceful Flight. He lives in Acushnet and has taught for 21 years at the Berklee College of Music, where he is the first and only Cape Verdean professor.

The Bedfords, circa 1973. *The Bedfords included a group of young, talented, local musicians, some of whom went on to achieve widespread fame. They toured extensively along the East Coast, performing in large clubs and concerts. They include (front row) Michael Pacheco on saxophone, vocalists Bobby Ferreira and Jeanna Antunes, Donald Hunt on bass and Mike Antunes on saxophone; and (back row) Paul Erickson on trombone, George Blier on trumpet, Jackie Santos on drums and Stephen Gonsalves on guitar.*

Tito Mambo and the Cyclones at Picadilly Lounge, 1965. *Lead vocalist Tito Mambo with New Bedford musicians Frank Perry on bass guitar, Bob Brock on tenor sax, Paul Nunes on drums, and Brian Souza on keyboard.*

Tito Mambo De La Cruz brought early, live rock to New Bedford via the Picadilly Lounge. A wild performer, he wore long hair before it was fashionable and performed outrageous parodies such as walking on water or getting shot by a band member and rising again from his coffin to finish his act. Local rockers remember him as having a strong influence on their music and lifestyle. The Cylcones, a local teenage band formed in 1958, also played at the Picadilly Lounge where they met Mambo in 1960. He had been playing with Jerry Lee Lewis, the Upsetters and others but decided to go on the road with the Cyclones. In New York City, Mambo left the Cylcones. Shortly after, the band signed with an agent that renamed them the Skyliners, a recently dissolved doo-wop band known for the hit *Since I Don't Have You.* "The agents ran the show," said member Paul Nunes. "They never heard us play. They looked at our studio photo and decided they liked the way we looked. They gave us the name The Skyliners, which they owned, and put us on the road. We didn't have time for studio work. The agents didn't want that. They just moved us around like cattle." Nunes spent the next 35 years on the road playing in show bands with Juri Christie and other local musicians.

The Raggamuffins, an electric folk rock band played legendary clubs in New York's Greenwich Village such as The Night Owl Café, The Cafe Wha, The Au Go Go and The Bitter End. The band included singer/songwriter Tom Pacheco, his brother Paul Pacheco on bass, Richard Marshall on drums, lead singer Sharon Alexander and Rick Hickman on lead guitar. They had two singles: "Four Days of Rain" / "It Wasn't Happening at All" and "Hate to See a Good Thing Have to Go" / "Parade of Uncertainty." They opened for The Doors in the same week that their "Light My Fire" hit #1 hit on the national charts.

Musicians consider Rick Hickman as one of the best rock guitarists to come out of New Bedford. While at New Bedford High Schools, he played in "The Walkers" with Rick Marshall on drums, John LaBrode on bass and Bruce Entwistle on keyboard and vocals. After it disbanded, he, Marshall, Bruce

The Skyliners, 1965. *The all-local band includes (left to right) Paul Bonneau, Juri Christie, Dick Rivet, Paul Nunes (seated) and Robby Vale, who was later replaced by another New Bedford musician, Jimmy Fonseca.*

The Ragamuffins, 1967. *Standing, left to right are Rick Hickman, Sharon Alexander and Rick Marshall. Seated are Tom Pacheco, and Paul Pacheco.*

Peter Grace, 1970.

Rick Hickman, 1975.

McCarthy Richards Band, 1979. *From left: guitarist Chris Richards, drummer John Borges, guitarist Butch McCarthy and bassist John LaBrode.*

Entwistle and Peter "Weed" Gimarese on bass formed RYBL. Hickman later studied at Berklee School of Music before heading to New York City. There, he joined the short-lived Raggamuffins. He worked as a studio musician and toured nationally with show bands and played throughout New England with smaller bands. He died at age 49 of complications related to cancer.

As a teenager, Peter Grace studied for a year under master-guitarist Richard Hickman at the Tony Pacheco guitar studios. After, from 1965 to 1968, he performed locally with The Wanderers, The Outcasts, The Spoils and The Roosevelt Dime, teaming up with musicians such as Bobby and Teddy Ferreira, Ray "Skippy" Sylvia, Mark Carney, Jim Phelan, Wes Abreau, David Mackler, Peter Gimarese and Mark Lafferty. In 1971, he played with the Boston-based band The Beacon Street Union, one of the Bosstown Sound groups. He later formed The Shakers with bassist Frank Goes and drummer Peter Blunsden. The band enjoyed a ten-year run. Its alumni included bassists Bill Botelho and Jack Maravell, guitarists Butch McCarthy and Mark Gidley, and drummers John Borges and Leo Dumas.

The McCarthy-Richards Band was among the region's leading rock groups in the late 1970s and early 1980s. It featured guitarists Eugene "Butch" McCarthy and Chris Richards. Known for producing original material, they played from Maine to New York. After the band broke up in the mid-1980s, McCarthy played with the Rhode Island band Warm Missiles and then The Shakers. Richards took a break before playing with Ken Lyon and the Tombstone Blues Band, and then a duo with local artist Ken Richards in The Stunners. In the 1990s, he had a solo act. In 2008, McCarthy began to write.

Rick Cormier started drumming during the 1960s at the age of ten, playing in rock bands as a teenager. During the 1970s, he wrote and performed 180 original songs (ballads and satire) for voice and guitar, had a cable TV show, recorded two albums, and landed the lead role in the musical "Hair." In the 1980s, Cormier switched his focus to synthesizers, resulting in more than 100 instrumental pieces. During the 1990s, he returned to his percussive roots and began hand drumming in what became one of the most successful drum circles in Massachusetts.

The South End's Bradley Cardoza founded a rock and roll group while he was student at Tabor Academy in Marion. Called the Fumin Humins, it was popular on Cape Cod. The group disbanded when its members went off to college.

Similarly, Jack Radcliffe played piano in a rock and roll band while in prep school. The Electras included several classmates at St. Paul's School in Concord, New Hampshire, including US Secretary of State John Kerry on bass guitar. They performed at school dances and debutante parties and pressed 500 copies of one record in 1961. Radcliffe later moved to ragtime piano while Kerry forged a political career. In his early days, Radcliffe played with Georgia country blues guitarist and singer Larry Johnson. His band, The New Viper Review, played blues, folk, rock and roll and jazz in the 1970s.

Jack Radcliffe at Tryworks, 1968.

Waterfront Festival, Pier 3, 1980. *"You'll feel better in New Bedford," was the slogan advanced by Mayor John Markey's Economic Development Commission to revive a flaccid tourist industry. In mid-July, "Discover New Bedford Days" sought to attract city residents and out-of-town visitors to the waterfront. While many visited festival booths, others were content to gawk from the tower leading to Route 18's pedestrian crossover.*

Feast of the Blessed Sacrament

The Feast of the Blessed Sacrament, celebrated annually in New Bedford for more than 100 years, is the reenactment of the *Festa do Santissimo Sacramento* observed in the villages of Maderia. Four Madeiran immigrants to New Bedford organized the first city *festa* at the Church of the Immaculate Conception during the first weekend of August in 1915. The founders were Manuel Agrela, Manuel Agrela Coutinho, Manuel Santana Duarte, all from the village of Estreito da Calheta, and Manuel Gomes Sebastião from Prazeres, the village due west of Estreito. The four men started the feast as a way to commemorate their safe passage to the United States and to honor the traditional festival of their native land. The New Bedford feast is now the largest Portuguese feast in the world and the largest ethnic festival in New England, attracting thousands of visitors each year.

The carne de espeto pit, 1980. *Day and night, feast goers flock to a massive 40-foot-long, make-your-own carne de espeto barbecue pit. A Portuguese version of shish kabob, this carne de espeto is made of sirloin chunks of beef that visitors season and then slide onto 8-foot-long skewers to grill over the gas-fired lava-rock pit.*

Grupo Folclorico Madeirense do Clube SS Sacramento at the Feast, 1980. *The local Grupo Folclorico, which was founded in 1979 by Dulce Reis, performs the Bailinho da Madeira (the Little Dance of Madeira)—the island's national song and dance—on Madeira Avenue near the feast grounds. The brinquinho musical instrument, emblematic of Madeira, accompanies the dancers, who wear traditional folk costumes. Made up of small, costumed puppets that are connected to castanets and mounted on a staff, the brinquinho produces a cheerful clang with vertical movements. The award-winning Grupo Folclorico's special interpretation of the historic dances of Madeira personifies Madeiran culture in dance and movement.*

The Centre Street Summer Festival, 1979. *In 1976, Mary E. Magnan founded the festival to promote the Historic District. On an August weekend, it united professional craftsmen with street entertainers in an atmosphere where specialty stalls supplied a wide variety of ethnic foods.*

The *Irene and Hilda* waits in line during Blessing of the Fleet, 1980. *Despite the appeal for divine protection, in October 1980, the* Irene and Hilda *was lost in high waves and 60-knot winds east of Nantucket. Captain William Rebello Sr., his son John, and four deckhands perished while trying to return to New Bedford.*

Blessing of the Fleet, 1980. *The Blessing of the Fleet has been celebrated continuously every year since 1969. In midsummer, when January's rough seas are faded memories, New Bedford fishermen gather family and friends on gaily decorated boats for a parade through the harbor and a blessing for the coming year. Typically administered by a Catholic priest, the ritual is a centuries-old tradition probably brought to New England by Italian and Portuguese fishermen. Here, Rev. Manuel P. Ferreira, pastor at St. John the Baptist Church anoints each boat as it passes by the starboard side of the Coast Guard cutter Bibb. Receiving a blessing in the photograph is the* Maria Angela, *built in 1977 and one of the newest boats to join the fleet. Based in New Bedford from 1973 until it was decommissioned in 1984, the Bibb was later sunk to serve as an artificial reef off the Florida coast. It previously had served in World War II and Vietnam. While based in the city, the Bibb carried out law enforcement and search-and-rescue patrols.*

The Photography of E. Milton Silvia

"A great moment caught on film has a clarity that's magic, an arrested moment in time. It delights the eye and pleases the brain. It becomes an old friend with each successive viewing.... A news photographer must work at speed in some difficult situations and still get that good composition with each subject. The challenge is to produce pictures that demand to be looked at—rich, meditative pictures." – Milton Silvia

In his 30-year career at the *Standard-Times* (1950s to 1980s), Edward Milton "Milt" Silvia captured on film the people and events from raging fires in the historic district to ships sinking in the Atlantic, from the worn hands of old men in prison to children smelling daffodils. His body of work is an insightful, photographic record of the times—as much a treasure of our heritage as any collection of writings or masterpiece paintings.

Silvia sought out local people in almost every conceivable setting—waterfront pubs, backstage at a burlesque show, playing in the park. A photojournalist extraordinaire, his love was the photo essay. When men were building the Braga Bridge in Fall River, he climbed to the top of the towering steel with his camera and shot the workers below. He documented immigrant families from the last days in their villages in the Azores, to their landings at Logan Airport and their emotional reunions with family members.

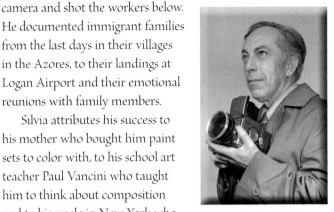

E. Milton Silvia

Silvia attributes his success to his mother who bought him paint sets to color with, to his school art teacher Paul Vancini who taught him to think about composition and to his uncle in New York who was an amateur photographer. As a young man, he was also influenced by the stark realism of the Farm Security Administration photographers during the Depression. Born in New Bedford, he died at 90, in 2006.

Over the years, Silvia had many opportunities to go with big newspapers in New York or Boston, but his family was here and the pull was strong to stay. "My years at the *Standard-Times* were the best years of my life. I love the New Bedford area. Once you have the sea in you, it's hard to let it go."

Men at work, circa 1960. *Photographer Milt Silvia was most proud of his portraits, particularly of people in the workplace. At right, Abraham Landau looks out his tailor shop window onto Pleasant Street. Landau was a Holocaust survivor of 13 Nazi labor and concentration camps between 1939 and 1945. He initiated the installation of the Holocaust Memorial at Buttonwood Park. At left, two lumpers in a fog of condensation haul fish from a dragger.*

John Durant, sailmaker, 1964.

Joseph Ainsley, Men's Mission, 1960.

William Kransler, antiques dealer, 1962.

At the **Durant Sail Loft** on the top floor of the Bourne Counting House, Merrill's Wharf, John Durant makes sails for the whaleship Charles W. Morgan.

Joe Ainsley, while superintendent of the Men's Mission for 38 years (1922-1960), gave assistance to 109,000 men. The mission was founded in the 1880s to "rally young toughs and old drunkards…to abandon their wicked ways and walk upright as Christians." The Mission provides lodging and baths for men at a minimal charge and operated a small store that sold goods picked up by its mission truck.

Antique dealer **William "Bill" Kransler's** shop at William Street and Johnnycake Hill was one of the nation's leading places that specialized in nautically-oriented or marine antiques. It generally carried a strong collection of decorative and utilitarian scrimshaw.

"The drama of the **Argo-Merchant** going down in Nantucket waters, I'll remember always. From the plane I could only see a spot through the clouds. I told my pilot, Norm Gingras, to go in so close, we would get spray on the windshield. He did and we got a spectacular picture. The wire services ran it big."

The 640-foot long Liberian oil tanker *Argo-Merchant* aground on shoals off Nantucket, December 1976.

Room with a view, 1965. Milt Silvia remembers: "I went up the stairs of a nearby hotel, knocked on this man's door and asked him if I could take a picture of the construction of the Kerwin garage from his window. Bill, who was not expecting company, was neatly dressed in tie and shirt, and he touched my imagination with his dignity and gentleness. He represents all the aged people who live alone in small rooms but make the best of it in their own way. He liked his little room that contained all his worldly possessions and looked out over New Bedford Harbor. 'From here,' he said, 'a man can look across the river.'"

Senator Edward "Ted" Kennedy obliges adoring fans at Bishop Stang High School, 1965. Kennedy visited the area often. On this November visit, he also stopped at New Bedford High School, where he urged students to be concerned about events in Vietnam. Regarding photography, Silvia opined: "I'm from the 'Documentary School,'" he says. "I like to film back streets, the seamy side of life. Being a news photographer fit my personality better than anything else I might have chosen. Being loose, flying around, that's me. I'm from the days of the photo essay. I tell the story in pictures."

Graduation procession, 1967. Mayor Edward F. Harrington, Lt. Governor Francis W. Sargent and a host of dignitaries lead New Bedford High School graduates down William Street. Graduation ceremonies took place at the Olympia Theatre on Purchase Street. The Class of 1967 was one of the last graduating classes to make "The Walk." In his commencement address, Sargent advised students to prepare for the evolution of "new technology."

First communion, 1966. *A young Cynthia Kaye Chamberlain receives communion from Reverend Constantine Bebis in the Greek Orthodox Church in New Bedford's North End. "The solemnity of the occasion, the spirituality, is brought out by the lighting of the window. I photograph the light and that becomes the picture," said Silvia.*

Demolition man at work, 1980. *While photographing the demolition of the Fontaine Pharmacy building at South Water and Cove Streets, Silvia playfully staged a shot, posing one of the demolition workers with a mannequin found lying in the pile. "They were very cooperative," he remembers.*

City Councilor William "The Watchdog" Saltzman, outside his fruit store, 1965. *A colorful and feisty figure in New Bedford politics, Willie Saltzman tirelessly opposed the construction of Route 18 connecting the North and South Ends, separating the waterfront from the rest of the city. Saltzman served as city councilor from 1965-1983 and from 1984 until his death in 1987. With his brother-in-law Leo Bromberg, he owned United Fruit Stores, one on Acushnet Avenue in the North End and the other on South Water Street—a business they started in the 1930s.*

Bishop Charles M. "Sweet Daddy" Grace's funeral service, 1960. *At Grace's House of Prayer, mourner Juliana Grace (left) grieves openly.*

Clyde Beatty-Cole Brothers Circus, East Rodney French Boulevard, 1967. Local youngsters stand in awe among the herd of 15 Asian circus elephants. After helping raise the poles for the white tents, the elephants relaxed before entertaining the crowd. Heading the animal display, the five in the center ring would kneel, stand on their heads and spin on small stools. Then they marched one behind the other, with their front feet balanced on the elephant in front, to the audience's oohs and aahs.

Ashley Ford Sales Grand Opening, Mount Pleasant Street, August 1964. Two young boys with bicycles pore over the booklet and dream of their first car—possibly a Ford! The company was forced to leave its old location at 1386 Purchase Street after its land was taken by eminent domain to construct a Route 18 off-ramp headed to the city center. Ashley Ford has been at this location for more than 50 years.

Free music lessons, 1966. Instructor Muriel Monteiro of the Ultramarine Band Club introduces young pupils to the clarinet while would-be trumpet players watch. From left to right, students are Marie Silva, Mary Ann Duarte, Arthur Burton, Ronald Livramento and Charlene Burton. The school began holding classes in 1965. Within a year more than 50 young students regularly attended the free Monday night sessions.

First day of class, Saint Anne's School, Emma Street and Brock Avenue, 1966. *Children often walked to and from school along city streets, with white-gloved traffic officers directing cars to wait while pupils kept to the crosswalk.*

Mobbed at Cook School, January 1971. *Youngsters smother Assistant Principal Dr. Herbert R. Waters Jr. on the first day of class following winter break. Dr. Waters went on to become the first principal of Carney Academy when the school opened in 1986.*

Going home, 1969. *South End children cover South Water on their return home from the first day of classes at Roosevelt Junior High School. Leading the pack are Peter Cabral, Dana Lopes and Steve "Jivey" Fernandes. Second row from left are Alfred "Rocky" Gomes, Kenny Soares and Vincent Rose. Following are Nellie Smith, Tony (last name unidentified), Barry Lima, Robert Pires, Donna Leighton, Mildred Ortega and Mary DePina.*

The Standard-Times Photographers

*I*t was John Lennon who said, "Life is what happens when you're busy making other plans." Indeed, it seems the most recent decades fly past us before we're able to really appreciate them. Photographs allow us to relive days gone by, with the reflection, grace and understanding that come with time.

In this next section, Spinner presents a broad collection of photographs of the 1960s and 1970s. Some of these are true masterpieces, most are drawn from the annals of the New Bedford *Standard-Times*. With these images we pay tribute to some of the city's great news photographers: Milt Silvia, Ed Rosa, Ron Rolo, Hank Seaman, Dave Crowell, Mike Valeri, Jack Iddon and so many others. Their daily craft gave them the opportunity to turn a wide lens on the city's many faces and places. Their work is a tour de force that chronicles the city from its celebrations to its daily routines, from its crimes to its good deeds, from its traditions to its one-a-kind events.

Other individuals also donated photographs, generously responding to Spinner's call to join in the creation of a pictorial slice-of-life retrospective of New Bedford.

We've chosen a fine selection from Spinner's collection of more than a million local images. The photo essay casts a caring eye on New Bedford, its people and their culture.

Standard-Times staff photographers, circa 1960. Seated: Ron Rolo and Dave Crowell; standing: Milt Silvia, Hank Seaman and Ed Rosa.

Young YMCA boxers, 1961. *Fifty-one youngsters, aged 10 to 15, trained under the supervision of coach Billy Bento. The boys competed for a spot in the Silver Gloves Boxing Tournament held at the YMCA. Proceeds went to the new YMCA Summer Camp, set to open in Mattapoisett in 1962.*

The New Bedford Kid, 1976. Eric Houtman hones his billiards skills at the Boys and Girls Club of Greater New Bedford at Jenney and North Streets.

Fast-draw contest at Common Park, 1964. The city offered an active summer recreational program administered by the park department, which also provided teenagers with summer employment. Supervising this contest is 15-year-old Tom Baroa (left background, wearing white shirt). The fast draw resulted in a stalemate, as both contestants shot each other.

Ice skating at Victory Park, 1967. Located on Brock Avenue in the South End, Victory Park pond at the Poor Farm provided an ideal winter skating surface.

Conveying books to new library from Cove Street, 1964. A gift from Sylvia Ann Howland Green Wilks, daughter of Hetty Green, financed the new Howland-Green Library. Workers used gravity roller conveyors to slide thousands of boxes of books from the old library at 164 Cove Street and transport them the two blocks to the new library at 3 Rodney French Boulevard. The South End Police Station later moved into the old library.

Restoring Ricketson's shanty in Brooklawn Park, October 1964. Members of the New Bedford Garden Club help spruce up the 12-by-14-foot shanty where Daniel Ricketson often retired to read, write and entertain literary guests. Despite their efforts, the shanty later fell into disrepair and the city dismantled it as a nuisance in 1981. Rumored to be somewhere in the city yard, locating it would be a major discovery.

Harbor Lights restaurant, Pier 3, 1964. Known as Harbor Lunch, the restaurant provided a quick meal or observation post for those working on the city piers.

United Fund Follies, 1968. Floodlights turn Purchase Street's night into day as people arrive at the Olympia Theatre for the sole performance of a United Fund Follies fundraising gala. The United Fund had set a record goal for the campaign of $669,820 to meet the needs of 34 participating agencies and the two-hour variety show featuring a cast of 100 and colorful costumes, helped generate enthusiasm in meeting that goal. A high-stepping chorus line of local "Rockettes" kicked off the program to the delighted applause of a full-house audience.

City of bars, Purchase Street, 1966. Six barrooms competed on this one-block strip between North and Hillman Streets. "Back in the early '60s when I opened my first tavern on Pleasant Street across from the hotel, there were bars everywhere downtown," remembered Jimmy Connors, local tavern owner, restaurateur and prizefighter. "You walk outside, there's a bar next door, across the street and all along Purchase Street—one after another. There was a lot to do in New Bedford. People would just go from bar to bar all night long." This Polaroid photograph, titled "Duggie's Tavern," was made by the New Bedford Redevelopment Authority as part of a property assessment of buildings earmarked for demolition.

Crisis at the gas pump, Kempton Street, 1974. *During the 1973 Arab-Israeli War, members of the Organization of Petroleum Exporting Countries (OPEC) imposed an oil embargo against the US by cutting production and causing prices to jump. Shortages caused retail gasoline prices to soar six-fold from September 1973 to March 1974. Some stations limited sales per customer or used odd-even rationing based on license plate numbers. To conserve energy, the government created the Strategic Petroleum Reserve, imposed a 55-mph highway speed limit and set fuel economy standards.*

Union Street during the January blizzard of 1964. *Winds up to 50 mph whipped the 14 inches of snow that fell in the city. Schools, factories and small businesses closed early to allow folks to get home and many remained closed during the cleanup. With a one-side parking ban in effect, more than 30 cars were towed from the path of the plows. Drivers without chains or snow tires posed a bigger problem when they got stuck and needed rescue. The blizzard grounded air transport and put a halt for a time to Union Street Railway and Almeida Bus Lines services.*

Purchase Street view from the Star Store third-story window, circa 1955.

Conductor Mitch Miller leads a "Sing Along with Mitch" Christmas concert, 1980. *Beginning in the late 1970s, the famous conductor held holiday sing-along concerts funded by the New Bedford Institution for Savings. On a crisp December evening, in front of the stage set up on the steps of the main library, an estimated 14,000 cheerfully sang along with Miller. The crowd included families with small children bundled against the cold.*

Holiday shoppers, Purchase and Union Streets, 1963. *Before large shopping malls and long before online shopping, residents strolled downtown and browsed local shops to find those special holiday gifts. The downtown bustled with shoppers laden with packages and bags walking along the festively decorated streets. Often, finding an available parking space meant adding another half-mile of walking to the besieged shopper.*

Salvation Army Band, 1964. *The Salvation Army organized in New Bedford in 1885. Its local band was formed shortly thereafter. Early band members acted as bodyguards with brass instruments and who protected Salvation Army street preachers. Their role rapidly evolved to one of actively promoting the Salvation Army's teachings. They took the same basic format as the traditional brass band. Many of Salvation Army bands played music specially arranged or composed to support the group's missionary work.*

Boy overwhelmed by Christmas toy choices at Saltmarsh's store, 1965. *Rifles, pistols, spy equipment for James Bond or the man from U.N.C.L.E., and guerilla warfare gear overwhelm Michael C. Oliver. A Napoleon Solo gun could morph from a compact pistol to a 29-inch-long rifle. Saltmarsh's also carried several walking dolls—including some that wet and needed changing—and toy ovens that could bake cookies, pizza and pretzels. Arthur J. Caetano, toy and hobby buyer, did his best to stay abreast of the latest gadgets, games and playthings.*

Star Store festivities, 1964. *A stripe-jacketed, swing combo entertains Star Store patrons, from women in curlers and people in 19th-century period costume to teenagers in school uniforms. In the 1960s, the store also installed an electric carillon, an automatic music machine made of many bells. A favorite during the holidays, it played popular Christmas songs.*

Christmas play, Parker School, 1968. *As part of their annual, end-of-year festivities, students at the John Avery Parker School put on a Christmas mini-ballet to the enthusiastic appreciation of delighted parents, family and friends.*

Purchase and William Streets, circa 1960.

Repairing a scallop dredge, circa 1979. *A scallop dredge consists of a heavy steel bar welded into a triangular-shaped frame. A bag made of welded steel rings hangs from the back of the frame. Dragging the dredge continuously along the seabed wears its parts. Once a scalloper is in port, welders perform key maintenance by checking and repairing breaks or weakened spots to minimize future downtime.*

Measuring rope at New Bedford Ship Supply, 1969. *The store clerk uses his arm span, roughly six feet, as an approximate measurement of a fathom or two yards. He pulls off the rope from a spool filled by Lambeth Rope Corporation, a well-known city manufacturer on Tarkiln Hill Road. Lambeth made braided, lead-core rope used extensively by trawlers. By the mid-1950s, Lambeth moved some operations to Kings Mountain, North Carolina.*

Salvaged, 3,100 horsepower Cooper-Bessemer diesel engine, Fish Island, 1964. *The salvage crew of Captain Edward O. Sanchez removed the engine from the 315-foot tanker* Dynafuel, *which sank off Cuttyhunk in 1963 after colliding with the Norwegian freighter* Fernview. *Engine rebuilding specialist David Hackett, left, and Edward O. Sanchez Jr., right, discuss final steps in preparing it for sale. Captain Sanchez' fleet of steel tugs, the only marine salvage operation between Providence and Quincy, specialized in recovering vessels from depths of less than 125 feet. Sanchez was known for tackling tasks others deemed impossible.*

Operating an ice crushing machine, 1965. *Crystal Ice's dockside machinery crushes large blocks of ice and blows the ice chips in bulk to the holds of fishing vessels. The company dates from 1957, at first providing services to the local fishing industry and later growing to meet ice needs throughout New England. Crystal Ice sells ice for a variety of uses, such as creating a winter wonderland at L. L. Bean and controlling concrete temperatures during hot weather at construction sites.*

M.C. Swift & Sons clothing store, 1980. *Moses Charles Swift went into the tailoring business in 1850. In 1852, at their Union Street store, he and partner Daniel B. Allen became known as M.C. Swift & Co. The company provided New Bedford area men with classic clothing. Here, company buyer Robert Gagnon fits a topcoat on store employee Roland LeClair.*

Silverstein's clothing store, 1980. *Lithuanian immigrant Barnet Silverstein founded the clothing store in 1900. For many years, it stood at Union and County Streets before moving to North and Cornell Streets. During the prosperous 1980s, Silverstein's doubled its local retail space. Here, Louis Silverstein adjusts a rack of jeans in a newly expanded section.*

"John the Cobbler," Rivet Street, 1980. *John Medeiros opened a cobbler shop on Rivet Street in 1927; little had changed inside the shop by 1980. Older men often gathered there, sitting on a bench, speaking in Portuguese and smoking. Medeiros worked standing behind the counter and sometimes joined in their talk. "I've been fixing shoes since 1917," Medeiros said. "My uncle taught me how. I used to get a dollar a week back then. I came here from Portugal in 1914. Came over here to Rivet Street in 1927. I used to make shoes for customers. Back then, people had their shoes custom made. Those were the best years for shoemakers. When I first came there were 110 shoemakers in this city. I remember the shoemakers had a picnic once, out in Acushnet. We all got together out there. Do you know how many shoemakers there were on Rivet Street? One down by Water Street, another on Acushnet and Purchase, one on Bonney Street, another on the corner of Mulberry, one on Bolton. Shoemakers all over the place. Everybody fixed shoes."*

Allen C. Haskell, New Bedford's premier horticulturist, 1967. *Haskell, born in New Bedford and a lifelong resident, graduated from Bristol County Agricultural High School. He could only visualize his plantings in two dimensions, the result of losing one eye to cancer at age two. His personal style, described as "painting with plants" enabled him to overcome that handicap. Haskell's plant paintings earned him countless ribbons and trophies. His creations graced gardens ranging from the White House on down.*

Louis Sylvia with "Centre St." on Centre Street, 1964. *New Bedford-born Louis Sylvia was a well-known marine painter. He studied at the Swain School of Design, the National Academy of Design, the Art Students League and also with painters Harry Neyland and Aldro Hibbard. From 1957 to 1965, he taught art at Roosevelt Junior High School. His marine paintings were featured in Yachting Magazine. Here he poses with his "Centre St." depiction of Centre Street in the 1800s. Some buildings remain unchanged.*

New Bedford Symphony Orchestra, summer concert, 1961. *Some 3,000 people came to hear the symphony perform a summer concert at Buttonwood Park. Many brought folding chairs while others listened from their cars. Under the baton of Conductor Josef N. Cobert, the symphony presented modern and classical pieces including George Frideric Handel's "Music for the Royal Fireworks."*

The Nutcracker Suite **rehearsal at Zeiterion Theater, 1980.** *A field trip to the "Z" gives young students the opportunity to watch a dress rehearsal.*

Polish folk dancing at a summer festival on Pier 3, 1964.

Cape Verden Vets Golden Clovers drum & bugle corps, May 1967. Band members (some unknown surnames), front row: Diane Luiz, Yvonne Campbell, Norma Rozario; second row: David Da Pina, Lorraine Rodriques, Tricia, Janet, Charlie Da Pina, John Hawkins; back row (staggered): Brenda Neves, Carla Mendes, Marlene Barros, Paula Pimental, Cindy, Phyllis Mendes, Queenie Victoria, Gail Monterio, Pauletta Grace, Joyce Soares and Betty Soares.

New Bedford Cordage fire, 1973.

Historic District gas explosion and fire, 1977.

In October 1965, the vacant **Pairpoint Building**, which was slated for demolition in the South Terminal urban renewal area, burned. Shortly after, the city razed the ruins to clear the land.

In January 1973, a 3-alarm fire destroyed a two-block complex in the West End that once housed the **New Bedford Cordage Company**. The buildings also had been marked for demolition to clear land for low-income housing.

In January 1977, gas explosions rocked the downtown **Historic District**. In near-Arctic winter weather, the ground had frozen deep enough that the 90-pound gas main had cracked, leaking gas into several buildings. Just before dawn, the thermostat in O'Malley's Tavern on Union Street clicked on and ignited the gas. A fireball shot 50 feet in the air, nearby buildings exploded and an inferno blazed. Firemen could not use water to douse the flames because it would freeze, causing the gas to build up elsewhere. While gas company crews worked to uncover and shut off the leak, firemen tried to contain the fires. No one was hurt. The tragedy drew attention to restoration efforts of WHALE, whose membership increased to 1,150 during the next three years. The blaze destroyed the recently restored Macomber-Sylvia Building, O'Malley's Tavern and the Eggers Building on William Street. The Mariners' Home and Seamen's Bethel survived intact. The Whaling Museum suffered broken windows. WHALE later bought and restored the damaged Sundial Building.

Pairpoint Corporation fire, 1965.

Pairpoint Corporation fire, 1965.

Repairing Butler Flats Light beacon, 1964.

Control Tower, New Bedford Airport, 1969.

Bridgetender at work, 1964.

Some New Bedford workers held lofty positions. The outer harbor's **Butler Flats lighthouse**, built in 1898, rose 53 feet above sea level. Technicians regularly serviced the bulb behind the stepped Fresnel lens; its lens is thinner than most conventional lenses in order make the lighthouse's beam visible over a greater distance. Butler Flats Light was automated in 1978.

At the New Bedford Regional Airport, Joseph E. Imondi stands in the steel-and-glass penthouse of the **air traffic control tower** that rises well above the runways that are located at 80 feet above mean sea level. From their perch, federal air controllers after 1958 supervised incoming and outgoing flights, monitoring planes in the air and on the ground.

Bridgetender Frank Montgomery climbs to a small shack above the swing-truss **New Bedford-Fairhaven Bridge** via a narrow stairway at the bridge's side and a catwalk. There, he uses levers to control the opening of the late 19th century span allowing fishing and recreational boats to move in and out of the inner harbor.

Built in 1859, the 24-foot **Palmer Island Light Station** was topped with a 4-foot high lantern. It was automated in 1941, three years after the lighthouse keeper's wife, Mabel Small, died in the 1938 hurricane. Since New Bedford regained the island in 1979, repeated vandalism has hindered the city's dogged restoration efforts.

Palmer's Island Light, after 1980s restoration.

Buttonwood Park pond, April 1966. *Young anglers crowd the spillway that dams three-mile long Buttonwood Brook to form Buttonwood Pond. With luck, they might catch stocked largemouth bass, chain pickerel, bluegills, pumpkinseed sunfish, black crappie or yellow perch, or even some accidentally introduced shiners. One young angler's cigarette dangles from his lips while he uses both hands to unhook a nice-sized yellow perch.*

Bowling on the green at Hazelwood Park, 1964. *By the early 1960s, followers claimed New Bedford was the only US city still playing this ancient English game. The first player tosses a small white ball called a "jack." Others try to put two balls called "woods," made of dense lignum vitae, as close to the jack as possible. Here, 94-year-old Joseph Taylor delivers a wood.*

Holy Family High School basketball team, 1969. *Holy Family's championship basketball team celebrates at the old Boston Garden after beating North Andover, 35-34, for the Class C Tech Tournament title. The tiny parochial New Bedford school with a student body of less than 90 boys ran a slow-down, deliberate game against the taller, faster, heavily favored and previously undefeated North Andover team. Players include John Gushue, Paul Healy, Ray Charette, Dennis Winn, Bill Walsh, John Goggin, Darryl Murphy, Tom Healy, Gary Dalbec, Steve Magnett, Paul Chevalier, Tim Donohue, Jim Lawless, and Tony El-Hillow. Also celebrating are coaches Jack Nobrega and John Brennan, Athletic Director Rev. Justin Quinn, team managers Bob Cayer, Michael Starkey and Chris Hendricks, and friends Patrick Walsh and Red O'Neill.*

Legal drag racing at Industrial Park, 1970. *A crowd lines the pit area along Duchaine Boulevard to watch drag racing. Faced with complaints about racing on Shawmut Avenue behind the airport and on Route 140, city councilors David Nelson and Mike Merolla and Mayor George Rogers created a venue for Sunday afternoon drag racing at the Industrial Park. Joe Jesus founded the New Bedford Performance Enthusiasts to organize the event.*

Sledding and tobogganing at Whaling City Municipal Golf Course, 1981.

New Bedford Half Marathon, 1979. *From small beginnings in 1977, the New Bedford Half Marathon grew into one of New England's important track and field events. Jim Ryan, Larry Finnerty, Marty Flinn and other friends helped organize the yearly events and create the tradition. The 1979 crowd, assembled on a blustery but sunny Sunday morning March 18, eagerly anticipates the starting gun. That year, Larry Olsen was the first man to cross the finish line in 1:09:08 and Ann Sullivan Hird was the first woman in 1:18:44. Life and running soon took on a faster pace. In 2015, those times would have kept both runners out of the top ten.*

Index

Symbols
1st Cavalry Division 152
2nd Infantry Division 154
10th Coast Artillery 158
23rd Coast Artillery Regiment 158
85th Evacuation Hospital 287
304th Infantry, 76th Division 137
323rd Army Band 246
555th parachute battalion 225

A
A-1 Restaurant 85
Abramson, Dr. Julius, Fisher, Ike 89
Abreau, Wes 329
Abreu, Augusto 244
Acadians 251
Acushnet 25, 28, 40, 246, 250
Acushnet Beach 103
Acushnet Cedar Swamp 298
Acushnet Fish Company 35
Acushnet Mill 13, 20
Acushnet Park 29, 92, 98, 102, 104, 114
Acushnet Process Co. 8, 40, 163, 167, 174, 287
Acushnet River 6, 22, 28, 40, 53, 68, 169, 266, 272, 276, 303
Acushnet Saw Mill Co. 298
Adam, Charles R. 250
Adams, Carole 227
Addie Mae, fishing vessel 18
Aerovox Corporation 5, 8, 28, 40, 167, 175, 287, 303
Agar, Augustus W. S. 53
Agrela, Manuel 332
Ahavath Achim Synagogue 82, 228, 268
Ahrens-Fox 96
Aiello Brothers 310
Aillery, Jan 318
Ainsley, Joseph 335
Ainsworth, Harry 316
Air Industries Flying School 200, 202
Air Raid Warden 163
Air-Tight Piston Ring Mfg. Co. 56
Air Transport Command 203
Akin, Joan LaFerriere 324
Albania 82, 135
Alderson, Eileen 318
Alert, ferry 320
Alexander, Edward 124
Alexander, M. Paul 99
Alexander, Sharon 328
Alfred J. Gomes Elem. School 290, 317
Aliança Liberal Portuguesa 246
Allen Beam Company 167
Allen, Daniel B. 351
Allen, Everett 28
Allen, Fred 123
Allen, Kenneth W. 178
Allen, Robert 133
Allen's Theater 97, 98
Allen, Woody 114
Allied Manufacturing Co. 168
Allison Engine 174
Al Lopes Orchestra 245
All the Brothers Were Valiant film 226
Almeida, Augusto and Clementina Jesus 292
Almeida Bus Lines 251, 344
Almeida, Candido "Notias" 244
Almeida, Edward C. 286
Almeida, Lois 160
Almeida, Manual, Theoff 89
Almeida, Peter 283
Almeida, "Snubby" 243
Alpar, schooner 33
Alper, Boris 89
Alpert, Michael 316
Alves, Antonio Rodriguez 133
Alves, Frank 160

Alves, John, Maria (Fernandes) 246
Alves, Julio "July" 191, 223, 243-245, 289
Alves, Paul 282
Alvo Aristocratas 130
Amandoles, Barbara 234
Amaral, Bob 324
Amaral, Edmund 111
Amaral, George 174
Amaral, Hilda 294
Amaral, José and Maria 294
Amaral's Linguiça Company 294
Amateur Orchestral Society 132
Amati diamond 156
Amati, Maria Patrice 156
Amelia, scalloper 136
American Bar Association 229
American Flexible Conduit Co. 304
American Friends Service Committee 260
American Gold Star Mothers 150
American Hope, fishing vessel 313
American Huarache Company 8
American Jazz Orchestra 248
American Playshoe Company 8
American Red Cross 148, 159, 162, 168-169
American Soccer League 106
Ames, Edmond B. 248
A.M. Nicholson, packet ship 134
Anapol, Frank 173, 306-307
Anapol, Joel and Walter 306-307
Anderson-Little Clothing 308
Anderson, Morris R., Scott 308
Andrade, Antonin "Boca" 131
Andrade, Bobby, David 282
Andrade, Joe 215, 245
Andrade, Maria Luisa 292
Andre, Edward 240
Andrew Robeson House 279
Andrews, Barbara 136
Andrews, Lucille 183
Angler 18, fiberglass fishing boat 47
angling 99, 356
Ann's Beauty Shoppe 97
Antunes, Jeanna 327
Antunes, Michael "Tunes" 216, 327
A & P 33, 69, 71, 83, 93
apparel industry 8, 25, 44-45, 104, 162, 171-173, 177, 256, 282, 306-309
Apponagansett Great Cedar Swamp 200, 203
Araujo, Ana 89
Araujo, Margie 131
Arcade Building 68, 70
Archambeault, Jean-Baptiste 120
Area Redevelopment Administration 320
Arey, Clarence W. 132, 159
Argentina 106, 107
Argo-Merchant, oil tanker 335
Arkwell, George 250
Arlans 43, 173, 191, 309
Army Air Corps 200
Army of the Potomac 122
Arnoff, Rabbi 89
Arnold, David 136
Arnold, Gellinore 136
Arruda, Caroline A. 287
Arruda, Frank 128
Arruda, Paulina 321
Art Perry Orchestra 240, 247, 252
Aseley, Marion 183
Ashenas, Joseph 159
Ashley, A. Davis 68
Ashley, Charles S. xii-1, 11, 12, 20, 50, 100, 107, 114, 316
Ashley Ford 338
Ashley, Jane 141
Ashley Park 23
Aston, Albert 241
Atlantic Fishermen's Union 187
Atlantic White Cedar 298

Atlas Tack 46, 116, 118
Aubut, Albert 160
Audette, Adeline, Alice 77
Auf Wiedersehen, rumrunner 16
Austin Street Salvagers 161
Australians, The 327
automobile dealerships 94
Avelar, Catarina 325
Avila, Adelia 100
Avila, Albertina, Fatima, Francisco, José 292
Avila's Concert Band 126
Avilla, Jorge 127
Aylwood, Jimmy 233
Azab Grotto Ban 129
Azorean Refugee Acts 292
Azores 15, 59, 81-82, 86, 109, 111, 130, 134, 157, 210, 232, 240, 246, 248, 292, 294, 304-305, 322, 325, 334
 Faial 292
 Pico 121
 São Miguel 109, 121, 130, 240
Azores Band 124
Azulay, Isaac 134

B
B-29 Band 131
Babbit, Isaac N. 179
Baby Boom 152, 183, 232, 314
Baez, Frank 293
Baines, Pauline 141
bakeries 82, 90, 155, 210-213
Baldo, Umberto Aníbal 84
Baldwin, Dorothy 141
Baldwin, Louise 183
Ball's Corner 78
Banks, Norma 163
Baptist, Jan 290
Baptista, George 191
Baptista, Howard "Howie" 224
Baptista, Jeff 283
Baptista, John Jr. 369
Baptista Antonio, José, Josephina, Manuel, Maria, Maria P., Martins, Virginia, 130
Baptiste, Mike 314
Baptiste, Ray 282
barbers 82, 250
Barboza, Felix "Phil Edmund" 243
Barboza, George 88
Bargasse, Jim 289
Barnes, Thomas C. 8
Barneys Joy Point 158
Barney, Virginia 183
Baroa, Diolinda 172
Baroa, Tom 341
Baron, Norman 160
Barron, Isaac 89
Barros, Jimmy 131
Barros, Lucille 232
Barros, Marlene 353
Barros, Mary 282
Barrows, Annie Edith, Arthur 93
Bartholo, Alipio C. 121, 246
Bartlett, Jennie 50
Barton, Marianne 162
Bastien, Kenneth 250
Batty, William 10, 12
Bauer, Daniel E. 29, 87, 102, 168
Baxter, Ruth 183
Baylies Flying Field 50, 51
Baylies, Frank L. 50, 51
Baylies Square 27, 78, 111, 152
Bay State Band 129, 247, 252
Bay State Furniture Company 178
Bay Village Housing Project 91
Bazzar, Josef 252
Beacon Mill 11, 26, 43
Beal, Fred 10-12

Bean, Wallen 289
Beaubian, Joan 156, 215, 235
Beaulieu & Mandeville 72
Beauregard, Lucien J. 164
Beaver Brown Band 327
Bebis, Constantine S. 337
Beckman, Carl, Charles Emil 42
Bedfords, The 327
Beetle Boatyard 46
Beetle, Carl, James, John H., Ruth 46
Beetle Cat Boat 46
Begnoche, Richard 222
Beidenkapp, Fred 11
Belcher, Teresa 253
Bell-Chords 250
Bellenoit, Domenica (Bollea) 27
Belleville Industries 303
Belli, John J. 286
Bellotti, Sue 318
Bellson, Louie 242
Bell, Thomas W. 97
Belotti, Richard "Dick" 224
Bendiksen, Matias 136
Bendiksen, Svanhild 253
Beneke, Tex 248
Benjamin Dawson & Son 180
Benjamin Rodman House 279
Bennett, Robert 128
Benoit, Stanislas T. 82
Bento, Billy 340
Bequia, British West Indies 156, 214
Bergeron Farm 18
Berg, Kirsten 253
Berklee College of Music 249, 323, 326-327
Berkshire Hathaway 171-172, 320
Bernard, Armand 98
Bernard, Father Stanislaus 89
Bernard, Ozzie 225
Bernice, eastern rig 33
Berry, Sarah E. 163
Bertha, packet ship 134
Bessette, Alphonse 43
Bessette, Donat 85
Bethel AME Church 214, 239
Betsey B. Winslow School 143
Bettencourt, George 292
Bettencourt, Manuel Jr. 292
Bettencourt, Manuel Sr. and Aldina 292
Bettencourt, Ted 240-242
Beyea, Basil 217
Big 4 Clothing Company 84
Big Value Outlet 309
Bisaillon, Eugene, Ralph 161
Biscari, Georgette 318
Bishop Stang High School 288, 336
Black Duck, rumrunner 16, 17
Black, Jake 129
blacklisting 223
Blackmore Pond, Wareham 139
Black Panther 260, 284-285, 287
Blessing of the Fleet 333
Blier, George 327
Blind Melba 111
Blue Laws 168
Blue Room 242, 244
Blue Surf, scalloper 313
Blunsden, Peter 329
Board of Commerce 7, 42, 53, 99, 173
Board of Engineers for Rivers and Highways 59
Board of Overseers of the Poor 15
boatbuilding 46-47
Boa Vista tower 271
Boelher, Stanley 314
Boino, Louis, Victor 154
Boisclair's Fish Market 83
Boisvert, Leda 162
Bolduc, Joseph 56

Bolger, Eleanor 233
Bonneau, Henry L. 82
Bonneau, Paul 328
Bonner, Walter 133
bookmobile 27
Booth Mill 45, 178
Borges, John 323, 329
Borges, Louis M. 129
Borg-Warner 301
Boston and Maine Airways 203
Boston Athletic Association 104
Boston, MA 17-19, 32, 33, 39, 44, 48, 52, 58, 77, 97, 104-105, 111, 114, 124-126, 133-134, 140, 155, 170, 184, 187, 195, 197-198, 202-203, 218, 225, 249, 286, 291, 301, 313-314, 329, 334
Boston Navy Yard 128
Boston University 229, 239
Botelho, Bill 329
Botelho, John 99
Botelho, Marion 15
Botelho, Robert 297
Bouchard, Alfred "Fred" Louis 73
Bouchard, J. Alfred 73
Bouchard's Tavern 73
Boucher, Alice, Laura 162
Boucher, Jack 101
Boucher, Laurier "Chick" 216, 244, 323, 327
Bourbeau, Adrien 99
Bourgeois, Ernest 315
Bourne Counting House 46, 335
Bourne Warehouse 279
Bourque, John J. 286
Bourque, Wilfred 95
Bousquet, John 206
Boutin, Marguerite 119
Bower, George 33
Bowie, Ennis 289
Bowman, Martin 99
Boy Scouts 89, 139, 160, 163, 223
Bradbury, Ray 156
Bradshaw, William 98
Brady, Florence 183
Braga, George 42
Braga, Tony 247
Bragg, Paula 324
Brais, Mable 163
Branchaud, Jerry 367
Brassard, Diane 233
Braudy, Oscar 159
Braudy's Department Store 76
Brault, Norbert Romulus 69
Brennan, John 356
Brenneke, David 212, 253
Brenneke, Martha, Martin, Rudolph 212
Brenneke's Pies 155, 211-212
Breton, Omer 174
Brewer, Basil 7, 156, 201-202, 217, 220-221, 223
Briden, John 250
Bridge Diner 85, 155, 205
Bridge Park 166
Briggs & Beckman, sailmakers 42
Briggs, Charles A. 135
Briggs, James C. 42
Briggs, Philip S. 56
Brightman, Omar 16
Bristol Arena 26
Bristol Building 63, 196
Bristol Community College 235, 290
Bristol County
 Agricultural High School 352
 House of Corrections 288
 Sheriff's Department 237
Bristol Electronics 287
Bristol Mill 6, 20, 22-24, 26, 72, 132
Brittany Dyeing & Printing 177
Britt, Frankie "Young" 109
Britto, Carol (Whitney) 249
Britto, João 131

360

Britto, Manny "Sheika" *131*
Britto, Richard A. "Rick" *326–327*
Britto, William "Bill" *244, 249, 323, 326*
Broadcasting State Band *129*
Brock, Bob *328*
Brockton Public Market *295*
Brodeur, Joseph H. *119*
Brodeur, Paul *223*
Bromberg, Leo *337*
Brooke, Edward W. *260, 283–285*
Brooker, Shelly *319*
Brooklawn Park *10, 23, 54, 66, 342*
  Storybook Land *231*
Brooks, Artie *112*
Brooks, Hyman *56*
Brothers, Armand *76*
Brow, Les *248*
Brown, Duane *316*
Brown, Edward *128*
Brown, Edward J. *249*
Brownell, Oliver G. *44*
Brown, Eugene F. *44*
Brown, "Panama" Al *109*
Brown & Poole *86*
Brown, Samuel *180*
Brown University *104, 106, 217*
Brown's (J.C.) Pharmacy *97*
Browne's Pharmacy *92, 216*
Bruce, Herman *311*
Brum, Theresa Sadek *319*
Brunswick Blue Jackets *247*
Buckley, James B. *304*
Buckley, Raymond A. *30, 31*
Bulgar, John *128*
Bullard, Catherine Crapo *279*
Bullard, John K. *278, 281*
Burgo, Arthur *160*
Burgo, Beverly *234*
Burgo, Joaquim "Jack" Antone *18, 19*
Burgo, Manual *89*
Burgo, Manuel "Manny" *225*
Burke, Kenneth *233*
Burleigh Club *132*
Burleigh, Henry Thacker *132*
Burnes, Andy *281*
Burnham, Melvin *250*
Burns Electronic Supply Co. *283*
Burrell, Harold *139*
Burrell, Linda Whyte (Toatley) *214*
Burton, Arthur, Charlene *338*
Burt's Grille *114*
Butler Flats Light *355*
Butler Flats lighthouse *95, 355*
Butler Mills *90, 175*
Butlers Point *158*
Buttonwood Acres *291*
Buttonwood Brook *356*
Buttonwood Park *22–24, 89, 98, 101, 163, 214–215, 218, 334, 352, 356*
Buttonwood Park Zoo *230*
Buttonwood Pond *98, 101, 356*
Buzzards Bay *40, 53, 61, 151, 163, 207*

C

Cabana, Esther *15*
Cabral, Antone *190, 191*
Cabral, John *99*
Cabral, Manny and Julie *245*
Cabral, Peter *339*
Cabral, Teresa Ana *246*
Cabrera, Ana *321*
Cachalot Council *139*
Cadieux, Adrian *159*
Cadieux, Arthur *160*
Caetano, Arthur J. *347*
Café Arpeggio *324*
Cafferty, John *327*
Callahan, Danny *233*
Calvin Clothing *307*
Camaradas Açorianos *130*
Camara, Joseph *250*
Camara, Manuel J. *77*
Camara's bicycle shop *77*

Cambra, Joseph F. *128*
Cameo Curtains *173, 307*
Cameron, Margaret E. *314*
Campbell Secretarial School *235*
Campbell, Yvonne *353*
Camp Edwards *23, 58*
Camp Maxim *139*
Canada *88, 104, 110, 115, 120, 134, 137, 166, 189, 241, 246, 300, 323*
Canadian scallopers *310*
Candleworks Restaurant *281*
Cannon, James *44*
Cannon Street Playground *91*
Canton, China *137*
Cape Cod Airlines *53*
Cape Cod Canal *23*
Cape Cod Ladder Mfg. Co. *178*
Cape Cod, MA *84*
Cape Cod Sportswear *307*
Capelinhos volcano *292*
Cape Verde *56, 88, 121, 131, 134, 245, 266, 269*
  Brava *90, 134, 228–229, 244*
  Fogo *244*
  São Nicolau *90*
Cape Verdean *10, 18, 88–91, 126, 131, 134, 155–157, 190, 214–215, 229, 240, 242–245, 251, 266, 292, 322–323, 327*
Cape Verdean Beneficent Association *18, 90, 131, 229*
Cape Verdean Memorial Hall *251*
Cape Verdean Relief Fund *229*
Cape Verdean Social Club *323*
Cape Verdean Ultramarine Band Club *90, 131, 242–244, 252, 338*
Cape Verdean Women's Social Club *90*
Cape Verden Vets Golden Clovers *353*
Cape Verde Serenaders *244*
Capital City Comedy Four *110*
Capital City Trio *110*
Capital Theater *116*
Capitol Candy Kitchen *73*
Car Barn *54–55, 196–197, 291*
Cardoza, Bradley *329*
Carleton Bell, packet ship *134*
Carmo, William *153*
Carney Academy *317, 339*
Carney, Claire T. *291*
Carney, Clara Heronica *132*
Carney Family Foundation *291*
Carney, Hugh *291*
Carney, Leo E. J. *1, 7, 91, 105, 200*
Carney, Mark *329*
Carney, Patrick *291*
Carney, Sergeant William H. *132*
Carney, William *99*
Carns, Barbara *324*
Caron, Joseph Adelard *120*
Carpenter, Clair F. *164*
Carreiro, Bobby *323*
Carroll, Henry M. *95*
Carroll, William A., William E. *56*
Carvalho, Altinho, Manuel Jr. *304*
Casa da Saudade library *292*
Casavant, Flavien *124*
Casey's Boat Yard *16*
Casimir Pulaski Park *79*
Casimir Pulaski School *317*
Casino Band *128*
Cathay Temple *137*
Catwalk *93*
Cawley, John J. *224*
Cawley Stadium *224*
Cayer, Bob *356*
Cayton, Manuel *123*
C. E. Beckman Sailmakers *42*
Cedar Street School *215*
Centeio, Gregory *89*
Central Labor Union of New Bedford *129*
Clevedon, freighter *58*
Centre Street Summer Festival *333*
Centro Católico Português *129*
Centro Monarchico Portuguez *121*
Cercle Champlain Social *83*
Cercle Gounod *112, 132–133*

C. F. Wing & Company *30, 62, 63*
Chabotte, George *163*
Chace, Malcolm, Jr. *171*
Chace, Sydney *123*
Chamberlain, Cynthia Kaye *337*
Chamberlain Manufacturing *245, 303*
Chambre de Commerce *162*
Champagne, Carl *233*
Champegny, Joseph *72*
Champegny Shoe Store *73*
Chapman Building *274, 275*
Charette, Ray *356*
Charles H. Cox Company *62*
Charles S. Ashley School *141*
Chas. E. Beckman, schooner *54*
Charles W. Morgan, whaleship *99*
Charlie Kerr Orchestra *240*
Charlie Wong's restaurant *137*
Chartier, Roland O. *154*
Chase, Charles *202*
Chase, Roger *173*
Chase, Thatcher *241*
Chassey, Vivian *141*
Chaussé, Aldège *69*
Chausse, Joseph *56*
Chedgzoy, Sam *106*
Cheetham, Eddie *323*
Cheney, Alouise *159*
Cherry & Company *62, 64*
Cherry, George *64*
Chesed Shel Emes Synagogue *276*
Chevalier, Paul *356*
Chevaliers of St. Louis *125*
Chick Boucher and his Cotton Pickers *253*
Children's Aid Society *239*
Children's Bathhouse *22*
Childs, J. S. *32–33*
China Clipper Restaurant *294*
China Hall *65*
Chinese *69, 71, 90, 137, 152, 294*
Chinese laundry *71, 90, 137*
Chin Yow Doo *137*
Choquette, Hormidas *70*
Choquette, Roland *160*
Christensen, Leslie *136*
Christie, Juri *328*
Christina J, dragger *311*
Christopher A. Church Mansion *68*
Chubby & the Realities *322*
Chubby & the Turnpikes *260, 322*
Citizen's Relief Committee *15*
City Band *127*
City Infirmary *22, 128*
City Mills *46, 90*
City Mission *25*
City Pier 3 *9, 22–23, 34, 36, 38, 166, 185, 219, 259, 331, 342, 353*
City Pier 4 *3, 23, 32–34, 36, 259*
Civil Aeronautics Adm. *155, 201*
Civil Aviation Authority *202*
Civil Defense *168*
Claire T. Carney Library *291*
Claremont Companies *291*
Clarence A. Cook School *141, 143, 145, 215, 233, 339*
Clarke, Patricia *183*
Clark, Gloria (Xifaras) *293*
Clark, Mary M. *287*
Clark's Cove *23–24, 26, 28, 57, 156, 228, 264*
Clarkson, Robert *222*
Clark's Point *22, 29, 46, 80*
Clark Street School *317*
Clarkwood Apartments *291*
Clasky Common Park *154, 218, 231, 287, 341*
Clattenberg, Ernie *36*
Clayton, Paul *261, 325*
Cleare Weave Hosiery Store *165*
Cleveland Symphony Orchestra *127*
Cliftex Corporation *173, 306–308*
Clinton, fishing vessel *168*
Cloutier, Denise *316*
Cloutier, Joseph *223*

Cloutier, Robella *216*
Club Madeirense S.S. Sacramento *72*
Club Royal Orchestra *128*
Clyde Beatty-Cole Brothers Circus *338*
coal *17, 22, 48, 50, 89–90, 191, 211*
Coastal Fisheries *186*
Coast Guard *9, 16–18, 154, 168, 286, 333*
  CG-290 *17*
  CG-2296 *16*
  Cutter Bibb *333*
  Cutter W380 or Yakutat *259, 286*
  Tug Acushnet *17*
Coaters, Inc. *177*
Cobert, Josef N. *352*
Cochran, William T. *217*
Coderre, Prudent *125*
Codman, Benjamin S. *300*
Codman Shurtleff, Inc. *300*
Coelho, Jackie *241*
Coffey, John W. *127*
Coffin Press *150*
Coffin, Richard *150*
Coggeshall Street Bridge *22, 28, 68, 99, 166, 195, 199*
Cohen, Abram *89*
Cohen, Benjamin *139*
Coimbra, Adolph "Doc" *242*
Coleus *326*
Collette, Ulric E. *73*
Collier, John *8, 119*
Colonial Funeral Home *283*
Colonial Gasoline station *95*
Colonial Restaurant Supply Co. *274*
Colonial Textile Company *45, 168, 178*
Colonial Theater *82, 98*
Columbia Electronics, Inc. *304*
Columbia Theater *114*
Comique Theatre *70, 98*
Community Development Block Grant Program *290*
Community gardens *26*
Compass Bank *274*
Conceição, Daniel *223*
Concordia Company *47*
Conley, Rev. Coleman *293*
Connolly, James L. *293*
Connors, Jimmy *225, 343*
Considine, Jimmy *233*
Continental Baking Co. *211*
Continental Screw Company *179*
Continuation Schools *143, 234–235*
Conward, Oliver *128*
Cook, James *255*
Coolidge, Calvin *252*
Coon, Lorraine *141*
Cooper, Everett *99*
Cordeiro, Francelina *130*
Cordeiro, João *246*
Cordeiro, João, Jr., Lillian, Vivian *130*
Cordeiro's Variety Store *130*
Coriolanus, passenger bark *134*
Cormier, Edythe *183*

Charles A. Russell, dealer of ice and oil, 1950s.

Cormier, Rick *323, 329*
Cornelius Callahan Co. *96*
Cornell, Alex *17*
Cornell Dubilier *8, 168, 175, 237, 244, 249, 287*
Cornell, Esther *221*
Cornell Hall *275*
Cornock, Sidney W. *110*
Correia, Abel *113*
Correia, Henry *26*
Correia, John, Jr. *154*
Correia, Joseph *253*
Correia, Walter *26*
Corson, Henry *92*
Costa, Alice *304*
Costa, Antone *241*
Costa, Dr. Goulart da *91*
Costa, Jeanne *282*
Costa, Jimmie *241*
Costa, Leandro J., Manuel *134*
Costa, Manuel J. "Manny" *225*
Costa, Maureen Berry *319*
Costa, Natalia *246*
Costa, Robert *222*
Costa, Ruth *141*
Costello, William E. *176*
Cote, Wilfred *180*
Cotnoir, Arthur B. *134*
Cotton, Dana M. *315*
cotton industry *4–7, 28, 41, 48, 58–59, 97, 127, 135, 147, 168, 171, 176–177, 190, 302*
Council of Women's Orgs. of Greater New Bedford *26*
Courosis, Arthur, George *73*
Coutinho, Manuel Agrela *332*
Couto, Jude *314*
Couture, Wilfrid *119*
Couza, Jim *324*
Cove Discount Center *309*
Covell, Addie Higgins (Ricketson) *132*
Covell, William P. *132*
Cove Road Playground *23*
Cox, Owen *19*
Coyne Industrial Laundry *302*
Crab Grass band *323*
craft unions *10*
cranberries *42*
Crane, Shepard *159*
Creole Sextet *245*
Creole Vagabonds *243*
Crocker, Samuel *46*
Crossley, Albert, Jr. *104–105*
Croteau, Paul "Truck" *324*
Crowell, Dave *340*
Crow Island *37, 119, 166, 167*
Crushed ice *186, 350*
Cruz, Julianna *90*
Cruz, Maria *90*
Cruz, Ricardo *314*
Cruz, Ronnie *289*
Crystal Café *243*
Crystal Ice *350*
Cuckoo Club *90*

Cummings Building 65, 287
Cunha, Florence 115
Cunha, Peggy 115
Curran, Mike 323
Curry, Kathleen 233
Curtis and Lawrence 110
Curtis, Billy 110, 133
Curtiss Flying Service 51, 53
Curtiss, Glenn 53
Curtiss NC-4 flying boat 53
Cushing, Cardinal Richard J. 129
Custodio, Jack 290
Custom House 16, 19, 279
Cuttyhunk Island 16, 63, 158, 320, 350
Cuvilja, Oswald 128
Cycledrome 104
Cyclones, The 328
CYO League 89

D

Dabrowski, Edward K. 288
da Costa, Jose 216
Dagny, fishing vessel 154
DaGraça, José, Pedro 131
Dahill Air-Hoist Aerial Ladder 96
Dahill, Edward F. 19, 96, 160
Dahlberg, Arnold E. 178
Daisy Cup Corporation 302
Dalbec, Gary 356
D'Alessandro, Marie 183
Daley, James 139
Daley, Thomas 72
Dallum, Marie W. 228
DaLuz, Genevieve 232
DaLuz, Manuel 314
D'Amore Construction Co. 91
Dance Bands Festival 241, 245
Dandurand Pharmacy 93
Dan's Pavilion 87, 102, 168
Da Pina, Charlie, David 353
Darcy, Homer 163
Dartmouth, MA 92, 217, 264-265, 309
Dartmouth Finishing Corp. 302
Dartmouth Manufacturing Co. 90
Dartmouth Mills 11, 302
Dartmouth, whaler 23
da Silva, Francisco Caetano Borges 121
DaSilva, Manny 314
Dauteuil, Paul A. 286
Davenport, Henry 212
Davenport, Holly 253
David, Annie 233
Davidsen, Hans, Serine 136
Davidson, James 294
Davidson's Meat Market 294
Davis, Al 19
Davis, "Dainty" Dora 115
Davis, Mary Lou 233
Davis, Maynard, Stanton 295
Dawson, Benjamin, Joseph 180
Dawson, Isaac 50, 51
Dawson's Brewery 50, 180
Days, Herbert 17
de Abreu, Plácido António Cunha 51
Debrosse Oil Co. 94
deCosta, Beverley 175
De Cotis, Roique 174
Deeb, Charley 76
DeGrasse, Bonnie Fermino 89
Delage, Alfred B. 114
Delano, Sara, Warren II 218
Delano, Sarah, Stephen 278
Delaware Rayon Company 41
Del Rios 322
Demello, John 294
DeMello, John B., Jr. 76
de Melo, José Pereira 246
Demers, Eva 307
Demers, Leopold "Young Paulie", Paul "Kid" 109
Dempsey, Jack 108
Denault, John 241
Dennison Memorial Building 25

DePasquale, Bernard 161
DePina, Barbara Fermino 89
DePina, Mary 339
Depot Café 205
DeRego, Rodney 318
Desaulniers, Joseph Arthur 120
DeSautels, John A. and Mary 95
Deschaine, Roland 118
Deshonge, Edwin 128
Desjardins, Yvette 112
DeSousa, John 324
DeSouza, William 223
Despres, Armanda 162
Desroisiers, Dennis 314
Desrosiers, Edmond H. 216
Des Ruiseau, Kip 159
Destremps, Louis E. 65
de Tai, Boboy 131, 244
Devault, Amozelie 162
Dever, Paul A. 165
Devlin, Robert, Josephine, Theodore 161
DeWalt, Earl 227
Dias, Antonio F. 134
Dias, Lionel F. "Leo" 110
Dias, Robert A. 224
Dinis, Edmund 321
Dion, Alfred 79
Dion, George J. 70
District of Columbia Infantry 124
Dizzy Gillespie Band 242
D.N. Kelley & Son 184
do Carmo, Charlie 283, 289
do Carmo, William "Bill" 90, 153, 289-290
documentary 217, 320, 325
Dolphin 24, boat 47
Donaghy Boys Club 138, 229
Donnelly, Elizabeth 12, 15
Donnelly, Jim 321
Donohue, Tim 356
Donovan, Francis 161
Donovan, Mary 287
Don Verdi Swing Band 131
Doolittle, Jimmy 51
Dorothy Earle 16
Dorsey, Tommy 113, 242, 323
Dottin, Duncan 282, 290
Double Bank Building 281
Doucette, Louis Jr. 32, 33, 36, 38
Doucette, Louis Sr. 18
Douglass Memorial AME Zion Church 214
Downing, Antoinette 278
Down to the Sea in Ships film 156, 226, 250
Downtown renewal 274-275
Doyle, Andrew P. 135
Draft Information Center 260
Drayton, Yvonne 214
Dream Warriors junior drum & bugle corps 251
Driscoll, Dennis 16, 19
dropouts 140, 232, 315
Duarte, Alvaro 243, 245
Duarte, John 90, 282
Duarte, John "Johnny" 244
Duarte, Laura 232
Duarte, Manuel Santana 332
Duarte, Mary 90
Duarte, Mary Ann 338
Duarte, Peter J. 56
Dube, Flora 141
Dube, Paul 189
Duchaine, Joseph P., Paul 213
Duff, Ernest R. 108
Duff family farm 50, 51
Duff, Mark 89, 173
Dukakis, Michael S. 287, 322
Duke, Johnny 248
Duke Oliver's Orchestra 243, 244
Dumas, Leo 323, 329
Dumont, Edward 85
Dumpling Light buoy 17
Dunbar, Joshua P., Reuben, William A. 123
Dundee, Johnny 109
Durant, Helen 183

Durant, John 335
Durant Sail Loft 227, 335
Dutra, Manny 212
Dworkin, Mark & Marilynn 287
Dyer, Kenneth 154
Dylan, Bob 325
Dynafuel, tanker 350
Dyre, Timothy I. 92
Dyson, Bobby 109
Dzedulevitz, Frank 241

E

E885, motorboat 17
E. Anthony & Sons 118, 202, 216, 321
Early, Dick 306
East Fairhaven Airport 50
Edgartown, MA 53
Edgewood Arsenal 174
Edith A. Kasan's Home Bakery 210
Edmonds, Phil 131
Ed Roderiques Orchestra 241
Edson Corporation 301
education 140-146, 232-235, 292, 314-319
Edvardsen, Arne, Thelma 136
Edwards, Antone T., John T. 134
Eggers Building 354
Eisenhower, Dwight D. 171, 218-220, 247
Eldred, Raymond H. 99
Eldridge, Linus S. 28, 32-39, 166, 219
Electralab Printed Electronic Corp. 301
El-Hillow, Tony 356
Ellen R. Hathaway School 316-317
Ellington, Duke 242, 260
Ellis, Ted 217
Ellison, Henry W. 68
Ell Vee Dee, Inc. 312
elm trees 88, 166
Elmwood Housing Dev. 276
Elsie Greenwood 104
Elwin, Jackie 115
Emergency Relief Adm. 128
Emilia Ramos 89
Emin, George A. 57
Emin Motor Car Sales 57
Empire Theater 27, 116, 227
employment 5, 9, 22, 27, 49, 129, 146-147, 162, 171-172, 179, 182, 240, 256, 282, 289, 304, 306, 341
England 69, 81-82, 110, 112, 124, 125, 127, 184, 210, 238, 324
  Lancashire 107, 125, 127
England, Nat A. 133
England, Walter 117
Enos, Mike 314
Entwistle, Bruce 328
Epstein, Abraham 89
Epstein Brothers 8
E.R.A. Band 128
Erickson, Paul 327
Erlbect, Max 252
Ernie's Venetians 130
Ervin, Gil 53
Esso gasoline station 276
Ethan Ames Mfg. 173
Evans, Charles 302
Evans, Jimmie 115, 207
Evelyn Parr 115
Exchange Club 188

F

Fabio, Zoe 289
Fado 246, 325
Fagerland, Selmer 136
Fairhaven 6, 16-17, 28-29, 33, 45-47, 50-53, 55, 77, 85, 89, 115, 136, 166-169, 173, 178, 189, 199, 205, 207, 218, 246, 264, 266, 283, 305, 308, 311, 317, 319
Fairhaven High School 252
Fairhaven Mills 199
Fairhaven train station 52
Falk, James 309
Fall River, MA 13-14, 54-55, 58, 107, 111-112, 116, 120, 123, 125, 129-130, 132-133, 139-141,
165, 171, 177, 191, 218, 229, 276, 283, 286, 308, 314, 324, 334
Falmouth, MA 18, 286
Family Welfare Society 83
Fargo Trucks 57
Farland, Therese 183
Farm Security Adm. 8, 119, 334
Farrady, Mary 72
Fauteaux, Pete 14
Fazendero, Mac 247
Feast of Saint John the Baptist 293
Feast of the Blessed Sacrament 332
feasts 293, 332-333, 338, 353
Fecteau, Clovis 252
Federal Aviation Agency 202
Federal Housing Adm. 58
Federal Music Project 98
Federal Writers' Project 98
Fédération Franco Américaine 82, 93, 157
Federation Hall 98
Federico, Carl 178
Feinstein, Hyman 309
Fermino, Albert "Burt" 241, 243, 245
Fermino, Anthony "Butch" 89
Fermino, Henry 89
Fermino, Joseph 191
Fernandes, Alfredo 266
Fernandes, Charles A. 29
Fernandes, Joseph E. 295
Fernandes, Mary 90
Fernandes, Steve "Jivey" 339
Fernandes Supermarkets 295
Fernley, John 107
Fernview, freighter 350
Ferreira, Bobby 327, 329
Ferreira, George 25
Ferreira, Lillian 163
Ferreira, Manuel P. 333
Ferreira, Milton 246
Ferreira, Teddy 329
Ferreira, Wayne 323
Ferro, Anibal 247
Ferro, Elsie 297
Ferro, Gilly 241, 247
Ferro, Jacintho A. 247
Ferro, Jesse 247, 297
Ferro, Joe (José) 245, 247, 253
Festa do Santissimo Sacramento 332
Field, Polly 234
Fifth Street Grammar School 110
Figas, Father Justyn 119
Figueiredo, Anthony 224
Finast Supermarkets 33, 300
Finkel, Max 181
Finnerty, Larry 358
Fire Department Training Tower 277
fires 96, 354
Firestone Defense Prod. 171, 176
Firestone Tire & Rubber Co. 11, 41, 61, 154, 171, 176, 287
Firpo, Luis Angel 108
First Baptist Church 214
First Congregational Church 78
First National Bank 65, 316
First National Stores (FINAST) 33, 300
fish auction 38, 154, 187, 288
Fisher, Edward 154
Fishermen's Union 188
Fisher, Ronald 161
Fishery Conservation and Management Act 313
Fish Forwarding Company Inc. 37
fishing industry 3-4, 9, 18, 29, 32, 35-38, 47, 60, 63, 90, 99, 139, 154-155, 167, 169, 176, 181, 184-189, 217, 219, 258, 259, 264, 266-269, 278, 310-313, 320, 325, 350
  blackback 32
  bluefin tuna 310
  bluefish 14, 98-99
  cod 32-33, 93, 186, 288, 311, 313
  fillet houses 33, 310
  haddock 32-33, 186, 288, 311, 313
  mackerel 34, 39

  menhaden 39
  quahogs 32-33, 35
  scallops 3, 32-34, 37-39, 136, 154-155, 186-189, 258, 296, 310-313, 350
  scup 36
  sea bass 36
  shad 36
  shark 36
  skate 36
  swordfish 33, 35, 38, 312
  whiting 36
  yellowtail 3, 32-34, 186-187, 258, 288, 310-312
Fish Island 34, 199, 350
Fish Transport Company 181
Fisk Rubber Company 11, 41, 176
Fitchenmeyer, Carl, Donald, Martin, Muriel, Shirley 161
Fitzgerald, Lillian 114
Fitzgerald, William J. 19
Five Bellhops 253
Flanagan, John J., Jr. 221
Fleetwing, fishing vessel 167
Fliege, George 206
Flinn, Marty 358
Flood, Dick 233
Flood, William 159
Florie, Tommy 107
Flynn, Mickey 115
Foley, Ronald 161
Fonseca, Jimmy 328
Fontaine, André D. 83-84, 93
Fontaine, Dorothy, Evelyn, Rene 83, 84
Fontaine, Laurina 84, 93
Fontaine, L.J. Oscar 133
Fontaine's Pharmacy 83, 84, 93, 337
Foote, Bob 53
Ford, Eddie 111
Ford, Gerald R. 229
Ford, Henry 56, 94
Ford, Sammie 115
Fort Devens 52
Fortes, Albert 282
Fortes, Lucy 90
Fortier, Dan 323
Fort Phoenix, Fairhaven 261, 263
Fort Rodman xi, 103, 151, 158-159, 166, 195
Forty Men and Eight Horses Drum Corps 126
Four Corners, downtown 62-63
Four Kings, The 245, 247
Fournier, J. Leonidas 85
Four Sharp Edges 250
Four Sisters, scalloper 154
Four Smoothies 250
Fox, George 132
Fox, Max 18, 19
France 50, 82, 116, 120, 133, 160, 238
Francis, Rev. Edmund G 89
Franco-American 69-73, 76, 251
Franco-American Chamber of Commerce 70
Franco-American Federation 76
Franco-American Radio Hour 119, 216
Franc Tireurs Marching Band 125
Fraser, Kitty "Kittens" 115
Frates, Albert 99
Frates Dairy Bottle 92
Frates farm & dairy 92, 369
Frawley, David E. 202
Fredette, J. Alfred, Louis N. 77
Fredette, Mary 162
Freedman Shoe Company 168
Freeman, Ethel, Harry 204
Freeman's Pharmacy 204
Freitas, Richard, Richard Jr. 248
French Band 122, 124
French Canadian 10, 57, 66, 68-73, 75, 79, 81, 119, 129, 132, 134, 140, 210, 214, 323
French Sharpshooters Club 83, 125, 252
Friends Academy 144
Friendship II, fishing vessel 168
Frostad, Ingvald 136

Fuller, Alvan T. 135
Fulton Fish Market 9, 33, 37
Fulton Supply Co. 250
Fumin Humins 329
F. W. Woolworth Co. 69, 71, 82, 85, 166, 257, 308

G

Gagnon, Robert 351
Gallant, Frank 253
Galvin, Herman 232
Galvin, Jiwe 244
Ganem, George 76
garages 57, 94, 314
Garcia, Wilfred 139
Gardner, Darius P. 44
Garry, Jean 114
Gar Wood Skating Rink 101
gas stations 49, 94, 160, 344
Gatenby, Scott 318
Gaudette's Pavilion, Acushnet 227
Gauthier, Ephrem G. 119
Gauthier's Furniture Store 97
Gauvin, Marion 216
Gebhard, Heinrich 249
Geggatt, Edna 141
Geller, Phyllis 318
Gene Marshall Band 247-248
Genensky, Dr. Jacob, Samuel 89
General Electric 57
Gentilhomme, Clemence 162
George L. Brownell Carriage Works 56
George, Louis 240
George N. Alden Ambulance Corps 159
Georges Bank 18, 32-33, 186, 189, 310, 312-313
George's Grille 201
George Shaw Company 295
German Band 247
Germany 18, 43, 91, 124, 132, 151, 163, 174, 184, 206, 211, 217, 225
Gibbs, John 128
Gidley, Mark 329
Gifford, Charles H. 44
Gifford & Co. 44
Gifford, Edward 123
Gifford, Mary 159
Gifford, Nella H. 238
Gifford, Sumner E. 95
Gifford, Winnifred 233
Gilly Ferro's Orchestra 247
Gimarese, Peter "Weed" 329
Gimong, Maria 246
Gingras, Norm 335
Gioiosa, Anastasia 141
Girl Scouts 89, 223
Giusti Baking Company 82, 210-211, 213
Giusti, Cesare, John, Joseph 213
Gleason, Jim 216
Glenn, Jack 320
Glenn Miller Orchestra 248
Gloucester, MA 33, 39, 313
Godelaer, Rev. John 89
Godreau, Rodolphe 132, 252
Goes, Frank 329
Goggin, John 356
Goggin, Mary F. 111
Golas, Chester 179
Goldberg, Harry, Julius 73
Golden Boys 111
Golden Clovers of the Verdean Vets 251
Golden Star Serenaders 130
Goldfarb, Samuel 89
Golub, Lisa 318
Gomes, Alfred J. "Lawyer" 89, 131, 229
Gomes, Alfred "Rocky" 339
Gomes, Domingo 191
Gomes, Donald 282, 289
Gomes, Guimar, Manuel, Maria 90
Gomes, Jack 323
Gomes, Maria Guimar 89
Gomes, Mary 89
Gomes, "Mingo" 131, 216
Gomes, Sabina 134

Gonsalves, Billy 107, 212
Gonsalves Brothers trio 131
Gonsalves, Charles 245
Gonsalves, John 250
Gonsalves, Louis 109
Gonsalves, Paul 131, 242, 244, 326
Gonsalves, Stephen 327
Gonzales, Anile 234
Goodwin, Caroline S. 182
Goodyear Tire & Rubber Co. 11, 40-41, 51, 106, 171, 176, 304
Goulart, Joseph 34, 35, 37, 38
Goulart Square 86
Goulart Square Business Assn. 86
Goulart, Walter 86
Gouveia Linguiça 294
Grace, Bishop Charles Manuel "Sweet Daddy" 135, 156, 169, 228, 256, 268, 337
Grace Building 245
Grace, Frank "Parky" 287
Grace, John 245
Grace, Juliana 337
Grace, Pauletta 353
Grace, Peter 329
Grace, Russ 233
Grace, Susan 296
Gracia, Dorothy 182
Gracia, George 139
Gracia, John F. 315
Grady, John C. 248
Gramas, Eugenia 114
Grand Army of the Republic 124, 239
Grand Banks 39
Gray and Sullivan's Orchestra 124
Gray, Edward, Henry Asa, Henry C., Leonard, Leonard C. 124
Graylords 241
Gray's Band 124
Gray's Band and Orchestra 124
Gray's Orchestra 124
Gray sports car 56
Great Depression 6-9, 13, 16, 18, 20-22, 26-27, 38, 40, 43, 45, 48, 50, 57-58, 63-65, 85, 90-91, 106, 117, 128, 133, 134, 138, 142, 147, 156, 174, 179, 197, 207, 229-230, 238, 246, 302, 334
Greater New Bedford Committee to End the War in Vietnam 260
Greater New Bedford Community Chest 223
Greater New Bedford Regional Vocational Technical High School 231, 317
Greater New Bedford Victory Garden Harvest Show 26
Great Quitticas Pond 23, 25
Great South Channel 186
Greek 63, 69, 71, 73, 82, 114, 266, 270
Greek Orthodox Church 337
Green, Col. Edward H.R. 50, 52-53, 57, 99, 108
Green, David 319
Greene and Wood 58-59, 167
Greene, Bobby 326
Greene, Fred C. 110
Green Front Band 246
Green, Hetty 50, 182, 280, 342
Greenstein, Max 72
Greenwood, Isie 105
Greyhound, packet ship 134
Griffin, Chet 115
Griffin, Edmund 128
Griffith, D.W. 84
Griffith, J. Frederick 133
Griffith, Thomas H. "Tommy" 111
Grimshaw, Imelda 216
Grinnell Mill 8, 178, 307
Grinnell, Peter S. 217, 278
Groebe, George, Henry 128
Groh, Dr. Herman 89
Grosswendt, Martin 324
Grupo Folclorico Madeirense 332
Grupo Santa Cruz 130
Gudgeon's Bakery 97
Guillet, Adrien S. 119, 216
Gulbransen, Edith 136

Gulecas, James 207
Gulf gasoline station 76, 276
Gulf Hill Dairy Bucket 92
Gulf Hill Farm 92
Gundersen, Frederick, Robert 179
Gundersen Glass Works 179
Gushue, John 356

H

Habid, Samuel 45
Hackett, David 350
haddock rash 186
Haddocks, Lloyd 282
Haddocks, Richard 216, 326
Haines, Sverre 136
Hall, Karl 283
Hall, William 222
Hamburges, Joseph 250
Hamid, Sophie 76
Hammond, Edgar B. 317
Hancock Industries 302
Handler, Morris 16
Haney, Carol 113
Hanson, John 233
Harbor Lights Restaurant 342
Harbor Lunch 342
Hardy, Charles 325
Harisee, George Darwish 76
Harisee's Grocery Store 76
Harney, Lucy 110
Harpoon, film 226
Harpoon Harmonizers 250
Harriman, Arthur N. 226, 232
Harrington, Arlene 161
Harrington, Edward F. 189, 230, 257, 266, 287, 290, 315, 336
Harrington, Joan 161
Harrington School 141
Harrington, Sheila 161
Harris Brothers 72
Harrison, Christopher 326
Harrison, John, John III, John Jr 326
Harris, William 'Undertaker' 128
Harry's Shoe Store 43
Harry the Hatter's 73
Hart, Leslie F. 19
Hartley, Catherine 183
Harvard Business School 181
Harvard Law School 229
Harvard Medical School 40, 174
Harvey, Ebenezer 132
Harvey Shoe Store 83
Haskell, Allen C. 352
Hassey, Ernest 104, 105
Hatch Street Studios 5

Hathaway, Chester 32
Hathaway, Edward R. 1, 118
Hathaway Mills 168, 171, 173
Hatton, Margaret 233
Hawes, Jonathan 123, 124
Hawes, Robert 202
Hawkins, George 161
Hawkins, John 353
Haworth, Dennis 125
Hayden, James R. 239
Hayden, Mary Ann 138, 229
Hayden-McFadden School 239, 317
Hayes, Lorin 123
Hayes, Will 110
Hazelwood Park 23-24, 100, 138, 156, 356
Healy, Brian 320
Healy, Pat 111
Healy, Paul, Tom 356
Heap, James Ogden 124
Heap, William H. 123, 124
Hearst, William Randolph, Jr. 51
Heck, Jody 324
Hedge Fence Shoal 116
Helmsmen, The 250
Hemingway Brothers Interstate Trucking Company 181
Hemingway, Joseph 181
Hemmings, William 250
Henderson, Eva 233
Henderson, Lou 189
Henderson, Regina 289
Hendricks, Chris 356
Henri-Chapelle American Cemetery and Memorial 164
Henry F. Harrington Memorial School 317
Henry Silva Band 245, 327
Henwood, Edgar 128
Herbert, Pauline 182
Herbert, Richard 139
Herman, Abram 89
Herman Melville Square 227
Herron, Wesley 212
Herter, Christian A. 168
H. E. Schmidt & Co. 43
Hetty Green's Counting House 280
Heys, Claude 163
Hibbits, Jack 104-105
Hickman, Rick 328-329
Hidden Bay 291
Hidden Brook 291
Higham's Drug Store 92
Higham, William 92
Hilario, Manuel 246
Hill, George 123, 124
Hillman, Henry T. 128, 129

Hill's New Bedford Band 122-124
Hilton Air Service 200-201
Hing Whang Chinese Laundry 137
Hinton, Walter K. 53
Hird, Ann Sullivan 358
Hirth, Paul 311
Hispanic Development Center 293
Hispanics 90, 229
Hitt, Charles 16
Hodgins, Mary 161
Hogan, Father John F. 237
Hoines, John, Karl, Ruth 136
Holmes, Rev. Guy Willis 135
Holmstrom, William 139
Holy Acre 272, 276
Holy Family Grammar School 161, 233, 317
Holy Family High School 104-105, 144, 287, 319, 356
Holy Rosary Church 68, 276
Homer's Wharf 34-35, 37, 147, 167, 259, 268, 310
Homlyke Bakery 211
Honeyman, Alice 141
Hong Kong 137
Hoover, Herbert 26
Horace Mann School 248
Hora Portuguesa 119, 247
Horne, Ruth 141
Horseneck Beach 16
Horvitz, Jacob 89
Hotel Harvey 250, 273
Hotte, Lenora 233
Houdini, Harry 112
House of Champions 225
House of Drums 323
House Un-American Activities Committee 232
Housing Act of 1949 266
Housing and Urban Dev. 91, 266
Houtman, Albert 128
Houtman, Eric 341
Houtman, Henry 241, 245
Houtman, Kenny 282
Houtman, Warren 283
Howard Baptiste 257
Howcraft, Gladys 14
Howdy Beefburgers 296
Howland-Green Library 342
Howland, Reuben R. 44
Howland School 140
Howland Street Club 88
Hudner's Market 82
Hughes, Bob 240
Hunt, Donald 327
Hunter, Lois 183

My Bread Bakery driver Alphonse Poyant (center) and colleagues, 1933.

Hunt, Herbert R. 64
Huntley, Chet 320
Hunt, Samuel C. 75
Hunt, Vera 216
Hurel, Gustave 120
Hurley, Andrew Sr., Andrew Jr., Barbara, Chester, Clifford, Clinton, Lloyd, 93
Hurley's Lunch 93, 155
Hurricane Barrier 169, 257, 259, 261, 263–265, 279, 311
hurricanes & storms 157
   1938 8, 23–24, 28–29, 46, 51, 53, 55, 58, 87–88, 92, 97, 99–100, 102, 205, 294, 355
   1944 166
   Great Blizzard of 1978 261
   Hurricane Carol, 1954 37, 47, 87, 166–169, 205
   Hurricane Donna, 1960 169
   Hurricane Edna, 1954 168–169
   January blizzard of 1964 344
   Valentine's Day Storm of 1940 55
Huston, John 156, 227, 325
Hyannis, MA 53, 200, 220

I

ice cream 50, 73, 92, 182, 204
Iddon, Jack 340
Ideal Ladies Undergarment Company 178
illiteracy 140
I. Margolis & Son 72
immigration 134–137, 292
Imondi, Joseph E. 355
Industrial Development Division 7, 42, 170, 173
Industrial Development Legion 7, 28, 40, 170, 175, 177
Industrial Workers of the World 82–83
infant mortality 152, 232
influenza epidemic 76, 238
International Longshoremen's Association (ILA) 190–191
International Sweethearts of Rhythm 157
Interstate 195 224, 255, 267, 276–277, 293, 312
Interstate Highway System 190
Ireland 82, 134, 210
Irene and Hilda, side trawler 333
Irish Americans 69
Irish House 266
Isaac Howland Jr. & Co. 280
Isaksen, Gail (Jacobsen) 188
Isaksen, Jane, Marian 253
Iskander, Gabriel 182
Israel, Louis 89
Italia, liner 59
Italy 82, 135, 164, 213, 217, 264
Izmirian, Claire 182

J

Jabotte, Palmelie 162
Jacintha, dragger 168
Jacintho F. Dinis Memorial Playground 87
Jack Simonsen 136
Jackson, Larry 324
Jacobsen, Kristine, Pete, Rasmus, Solveig 136
jacquard weaving 5, 43
Jacques, Barbara, John, Milton, Shirley 161
Jalbert, Claude 76
James Cunningham, Son & Co. 56
James P. Murphy Memorial Club 104
Janiak, Mitchell S. 164
Janiak, Walter "Zyggie" 104, 320
Jardin, Kristina 316
Jarry, Roger 83
Jarvis, Frank 63
Jaskolka, Anna 113
Jaslow, Richard 318
Jason, Albert 117
Jason, Antone, Joseph 99
Jason, Joseph P. 17
Jason, Paul 230
J. C. Mendes Company 170
J.C. Rhodes 301
Jeffries, Cheryl 324

Jenkins, Lester I. 118
Jennings, Ernest 99
Jeremiah, Paul 324
Jesus, Joe 357
Je T'Aime, rumrunner 18
Jewish 69, 71–73, 82–83, 89–90, 155, 323
J.G. McCrory 69, 82
J. Henry Smith, fishing vessel 167
Jimmy Barros band 322
Jimmy Connors Irish Pub 225
Jimmy Connors Tavern 225, 241
Jimmy Evan's Flyer 155
Jimmy Lomba's Orchestra 244
Jireh Swift School 78
Joblon, George 177
Jodoin, Romie 369
Joerres, Charles F. 111
John Avery Parker School 231, 316, 347
John B. DeValles School 27, 138, 143, 252
John C on Pier 3 297
John Halliwell Memorial Park 100
John H. Clifford School 317
John I. Paulding Company 304
John J. Cawley Stadium 22
John J. Duane Company 269
John M. Hathaway, schooner 32
Johnny Duke Orchestra 248
Johnny Rogers and His Band 245
Johnny's Diner 207
John R. Manta, whaler 9, 30–31, 134
Johnson, Ellsworth A. 133
Johnson, Lyndon B. 286
Johnson, Martin 154
Johnston, Harrie 249
Johnston, Henry 129
Jolly Whaler, restaurant 296
Jolly Whalers 250–251
Joncas, Oscar A. 119
Jones, Edith 175
Jordan Hall 326
Joseph Abboud Manuf. 5, 306
Joseph, Annie 76
Joseph Hamel's Orchestra 129
Joseph, Ira 239
Joseph, Nahum 76
Joseph Z. Boucher's Real Estate 97
Jospé, Maurice 281
Jowdy, Rev. George A. 29
Józef Kulig Warsaw Orchestra 128
J. S. Thomas Building 86
Julia K, fishing vessel 167

K

Kaczor, Josephine 12
Kalife, Alex 173
Kalife, Alex, Jr. 307
Kaplan Brothers Furniture 73
Karmøy Island, Norway 39, 136, 186
Kaufman, David 89
Kavanaugh, Joseph M. 128, 252
Kavanaugh's Orchestra 128, 240
Kay Windsor Factory Outlet 308
Keene, Henry R. 301
Keith, Hastings 283, 312
Keith Junior High School 315
Kellaway, Richard 324
Kelley's Boatyard 29
Kelly, Arthur 53
Kelly, Theresa 161
Kennaway, Joe 106
Kennedy, Edward M. 257, 292, 336
Kennedy, John F. 169, 219–221, 227, 247, 256, 312, 320
Kent State University 288
Kerry, John F. 329
Kettle, Acushnet 242
Kilburn, Clifford H. 46
Kilburn Mill 169, 176, 177
King, Clara 214
King George V 112
King, Herbert "Herbie" 326
King, Margaret 117
King, Martin Luther, Jr. 256, 326

Kings Mountain, NC 350
King, Tom 46
King, Walter L. 56
Kinney, Jocelyn 253
Kinyon-Campbell School 235
Kinyon Commercial and Short-Hand School 146, 235
Kinyon, William H. 146
Kirby, Gladys 183
Knights of Columbus 108
Knowles, Alice (Tiffany) 148
Knowles, Arthur 230
Knowles, Helen 175
Knox, Gordon 320
Knutsen, Solveig 188
Kobak, Joe 221
Kocur, Ed 314
Konarka Technologies Inc. 300
Korean War 152, 154
Korean War Veterans' Mem. Roadway 154
Kosciuszko Square 78, 95
Kransler, William "Bill" 335
Kravates, Josephine 173
Kroudvird's (Abram) Sanitary Bakery 73, 83, 155, 210
Krumbholz, George B. 128
Ku Klux Klan 135
Kulig, Alfred 128
Kulig, Józef 128
Kwiatkowski, Zygie 180
Kydd, William L., Sr. 214

L

Labarge, Matthew 316
Laberge, Raymond 160
Laboa, Manuel 253
LaBonte, Hervey 241
LaBrode, John 328, 329
LaChapelle, Marie 233
Lafayette Escadrille 50
Laferriere, Alice 160
Laferriere, Anita 100
Lafferty, Edward J. 57
Lafferty, Mark 329
La Flamme Cobblers team 106
Lague, Michael 318
LaJoie, Donald 161
Lajoie, Normand 224
LaJoie, Paul 161
Lakeville, MA 112, 125
Lalime, Napoleon 99
Lalime's Pirates 99
Lambeth Rope Corporation 350
Lamoureux, Stanislas 92
Landau, Abraham 334
Landry, Armand J. 112
Landry's Magic and Joke Shop 112
Landsvik, Jack, Robert 136
Langford, Shirley 100
Langhan, Joe 321
Langlois, Aldemar P. 249
Langlois, Paul A. 286
Lang, Marguerite "Gig" 238
Languerand, Rose 183
LaRocque, Bernice 183
Larrivee, Leo E. 104–105
Larsen, Karl, Tom 136
Larseu, William 42
Law, George J. 250
Lawler, Francis J. 217, 226–227, 231, 236, 256, 276
Lawless, Jim 356
Lawrence, Lou 110
Lawton, Charles, Horace 62
Lawton's Corner 62
Laycock, Ernest 135
Lazarus, Shirley 182
Leach, Susan 253
Leaming, Abigail 318
Leary, Frank J. 7, 173
Leavitt, William 249
Lebanese 71, 86
Leblanc, Albanie "Bennie" 113

Leblanc, Charles I. 72
LeBlanc, Doris 216
LeBlanc, Jeannette 119
LeBlanc, Lorraine 318
Leblanc, Silvio H. 250
LeBlanc, Stella 113
L'Echo Publishing Company 120
LeClair, Roland 351
Ledvina, Eleanor 141
Lee and Lawrence 110
Lee, Jack 110
Legg, Corrine 183
Leighton, Donna 339
Leighton, George N. 138, 229
Leite, Antonio 300
Lemenager, Edgar 119
LeMoine, Emile 216
Len Gray's Orchestra 124
Leonard's Wharf 59, 259
Leon Lowenstein and Sons 172
LePage, Jeanne 233
LeTendre, Ernest 161
Letourneau, Raymond "Rabbit" 224
Leung, Don, William & Dick 294
Levesque, Albert 206
Levesque, Oglare 162
Levy, Abraham 89
Lewin, Charles J. 217
Lewis Cup 106
Lewiston, ME 84, 111
Liberty Hall 190
Liège, Belgium 164
Lighthouse Oil Company 95
Liinus S. Eldridge & Son 3, 9, 32–36, 166, 219
Lilley, James 123
Lima, Barry 339
Lima, Lester 260, 283–284
Lima, Marie, Rose 283
Lincoln, Abraham 23, 122
Lincoln Hotel 96
Lincoln Park 112, 124, 129, 157, 236, 240–241, 244, 248, 327
Lincoln Stores 63
Lindbergh, Charles 50–51
Linehan, John 188
linotype machines 120, 221
Lionel Soares Orchestra 241
Lipp, Stan 320–321
Lipson's Shoe Store 97
Lisbon Sausage Company 294
Lissak and Company 173
Lissak, Nathan 173
Lithuanian 84, 351
Little Quitticas Pond 23, 25
Little Theater Group 314
Litz, Trudy 63
Livesey, Albert 110
Livramento, Jimmy, Joaquim do 131
Livramento, Joseph 131, 243, 244, 326
Livramento, Maria L. 90
Livramento, Ronald 338
Livraria Colonial bookstore 86
Lobato, António José Gonçalves 51
Local 214 American Federation of Musicians 242–243, 246–247, 253, 327
Lodge, Henry Cabot, Jr. 218, 220
Lomba, Jimmy 243, 244
Lomba, John Da 134
Lomba, Johnny 243, 245
Lomba, Raymond "Ray" 243–244
Lomba, Ronnie 282
Lomba, Roy 131
Lomba, Walter 232
Long Island, NY 50, 114, 166
longshoremen 155, 190–191
Loose-Wiles Biscuit Company 211
Lopes, Al 245
Lopes, Arthur 289
Lopes, Betty Ann 232
Lopes, Bumby 289
Lopes, Dana 339
Lopes, Frank 269
Lopes, James, Jr. 154

Bobby Watkins football card, 1955.

Lopes, Jamie 282
Lopes, John 191
Lopes, Joseph S. 246
Lopes, Stephen 222
Lopes, Tom 89
Lopez, Armando 118
Lord, Betsey 183
Lord, Joseph 123
Lorraine, Frederick 205
Lorraine's Coffee Shop 155, 205
Louie's on the Wharf 310
Louis Giusti's Wharf Diner 310
Louis, Joe "The Brown Bomber" 225
Lowell, Jean 182
Lowe's Theater 129
Lowry, Ted "Tiger" 225
Lubin, Hillard L. 202
Luiansky, Bernard 89
Luiz, Diane 353
Luiz, Guilherme M. 86, 121
Luke, Richard 302
Lumbard Volunteers 182
Lumiansky, Dave 109
Lumiansky, Harry 89
Lunds Corner 55, 78, 195
Luzitano Club 129
Luzo American Soccer Assn. 292
Lyman, Catherine 218
Lynch, Margaret 233
Lyonnais, Donna 316

M

Macabello, George 241
Macedo, Abílio Monteiro de 134
Machado, Arbone 127
Machado, Manuel 241
Machito Orchestra 243
Mackler, David 329
Macomber-Sylvia Building 354
Madeiran Folkloric Group 130
Madeira, Portugal 72, 77, 82, 130, 157, 240, 247–248, 295, 332
   Funchal 130
Madsen, Phyllis 183
Magnan, Mary E. 233
Magnant, Joseph A. 154
Magnett, Jim 289
Magnett, Steve 356
Maguire, Catherine 183
Mahan, Lois 183
Mahoney, Frank 233
Maiocco, Carmen 73
Majorka, Mildred 253
Malcolm Chace Jr., 171
Maloney, Thomas 117
Mandell, Bertha 238
Mandly, Antone J. 30, 134
Mandly, Henry, Laura P. 134

Manelis, Louis 89
Manning, Frank 12, 14
Manning, Leonard C. 111
Manomet Mills 5, 41, 173–174, 303, 307
Manty, Charles 109
Manuel Sylvia's hardware store 77
Ma Raffa's Restaurant 297
Maranville, Walter J. "Rabbit" 111
Maravell, Jack 329
Marciano, Rocky 225
Marcus Lowe chain 75
Margaret, packet ship 134
Maria Angela, fishing vessel 333
Marine Park 23, 29, 105, 166
Markey, John A. 278, 331
Marquis, Hermindale 162
Mars Bargainland 309
Marscot Plastics 47
Marshall, Antone 110
Marshall, Gene 240, 241
Marshall, John, Peter, Rita 233
Marshall, Rick 328
Martha Briggs Educational Club 214, 239
Martha D. Webb Missionary Society 214
Martha's Vineyard 18, 32, 50, 52–53, 116, 155, 195, 198, 202–203
Martin, Winnifred 184
Mary B. White School 25, 96
Mary J. Hayes, dragger 37, 167
Mary J. Landry, fishing vessel 167
Mary R. Mullins, trawler 33
Mary, schooner 32
Masonic Band of New Bedford 129
Masonic Building 92
Masonic Temple 283
Mason's Furniture 65
Massachusetts Air Industries 201–202, 220, 234
Massachusetts Arts Council 325
Massachusetts Bar Association 229
Massachusetts Development Corp. 170, 178
Massachusetts Housing Finance Agency 285, 291
Massachusetts Maritime Academy 158
Massachusetts National Guard 249
Massachusetts Pocketbook and Leather Goods Wage Board 45
Massachusetts State Federation of Labor Convention 45
Massachusetts State Firemen's Assoc. 96
Massachusetts State Guard 50
Massachusetts Volunteer Infantry 46, 122
Massachusetts Volunteer Militia 124
Massasoit Motors Company 56
Masseuet Quartet 133
Mathieson, Paul 33
Mattapoisett, MA 32, 55, 93, 118, 137, 340
Matt Perry Band 240
Maudsley, George A., III 286
Mauricia family 119
Mauricia, Juliette 232
Maxie's Delicatessen 297
Max, Louis 18
May, Alvin 128
Mayflower Airlines 203
McAlpine, June 141
McBratney, John Greer 287
McCarthy, Eugene "Butch" 329
McCarthy, Mildred 183
McCarthy, Pat 225
McCarthy-Richards Band 329
McCarty, William H. 15
McCauley, Thomas C. 133
McCord, Semenya 326
McDermott's Fish Market 97
McGee's Photo Supply, 165
McGrath, Betty Moore 133
McGregor Scotch hams 294
McKenna, Eileen 98
McKenna, John 233
McKenna, John J. 161
McLeod, Elinor 183
McLeod, Samuel D. 12, 15

McNally, Patricia 318
McPartland, Marian 249
M.C. Swift & Sons 351
Meaney, Edward 161
Meaney Hall 82, 83
Meaney, Thomas J. 82
Mechanics Bank 281
Medeiros, Ernest 130
Medeiros family farm 265
Medeiros, João 311
Medeiros, John 351
Medeiros, Manuel 294
Medeiros, Phillip 207
Medeiros, Richard 297
Medeiros, Tony 324
Mee, Joanne 115, 207
Mello, Brian 323
Mello, Charles 134
Mello, Egidlio 245
Mello, Manuel C. 177
Mello, Pat 290
Mello, Rosalina 159
Mello, Serafim E. 211
Mello's Market 169
Melville, Herman 156, 227
Melville Towers 273
Mendes, Carla 353
Mendes, Phyllis 353
Mendoza, Joe, Louis 240
Men's Mission 335
Mercantile Wrecking Company 116
Mercer Brothers 211
Merchant Marine 184
Merchants National Bank 62, 65, 206, 281
Merolla, Michele E. 282, 357
Merrimac, MA 50
Merritt-Chapman & Scott 23
Mertie B. Crowley, fishing schooner 18
Messier, Pierre 129
Methodist Episcopal Church 96–97, 135
Metivier, Karen 316
Metropolitan Motors 18
Metthe, Oliva 56
Meunier, Barry 223
Meunier, Blanche 95
Michaud, Gloria 183
Mickelsen, Helena, Leif, 136
Mickelson, Charles 206
Mickelson, Harvey 224
Midttun, Sig, Toralf 136
Miggins, George 128
Millbury, MA 72
Miller, Evelyn 141
Miller, Harry 56
Miller, Mitch 146
millinery 69, 77, 82, 146
Millside Bakery 211
Mirsky, Samuel H. 160
Mishaum Point 158
Mitchel, Armand 180
Mitchell, Walter 118
Mitch, Joseph 43
mobile telephone 221, 319
Mobilgas 94
Moby Dick film 156, 226–227
Moby Dick Restaurant 296
Model Cities 283, 290
Modern Venetian Blinds Company 178
Mohawk Carpet Mills 41
Monarch Clothing Company 309
Monarch Wash Suit Company 8, 173
Moniz, Joseph, Jr. 211
Moniz, Manuel, Jr. 154
Moniz, Richard 211
Monteiro, Antonio 243
Monteiro, Frank "Chico" 243–245, 326–327
Monteiro, Garcia 121
Monteiro, John 282, 289
Monteiro, Muriel 338
Monteiro, Pedro 243
Monteiro, Richard 223
Monte, Joseph J. 91
Monte Pio Hall 91, 131, 242

Monte Playground 91
Monterio, Gail 353
Monterio, Peter 245
Montgomerie, James Baird "Jimmy" 106
Montgomery, Frank 355
Montron, Hannibal 191
Monty, Omer 105
Moore, Claire 161
Moore, Francis C. 25
Moore, Jean 141
Moore, Marguerite 183
Moore, William F. 224
Moraes, Emilia 246
Morde, Theodore A. 217
Morgan, Lois 183
Morrison, James 154
Morrison, Joanne 318
Morse, Albert 250
Morse Twist Drill 26, 90, 99, 125, 179, 246, 291, 304
Mortenson, Robert 305
Mosher, Florence 159
Mostrom, Philip 53
Motta Building 78
New Bedford Aero Club 200
Motta, John C. 78
Mount Pleasant Playground 23
Mount Pleasant Reservoir 125
Mount Pleasant School 141
Moura, Domingos 26
movies 84, 89, 98, 110, 129, 156, 226–227, 250, 305
Mt. Vernon, NY 118
Muhlberger, Elizabeth 183
Mullins, Daniel 28, 32–33, 35–37
Mullins Fishing Gear 36
MultiLayer Coating Technologies 300
Municipal Bathing Beach 156
Municipal Golf Course 27, 357
Munro, Dr. Donald 97
Munson Steamship Line 59
Murdock, William 10, 11, 15
Murphy, Anne Marie 233
Murphy, Darryl 356
Murphy, James P. 104, 105
Murphy, Jimmy 233
Murphy, Rosemary, Susan 253
Murray, Winifred 233
Muse, Mikel 136
Music 122–133, 240–251, 322–329
Music Corp. of America 248
Mutterperl, Raphael 45
My Bread Baking Company 211, 213, 363

N

NAACP 133, 214
Nantucket 33, 50, 52–53, 62, 90, 154–155, 186, 195, 198, 202, 203, 311–312, 333, 335
Nantucket, lightship 229
Nantucket Shoals 33
Nantucket sloops 33
Nantucket Yacht Club 240
Napoleon, Phil 249
Napoli, Filippo 249
Narragansett Airways 200
Nashawena Island 158
Nashawena Mills 5, 8, 10, 40, 171, 175, 178, 306
Nash Road Pond 61
N.A. Textile Company 8
National Airmail Week 50
National Amateur Cup 106, 115
National Amateur Soccer Cup 107
National Band 252
National Biscuit Company 211
National Challenge Cup 106
National Committee to Combat Fascism 284
National Guard 12, 23, 158, 168, 261, 286, 288
National Ice Cream Week 50
National Marine Fishery Service 313
National Music Week 252
National Peace Day 287
National Register of Historic Places 280
National Silver Co. 171, 178
National Soccer Hall of Fame 107

National Spun Silk 173
National Student Marketing Corp. 307
Native Americans 68, 80, 214, 298
Naushon Mills 8
NBC Symphony Orchestra 248
Needle Trades Action Project 306
Neild Mill 97
Nelson, Alma 183
Nelson, David R. 282, 357
Nelson, John B. 128
Nelson, Miriam 104
Neptuners 250
Netinho, Frank 304
Neto, João and Filomena 292
Neto, John 292
Neto, Manuel F. 292
Nettuno, Rome, Italy 164
Neves, Brenda 353
Neves, Frank 206
Neves, Lolita 282
Newall, Leon 224
New Bedford 35, cruising-racing yacht 46
New Bedford-Acushnet Airport 50
New Bedford Aero Club 200
New Bedford All Stars 326
New Bedford Amateur Radio Club 118
New Bedford American Legion 137
New Bedford & Fairhaven Street Railway 196
New Bedford Arts Center 326
New Bedford Athletic Field 78
New Bedford Band 122, 123, 124
New Bedford Black Cats 106
New Bedford Boys (and Girls) Club 137–139, 214, 225, 229, 341
New Bedford Brass Band 122
New Bedford Business Park 298
New Bedford Centennial Week 104
New Bedford Chamber Music Society 133
New Bedford City Hall 22, 170, 274, 288, 316
New Bedford Civic Chorus 132
New Bedford Concertina Band 127
New Bedford Cordage Co. 176, 191, 354
New Bedford Cotton Mfgs. Assn. 10–13
New Bedford Country Club 236
New Bedford Day Nursery 233
New Bedford Defenders 106–107, 115
New Bedford Defense Products 154, 303
New Bedford-Fairhaven-Acushnet Airport 50
New Bedford-Fairhaven Bridge 28–29, 106–107, 109, 195, 199, 266, 355
New Bedford Fillet Company 35
New Bedford Fish Company 32–33
New Bedford Five Cents Savings Bk. 62, 65
New Bedford Folk Festival 324
New Bedford Free Public Library 22, 223, 252, 287, 316, 325
New Bedford Garden Club 342
New Bedford Gas & Edison Light Company 35, 37, 128, 167
New Bedford Guards Brass Band 122
New Bedford Half Marathon 258
New Bedford Haydn Society 132
New Bedford High School 22, 23, 104–106, 113, 118, 131–140, 142, 159, 217, 224, 229, 233, 246, 249, 260, 291, 315, 317–318, 322–323, 336
New Bedford Historical Society 214
New Bedford Hockey League 101
New Bedford Home for the Aged 239
New Bedford Hosiery Company 8
New Bedford Hotel 118, 131, 136, 151, 208, 227, 245, 248, 272–273, 296
New Bedford Housing Auth. 58, 91, 290
New Bedford Industrial Development Commission 170, 217, 257
New Bedford Industrial Foundation 170, 298
New Bedford Industrial Park 298–301, 357
New Bedford Industrial Plan Inc. 170
New Bedford Institute of Tech. 229, 234
New Bedford Instn. for Savings 62–63, 346
New Bedford Labor Council 306
New Bedford Lumber Company 167

New Bedford Mfg. Company 49
New Bedford, Martha's Vineyard & Nantucket Steamboat Co. 53
New Bedford Municipal Beach 24, 98, 100, 104, 168
New Bedford Municipal Garage 22
New Bedford Municipal parking lot 56
New Bedford Musical Association 132
New Bedford Musical Ensemble 326
New Bedford Orchestral Club 132
New Bedford Performance Enthusiasts 357
New Bedford Pirates 106
New Bedford Police Department 15, 45, 83, 112, 215, 276, 282, 290, 316, 342
New Bedford population 60, 142, 145, 232
New Bedford Power Boat Club 29, 83
New Bedford Protecting Society 180
New Bedford Rayon Company 28, 41, 174
New Bedford Redevelopment Authority 255, 257, 266–275, 280–281, 285, 290, 312, 343
New Bedford Reel 125
New Bedford Regional Airport 23, 51, 104, 200–203, 298, 356
New Bedford Revolver & Rifle Club 165
New Bedford Salvage Committee 160
New Bedford Scallop Festival 188
New Bedford School Superintendent 239
New Bedford Seafood Company 34
New Bedford Sealer of Weights and Measures 44
New Bedford Ship Supply 136, 350
New Bedford Shortwave Radio Club 118
New Bedford Shuttle Company 291
New Bedford Symphony Orchestra 132, 246–247, 249, 352
New Bedford Textile Council 10–13
New Bedford Textile Institute 137, 147, 154, 234
New Bedford Theatre 110, 115–118, 227, 237
New Bedford Veteran Firemen's Association Fife and Drum Corps 127
New Bedford Village Four Quartet 115
New Bedford Vocational School 22, 24, 104, 106, 128, 146, 160, 162, 217, 225, 234, 287, 314–315, 319–320
New Bedford Water Department 22, 25
New Bedford Whalers 106–107, 111
New Bedford Whaling Museum ix, 227, 257, 278, 316, 325, 354, 371–372
New Bedford Whaling National Historical Park 257, 259
New Bedford Women's Defense Corps 163
New Bedford, Woods Hole, Martha's Vineyard and Nantucket Steamship Authority 198
New Bedford Yacht Club 28
New Brunswick 113, 251
New Deal 58, 98, 220, 250
New England Amateur Athletic Union 225
New England Auto Radiator Co. 56
New England Central Airways 200
New England Conservatory 323, 326
New England Conservatory of Music 248, 326
New England Garde Drill Championships 125
New England League 107
New England Midget Auto Racing Association 224
New England Pajama Company 45
New England Steamship Company 53
New England Telephone & Telegraph 155
Newfoundlanders 35, 36, 38, 203
New Haven Railway 197
New Jersey 310
Newport Jazz Festival 242, 248
Newsham, Enoch 196
Newsham, Robert 222
newspapers
  A Alvorada 86, 121
  Alpha 229
  Alvorada Diária 121
  Anderson Herald 188

A Restauração 121
Boston Globe 17, 111
Cape Cod Times 221
Cape Cod Standard-Times 160, 220–221
Correio Portuguez 121
Dayton Daily News 27
Diário de Notícias 86, 121
Evening Standard 10–13, 108, 118, 220
Fairhaven Star 51
L'Ami du Peuple 120
L'Echo 120, 132
L'Echo de la Presse 120, 132
L'Echo du Soir 120
Le Journal 120
Le Messager 120
Le Petit Journal 120
L'Indépendant 120
Morning Mercury 26, 44, 90, 137, 220
New Bedford Times 11, 220
New York Times 37, 184
O Independente 121
O Jornal 121
O Novo Mundo 121
O Thalassa 121
Portuguese Times 121
Progresso 121
Protecteur Canadien 120
Providence Journal 9
Standard-Times ix, 26, 28, 32, 45, 98, 110, 112, 117–118, 138, 151, 153, 156, 160–161, 170, 201, 214, 217–218, 220–223, 250, 253, 260, 266, 293, 306, 316, 321, 334, 340
Sunday Herald 124
Trybuna Polish Weekly News 120
New Viper Review 329
New York Bakery 211
New York Boat Show 46
New York-Hyannis line 53
New York, New Haven & Hartford Railroad 48, 195
New York, NY 9, 33, 35, 37, 39, 44–45, 53, 95, 105–106, 110–111, 113–114, 119, 129, 132, 172–173, 175, 178, 181, 184, 186, 191, 203, 215, 228, 238, 242, 246, 248, 277, 306, 325, 328, 329, 334
New York Sea Grill 137
New York Shoe Store 83
New York Symphony Orchestra 132
Nickerson, Howard 188, 312
Nicolaci, Domenick and John 306–307
Nicolaci, Pasquale 307
Nielson, Gary 319
Nielson, Hal 221
Nixon, Richard M. 323
Nobrega, Jack 356
Nobska, steamship 198
Nogueira, Joseph 207
Nolin, Mrs. Pierre 162
Nollette, Helen 286
Nonquitt Mills 8, 173
Nordlyset (Northern Lights) Society 136
Noreen, scalloper 189
Normandin Junior H.S. 114, 142, 168, 232, 319
Normandy Print Works 177
Norris, Minnie 72
Nortek 304
North Congregational Church 62, 133
Northeast Airlines 200, 203
North End 6, 12, 19, 23, 25, 28–29, 47, 66, 68, 72–73, 77, 79–80, 112, 124, 132–133, 162–164, 170–171, 176, 205, 238, 269, 276, 280, 290, 293, 298, 308, 337
North Korea 152
North Terminal 171, 257, 272–274
Norton, Ruby 114
Norton, William 288
Norwegians 35, 39, 134, 136, 155, 179, 186, 189, 227, 253, 350
Notre Dame Church, Fall River 133
Nova Scotia 38, 93
Nu-Era Gear Corporation 301
Nunes, Eddie 216
Nunes, Paul 323, 328

Nye Oil Co. 256
Nye, William F. 94
nylon riots 165

O

Oak Grove Cemetery 22, 325
Oarsmen 250
Ocean House hotel 16
O'Connor Orchestra 129
O'Connor, Tom 129
octopus 273
Office of Defense Transportation 196
Office of Economic Opportunity's War on Poverty 289
Office of Price Administration 184
Official Ground Forces Orchestra 248
Offley, Jack 302
Ohio State University 224
Okolski Square 164
Okolski, Stephen Walt 164
Old Bedford district 88
Old Colony Aviation 200, 201
Old Colony Railroad 52, 197, 280
Old Colony Transportation Company 181
Olden, Andrew 136
Olden, Henry T. 50–51, 53, 104, 200
Oldfield, Estelle 159
Old Home Bakery 211
Old Rochester Regional School 244
Oliveira, Francisco 119, 247
Oliveira, Isadore 243
Oliveira, Jacqueline 234
Oliveira, Jesse 305
Oliveira, Leroy 232
Oliver, Arnold 106, 107
Oliver, Duke 243
Oliver, Garrison 128
Oliver, Michael C. 347
Oliviera, Francisco 247
Ollivierre, Audrey 233
OLOA Club 89
Olsen, Gerda 136
Olsen, Larry 358
Olympia Building 207
Olympia Theatre 62, 112, 114, 116–117, 129, 204, 226, 237, 274–275, 315, 324, 336, 343
Olympic Games 104
O'Malley's Tavern 354
Oman, Barbara 141
Omega Aircraft 202
Omerod, James 123
ONBOARD 214, 289
O'Neill, Catherine 183
O'Neill, Red 356
Opdyke, George 44
Ornellas, Frank, Virginia 130
Orpheum Barber Shop 84
Orpheum Theater 83–84
Ortega, Mildred 339
Osgood Bradley Car Company 54, 162, 195
OSS (Office of Strategic Services) 217
Ostensen, Eddy 136
Otis Air Force Base 231
Ottaway, James H., Jr. 221
Ouellette, Lucien 159
Our Lady of Assumption Church 89, 293
Our Lady of Fatima Parish 79
Our Lady of Fatima Youth Services 266
Our Lady of Mount Carmel 82
Our Lady of Perpetual Help 72
Our Lady of Purgatory Church 29
Our Lady of the Immaculate Conception Church 72
Outcasts, The 329
Owen, Charles D., II 43
Owen, Walter 227

P

Pacheco, Antonio "Tony" 322
Pacheco, Ernest 173
Pacheco, Frank 109
Pacheco, Jose 127
Pacheco, Mariano M. 97

Pacheco, Michael 327
Pacheco, Paul, Tom 323, 328
Pacheco, Tony 323
Pacific Oil Company 95
Padanaram, MA 55
Padelfor, Barbara 253
Page Mill 26, 28, 309
Page, Patti 216
Pairpoint Glass Corporation 90, 179, 256, 267, 269, 279, 354
Paiva, John 292, 294
Paiva, Maria 292
Palace of Sweets 73
Palestine, Herbert 309
Palestine, Jacob, Lester, William 173, 309
Palmer Island Light Station 355
Palmer, James 139
Palmer Scott Boat Company 47
Palmer's Island 29, 61, 90, 355
Panaretos, Peter M. 73
Papazian, Adrienne 287
Papineau, Clarence C., Norbert A. 164
Papineau Square 164
Papkin, Hyman 82, 89
Pa Raffa's restaurant 95
Paramount Restaurant 207
Paramount Theater Orchestra 240
Parisi Fillet 310
Parker House Hotel 212
Parker Street Dump 317
Parker Street School 141
Park, Irene 183
Park Motors 168
Parry, Arthur J. 125
Parry & Haworth's Orchestra 125
Parry's Orchestra 125
Parsons, Frank 35, 37, 38, 39
Parson's Laundry 215
Passionada film 325
Pastime Theater 114
Pata, Madalena 325
Patnaude, Edmond 72
Patriots Day Parade 126
Paulric Artists Bureau 248
Pawtucket, RI 107, 110, 146, 242
Payette, Raoul "Ralph" 206
Payson, Linda 183
PCBs (polychlorinated biphenyls) 175, 261, 303
Peace & Harmony Social Club 83
Pearl Harbor 150
Pearl Street Depot 49, 52
Pearly Baker Band 324
Pease, Luther 250
Peck, Gregory 156, 227
Peckham, Samuel J. 127
Pedersen, Ethel 136
Pedersen, Gunnar, Peder, Serene, Theodore 136
Pederson, Gunnar 154
Pedro Monteiro 326
Peel, Raymond 301
Peirce, Charles Edward 46
Peirce, Edward C. 170
Peirce & Kilburn 46, 184, 189
Peirce, Maggi Kerr 324
Pelletier, Gerald 250
Pelli, Joe 253
Pelli, Sal 253
Pemaquid Mill 15
Pennsylvania 5, 35, 118, 172
Pepin, Cora 162
Pep, Willy 225
Pequod Lounge 279
Pereira, Manuel A. 130
Perini Construction 265
Perkins, George 278
Perreira, Joseph 347
Perry, Alice L. 221
Perry, Anthony 99
Perry, Anthony J. 252
Perry, Armand F. 234

Perry Brothers Orchestra, Arthur ("Art"), Gus (Augustus), Jackie (Antonio), Joseph ("Joe"), Manuel ("Matt"), "Pee Wee" 240
Perry, Charlie, Sr. 282
Perry, Francis 240
Perry, Frank 328
Perry, Gilbert 99
Perry, Johnny 244
Perry, Joseph 177
Perry, Samuel 123
Perry's Grove, North Dartmouth 129
Peters, Joe 253
Peterson, Hal 320
Peters, William 104
Pete's Auto Body Shop 56
pharmacies 83–84, 92–93, 204
Phelan, Jim 329
Philadelphia, PA 39, 107, 124, 133, 181, 228, 240
Phil Edmond Band 242
Philharmonic Orchestra 132
Phillips, Arthur R. 178
Phillips, Jim 320
Picard, Matthew 316
Picadilly Lounge 241–242, 328
Piche, Armand 85
Piedade, Antonio 247
Pieraccini's Variety Store 284
Pierce Mill 8
Pilkington, Harold 84
Pimental, Paula 353
Pina, Domingo "Mingo" 245
Pina, Eugene M. 232
Pina, Henry 88
Pine Grove Cemetery 69, 228, 317
Pinkerton, Sue 287
Pinto, Augusto 12
Pinto, Eddie 241, 245
Pinto, Rose Tavares 289
Pires, Joseph A. 296
Pires, Robert 339
Pitta, Dr. João Carlos da Silva 305
Pittle, Anne 252
Pittsley, Herbert F. 179
Piva, Agnes 141
Piva, Manuel 245
Piwowarczyk, Walter 241
Plainville 22, 200
playgrounds 91, 138
Pline, Richard 278, 290
Plymouth Glee Club 133
Plymouth, MA 68, 280, 308
Pneumatic Aerial Fire Appliance Co. 96
Pochsha Swamp 23
Poirier, Alice 162
Poirier, Charles A. 15
Poisson, Avila 83
Poitras, Norman J. 224
Poitras, Rene G. 154
Polaroid Corporation 174, 300
Police Traffic Tower 22, 24
polio epidemic 182–183, 218, 232, 238, 248
Polish 11, 15, 69, 71–72, 79, 81–83, 95, 104, 113, 119–120, 126, 157, 164, 189, 211, 240, 252, 353
Polish American War Veterans 165
Polish Hour 119
Polish National Alliance 82, 157
Polish National Building 82
Pollard, Albert 250
Pollitt, Robert 139
Pollock Rip 39, 154, 189
Ponte, Frank 99
Pontes, Frank "Pawpaw" 245
Poole, Dorothy 183
Poor Farm 26, 341
Pope, Marilyn 141
Pope's Island 28, 55, 105, 155, 166, 181, 188, 196, 199, 205, 308
Poplack, Samuel L. 305
Port Hunter, freighter 116
Portugal 81–82, 86, 88, 121, 126, 130, 134, 210, 246–247, 292, 294, 321, 325, 351

Portugal-America Band 247
Portuguese 10–11, 15, 35, 51, 71–72, 77, 82, 84, 86, 89–91, 113, 119, 121, 126, 130, 134, 140, 144, 155, 157, 211, 214, 229, 240, 243, 246, 252, 266, 288, 292, 295, 305, 321, 325, 332–333, 351
Portuguese American Band 128, 246, 252
Portuguese aviators 51
Portuguese Band of New Bedford 124
Portuguese feast 72, 332
Portuguese Hour Orchestra 247
Portuguese Instrumental Trio 244
Portuguese National Club 83
Portuguese Navy Yard 90
Potomska Mills 20, 23, 80, 90, 101
Poulos, Leslie, Lisa, Linda, Marilyn, Tom 297
Poulos Pharmacy 297
Powell, Phillip S. 53
Poyant, Alphonse 363
Poyant, George, Leon 73
Poyant Shoes 73
Pratt & Whitney 174
Prescott, Helen W. 238
Presidential Heights Federal Housing Project 61, 119, 236
Prince Kavanaugh and his Orchestra 128
Prince Rajah Sigmund 114
Pring, Robert E. "Bobby" 248
Private Hermano P. Vieira Square 169
Progress, schooner 18
Prohibition 9, 16–19, 43, 50, 92, 134, 180
Providence, RI 9, 13, 52, 54, 62, 84, 110, 130, 171, 197, 218, 236, 250, 278, 321, 322, 350
Provincetown, MA 39, 62
Provost, Delia 162
P & R (Pennsylvania & Reading) Wharf 35, 37
Pruneau, Yvette 163
Puerto Ricans 90, 293
Pulaski Park 79
Pumilia, Peter 250
Puritan Grocery Stores 69
Purrington, Frederick R. 286
Puryear, Earl 109

Q

Quaker Oats 272
Quakers 12, 88
Quebec Province, Canada 69, 81–82, 93, 109, 119, 124, 251
Queen, Harry 89
Queen, Louis 309
Query's Drug Store 215
Quincy, MA 86, 104, 350
Quinn, Justin 356
Quisset Mill 90, 107, 267
Quitticas Pumping Station 23
Quonset Point, RI 200, 201

R

Radcliffe, Jack 324, 329
radio station
  NBHS W1HUM 118
  WBBG 118
  WBSM xi, 216, 282, 320–321, 325
  WDAU 118
  WEEI 114
  WFBN 118
  WFMR 166–167, 325
  WGCY FM 321
  WI-ZE 118
  WJAR, Providence 130
  WJFD, Portuguese 321
  WJZ 108
  WNBH xi, 118–119, 130, 160–161, 166–167, 216, 220, 320
  WSAR, Fall River 130
  WSMU, UMD 326
Raggamuffins, The 323, 328
Rainone, Al 240
Ralph Saxon's Orchestra 248
Ralph's Lunch 155, 206
Ramalhete, Evelyn 234

Ramon Argueso Orchestra 244
Ramos, Alfred 160
Ramos, Epifano "Peefonte" 131
Ramos, Joe 243
Ramos, Josephine 141
Ramos, Milton 89
Ramos, Tony 88
Ramos, William "Smiley" 225
Rampias, John 73
Ramsden, George 128
Rankin, David 324
Raposa, Armando 131
Rapoza, Eddie, Gus, Leonard "Lenny", Manny, Tony 240
Rapp, Lenny 240
Rauch & Lang 57
Rau, Gustavus 124, 125
Ray and Joe's Delicatessen 204
Ray Lomba's Latin-American Combo 245
rayon industry 5, 41, 177
Read, Albert C. 53
Read, Alexander 92
Read, William F. 44
ready-made clothing 44
Rebello, Charlie, Gil, Manuel 26
Rebello, John 26, 333
Rebello, William, Sr. 333
Reconstruction Finance Corporation 8, 58
Recordações da Madeira 130
Red Feather agencies 223
Redstart, scalloper 168
Reed, Lorraine 182
reed maker 43
Refuse, Albert "Al" 212
Regina Pacis Center 293
Regis, Margherita 141
Reisch, Sadie 12
Reis, Doreen 316
Reis, Dulce 332
Reis, Pauline V. 234
Reiter, John W. 124
Reiter's Band 122
Remington, Walter H. B. 89, 252
Reserve Officers' Training Corps 148
Rett, Eileen 183
Revere Copper & Brass 28, 47, 128, 168, 170–174, 217, 287, 304
Rex, Donald 279
Rex Monumental Works 86
Rex, Samuel Thomas 86
Reynolds/Mercury building 279
Reynolds, William J. 18
Rhodes, Shirley 183
Ribeiro, Albert 282
Ribeiro, Clyde 283
Ribeiro, Joe 241
Ribeiro, John 282
Richard, Arthur, Johanna 26
Richards, Chris 329
Richards, George D. 123
Richards, Ken 329
Rich, Buddy 327
Richfield 94
Richmond, Anthony D. 92
Richmond Oil 95
Richmond, Samuel P. 210
Richmond, Virginia 183
Rickenbacker, Eddie 51
Ricketson, Daniel 342
Ricketson, Frederick F. 97
Riendeau, Edward 205
Ringside Café 206
Ríos, Roberto 323
Rioux, Lucília Mota 246
Rita, Joseph 181
Rivard, Patricia 236
Rivard, Raymond 236–237
Riverside Cemetery, Fairhaven 218
Rivet, Dick 328
Riviere, Alexander 29
R. M. Bradley Co. real estate 170
Robbins, Annie 141
Roberge, Edmund 224

Roberts, Mark 324
Roberts, Philip 160
Robideau, Wilfred 117
Robillard, Eugenie 82
Robinson, Edward Mott 280
Robinson, Elsie 150
Robinson, Michael S. 124
Robitaille, Hector J. 235
Rocha, Antone 250
Rocha, Caroline 90
Rocha, João R. 121
Rocha, Lorraine 233
Rochester Air Field 104
Rochester, MA 53
Rockdale School 145
Rock, J. O. 133
Rockman, Benjamin 180
Roderick, Gilbert, Jesse F. 99
Roderiques, Dimas 223
Roderiques, Manny 222
Rodman Candleworks 281
Rodman Job Corps Center 289
Rodman, Samuel 281
Rodman's Wharf 46
Rodney Metals 178, 304
Rodrigues, Amalia 246
Rodrigues, Antonio, Joan, Nina 294
Rodrigues, Cindy 306
Rodrigues, Ed 241
Rodrigues, Elena 183
Rodrigues, Kevin 246
Rodrigues, Sonny 245
Rodrigues, Lorraine 35
Rogers, Annie 183
Rogers, Frank 131
Rogers, George 282–283, 292, 300, 357
Rogers, Joe, John C., Sr. (Johnny DeMarguida) 245
Rogers, Wendy 316
Rolo, Ron 340
Romanowicz, Rita 183
Romaria da Camacha 130
Romeo's Diner 85
Rooney, John P. 133
Roosevelt Dime 329
Roosevelt, Franklin D. 20, 112, 180, 207, 218, 250
Roosevelt, Franklin, Jr., James 218
Roosevelt Junior High School 142, 168, 215, 239, 339, 352
Rosa, Ed 340
Rosario, Joseph "Cab" 191
Rose, Barbara J. (Oliveira) 248
Rose Bowl 224
Rose, Derek 320
Rose, Edmund 301
Rose, Ethel 234
Rose, John 191
Rose, Manuel, Jr. 244, 286
Rose, Manuel "Manny" 131, 242, 244
Rosenberg, David 173
Rose, Vincent 339
Rotch Counting House 280
Rotch Spinning Company 41
Rotch's Wharf 23
Rotch, William, Jr. 280
Rothberg, Madelaine 216
Round Hill 51, 53, 99, 108
Rousseau, Arthur D. 111
Rousseau, Jean, Robert 233
Route 18 338
Royal Fruit Store 83
Royal Shoe Company 173
Royal Theater 83, 84
Roy, Roland 245
Rozario, Cab 241, 244, 245
Rozario, Norma 353
Rozario, Sebastian 89
Rubenstein, Jack 12, 14
Rudd, Robert E. 302
Rugg, Elizabeth S. (Holmes) 238
Ruggles, John A., Jr. 68
rumrunning 9, 16

Runyon, Damon 156
Rural Cemetery 21–22, 24, 86
Rushton, Thomas 286
Russell's Mills Village 265
Russell, Charles 361
Russell, Wing 92
Russian 69, 71, 81–84, 109, 116, 120, 323
Russian Symphony Orchestra 132
Russo, Domenico F., Joseph, Morris 178
Ruth B. McFadden 239
Ryan, Jim 358
Ryder, Ted 76
Rymszewicz, Wanda 183

S

Sabby Lewis Band 242
Sacco and Vanzetti 135
Sadler, Irene 140
Sadow, Laurence 73
Sadow's clothing store 73
Sagres Beer 246
Sagres, training ship 261
St. Ambrose Episcopal Church 214
St. Anne's Church 82
St. Anne's School 339, 367
St. Anthony of Padua Church 61, 66, 68, 133, 316
St. Anthony's High School 144
St. Clair, George 154
St. Eustatius, Netherlands Antilles 128
St. Hedwig's Church 82
St. Hyacinthe School 144, 233
St. Hyacinthe Church 82
St. John, Delphis D. 56
St. John the Baptist Church 89, 325, 333
St. John the Baptist School 144
St. Joseph Church 68, 79
St. Kitts 128
St. Lawrence Martyr Church 124, 133, 101, 287
St. Louis Opera Company 112
St. Luke's Hospital 19, 22, 182, 183, 287, 305
St. Martin's Episcopal Church 82
St. Mary's Church 28
St. Mary's Home Boys Harmonica Orchestra 237
St. Mary's Home for Children 18, 227, 236–237
St. Mary's School 249
St. Stephen's Day 136
St. Theresa's Church 69, 79
St. Vincent Island 128
St. Vincent, steamer 134
Ste. Thérèse du Lac chapel 79
Sal Pelli Trio 253
Saltmarsh's 257, 347
Saltonstall, Leverett 169, 218
Saltzman, William 73, 276, 282, 337
Salvador, Constantino 294
Salvation Army 168, 322, 347
Salvation Army Band 347
Sam Kee & Co. 137
Sampson, Isaac 46
Sanborn, Dana 118
Sanchez, Edward O., Edward O., Jr. 350
Sanchez, Mike 243, 244
Sandburg, Carl 325
Sanders, Patty (Pacheco) 323
Sanson Joy, swordfisher 312
Santo Christo Club 106, 107
Santos, Ernesto 127
Santos, Joaquim "Jackie" 323, 327
Santos, John 244
Santos, Louis 99
Santos, Manny 323
Santos, Manuel, Maria "Bach" 89
Santos, Mariano 127
Santos, Mildred 104, 105
Santos, Vasco 160
Sargent Athletic Field 132
Sargent, Francis W. 336
Sassaquin 55, 79, 305
Sassaquin Hospital 55, 305
Sassaquin Pond 79
Sassaquin Sanitarium 128
Saudades da Madeira 130
Saulnier, Al 13
Savaria, Rolande 233
Savoie, Gladys Reynolds 170
Savoy Theater 98
Saxon, Lillian, Ralph 248
Scallop Advertising Fund 188
scallop dredge 39, 186, 350
scallops *See fishing industry*.
Schaefer Equipment Co. 300
Schellenberg, Albert 109
Schick, Katherine, Leo, Stanley 72
Schick & Son Funeral Home 72
Schillinger House 249
Schmidt, Hugo E. 43
Schuster, Betsy 318
Schwartz, Danny 326

Sconticut Neck 29, 207
Scott, Myron 27
Scott, Palmer 47
Scovill Fasteners 301
S.C. Pease & Sons 56
Seafood Council 188
Seafood Producers Association 187
Sealtest Ice Cream 201
Seaman, Hank 340
Seamen's Bethel 227
Seamen's Memorial Scholarship fund 229
Searle, Charles T. 123
Searle, Josephine T. 133
Sears Roebuck & Company 63
Sea View Fillet 310
Seaview Fish Company 7, 34, 35
Sebastião, Manuel Gomes 332
Seemenski, Phyllis 183
Semedo, Mary Santos 89
Semiansky, Harry 206
Senna, Charles, Clarence "Tony", Manuel J. 114
Senna, Joseph "Jedge" 191, 242–243, 245
Sequin, Allen A. 152
Seven Blends 326
Seven-Up Bottling Company 302
Sewing Project 25
Shapiro, Avis 253
Shapiro, Herman, Hyman, Israel 84
Shapiro, William 89
Sharpshooters Drum & Bugle Corps 125
Sharpshooters Hall 242
Shaw, Barbara 141
Shaw, Betty 115
Shawnbeck, Gerry 33
Shaw's 295
Shea, Dorothy 165
Shee Yuen 137
Shepley, Janet 318
Sher, David 50
Sherman, Anne 253
Sherman Antitrust Act 39
Sherman, Billy, Dennis 311
Sherman, Harry, Phillip 16
Sherman, William T. 122
Sher's Company Auction Sales Room 274
Sher's furniture store 274
Shimizu, Roy E. 268–269
Shubert, Al "Bearcat" 109
Shulman, Mike 12
Shuster, Solomon 89

Jerry Branchaud, second row from right, third seat, poses with classmates at St. Anne's grammar school, 1947.

Sicily-Rome American Cemetery 164
Sid Wainer Fruit 43
Siegal, Calvin 307
Siegal, Charles, Max 173
Siegel, Harry 315
Sig Midttun's bakery 155
silk industry 5, 11, 41, 171, 177
Silva, Anna 90
Silva, Benjamin 232
Silva, Danny 186
Silva, Frank 130
Silva, Freddie 245, 327
Silva, Henry 244
Silva, Jesse L. 25
Silva, Joseph 160, 327
Silva, Manuel 99, 191
Silva, Manuel "Gelina" 131
Silva, Marie 338
Silva, Mike 131, 242, 245
Silva, Sabina 90
Silva's Market 284
Silva, Tony 206
Silveira, Eddie 283
Silver Gloves Boxing 340
Silver Shell Beach 29
Silver Star Cafe 271
Silverstein, Anna, Bernard, David, Harry, Joseph, Stephen 84
Silverstein, Barnet, Louis 84, 351
Silverstein's clothing 351
Silvia, Alice D. 233
Silvia, E. Milton "Milt" 334-340
Silvio's Barber Shop 250
Simmons, Jill 324
Simmons, Manny 282
Simmons, Manuel 25
Simonsen, Pauline 136
Sinatra, Frank 113, 248
Sirois, Andre 77
Sisson, George 99
Sisson, Otis A. 79, 124
Sisson's Donuts 211
Sister Anne, SSD 233
Sisters of St. Francis 236
Skipper Restaurant 248
Skyliners 191, 241, 243, 245, 247, 326
Skyliners (1965 doo-wop) 328
Slocum & Kilburn 118
Small, Arthur A. 29
Small, Mabel 29, 355
Smith, Ann 233
Smith, Bill 19
Smith Brothers Brewery 43, 180
Smith, Charles W. 178
Smith College 290
Smith, Elizabeth 161
Smith, Ernest 42
Smith, Evelyn 234
Smith, Israel 122, 124
Smith, James F. 43, 180
Smith, Joseph T. 43
Smith, Nellie 339
Smith, Peter 233
Smith's Lounge 241
Smith's New Bedford Quadrille Band 124
Smithsonian Institution 53
Smith, William 161
Smith, William C. 217
Smoking Rocks 80
soapbox derby 27
Soares, Avelino "Boboi" 244-245
Soares, Betty 353
Soares, Joseph 191
Soares, Joyce 353
Soares, Kenny 339
Soares, Lionel 241
Soares, Maria 90
Soares, Mary Beth 324
Soboski, Stanley 240
Société des Quarante Hommes et Huit Chevaux 126
Société l'Assomption Bugle & Drum Corps 251

Society for the Preservation and Encouragement of Barber Shop Quartet Singing in America (SPEBSQSA) 250
SOCONY (Standard Oil Company of New York) station 95
soda fountains 82, 92, 116, 204
Sol-e-Mar Children's Hospital 128, 227
Solemar development 291
Solomon, Charles "King" 18
Songs of Norway Singers 253
Sorrelle, Joseph, Jr. 69
Soule Mill 97, 177
Sound Airways 50, 53
Sousa, Fernanda 161
Sousa, Hope 161
Sousa, John Phillip 247
Sousa, Natalia 161
South Bedford 80
South Central 88-91, 153, 190, 266-270
Southeastern Massachusetts Technological Institute 371
Southeastern Massachusetts University 284, 287-288, 291, 326
Southeastern New England Golden Gloves 225
South End 10, 12, 24, 69, 73, 75, 80-84, 86, 93, 107, 115, 132-133, 138, 215, 222, 229, 238, 248, 252, 289-290, 293, 309, 329, 339, 341-342
South End Social Club 83
South Primitive Methodist Church 133
South Station 197
South Terminal 266-271, 274, 310, 312
Southworth, Betty 141
Souza, Brian 328
Souza, Eunice 141
Souza, Herbert 227
Souza, Joe 139
Souza, Ralph 136
Souza, Randall 316
Souza, Roger 89
Souza, Tony 278
Soviet Union 189, 312
Spanish-American War 126
Spence, Ernie 98
Spigliano, Hank 213
Spinner, Dorothy 283
splicing twine 36
Spooner, Charles 124
Spoor, Wilfred 160
Spouter Inn Restaurant 296
S. P. Richmond & Co. Bakery 210
Springfield, MA 39, 111, 140, 165, 181, 203
Sprott, Edward 128
Sprott, George 128
Squires, William W. 118
S.S. Kresge 63
SS Munindies, freighter 59
SS Munmystic, freighter 59
Stack, Eddie 248
Stanton, Lynn Riley 319
Stanton, Seabury 171
Star Garment Mfg. Company 8
Starkey, Michael 356
Star Orchestra 131, 243
Star Store 62, 65, 257, 345, 347
State Band 129
State Pier 34, 58-59, 166-168, 190-191, 227, 259
States Nitewear Mfg. Company 5, 306
State Theater 116-117, 226-227, 237
Steamship Pier 259
Stearns-Knight 57
Stefanik, Mitchell 180
Steiger-Dudgeon Company 62, 252
Sterling, Stanley, Jr. 128
Standard-Times' Newspaper Boys Band 223
Stetson, Edward J. 250
Stevenson's Dry Goods Store 83
Stevens, Robert M. 284
Stokely Brothers & Co. 7, 42, 173
Strand Leather Company 8
Strand Theater 27, 75
streets
   Acushnet Avenue 44, 50, 54-55, 63, 66,

    68-69, 71-73, 75-79, 83, 85-86, 91-92, 94-95, 97-98, 111, 129, 131, 137-138, 152, 154-155, 164-165, 205-206, 242-245, 252, 255, 266, 272-274, 276, 305, 308, 337
Allen 130, 143
Ark Lane 166, 308
Arnold 55
Ashley Boulevard 66, 78, 92, 95, 276, 317
Beetle 75
Belleville Avenue 8, 26, 28, 41, 66, 77, 135, 164, 166, 173-175, 224
Blackmer 284
Bolton 86
Bonney 87, 211, 309
Braley Road 79, 298
Bridge Street, Fairhaven 50
Brock Avenue 80, 83, 85, 102, 142, 160, 339, 341
Brook 23, 173, 180, 306-309
Bullard 69
Cannon 44, 91
Cedar 214, 215, 239, 282-283
Cedar Grove 72, 277
Central Avenue 78
Centre 280, 281, 352
Church 41, 61, 298
Clark 291
Coffin Avenue 97, 173, 213
Coggeshall 22, 26, 28, 43, 45, 66-70, 77, 99, 104, 135, 166, 178, 180, 195, 199, 224, 277
Collette 230
Commercial 280
Conway 270
Cornell 351
Cottage 282
County 11, 28, 31, 68, 87-88, 92, 142, 144, 211, 216, 223, 231, 238, 261, 274, 277, 285, 320, 351
Court 214, 317
Cove 28, 81, 83, 87, 164, 171, 238, 267, 271, 309, 337, 342
Cove Road 11, 24, 29, 68, 87, 168-169, 238, 264, 294
Cross 92
Dartmouth 86, 181, 211, 240
Deane 43, 69, 173, 307, 309
Delano 82
Division 82
Duchaine Boulevard 298, 357
Duncan 68
Durfee 77, 101
East Rodney French Boulevard 29, 45-46, 87, 90, 102, 169, 175-178, 264, 338
Elm 62, 273, 275, 283
Emerson 212
Emma 339
Eugenia 26
First 266
Front 22, 43, 66, 88, 94, 163, 213, 250, 280
Granfield 135
Grape 21
Griffin 91, 128, 171, 263
Grinnell 46, 54, 169, 269, 270
Hamilton 250, 281
Hampton Court 22
Hathaway Road 26
Hawthorn 157, 182
Hawthorn Terrace 157
Hazard 210, 213
Healey 306
Hicks 252, 276
High 166, 199
Hillman 272, 343
Holly 76
Howard 238
Howland 82, 88, 91, 169, 228, 267-270
Jenney 341
Jouvette 28, 248
Katherine 143
Kempton 18, 22, 57, 88, 95, 212, 215, 228, 236, 239, 260, 282-285, 344
Kenyon 255, 260
Kilburn 8

Leonard 46, 89
Liberty 317
Locust 320
Logan 22, 47, 68, 276
Madison 89, 91, 109
Market 108, 137, 225
Maxfield 85, 297
Middle 55, 207, 215, 269, 272-273, 275
Middle Point Road 80
Middle Road, Acushnet 50
Mill 22, 57, 95, 280
Mill Road, Fairhaven 50
Morgan 144
Mount Pleasant 23, 26, 55, 61, 68, 145, 164, 200, 338
Mulberry 351
Myrtle 277
Nash Road 61, 68-69, 76, 97, 177
New Plainville Road 164
North 341, 343, 351
North Front 22, 66, 76, 94, 163, 167, 178, 213, 260, 307
North Second 199, 273, 279
North Water 166, 173, 257, 281, 297, 308
Old Plainville Road 200
Orchard 24, 41, 88, 138, 143, 169, 292
Palmer 109
Parker 141, 212, 316
Pearl 49, 52, 107, 213, 218, 231, 277
Peckham Road 79
Penniman 277
Phillips Avenue 29, 73, 77, 97
Phillips Road 78
Plainville Road 51, 200
Pleasant 22, 56, 65, 68, 88, 92, 96-97, 108, 110, 113, 115, 135, 137, 145, 207-208, 218, 220, 222, 225, 238, 250, 252, 272-275, 287, 297, 305, 334, 343
Pontiac 50
Portland 102
Potomska 14, 88, 266-267, 269-270, 293
Potter 177
Prospect 267, 280
Purchase 43, 62-65, 116, 124, 137-138, 165-166, 180, 195-196, 204-207, 210, 213, 218, 229, 272-273, 276-277, 280, 287-288, 291, 294-296, 336, 338, 343, 345, 346, 349
Riverside Avenue 28, 174, 307, 309
Rivet 26, 54, 81-83, 86, 112, 233, 351
Rockdale Avenue 21, 95, 101, 181, 272, 294-295, 297
Rockland 155
Rock O'Dundee Road, Dartmouth 265
Rodney 46
Rodney French Blvd. 22, 82, 85, 164, 342
Rose Alley 281
Route 140 357
Russell 110
Sawyer 77, 97, 164, 173
School 88
Sears Court 65, 93, 319
Seventh 88
Shawmut Avenue 26, 51, 200, 357
Sixth 88, 89, 132, 274
Smith Neck Road 47
South 46, 90, 138, 267, 269, 270
South First 15, 25, 90, 267, 269, 270, 293
South Front 267, 270
South Second 82, 88, 91, 137, 186, 206, 266-268, 270-271, 274, 279, 294, 308
South Sixth 89, 148, 283
South Water 13, 14, 69, 73, 80-86, 89, 93, 155, 168, 169, 210-211, 213, 266-267, 269-271, 274, 284, 290, 337, 339
Sycamore 96
Tallman 8
Tarkiln Hill Road 28, 68, 78, 92, 142, 350
Tinkham 76
Union 44, 49, 55, 62-65, 92-93, 98, 116, 148, 155, 162, 164, 167, 195-196, 206, 208, 210, 216, 218-220, 241, 259-260, 274, 280, 288-289, 291, 297, 320, 344, 346, 351, 354

Viall 164
Victoria 92
Walnut 88, 91, 193, 244, 268
Wamsutta 6, 272, 276
Washburn 22, 94, 211, 224, 255
Water 28, 89, 92, 118, 351
Weld 276, 291
Westland 50
West Rodney French Boulevard 83, 98, 156, 169
William 62-65, 108, 204, 220, 274, 279, 281, 286-287, 315, 319, 335-336, 349, 354, 371
Wing 89, 245
Wood 28, 95, 167
S. T. Rex and Company 86
String Ensemble 253
Stuart Anderson 308
Stunners, The 329
Suggs, Edward "Chic" 109
Sullivan, Agnes (Kerns) 207
Sullivan, Daniel J. 124
Sullivan, John 11
Sullivan, Mary Louise 183
Sullivan's Band 122, 124
Summerfest 324
Sunbeam Bread 213
Sunbeam, packet ship 134
Sunnyside's bakery 155
Superfund cleanup site 175, 261
Supreme Judicial Court 284
Sutherland, Aldea 77
Swain School of Design 147, 287, 322, 352
Swanson, Fred 252
Sweeney, Patrick 179
Sweet Adelines International (SAI) 250
Swift, Arnold F. 133
Swift, John 123
Swift, Margaret M. 133
Swift, Moses Charles 351
Swithin Brothers marble works 86
Sykes, Albert, Raymond 161
Sylvan Grove 79, 124
Sylvia, Alice 232
Sylvia, Arthur 191
Sylvia, Barry 233
Sylvia, Dennis A., Natalie (Hemingway) 63
Sylvia, Dorothy L. 163
Sylvia, Ed 93
Sylvia, Frank 202
Sylvia, George 36
Sylvia, Henry 244
Sylvia, Joseph 190
Sylvia, Joseph J. 159
Sylvia, Joyce 318
Sylvia, Kathleen 233
Sylvia, Louis 352
Sylvia, Ray "Skippy" 329
Sylvia, Sylvia Ann (Rapoza) 240
Symphony Music Shop 326
Syrian 71, 76
Szubzda, Emil 120

T

Taber, Edward T. 44
Taber, John 252
Taber Mill 8, 11
Taber, Read & Gardner 44
Tabet, Henry, Marie 76
Table Talk Pie Company 211-212
Taft, Robert A. 220
Tallman, Peter 305
Talmage, A. A. 13
Talmage, Lucille 145
Tamits, Frank 253
Tatelbaum, Matthew 309
Taunton, MA 50, 52
Tavares 260, 322-323, 326-327
Tavares, Antone "Chubby," Arthur "Pooch," Feliciano "Butch," Feliciano "Flash" Vierra," John, Lorae, Perry Lee "Tiny," Ralph Vierra 322
Tavares, Hoxie 190
Tavares, Jack 191

Tavares, Marlene 282, 289
Taylor, Joseph 356
Taylor, Leslie 139
Taylor, Philip 161
Taylor Shoe Company 173, 308
Taylor, Truman 321
Taylor, William 161
Taylor, William F. "Billy" 224
teacher salaries 141
Tebbetts, Art 324
Teddy Bettencourt's 241
Teledyne Inc. 304
Telesmanick, Leo 47
Temple Landing 285
Temple, Louis 285
Tetzner, Herman 43
textile industry 4–14, 20, 22, 28, 41, 43, 48, 54, 58, 60, 63, 66, 68, 72, 80, 85, 109–110, 113, 124, 128, 130, 134–135, 154, 166, 168, 171–172, 176–178, 190, 213, 219, 238, 240, 243, 267, 273, 306
    Southern competition 6–7, 11, 13, 41, 166, 225, 306
Textile Mills Committee 10–15
Textile Strike of 1928 10–15, 54, 58, 76
    strike songs 15
Textile Workers Union of America 13, 171
Theatre Comique 70, 98
Theberge, Stephen 160
Thibodeau, Anna 162
Third District Court of Bristol County 45
Third Massachusetts Regiment 124
Thomas, Agnes Lopes 89
Thomas, Al 109
Thomas, Anthony 233
Thomas, Arthur, George J. 144
Thomas Donaghy School 138, 145
Thomas, Jane (Galligan) 296
Thomas, Joe 109
Thomas, Joseph S. 86
Thomas, Stephen 233
Thomas, Thomas 109
Thomaston, ME 33, 154
Thomas, Tony 109
Thom McAn Shoe Co. 69
Thompsen, Kristi, Margit, Solveig 136
Thompson, Donald 12
Thompson, Father William D. 237
Thompson Street School 292, 317
Thornton, Elisha 92
Three Glenns, The 113
Tide Water Oil 94
Tierney, H. William, Jr. 56
Tifereth Israel Synagogue 89
Tighe, Helen, Margaret 183
Tilton, George Fred 99
Timber, Everett 128
Times Building 208, 273
Tinkham, Bill 129
Tiny's Lunch 270
Tip Top Lunch 73
Titanic, RMS 84
Titleist golf ball 40
Tito Mambo 328
Tobey family 79
Tobin, W. Maurice 129
Tolentino, Frank 233
Tonnessen, Rasmus, Sally 136
Tony Pacheco Folk Minstrels 323
Tony Pacheco Guitar Studio and Music Store 322
Tony Trio 323
Topolewski, Carol 318
Torres Oil Company 95
Touraine Hotel 75, 76
Toy Mee 137
Trahan, James Albert "Al" 112, 113
Trahan, Robert 222
Tranmer, Olive A. 133
Tran Nhat Duat, renamed *Yakutat* 286
transportation 48–5, 181, 195–203
Travers, Charlie 16, 17
Travers, Gil 253

Travers, Gilbert 130
Travers, Louis 99
Treble Clef, The 132
Tremblay, Arthur 202
Tremblay, Romeo 206
Treot, Helen 132
Tri County Symphonic Orchestra 247
Trimont Dredging Company 59
Trimount Plastics Company 170
Trinitarian Congregational Church 133
Tripp, Edward 99
Tripp, Howard B. 95
Trobonae, Jonny 245
Trojan Athletic Club 99, 108
trucking, refrigerated 33, 36, 49
Tru-Line Dress Company 8
Truman, Harry S. 152
Tryworks Coffee House 261, 324, 329
Tschaen, Elsie, Raymond, Jr., Raymond, Sr. 204
tuberculosis 305
Tuna União Portuguesa 247
Turkish 74, 82, 93, 135, 217
Turner, Lloyd 240
Turnpikes, The 322
Tuttle, Clifford H., Jr. 303
Twarog, Janice 318

U

UMass Dartmouth 107, 224, 229, 290, 291, 323, 324, 326
Uncatena, sidewheel steamer 53
Underground Railroad 88
Unholy three 161
Union Baptist Church 214
Union Cornet Band 122, 124
Union Hall, Fairhaven 33
Union Hospital 305
Union Motor Corporation 57
Union National Band 124
Union of Franco American Guards of New England 125
Union Saint-Jean-Baptiste d'Amérique 120
Union Street Railway 49, 54–55, 64, 162, 195–196, 208, 291, 344
    Bus Terminal 55
    Car barn 55
United Front 282, 289
United Front Homes 285
United Fruit Stores 73, 83, 337
United Fund Dev. Corp. 285
United Fund Follies 343
United House of Prayer for All People 156, 228, 337
United Pilgrim Church 324
United Social Club 88, 90, 243, 268
United States Football Association 106
Unity Chorus 133
Universal American Corp. 304
Universalist Church 133
upholstery 315
urban renewal 260, 266–275, 278–281
urban riots 282–285
Uruguay 106–107
US Army Chemical Warfare Service 40, 174
US Army Corps of Engineers 169, 264–265, 311
used car dealerships 49
US Employment Service 162
US Housing Authority 58
US Naval Reserves 52
US Post Office 42, 229, 273–274, 308, 316

V

Vagabonds, The 253
Valentin, Jose 294
Valeri, Mike 340
Valerio, Manuel C. 127
Vale, Robby 328
Valley Falls Company 171
Vancini, Paul 334
Van Norman Industries 304

Varkeros drum and bugle corps 251
vaudeville 4, 62, 75, 84, 110–116, 129, 133
Velie hearse 56
Ventor, Joe 191
Vercellone, Bernard "Nino", Irene 205
Verda-Tones 245
Verdi, Don 243
Verissimo, Scott 316
Vermilya, Irving 118, 119
Verville, Anthony Paul 322
Veteran Firemen's Association 160
Viau, Antoine J. 205
Victoria, Queenie 353
Victory Key Campaign 160
Victory Park 214, 341
Vieira, Alfred 316
Vieira, Hermano P., Square 169
Vieira, Lucindo 127
Vieira, Manuel, Manuel, Jr. 129
Vieira, Rev. Antonio 82, 121
Vieira, Vickie Tavares 322
Vieira, Wayne 297
Viens, Edgar 216
Vien Theater 75
Viera, Ethel 183
Viera, Frank 139
Viera, Manuel 252
Viera, Theophile "Tiffy" 131
Viera, Vick 245
Viera, William 110
Viereck, Marion 159
Vietnam War 152, 259–261, 286–287, 336
Vigeant, George, Sr. 181
Vigilant, whaling bark 124
Vikre, Rasmus 136
Villa, Pancho 109
Vinagre, Ana 325
Vinagre, José 246, 325
Vincennes, France 51
Vincent, Melville 105
Vineyard Haven, MA 53
Viseu airport, Portugal 51
Vivian and Fay, fishing vessel 167
Volpe Construction Co. 305
von Ledebur, Friedrich 156, 227
von Papen, Franz 217

W

Waite, Beatrice C. 163
Waldorf Cafeteria 206
Walecka, Norris 222
Walker, Izaura 307
Walkers, The 328
Wallner's Bakery 211
Walsh, Bill 356
Walsh, David 207
Walsh, Patrick 356
Walthour, Jimmy, Jr. 105
Wamsutta Club 250, 320
Wamsutta Mill blocks 22
Wamsutta Mills 6, 22, 168, 171–172, 246
Wanderers, The 329
Wanderer, whaling bark 63, 134
war bonds and stamps 26, 162
Ware, Norman 11
War Manpower Commission 176
Warren, Russell 281
war salvage campaign 150
Warsaw, Poland 128
Washington Club 11, 12, 15, 127
Washington, Lori 316
Washington Social & Musical Club 83, 132
Waterfront Historic District 278
Waters, Everett T. 132
Waters, Herbert R., Jr. 339
Watkins, Helen 244
Watkins, Rillis, 224
Watkins, Robert A. "Bobby", Jr. 224, 364
Waverly Hotel 75
Weeden Manufacturing Co. 179
Weeden, William M. 179
Weeks, Allen 40

John Baptista Jr. enjoys a moment with longtime Frates Dairy server Romie Jodoin, circa 1975.

Weiner, Moses 82
Weitzman, David 89
Weld Square 48, 52, 68, 76, 94, 196–197, 276–277
    Barbershop 76
    Depot 52
    Pharmacy 76
Welles, Orson 227
Wengraf, Richard 278
West, Alice 141
West End 22, 155–157, 214–215, 223, 239, 260, 269, 274, 282–285, 354
West End Branch Library 215
West End Day Nursery 215, 239
West End Public Market 215
West End Youth Center 215
Westerly, RI 86
West Wind II, dragger 312
whaleboat races 98–99
Whale Furniture Mart 168
Whalers Drum & Bugle Corps 251
WHALE (Waterfront Historic Area LeaguE) 259, 278–281, 354
Whaling City Cable TV 321
Whaling City Marine 300
Wharfinger Building 22–23, 38, 166, 289
Wheaton College 327
White, Beverly 183
White, Linden 11
White, Vivian 253
Whitman Mills 6, 8, 13, 20, 42, 173, 252, 309
Whitman, William 5
Whittaker, Albert 250
Whyte, Leonora Kydd 156, 214
Whyte, William Darcey 109, 214
Wicherski, Frank 179
Wilcox, Raymond H. 161
wildlife 298
Wild Root Barbershop 270
Wilhelmsen, Bonnie 253
Wilkinson, David 123
Wilks, Henrietta Sylvia Ann Howland Green 182, 342
William A. Graber, packet ship 134
William Coulson Company 65
William Crabtree 301
Williams, Elnora M., Moses H. 239
Williams, M. Jennie, Ralph 150
Williams, Ray 215
Willis, Ellis 89
Willis Point 171
Willow Tree Restaurant 92, 297
Wilson, Earle D. 138
Wilson, William D. 133
Winchester hardware store 116
Wing, Joseph 44
Wing Lee 137
Wing Lee & Sons Laundry 137
Wing, William R. 44
Winn, Dennis 356
Winsegansett Heights 29
Winterbottom, Martha 183

Wollison, Esther 133
women during war 163
Woodcraft Project 25
Wood, Eldridge Everett "Ev" 250
Wood Pussy, catboat 47
Woodrow Wilson Hall 82, 157
Woods Hole, MA 16, 53, 154, 195, 198
Woods Hole, Martha's Vineyard & Nantucket Steamship Authority 195, 198
Wood Street Bridge 28
Woo Shee Chin 137
Worcester, MA 16, 54, 113, 162, 165, 212
Worden, Curt 320
Workers International Relief 11, 14
Workingmen's Club 132
Work Projects Administration 23
Works Progress Administration 20–27, 43, 98, 101, 155, 156, 159, 162, 200, 207, 238
World Cup 106, 107
World War I 18, 26, 40, 51, 86, 91, 110, 120, 126, 132, 137, 150, 163, 173
World War II 8, 46–47, 58–59, 63, 104, 113, 120, 129, 131, 133, 150, 152–155, 157–158, 164–165, 170, 172, 176–177, 183–184, 186, 190–197, 200, 203, 206, 211–212, 217–218, 223–224, 238, 240, 246–248, 251, 259, 266, 291, 305, 310, 315, 322, 333
Worley Bedding & Furniture Factory 308
Worley, John L. Sr., Patrick 308
Worthington's bakery 155
Wright Aeronautical 174
Wright, John 127
Wright, Tootsie 131, 244
Writers Guild of America 223
WTEV, television station 220, 295, 320–321
W. T. Grant Company 63
Wyatt, Eva Rosetta 133

X

Xavier, Manuel das Neves 121

Y

YMCA 113, 132, 159, 223, 274–275, 340
YMCA Summer Camp 340
Young Musicians Music Festival 249
Young, Philip E. "Skipper" 40
Young, Richard B. 169, 174
Youth Craft 173, 307
YWCA 14, 132, 139, 214, 223, 314

Z

Zeiterion Realty Corporation 116
Zeiterion Theater 116, 325, 327, 353
Zeitz, Barney, Carl, Fannie, Fisher, Frank, Harry, Kopel, Morton, Phillip 116
Zeitz Building 116
Zerbonne, Richard 233
Ziegfeld Follies 114
Zimon, Anthony 318
Zinno, Dave 326
Zolt, Dorothy 141

Selected Bibliography

Books, pamphlets and articles

1938 hurricane pictures: from Falmouth to Fall River and New London areas, mostly in and about New Bedford. New Bedford: Reynolds Printing, 1938.

1938 hurricane: mostly new large unpublished before and after photos in vicinity of New Bedford, Cape Cod, Martha's Vineyard. New Bedford: Reynolds Printing, 1939.

Acushnet Process Company. *Apco News Hurricane Edition*. New Bedford: 1954.

The Aerovox Corporation. *Hurricane "Carol" August 31, 1954*. New Bedford: The Aerovox Corporation, 1954.

Allen, E. S. *Children of the light : the rise and fall of New Bedford whaling and the death of the Arctic fleet*. Boston: Little Brown, 1973.

Allen, E.S. *A Wind to Shake the World: The Story of the 1938 Hurricane*. Boston: Little Brown, 1976.

Arato, C. A. et al. *Safely moored at last: cultural landscape report for New Bedford Whaling National Historical Park*. Boston: National Park Service, 1998.

Ashley, C. W. *The Yankee Whaler*. Boston: Houghton Mifflin Company, 1938.

Atlas of the City of New Bedford Massachusetts. Boston: Walker Lithograph and Publishing Co. 1911.

Avila, G. C. *The Pairpoint Glass Story*. New Bedford: Reynolds-Dewalt, 1978.

Barnes, J. et al. *A Nossa Vida: The Portuguese Experience in America*. New Bedford: Southcoast Media Grp., 2006.

Beers, F. W. *Atlas of Bristol Co. Massachusetts*. New York: F.W. Beers & Co., 1871.

Belisle, A. *Histoire de la presse Franco-Américaine*. Worcester: Ateliers typographiques de L'Opinion Publique, 1911.

Blasdale, M. J. *Artists of New Bedford: a Biographical Dictionary*. New Bedford: Old Dartmouth Hist. Soc., 1990.

Boss, J. A. and J. D. Thomas. *New Bedford, a Pictorial History*. Norfolk: Donning Co., 1983.

Burgess, J. H., ed. *New Bedford, Massachusetts, World Famous as the "Whaling City" Leading in Manufacture of Fine Cotton Cloth*. Souvenir 1909. n.p., n.d.

Burgess, J. H., ed. *The South End, the Rapidly Growing and Constantly Advancing Section of New Bedford, Massachusetts*. Souvenir 1909. n.p., n.d.

Cabral, S. L. *Tradition and Transformation: Portuguese Feasting in New Bedford*. New York: AMS Press, 1989.

Chartier, A. B. *French New Bedford: a Historical Overview of Franco-Americans of New Bedford, Massachusetts*. New Bedford: Assn. Canado-Américaine, 1993.

Church, A. C. *American Fishermen*. New York: W. W. Norton, 1940.

Clayton, B. and K. Whitley. *Guide to New Bedford*. Chester, Ct.: Globe Pequot Press, 1979.

Coltman, B. *Paul Clayton and the Folksong Revival*. Lanham, Maryland: Scarecrow Press. 2008.

Consecration of Saint Lawrence Church. New Bedford: St. Lawrence Martyr Parish, 1953.

Conant, L. D. *New Bedford Pictorial: a Picture Roster of the Union Street Railway*. Forty Fort, PA.: H.E. Cox, 1980.

Corps of Engineers, US Army Engineer Division, New England. *Ground Breaking Ceremonies, New Bedford-Fairhaven-Acushnet Hurricane Barrier, November 17, 1962*. S.l.: Corps of Engineers, 1962.

Crapo, H. H. *The Story of Cotton and its Manufacture into Cloth in New Bedford*. New Bedford: Old Dartmouth Historical Society, 1937.

Dallum, M.W. *Daddy Grace, A Celebrity Preacher and His House of Prayer*. New York: NYU Press, 2009.

Dewar, M. E. *Industry in Trouble: The Federal Government and the New England Fisheries*. Philadelphia, PA: Temple University Press, 1983.

Dias, E. "Daniel Ricketson and Henry Thoreau." *The New England Quarterly*, 26, n. 3. (1953).

Down to the Sea for Fish. New Bedford Fishing Fleet booklet. New Bedford: Reynolds Prntg. Co., 1939.

Ellis, L. B. *History of the Fire Department of the City of New Bedford, Massachusetts, 1772-1890*. New Bedford: E. Anthony & Sons, 1890.

Ellis, L. B. *History of New Bedford and its Vicinity, 1602-1892*. Syracuse: D. Mason & Co., 1892.

Festa do Santíssimo Sacramento 100 Anos – 100 Years Feast of the Blessed Sacrament. New Bedford: Museum of Madeiran Heritage, 2014

Gartaganis, A. J. *The history of the Greek community in New Bedford, Massachusetts, 1885-1915*. New Bedford: A.J. Gartaganis, 1993.

Gartaganis, A. J. *The history of the Greek community in New Bedford, Massachusetts, 1915-1955*. New Bedford: A.J. Gartaganis, 2000.

Gartaganis, A. J. *The History of Movie Houses in the Greater New Bedford Area of Massachusetts during the Twentieth Century*. New Bedford: Privately Published, 2005.

Georgianna, D. and R. H. Aaronson. *The Strike of '28*. New Bedford: Spinner Publications, 1993.

Gibson, C. D. "Victim or Participant? Allied Fishing Fleets and U-Boat Attacks in World Wars I And II." *The Northern Mariner/Le Marin du nord*, 1 (1991): 1-18.

Gifun, F. V. *New Bedford's Church: The First Unitarian Church in New Bedford*. Dartmouth: Progressive Press, 2011.

Goethe, W. H. G., E. N. Watson and D. T. Jones, eds. *Handbook of nautical medicine*. Berlin: Springer-Verlag, 1984.

Gonsalves, Jennifer. "Looking at the Urban Renewal Program of the 1960s through the Lens of the South Terminal Redevelopment Project in New Bedford, Mass." Unpublished master's thesis in community planning, Univ. of Rhode Island, 2004.

Grieve, R. *New Bedford Semi-Centennial Souvenir*. Providence: Journal of Commerce Co., 1897.

Grover, K. *The Fugitive's Gibraltar: Escaping Slaves and Abolitionism in New Bedford, Massachusetts*. Amherst: University of Massachusetts Press, 2001.

Grover, K. *MHC Inventory Form: Acushnet Avenue Area*. Boston: Mass. Historical Commission, 2011.

Hall, E. W. and Old Dartmouth Historical Society. *New Bedford Furniture*. New Bedford: Old Dartmouth Historical Society, 1978.

Halter, M. *Between Race and Ethnicity, Cape Verdean American Immigrants, 1860-1965*. Chicago: University of Illinois Press, 1993.

Hayden, J.M. *The Presence of the past: the ancestors and descendants of Michael James Hayden and Mary Ann Flanagan*. Saskatoon, Saskatchewan: J. M. Hayden, 1996.

Hayden, R. C. *African-Americans and Cape Verdean-Americans in New Bedford: a History of Community and Achievement*. Boston: Select Publications, 1993.

Heath, K. *The Patina of Place: The Cultural Weathering of a New England Industrial Landscape*. Knoxville: University of Tennessee Press, 2002.

Hegarty, R. B. *New Bedford's History*. New Bedford: R. B. Hegarty, 1959.

Hegarty, R. B. and Free Public Library. *A List of Log Books of Whaling Voyages in the Collection of the Melville Whaling Room in the Free Public Library*. New Bedford: Reynolds-Dewalt, 1963.

Hemingway, Natalie S., *East Fairhaven (Naskatucket) Massachusetts History, Book 1 & Book 2*, Fairhaven: self-published, 2010, 2011.

Hough, H. B. *Wamsutta of New Bedford, 1846-1946; a story of New England enterprise*. New Bedford: Wamsutta Mills, 1946.

Howland, L. *The New Bedford Yacht Club: a history*. South Dartmouth, Mass.: The New Bedford Yacht Club, 2002.

Hurd, D. H. *History of Bristol County, Massachusetts*. Philadelphia: J. W. Lewis & Co., 1883.

J. H. Beers & Co. *Representative Men and Old Families of Southeastern Mass*. Chicago: J. H. Beers & Co., 1912.

Jobe, B., G. R. Sullivan and J. O'Brien. *Harbor & Home: Furniture of Southeastern Massachusetts, 1710-1850*. Lebanon: Univ. Press of New England, 2009.

Katz, J. "Opportunity, Exclusion, and Immigrants: Textile Workers in New Bedford, Massachusetts, 1890-1930." A.B. Honors thesis, Harvard University, 1974.

Kelley, J. F. and A. Mackie *History of the Churches of New Bedford*. New Bedford, E. Anthony & Sons, 1869.

Kennedy, D. A. *City of New Bedford Historic Mill Inventory 2008*. New Bedford: MediumStudio, 2008.

Laham, L. *Rodman Candleworks, Double Bank Building, United States Custom House: Historic Structures Report*. New Bedford: Historic Architecture Program, Northeast Region, National Park Service, U.S. Department of the Interior, 2011.

Leading Manufacturers and Merchants of Eastern Massachusetts. 1887. New York, International Pub. Co.

Maiocco, C. *The Avenue, Memories of Acushnet Avenue*. New Bedford: privately published, 1992.

Maiocco, C. *The Center, downtown New Bedford in the 1950's*. New Bedford: privately published, 1998.

Massachusetts Historical Commission. *Historic & Archaeological Resources of Southeast Massachusetts. A Framework for Preservation Decisions*. Boston: Massachusetts Historical Commission, 1982.

Massachusetts Historical Commission. *MHC Reconnaissance Survey Town Report, New Bedford*. Boston: Massachusetts Historical Commission, 1981.

McCabe, M. and J. D. Thomas. *Julio J. Alves, Sr. Scholarship Souvenir Booklet*. New Bedford: Spinner Pub., 1985.

McCabe, M. and J. D. Thomas. *Not Just Anywhere: The Story of WHALE and the Rescue of New Bedford's Waterfront Historic District*. New Bedford: Spinner Publications, 1995.

McDonald, C. *The Military History of New Bedford*. Charleston: Arcadia Publishing, 2001.

Medeiros, P. *New Bedford Mansions: Historic Tales of County Street*. Charleston: The History Press, 2015.

Michelsen, B. F. *Story of New Bedford Fire Department*. New Bedford: Reynolds Printing, 1927.

Mulderink, E. F. *New Bedford's Civil War*. New York: Fordham University Press, 2012.

National Park Service. *Behind the Mansions: The Political, Economic, and Social Life of a New Bedford Neighborhood*. County-sixth neighborhood study, Boston: National Park Service. 2006.

The New Bedford Mercury. 1907. One hundredth anniversary supplement. New Bedford, Mass.